KV-375-497

Northern Ireland
Environment and Natural Resources

Northern Ireland
Environment and Natural Resources

Edited by

JAMES G. CRUICKSHANK

and

DAVID N. WILCOCK

PUBLISHED BY:
THE QUEEN'S UNIVERSITY OF BELFAST
AND THE NEW UNIVERSITY OF ULSTER

© The Queen's University of Belfast
and the New University of Ulster 1982

All rights reserved. No part of this publication may be
reproduced, stored in a retrieval system, or transmitted in any
form or by any means, electronic, mechanical, photocopying,
recording, or otherwise, without the prior permission of the
Copyright owner.

First published 1982

ISBN 0 85389 212 1

Phototypeset by Mayne, Boyd & Son, Ltd., Belfast

Contents

The Contributors

from the Queen's University of Belfast

W. James Armstrong, BA, MAgrSc	*Lecturer in Geography.*
Nicholas L. Betts, BA	*Lecturer in Geography.*
Patrick J. S. Boaden, BSc, PhD	*Director of Marine Biology Station, Portaferry, County Down.*
Ronald H. Buchanan, BSc, PhD	*Director of the Institute of Irish Studies, and Reader in Geography.*
Robert Common, BSc, PhD	*Reader in Geography.*
James G. Cruickshank, BSc	*Senior Lecturer in Geography.*
Roy W. Tomlinson, BSc, PhD	*Lecturer in Geography.*
Mrs J. A. Whatmough, BSc	*Warden of the Murlough National Nature Reserve, and of the The Queen's University Field Centre.*

from the New University of Ulster, Coleraine, County Londonderry.

Richard W. G. Carter, BSc, DPhil	*Senior Lecturer in Environmental Science.*
Alan C. Hamilton, BA, PhD	*Lecturer in Environmental Science.*
Palmer J. Newbould, BA, PhD	*Professor of Environmental Science.*
John C. Roberts, BSc, PhD	*Senior Lecturer in Environmental Science.*
David N. Wilcock, BA, PhD	*Senior Lecturer in Environmental Science.*
R. Brian Wood, BSc, PhD	*Professor of Biology and Director of the Limnology Laboratory, Traad Point, Ballyronan, County Londonderry.*

Acknowledgements

The most important acknowledgement, that the editors and contributors wish to make, is to the two universities – The Queen's University of Belfast and the New University of Ulster at Coleraine (Garfield Weston Trust) – for their financial support in making possible this publication. The collection of essays is a major, joint venture in which the two universities share equally in material contributed and in their financial sponsorship. All of those involved in the joint project wish to record publicly their thanks and appreciation to the two universities.

Linked with the first acknowledgement, the editors also wish to thank Professor W. Kirk, Department of Geography, The Queen's University of Belfast, and Professor P. J. Newbould, Professor of Environmental Science in The New University of Ulster, for their assistance in negotiating with their respective universities and for promoting the publication in a variety of ways.

Acknowledgement of technical assistance from many people in typing the scripts must be nameless because of their number, but nevertheless is most sincerely appreciated by the contributors. The typists were mainly secretarial staff of the School of Biological and Environmental Studies NUU, and of the Department of Geography QUB.

Thanks are due also to the cartographers of the Department of Geography, The Queen's University of Belfast, – Maura Pringle, Ian Alexander and Gill Alexander – who created the seventy line drawings of the book. Photographers Michael Collins and Trevor Molloy were responsible for printing these. The photographs were taken by R. W. G. Carter, J. G. Cruickshank, N. C. Mitchel and D. N. Wilcock, unless otherwise acknowledged. N. C. Mitchel took all the air photographs. Particular thanks for additional proof reading and other technical assistance must go to Fran Wilcock and Margaret Cruickshank.

Throughout the book, individual authors have their own acknowledgements at the end of their respective chapters. These are acknowledgements for specialist advice and data, and are additional to this general acknowledgement.

Foreword

The decade of 1970–1980 has seen world-wide changes in attitudes toward the protection and management of the natural environment. These changes are reflected in government legislation to protect the environment, in new research techniques of environmental measurement and evaluation, in greater public awareness of environmental issues, and in advances in environmental education. Northern Ireland has participated in these world-wide trends and this collection of papers prepared by physical geographers, environmental scientists and biologists, aims to show how the measurement, evaluation and management of processes and resources in Northern Ireland's natural environment have evolved in the recent past. It also attempts to identify existing problems of environmental management, and to suggest future trends.

The approach adopted by individual authors varies throughout the book, and no attempt has been made to enforce the same method of treatment. Each contributor was asked to write about a particular environmental system, or aspect of environmental management, which he or she had already studied in some detail and to present the major issues as he or she saw them. The book is divided into two sections; the first seven essays are concerned with the aquatic environment and are introduced by a chapter describing the climatic framework within which water resources have to be managed. The last six essays are concerned with the natural resources of the terrestrial environment.

Throughout the book the emphasis is on environment and natural resources from a management, and not from an economic development, point of view. Thus, there are no chapters on agriculture or manufacturing industry. Economic themes as they relate to management do however recur throughout the book: the need for more cost-benefit studies in different aspects of water management, the need to balance short-term economic gain against long-term economic security in the nearshore fishing industry, the choice between pump-storage and gravity-fed water supply schemes. These and other issues show how tightly bound together are economic and environmental considerations, and how important is the application of certain economic techniques to environmental management. Because policy-making and decision-making about the physical and biological environment have to be seen in an economic context, the introduction is on this theme.

A brief word at this stage about legislation in Northern Ireland during the early 1970s is perhaps appropriate to guide the reader through this sometimes complex aspect of environmental management. In 1972 the Northern Ireland Parliament was suspended. Under the terms of the Northern Ireland (Temporary Provisions) Act of the same year it became possible to make laws for Northern Ireland by means of Orders in Council. These have the same status as earlier Public General Acts of the Northern Ireland Parliament. In references at the end of each chapter Orders in Council are therefore indexed under Northern Ireland Parliament.

In 1973, under the Ministries (Northern Ireland) Order a Ministry of the Environment for Northern Ireland was first created. Like all other Ministries of the Northern

Ireland Parliament at Stormont, this Ministry became a Department in 1973 under the terms of the Northern Ireland Constitution Act. Under this Act of the Westminster Parliament, the Ministry of Agriculture became the Department of Agriculture, the Ministry of Commerce became the Department of Commerce etc. Finally, on the 1st of January 1974, under the terms of the 1973 Departments (Transfer of Functions) Order for Northern Ireland, the former Ministry of Development was re-designated the Department of Housing, Local Government, and Planning. At the same time the recently-formed Department of the Environment for Northern Ireland took over many of the responsibilities of the former Ministry of Development, including those for water supply, sewerage and the preservation of historic buildings.

Throughout the book an attempt has been made to keep terminology simple in order to appeal to as wide a readership as possible. References are quoted in non-abbreviated form. We hope that the book will be of interest to specialists in the field of environmental management, to teachers, students and the general public. We hope that it will raise the level of public information and that it might make a small contribution to the maintenance and improvement of the rich, diverse and beautiful, natural environment of Northern Ireland.

JAMES G. CRUICKSHANK
DAVID N. WILCOCK
Editors
April, 1982.

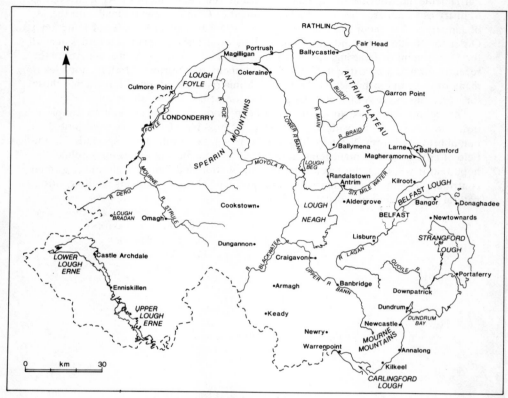

Principal place-names used in the text.

An Introduction:
The Economic Perspective

W. JAMES ARMSTRONG,
Lecturer in Geography, The Queen's University of Belfast

The objective of this introduction is to present an economic perspective on the problems of natural resource management in Northern Ireland. In particular, the aim is to place natural resources in a framework of economic, social, locational and political factors that constrain use, consumption, or productivity of the resources. Agriculture will serve as the first example of the economic development of soil, vegetation and climate. It illustrates also certain aspects of competition for, and government influence in, the management of these resources.

Ginsberg (1965) notes that natural resources:

> "in their widest sense include all the freely given natural phenomena of nature within the zone of man's activities ... extending about 12 miles above the surface of the earth and 4 miles below it, plus the additional non-material quality of situation or location."

It is clear from this definition that the term "natural resources" includes the climate and soil in which plant growth takes place. They must therefore play an important role in determining the potential for agricultural production, an economic activity which currently employs some 9.7% of Northern Ireland's workforce and contributes 5.6% of the Gross Domestic Product. In the United Kingdom as a whole, the proportions are 2.7% and 2.5% respectively. These figures illustrate the fact that agriculture plays a more important role in the Northern Ireland economy than in the U.K., but that there is greater productivity disparity between agriculture and other sectors of the economy in Northern Ireland. During the period from 1970-78, net farm income in Northern Ireland was 36% below the United Kingdom average. These features are a reflection of the utilization and allocation of resources within the agricultural sector.

Some 45% of all land in Northern Ireland has been defined as Less-Favoured under EEC Directive 268/75, as compared to 30% in the rest of the U.K. If it is accepted that the main criterion used in the definition of the areas is the existence of a difficult physical environment, then it would appear that Northern Ireland agriculture is faced with a natural resource disadvantage. Despite the fact that the definition was not based on any environmental survey, the distribution of these Less-Favoured Areas shows a marked correlation with the Mournes, Sperrins and Antrim plateau, while the large area in Fermanagh is associated with poorly drained land. Adverse climatic and soil conditions in the uplands restricts the choice of enterprise to livestock breeding. The lack of improved land (due to steep slope, rock outcrop and poor soil drainage) combined with adverse climatic conditions for fodder conservation in summer, means that winter stocking densities have to be maintained at a low level, forcing the farmer to sell the progeny of the breeding herd on a buyers' market in the autumn. At the same time the summer stocking levels are often well below total grazing capacity.

Currently, average farm size in Northern Ireland (16 ha) is much smaller than in England and Wales (47 ha) and Scotland (54 ha). Some 47% of all holdings are classified as part-time in the sense that they provide less than 200 standard man days of labour per year. This means that there must be considerable underemployment of the agricultural labour force which in itself would help to explain the productivity disparity already mentioned. A similar proportion of farms in the Less-Favoured Areas fall into the part-time category, and this may also indirectly affect productivity and income levels in that the small area of improved land available would not justify the large-scale capital expenditure on silage making equipment and buildings for in-wintering, which would help the farmer to overcome some of the limitations of his physical environment. Finally, the Farm Management Standards for Hill Breeding Cows, published by the Department of Agriculture for Northern Ireland, show that in 1978-79 some 50% of surveyed farms obtained gross margin profits which were £37 per cow below average. Whatever the cause, lower levels of farm management also may contribute to the lower levels of productivity and to lower incomes achieved in Northern Ireland's agricultural sector.

From this brief description of the factors involved, it is clear that there are complex inter-relationships between natural resource endowment, farm size structure, levels of capital investment in buildings and equipment, management standards and farm performance. It would therefore be difficult and perhaps unrealistic to consider natural resources as an independent variable in analysing current economic performance and prospects for economic development. It is also clear that there is need for improvement and adjustment in the part played by these variables. Since the 1930s it has been accepted that this process of adjustment should be guided and controlled by government.

Production grants in the form of an annual payment for each Hill Breeding Cow and Hill Ewe kept on the farm have been a consistent feature of government policy. On economic grounds, these grants could be justified as an incentive to farmers to increase stocking levels, and hence increasing national self-sufficiency in these products. They have also played an important social welfare role in that they represent direct income supplement to small farmers operating under difficult physical conditions. The current (1979-80) level of payment is £54.87 per Hill Cow and £4.25 per Hill Ewe, while the total expenditure is about £9 m.

Under a variety of schemes, farm improvement grants have been made available to encourage farmers to increase the productive capacity of their farm resources. They can be subdivided into incentives to improve capital infrastructure such as buildings and roads, and those encouraging the improvement of land by reclamation, drainage, fencing, re-seeding, liming and increased fertilizer application. The total expenditure in 1979-80 was £23 m, of which the spending was £10 m on land improvement and £13 m on other improvements. Finally, in an attempt to encourage the amalgamation of small farmers into large and more viable units, early retirement incentives were offered to farmers in the older age category, while amalgamation grants were made available to potentially viable farm units to aid the purchase and equipping of more land. Expenditure in this scheme in 1979-80 was only £87,000.

In pragmatic terms, the relative levels of expenditure on these policy measures may provide an indication of the priority given to them by the Government. For example, from a purely economic viewpoint, the amalgamation of farms into more viable units may represent a cost effective and direct method of improving both levels of output and farm incomes. However, the relatively small level of expenditure may reflect the Government's reluctance to follow aggressively a policy which would encourage rural depopulation and add to the already considerable burden of job creation in manufacturing and other sectors of the economy. The Government therefore, in formulating a policy to encourage adjustment in resource use in agriculture, is given the responsibility of interpreting the overall objectives or needs of society. The policy itself may involve a trade-off among economic, social and regional policy objectives.

It would be expected that the list of grant-aided farm improvements and the relative expenditure on each one would reflect an empirically based definition of the real bottlenecks to improvement. In this sense the greater emphasis placed on land improvement, would suggest that this is seen by the Government as the main constraint, and it is particularly so in the Less-Favoured Areas where higher rates of grant are available for this purpose. In addition, a specific programme for the development of agriculture in the Less-Favoured Areas of Northern Ireland is being negotiated in the Council of Ministers in Brussels. The total investment aid will be £86 m paid over 10 years. The breakdown of proposed expenditure again shows that considerable emphasis is given to land improvement schemes.

However, the wisdom of this strategy may be questioned from a number of points of view. Firstly, most empirical studies of farming conditions in the Less-Favoured Areas would suggest that small farms, lack of investment in buildings and equipment, inadequate marketing arrangements and poor management standards are also important and very much inter-related constraints. It might therefore be suggested that these farm improvement schemes should be much more broadly based, giving perhaps equal emphasis to education, the promotion of co-operation, improvement of marketing structures and investment in buildings and equipment. This may involve a diversion of funds away from land improvement. Secondly, it has been claimed that the environmental impact of drainage and reclamation schemes on natural habitats of scientific and educational value, wildlife and landscape amenity have not been adequately assessed. Thirdly, it has been questioned whether the benefits of increased output can be sustained for a sufficient period to justify the initial capital outlay. Such comments are of particular relevance in the Less-Favoured Areas where there are competing demands for land. For example, an expansion in the tree-planted area may not only provide alternative sources of employment and income, enhance landscape amenity, improve recreational facilities, but also make an important contribution to reducing the nation's heavy reliance on imported timber.

In a review of the afforestation programme for Northern Ireland in 1971, a planted target of 90,000 hectares was set for the year 2000. By 1979, 52,245 hectares had been planted, most of this being in the Less-Favoured Areas. However, in recent years the rate of planting has slowed down considerably, and it is unlikely that the target for 2000 AD will be achieved. The reduction in the rate of planting is largely attributable to a fall in the rate of land acquisition as the Forest Service, Department of Agriculture for Northern Ireland, finds difficulty in competing with farmers in the market for land. It might be suggested that this competitive edge which farmers have obtained is due to the subsidization of profits from production grants, which may account for up to 50%

of net farm income. Government intervention in the agricultural sector may therefore have distorted the market allocation of land in its favour.

Although it may be possible to justify subsidization of afforestation on similar social and economic grounds, there has been no explicit policy decision to this effect. Furthermore, most attempts to assess the relative merits of forestry and upland farming as alternative forms of land use, have tended to concentrate on economic criteria. Not only does this approach ignore the potential social, environmental and recreational benefits of forestry, but it is also fraught with discounting problems due to the long term nature of investment in forestry.

The Northern Ireland Development Programme 1970-75 notes that Northern Ireland's

"large supply of water can be expected to become an increasingly important industrial asset".

In Chapters 2 and 4, dealing with Northern Ireland's rivers and loughs respectively, both the quality and quantity of water resources are examined against the background of present and future patterns of consumption. The global water budgets for Northern Ireland would suggest that it is a plentiful resource. However, while water in situ might be described as a "freely given" natural resource, it does also possess that additional "raw-material quality of situation and location". Where the location or quality of supply does not coincide with the major points of consumption, considerable cost may be involved in storage, pumping, quality control and pipeline. These may be described as the internal costs of a water supply scheme. The manipulation of the natural hydrology of the catchment or donor area could also incur environmental costs, which may be described as external costs. These may be incurred by the local population, other catchment users such as anglers, or the whole community.

Belfast Urban Area now accounts for about one third of total water consumption. The Department of the Environment for Northern Ireland have considered two alternative methods of meeting future needs. One involved drawing further on the Mourne Catchment Area by constructing a new dam at Kinnahalla, the other would use Lough Neagh water by pumping from Tunney Point. An examination of the relative engineering, or internal costs, suggested that the Kinnahalla Dam was the best alternative and detailed proposals for this scheme were published.

A pressure group was formed in the South Down area to oppose this scheme and a public inquiry was held early in 1980. During the inquiry, two aspects of the DoE's decision-making procedure were questioned. Firstly, it was suggested that their forecasts of annual yield were over-estimated. Secondly, that particularly during periods of low discharge, the scheme would draw so heavily on the upper reaches of the Bann catchment, that there would not be sufficient water left for flushing. The scheme would therefore lead to further environmental deterioration in the Bann, with depletion of fish stocks and a general loss of amenity. These criticisms were never fully accepted by the DoE, but they did abandon the proposal, the reason given being unforeseen high costs. It was later disclosed that the cost of preparing this plan and the subsequent inquiry was £750,000. It might be suggested that this money may have been better spent on a more thorough investigation of both the internal and external costs of the two schemes, before specific proposals were made.

Much publicity has been given to the fact that energy costs in Northern Ireland have been higher than in the rest of the U.K. It would seem that there are two main reasons

4

for this. Firstly, 90% of electricity generation is dependent on oil, which has escalated in price, and secondly, the investment in generating capacity has turned out to be much greater than that required. At face value this may suggest another example of poor decision-making by both the Government and the Northern Ireland Electricity Service. However, in 1965, when the decision was made to construct an oil fired generating station at Kilroot with a capacity of 1,200 megawatts per annum, the situation was considerably different from that of today. In the period before this decision was taken, industrial consumption of electricity had been increasing at 8% per annum. Assuming a continuation of this trend the total capacity of the new station at Kilroot was defined on the basis of an expected overall growth rate in consumption of 9–10%. While oil dependent systems were economically justified in 1965, the rapid increase in oil prices since the early 1970s could not have been foreseen. Not only has this increase in oil prices been reflected in an increase in electricity costs, but it has also helped to create a recession in world trade, which in combination with the civil disturbances in Northern Ireland, has considerably reduced the rate of industrial growth and therefore growth in demand for electricity. What this current problem of high energy costs does reflect (despite recent guarantees by the U.K. Government to reduce the difference), is that such long term investment plans inevitably involve prediction of future trends in demand and costs of production, and therefore resource allocation decisions are made under conditions of bounded uncertainty.

In economics, a resource is defined as an entity which can generate production for which there is some demand. When that demand is translated into a price which is high enough to provide an acceptable return on investment after production costs have been deducted, the resource will be utilized. The possibility of using local, and freely given, natural resources such as lignite, peat, solar energy, wind, tidal energy and wave action, to generate electricity has been investigated in the past, but excessive production costs suggested that they were not viable alternatives to imported oil or coal. However, subsequent increases in the price of these alternative fossil fuels, have created renewed interest in the utilization of these resources. In Chapter 11, their possible contribution to annual energy production is examined in some detail and a possible energy system for the year 2000 is suggested.

Once again, in this and other chapters, it is stressed that there are external costs and benefits to be considered. For example, dealing with alternative energy sources, in Chapter 5 (Estuarine and Inshore Waters), the environmental impact of constructing a tidal barrage from Strangford to Portaferry on the estuarine ecology of Strangford Lough is examined. Chapter 9 (Peatland) suggests that the exploitation of peat for this purpose would create employment in rural areas, although there would be costs involved in the destruction of sites of ecological interest.

During the 1970s the objectives of development have become more comprehensive than merely trying to obtain the maximum growth of Gross Domestic Product. For example, the Northern Ireland Development Programme 1970-75, states that the need for recreation is becoming an increasingly important part of people's lives while the quality of life and of the environment is of great importance in attracting new industry and tourists to the region. The same report suggests that the:

> "Ulster countryside is probably the region's greatest asset in providing leisure facilities for the people and in attracting tourists".

Chapter 12 deals specifically with an appraisal of landscape as a resource in Northern

Ireland, and Chapter 4 examines the potential for the development of tourism on our loughs. In evaluating coastal resources, Chapter 6 stresses their recreational and amenity value. Sites of ecological interest on the estuaries, the peatlands and uplands are defined in Chapters 5, 9 and 10 respectively.

Most of the authors would agree with the view that the greater pollutions of the twentieth century are fortunately absent from Northern Ireland. Equally, they would agree that there are many actual and potential sources of pollution that need to be carefully monitored and controlled. For example, the disposal of increasing quantities of slurry and silage effluent, and the increased use of artificial fertilizers which have accompanied the intensification of agricultural production, pose a considerable threat to the water quality and ecological habitat of our loughs and rivers. The part played by the disposal of industrial effluent in polluting the rivers and coastal waters is also examined and the need for careful monitoring of this activity is emphasised. Sporadic residential development in areas of outstanding natural beauty, the excessive development of poorly sited and poorly landscaped caravan parks on the coast, the widespread occurrence of unofficial refuse tips and many other threats to the high amenity value of the countryside are also noted.

Most of these threats to the quality of the environment are external costs arising from other forms of resource use, where the allocative decisions and management practices are largely determined by internal cost considerations. The need for the adoption of integrated resource management plans, which would be based on an examination of all costs and benefits deriving from resource allocation, and which would reconcile the economic, social, and environmental needs of society, is reiterated on many occasions.

In this, as in all the other resource management problems discussed in this chapter, the responsibility for planning and controlling the use of natural resources lies with the Government. By way of conclusion, therefore, it would be useful to review the decision-making problems that arise, and the possible contribution of this volume of essays in that area. Whitby *et al.* (1974) have suggested that the decision-making process can be broken down into five stages: description, prediction, evaluation, review of policy measures and decision.

In the descriptive stage the quantity and quality of known, and freely given, natural resources should be assessed. This is a basic objective adopted in each of the twelve chapters. In some cases it may be possible to present this information in quantitative terms. For example, in Chapter 2 (Rivers) it has been possible to provide an estimate of the quantity and quality of water available. On the other hand, in the case of some resources, such as landscape amenity, it has so far proved impossible to devise an objective method of evaluating that intangible resource, so much more emphasis is placed on the research problems involved in measurement. At this stage there should also be a description of the economic, social and environmental consequences of present patterns of resource use. Since most of the authors are environmental scientists, physical geographers or biologists, it is to be expected that they stress the physical or environmental consequences. However, it is important to remember that at this stage all that is required is a statement of possible sources of conflict, or costs and benefits. The evaluation of the relative importance of these costs and benefits to society is a problem which largely lies outside their expertise, although some may be tempted to express value judgments of their own. Finally, as discussed earlier, natural resource endowment is simply one of a whole series of inter-related factors which in combination influence economic, social and environmental conditions. However tempting it might be to the environmental scientists, it would therefore be unrealistic to view natural resources as an independent variable in this context.

The predictive stage will involve the definition of future relationships between supply and demand for natural resources. Such prediction will involve the quantification of such variables as population growth, changes in consumption patterns, disposable incomes and leisure time and the impact of technological change. All this is clearly outside the scope of interest of the environmental scientist, but he can make important contributions at this predictive stage in the identification of the future physical, or environmental, state if present patterns of resource use continue. However, as noted in this chapter in relation to the provision of energy, the problems of making accurate predictions limit the effectiveness or success of long term resource allocation decisions.

In the third stage, the desirability or otherwise, of present or expected economic, social and environmental conditions, must be evaluated on the basis of the overall objectives of the community. In the context of evaluating the need for environmental protection, Whitby *et al*. (1974) put the case very succinctly by pointing out that:

> "In an economic framework, the claims of the 'environmentalists', for example, that ecological stability is a desirable goal in itself, can be relevant as goals only if they are chosen by society . . . Decisions involve 'trading off' such objectives against others, or measuring the costs of policy options in comparison with other means and levels of control. Pollution problems do arise and they can be described in terms of physical relationships. But they will only be controlled where there is an effective demand for their control, sufficient to cover the cost of doing so."

The definition of what constitutes an efficient allocation of resources is therefore dependent on what the objectives or demands of society happen to be. A major part of economic theory is based on a definition which assumes that the price of goods in the market place reflects these objectives and that the allocation of resources can be left to the decisions of individuals who are guided by market price. However, it is now widely accepted that the price in the market place may not adequately express society's objectives. For example, landscape amenity or outdoor recreational facilities are goods for which it is difficult to define a price, and are not often included in the profit and loss accounts on which private decisions are based. Alternative methods of evaluating these goods have to be devised and increasingly sophisticated methods of cost benefit analysis are being devised for this purpose. It is clear that there is a need for the application of this type of technique to an appraisal of many aspects of natural resource use in Northern Ireland. Where environmental costs or benefits of an educational or scientific nature are involved, then it can be argued that the environmental scientist is in a well-qualified position to evaluate them. For example, the ecological importance of Strangford Lough is assessed in Chapters 5 and 11, and used as a factor in the consideration of tides as an additional energy source.

In the fourth stage of this decision-making process, it will be necessary to review the existing policy measures to see if they are likely to induce the resource allocation objectives. In this introduction, it has been stressed that there is a need for a review of the measures which are used to adjust and improve the use of resources in the Less-Favoured Areas of Northern Ireland. In Chapter 12 there is an appraisal of rural land use planning legislation which would also suggest that important changes should be made.

Finally, the decisions about which objectives and policy measures should be adopted must, ultimately, be left to the politicians. While it is easy to advocate the adoption of a more scientific and quantified approach to resource management, where the relevant costs and benefits cannot be quantified with reasonable accuracy, the politician must be left to interpret the needs of society in these respects. Furthermore, the objectives of society may often be mutually exclusive. For example, in Northern Ireland it might be said that the objectives of resource allocation should be to provide more employment, improve incomes, lower the costs of living, create social and political stability and improve the quality of the environment. However, the achievement of any one of these goals may involve a trade-off against other objectives; possibly industrial development might be encouraged by relaxing control over such things as siting, location, building design or even the disposal of effluent, but the quality of the environment may suffer in consequence. In interpreting the needs of society, the politician may draw upon the advice of advisory committees or civil servants. Ultimately therefore, the extent to which efficient resource allocation decisions are made, depends on the efficiency and objectivity of the administrative, advisory and political systems.

REFERENCES

Armstrong, W. J., McClelland, D. and O'Brien, T., 1980. *A Policy for Rural Problem Areas in Northern Ireland,* Ulster Polytechnic.

Ginsberg, N., 1965. Natural resources and economic development, Chapter 6, *Readings in Resource Management and Conservation, (Edit.)* I. Burton and R. W. Kates, University of Chicago Press, 404–22.

H.M.S.O., 1965. A ten year programme for electricity supply in Northern Ireland, Command Paper 478.

H.M.S.O., 1970. *Northern Ireland Development Programme 1970-75,* Belfast.

H.M.S.O., 1976. *Forestry in Northern Ireland,* Command Paper 550.

Whitby, M. C., Robins, D. L. J., Tarsey, A. W., and Willis, K. G., 1974. *Rural Resource Development,* Methuen, London.

CHAPTER I

Climate

NICHOLAS L. BETTS
Lecturer in Geography, The Queen's University of Belfast

Synoptic climatology of Northern Ireland

The general circulation

The climate of Northern Ireland owes much to a mid-latitude oceanic position on the western side of a land mass, the maritime influence being enhanced by heat transfers from the neighbouring relatively warm surface waters of the North Atlantic Drift to the overlying atmosphere (Perry and Walker, 1977).

The other dominant factor is the close proximity to the tracks of depressions with their associated frontal systems, often occluded, passing over the country. These depressions usually form along the polar front, although its presence is not a prerequisite for cyclonic activity, and they represent the main mechanism for the transport of mild air from the Atlantic Ocean.

The mean surface pressure pattern is characterized by a west to south-west airflow between the sub-tropical high pressure cell of the Azores area and the Icelandic low, a statistical feature representing the zone in which mobile depressions reach their greatest intensity. Although the main depression track lies between Scotland and Iceland, individual lows frequently cross Northern Ireland, and Rohan (1968) has determined that on average 170 fronts pass over south-west Ireland each year. This extremely mobile atmospheric circulation produces a great variation and rapidity of change of weather types over Northern Ireland. Nevertheless, marked deviations from the normal zonal pressure pattern occur, producing anomalous weather which may persist over considerable periods.

The exact position of the depression tracks and the general surface pressure distribution in the vicinity of Northern Ireland is dependent greatly upon the meandering, high velocity, upper westerly airstream, which attains a maximum intensity at the 300 millibar level, or about a height of 9 km. Variations in the strength and latitudinal position of this airflow, together with alterations in the amplitude and wavelength of the upper waves, produce departures from the climatic norm.

The upper atmospheric pattern consists of a warm ridge extending north-eastwards from the Azores high and a cold trough changing in position between a mid-Atlantic location and longitudes 30–40°E. On occasions when a strong zonal flow dominates

9

the Atlantic sector, there is little evidence of this trough. Generally, if the axis of the trough is located in mid-Atlantic, Northern Ireland experiences mild and usually wet weather. When located over or to the east of the country, colder, showery conditions prevail. With a decrease in wavelength, accompanied by increasing amplitude of the upper waves, the warm ridge extending over Northern Ireland and on towards Scandinavia may become enlarged, producing a 'blocking' situation with increased meridional airflow and weather which is often drier than normal. During this blocking of the westerlies, the upper jet stream still exists, but meanders around the high pressure ridge and low pressure trough, with its surface expression, the polar front, following in similar fashion. As a result, cyclonic activity occurs along tracks of north-south alignment, rather than along the more usual west-east track. Boucher (1975) and Lamb (1972a) have outlined case studies showing the relationship of surface weather to the middle troposphere westerly flow.

The fluctuating upper airflow pattern shifts between two extreme stages: a 'high index' circulation is associated with strong zonal movement (Figure 1.1a) while a 'low index' situation is characterized by meridional airflow (Figure 1.1b). The climate of an individual period of the year is usually determined by the relative dominance of one of these two forms of circulation. Overall, years when a 'high index' predominates are warmer and wetter than average, whilst 'low index' circulations tend to produce greater climatic variability, dependent upon the location of the upper trough.

De la Mothe (1968) has indicated that the upper airflow pattern follows a fairly common sequence at certain times of the year, producing a recurrence of distinctive features of the climate. Often, the upper westerly airflow is in a 'high index' phase during December and January, with associated depressions at the surface progressing rapidly eastward accompanied by strong winds and appreciable frontal rainfall over Northern Ireland. A gradual shortening of the upper wavelength then follows during the spring, and in association, a blocking pattern becomes prevalent. This is associated with an extension of the continental anticyclone towards Northern Ireland which prevents the advance of depressions, and accounts for a greater frequency of dry spells in spring than at other seasons. Towards late-June there occurs a renewed increase of the wavelength pattern aloft, and a return of the westerly airflow, although associated depressions are often quite shallow and progress less rapidly than in winter, and may sometimes remain almost stationary for several days. In September, the progressive pattern is often interrupted by a spell of anticyclonic weather, and in recent years, early and middle October has also experienced settled weather (Clark, 1979). From mid-October on, however, progressive stormy weather is the most prevalent situation, although long spells of a particular weather type are less common at this period of the year (Lamb, 1950). With the variability of weather in oceanic middle latitudes, several of the above mentioned features may not occur during the course of an individual year.

Weather types over Northern Ireland

A useful approach to the analysis of weather characteristics is the daily categorization of the circulation pattern over an area. The circulation pattern over the British Isles has been classified daily, from 1861 to date, using the criteria adopted by Lamb (1950, 1972b) and a modified catalogue for Northern Ireland is near completion. The classification for the British Isles overcomes some of the inadequacies of the more

(a)

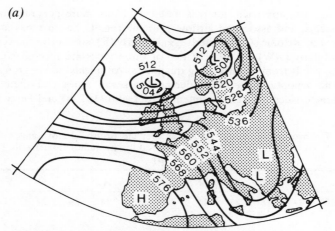

Figure 1.1 *(a)* 'High-index' zonal circulation at 500 mb over the Atlantic and Western Europe. (Derived from Europäischer Wetterbericht, 00.00 hrs. 17 December 1979).

(b)

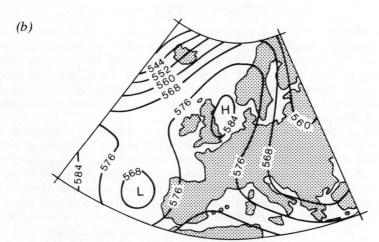

Figure 1.1 *(b)* 'Low-index' meridional circulation at 500 mb over the Atlantic and Western Europe. (Derived from Europäischer Wetterbericht, 00.00 hrs. 21 August 1976).

traditional air mass approach, for it is based upon the more general movement of pressure systems, and associated airflow over the region. Seven types are defined: anticyclonic (A), cyclonic (C), northerly (N), easterly (E), southerly (S), westerly (W), and north-westerly (NW). Hybrids of two or three types are recognized, the latter cases sharing winds from neighbouring quadrants. An unclassifiable grouping is also included. The synoptic patterns producing the seven types and their associated weather characteristics are well documented by Lamb (1972b) and Perry (1976).

TABLE 1.1

The average percentage frequency over the British Isles of Lamb's seven weather types, 1941-70. (Derived by the author from Lamb, 1972b)

	J	F	M	A	M	J	J	A	S	O	N	D
W	26	24	18	22	15	24	27	24	29	27	24	31
NW	5	5	4	5	4	5	9	5	4	4	6	8
N	8	9	7	9	10	8	8	8	5	5	9	7
E	8	12	13	10	13	7	4	5	5	7	7	6
S	12	7	13	7	8	6	4	5	9	12	9	9
A	21	24	28	29	25	27	25	22	25	29	22	21
C	16	15	12	14	20	19	20	26	18	13	19	14

Table 1.1 reveals marked seasonal variations in the average frequency of each of Lamb's weather types over the British Isles. Particularly evident is the December peak of westerly circulation, and the maximum occurrence of the cyclonic type in mid-summer. Lamb (1972b) has shown that there have been changes in the frequency of the various weather types since 1861, especially the westerly type, resulting in climatic changes, to be discussed later.

Meteorological network and records

Armagh Observatory possesses the longest continuous series of meteorological records in Northern Ireland, dating back to 1794, although weather diaries exist from earlier periods. One such diary is that of Thomas Neve from Ballyneilmore, County Londonderry, for the years 1711-25 (Dixon, 1959). The lack of standardization of meteorological instruments and general observational procedures requires caution in the analysis of early records, although by the 1880s a fairly homogeneous station network had been achieved (Rohan, 1975).

Expansion of the observational network was slow during the first half of this century, but with the establishment of the Belfast Meteorological Office in 1961 to develop and maintain standards set by the World Meteorological Organisation, there followed a rapid development of both rainfall and climatological stations. Table 1.2 shows this growth, with consideration given only to those stations currently in use (June 1980). The intensification of the network in the 1960s provided a significant increase in the number of both upland stations (those above 150 m O.D.) and climatological stations. Since 1970, the policy of the Belfast Meteorological Office has been to improve the quality of instrumentation, rather than to greatly expand the network. Apart from the requirement of additional upland stations, the general meteorological coverage of Northern Ireland is satisfactory.

TABLE 1.2

Development of the meteorological network in Northern Ireland.
(Water Service, 1980)

Period	Type		No. of stations established at heights of m O.D.		
	R	C	Below 150 m	150–300 m	Above 300 m
Before 1900	9	3	8	4	0
1900-49	30	5	22	6	7
1950-59	11	4	10	2	3
1960-69	117	30	100	32	15
After 1970	43	18	51	9	1
Total	210	60	191	53	26

R = Rainfall stations (daily/weekly/monthly recording)
C = Climatological recordings in addition to rainfall. This category includes stations
    recording for Potential Transpiration calculations.

The variability in length of records at climatological stations in Northern Ireland makes it difficult to ensure a common time base for the description of mean conditions relating to all aspects of individual climatic elements. In the following account figures have been derived for the standard climatological period 1941-70 where this was possible, but occasionally averages have been obtained from data relating to a shorter period. All time references are based on the 24-hour system, and all times are GMT.

Wind

Wind direction

Figure 1.2 presents 12-point wind roses for four stations, selected to give a broad impression of wind distribution over Northern Ireland. Aldergrove (1957-76), Ballykelly (1957-67), and Kilkeel (1964-69) data are from continuous recording equipment at an effective height of 10 m O.D. whereas the Castle Archdale (1949-56) readings comprise observations measured over 5 minutes, taken at 03.00, 09.00, 15.00 and 21.00 hours.

Figure 1.2 clearly shows that the predominant wind directions are generally between 200°–220° and 260°–280° (west), although the surface airflow is modified by relief features. Glassey and Durbin (1971) for example, suggest that winds at Ballykelly may be funnelled along the Foyle Valley thus producing maximum frequencies in the range 230°–250°. Similarly, the Roe valley provides a natural path for southerly winds (170°–190°). The least frequent winds at Ballykelly are from 50°–70°, and at Kilkeel from 350°–010°, a possible reflection of the shelter effect provided by the North Derry hills and Mournes respectively. At Castle Archdale high frequencies of winds in the ranges 140°–160° and 290°–310° suggest a channelling effect through the Lough Erne lowland.

Analysis of wind directions throughout the year reveals a marked spring maximum of northerlies. Winds from 140°–160° have a well-defined summer maximum at each station, particularly Aldergrove and Castle Archdale. There is a distinct winter maximum for winds between 170° and 220°, and a pronounced summer maximum for those between 260° and 340°.

13

Plate 1.1 Meteorological equipment at the New University of Ulster. A Campbell-Stokes sunshine recorder can be seen on left, a continuous rainfall recorder in the right foreground and a series of anemometers mounted at different heights on the mast in the background. The latter enable profiles of windspeed to be recorded continuously.

Wind speed

Close proximity to the paths of depressions over the Atlantic means that Northern Ireland generally experiences stronger winds than southern areas of the British Isles. The effects of relief may result in the values of mean wind speed at an individual station only being representative of that location, but generally, mean wind speed decreases with distance inland. This pattern is due to land exerting a greater frictional force upon the surface wind than the ocean. The annual average wind speed ranges from more than 13 knots on the North Antrim coast to under 8 knots at sheltered inland sites. June to September is the period of lowest mean wind speed, while highest

Plate 1.2 Three types of raingauge at the New University of Ulster. In the foreground, the raingauge is installed at ground level and surrounded by an anti-splash grid. In the centre, the raingauge stands 12 inches above ground level. In the background, the raingauge is protected by a turf wall, a typical installation in exposed locations. All three raingauges are read once every 24 hours. Refer to 'Precipitation' section, pp. 28–34.

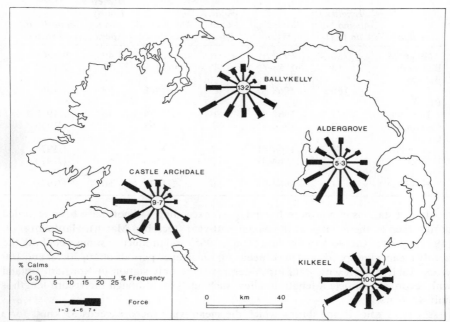

Figure 1.2 Annual percentage frequency of the force and direction of wind at selected stations.

velocities are most frequent between November and March. The wind regime, however, displays considerable variation from year to year, dependent upon prevailing synoptic pressure distributions.

Wind speed, like wind direction, varies continuously, and although it is unusual for the mean wind speed to attain force 8 (34–40 knots) inland, gusts exceeding force 9 (over 47 knots) are not uncommon. Table 1.3 presents the highest hourly mean wind speeds and the highest gust speeds recorded at selected stations with at least 10 years of record. Despite the sheltering effect of the mountains of Sligo, Leitrim and Donegal, severe gales are occasionally experienced throughout Northern Ireland. The greatest intensities are reached along the Londonderry and Antrim coasts, although the County Down coastline experiences storms associated with the very strong south-east to east winds. Indeed Figure 1.2 clearly shows that the strongest winds do not blow solely from the south-westerly quadrant. The highest hourly mean speeds so far recorded in Northern Ireland at low altitudes have not exceeded 54 knots, whereas recordings in excess of 65 knots have been monitored over north-west Scotland, and south-west England. Upland sites in Northern Ireland have probably experienced hourly mean speeds of such force, but the paucity of such stations, and short length of records prevent a meaningful discussion of wind speeds at high altitude over the country.

TABLE 1.3

Extreme wind speeds in knots recorded by anemograph stations in Northern Ireland. (Data from Meteorological Office, Belfast)

Station	Height of Anemograph m O.D.	Recording Period	Highest Gust Speed	Month/year occurrence	Highest Hourly Mean Speed	Month/year occurrence
Aldergrove	80	1927-81	76	9/1961	49	9/1961
Ballykelly	13	1958-71	92	9/1961	53	2/1963
Ballypatrick Forest	166	1968-81	82	1/1968	53	1/1968
Belfast Harbour	21	1967-81	80	1/1976	46	1/1978
Carrigans	129	1964-81	81	11/1965	45	1/1965
Castle Archdale	79	1964-81	87	1/1974	48	1/1974
Kilkeel	36	1964-81	108	1/1974	54	1/1974
Orlock Head	51	1968-81	80	1/1974	56	1/1978

At most stations in Northern Ireland, gusts exceeding 64 knots have been recorded during each of the months of the winter half-year (October–March). Hardman et al. (1973) updated the work of Shellard (1962, 1965) and produced estimates of both the hourly mean wind speeds and gust speeds for recurrence periods of 10, 20, 50 and 100 years. Table 1.4 presents data for Aldergrove, the only station in Northern Ireland with records of sufficient length to allow such analysis, although the record length is only 43 years.

A 'day of gale' is one during which the mean wind speed exceeds 33 knots for a period of at least 10 consecutive minutes at a standard height of 10 m above the

TABLE 1.4

Estimated extreme wind speeds in knots at 10 m above the ground at
Aldergrove (after Hardman *et al.*, 1973).

Maximum gust speeds						*Maximum hourly mean speeds*					
Av. annual max.		*Speeds likely to be exceeded only once in stated no. years*				*Av. annual max.*		*Speeds likely to be exceeded only once in stated no. years*			
	10	20	50	100 years			10	20	50	100 years
61.6		72	77	82	87	35.1		42	45	49	51

ground. The greatest frequencies of days with gales are to be found along the exposed coasts of north Antrim and County Down, averaging 18 each year. This contrasts with inland, low-lying sites, for Aldergrove averages only 4 days each year, and Moneydig (near Garvagh, County Londonderry) and Armagh, 6 and 7 respectively. The frequency of gales increases with altitude, but even on the highest sites, the annual average never exceeds 40 days. The variation in frequency from year to year is of course considerable, but gales are most frequent during the period November to March. Generally, gales in summer are less severe than those occurring in winter. Nevertheless, events such as one gale in July 1978 during which hourly mean wind speeds of 38 knots and a maximum gust of 60 knots were recorded at Kilkeel, emphasize the possibility of intense storms at any season.

Solar radiation, sunshine and cloud

Solar radiation

The source of energy behind atmospheric circulation on earth is solar radiation, and the small fraction of total solar radiation intercepted by the earth is scattered or absorbed within the earth's atmosphere, reflected back into space or absorbed by the earth's surface. Solar radiation received at the earth's surface therefore comes from many directions. The term global solar radiation is used to denote the rate of receipt of solar energy on a plane surface, usually horizontal, coming from the whole hemisphere. It is made up of contributions directly from the sun, and also diffuse amounts from the sky.

Measurements of radiation, usually carried out with a thermopile instrument, are very few, and none exist over a long period in Northern Ireland. Figure 1.3*a* shows the annual variation of mean daily totals of global solar radiation, and Figure 1.3*b* the ratio of mean daily diffuse solar radiation to mean daily global solar radiation at Aldergrove over the period 1968-77. A marked difference between winter and summer global solar radiation receipt is apparent, caused by the geometrical aspects of the earth's rotation and orbit. With the predominance of cloud cover throughout the year in Northern Ireland, the diffuse component expressed as a percentage of the global value is shown to be of great importance.

Sunshine

The duration of 'bright sunshine' is measured by a Campbell-Stokes type sunshine recorder. (See Plate 1.1 on p. 14).

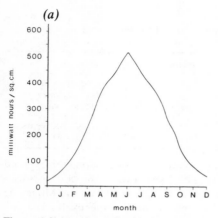

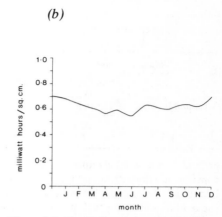

Figure 1.3 *(a)* Annual variation of mean daily totals of global solar radiation at Aldergrove, 1968-77.

Figure 1.3 *(b)* Ratio of mean daily diffuse solar radiation to mean global solar radiation at Aldergrove.

Monthly averages of the mean hours per day of duration of bright sunshine for selected stations over the period 1941-70, are given in Table 1.5. With the constantly changing declination of the sun throughout the year, and a corresponding annual variation of day length, there exists a marked annual regime in average daily sunshine duration. Values show a significant rise in April and an equally marked fall in September, with May the sunniest month, and June also experiencing significantly high amounts, a reflection of the high frequency of drier airflows at this time of the year. Relatively low July and August averages correspond to the comparative wetness of the summer season, although December is the dullest month.

Also apparent is the relatively small percentage of bright sunshine that reaches the instruments in Northern Ireland. Annual sunshine values are only about 28% of possible amounts, ranging from a minimum of 17% in December to a May maximum of 38%.

Over the year as a whole, the duration of bright sunshine is between 3.3 and 3.8 hours a day, with coastal areas having the highest values. In upland areas the enhancement of cloudiness, particularly on windward slopes, results in lower sunshine

TABLE 1.5

Average daily bright sunshine in hours, 1941-70. (Data from Meteorological Office, Belfast)

Station	J	F	M	A	M	J	J	A	S	O	N	D	Year
Aldergrove	1.4	2.4	3.3	5.1	6.2	5.8	4.4	4.4	3.5	2.5	1.9	1.1	3.5
Armagh	1.5	2.4	3.4	4.9	5.9	5.5	4.1	4.3	3.5	2.7	1.9	1.2	3.5
Ballykelly	1.6	2.7	3.5	5.3	6.3	5.7	4.3	4.7	3.7	2.8	2.0	1.2	3.7
Bessbrook	1.7	2.6	3.3	5.0	6.1	6.0	4.7	4.7	3.6	2.8	2.0	1.3	3.7
Castle Archdale	1.6	2.6	3.2	4.9	6.0	5.4	4.3	4.5	3.6	2.6	2.1	1.4	3.5
Hillsborough	1.5	2.4	3.2	4.8	6.0	5.9	4.4	4.4	3.5	2.7	1.9	1.2	3.5
Kilkeel	1.8	2.6	3.3	5.4	6.5	6.5	5.0	4.9	3.8	3.0	2.0	1.4	3.8
Lough Bradan	1.4	2.3	3.2	4.7	5.6	5.2	3.9	4.2	3.5	2.5	2.0	1.3	3.3

amounts than on neighbouring lowlands. Estimates at the few upland stations possessing sunshine recorders suggest that less than 25% of the possible annual bright sunshine is received.

Cloud

Cloud cover not only influences the receipt of bright sunshine by day, but it also controls night temperatures, for clear skies under favourable synoptic conditions are associated with lower night temperatures and the occurrence of phenomena such as dew, frost or fog. Observations are made of cloud type and the amount of cloud, which is measured in terms of oktas of the sky covered.

TABLE 1.6

Average amount of cloud in oktas at Aldergrove, 1941-70. (Data from Meteorological Office, Belfast)

J	F	M	A	M	J	J	A	S	O	N	D	Year
6.0	5.7	5.5	5.2	5.5	5.7	6.3	6.2	5.8	5.8	5.0	6.1	5.8

Table 1.6 provides monthly and annual averages of cloud amounts at Aldergrove for the period 1941-70. These values are fairly typical of Northern Ireland, the mean annual value of 5.8 oktas emphasizing the cloudy conditions so typical of a midlatitude maritime climate. July is the cloudiest month, closely followed by August, and a secondary maximum occurs from November to January. The clearest period is from March to May. Increased cloudiness over uplands gives values well in excess of those for Aldergrove, and since humidity also increases with altitude, the uplands tend to be very wet.

Barrett (1976) shows the cloudy nature of Northern Ireland, but even so, the incidence of heavily overcast skies (7–8 oktas cloud cover) is somewhat less than in Wales, northern England and Scotland, and only a little higher than in southern England. Days with relatively clear skies (0–2 oktas cloud cover) are experienced with a markedly lower frequency in Northern Ireland than in southern England due to the more frequent occurrence of anticyclonic weather and the general lack of relief in the latter area. However, Northern Ireland also compares unfavourably in relation to much of Wales, northern England and Scotland. Within Northern Ireland, the number of days experiencing little cloud cover increases eastward, and ranges from 27 days per year in the west, to over 46 days on the Down coast. This pattern is partly a reflection of topography.

Temperature

In Northern Ireland, the relatively high average temperature for such a northerly latitude, and the rareness of extremes, results from an oceanic position in the mid-latitude westerly wind belt, and exposure to the effects of the North Atlantic Drift. It is during departures from the normal zonal circulation over varying time periods that extremes of temperature are recorded.

The extreme oceanic regime of Northern Ireland is indicated by the application of Conrad's (1946) Continentality Index upon temperatures at selected stations. The formula, which takes account of the annual range of mean temperature and the

TABLE 1.7

Monthly and annual values of mean daily maximum, mean daily minimum and mean daily air temperature for selected stations, 1941-70. (Data from Meteorological Office, Belfast)

Station	Altitude Values m O.D.	Mean Daily Values °C	J	F	M	A	M	J	J	A	S	O	N	D	Yr
Aldergrove	68	Max	5.8	6.5	9.0	11.8	14.7	17.4	18.1	18.0	16.0	12.9	8.9	6.7	12.1
		Min	1.2	1.1	2.4	3.9	6.1	9.2	10.7	10.5	9.3	7.2	3.9	2.5	5.7
		Mean	3.5	3.8	5.7	7.9	10.4	13.3	14.4	14.3	12.7	10.1	6.4	4.6	8.9
Armagh	62	Max	6.7	7.4	10.0	12.7	15.5	18.3	19.0	18.8	16.8	13.6	9.5	7.6	13.0
		Min	1.2	1.2	2.6	4.0	6.3	9.2	10.8	10.6	9.2	6.9	3.5	2.1	5.6
		Mean	3.9	4.3	6.3	8.3	10.9	13.7	14.9	14.7	13.0	10.3	6.5	4.9	9.3
Ballykelly	2	Max	6.8	7.2	9.4	11.8	14.7	17.6	17.5	17.6	16.3	13.6	9.3	7.4	12.4
		Min	2.0	1.8	3.5	4.4	6.8	9.7	10.8	10.6	9.7	8.1	4.3	3.0	6.2
		Mean	4.4	4.5	6.5	8.1	10.7	13.7	14.1	14.1	13.0	10.9	6.8	5.2	9.3
Castle Archdale	66	Max	6.4	7.0	9.4	11.4	14.8	16.9	17.9	17.9	16.2	12.8	9.5	7.5	12.3
		Min	1.9	2.0	3.1	4.7	6.7	9.6	11.3	11.1	9.7	6.9	4.4	3.0	6.3
		Mean	4.1	4.5	6.2	8.1	10.7	13.3	14.7	14.5	12.9	9.9	6.9	5.4	9.3
Hillsborough	116	Max	6.1	6.4	8.6	11.3	14.0	16.8	17.7	17.6	15.7	12.7	8.9	7.2	11.9
		Min	1.2	1.1	2.1	3.8	5.9	8.5	10.3	10.2	9.1	7.0	3.5	2.2	5.4
		Mean	3.7	3.7	5.3	7.5	8.9	12.7	14.0	13.9	12.4	9.9	6.2	5.7	8.7
Kilkeel	18	Max	6.9	6.8	8.6	11.1	13.5	16.2	17.3	17.6	15.9	13.3	9.8	8.1	12.1
		Min	2.9	2.4	3.5	4.9	7.2	9.8	11.1	11.2	10.0	8.3	5.3	4.1	6.7
		Mean	4.9	4.6	6.1	8.0	10.3	13.0	14.2	14.4	13.0	10.8	7.5	6.1	9.4
Moneydig	34	Max	6.2	6.9	9.4	12.1	14.8	17.4	18.1	18.1	15.2	13.2	9.2	7.2	12.4
		Min	0.7	0.6	2.0	3.5	5.6	8.8	10.2	9.9	8.6	6.5	3.0	1.9	5.1
		Mean	3.5	3.7	5.7	7.8	10.2	13.1	14.1	14.0	11.9	9.9	6.1	4.5	8.7
Parkmore Forest	235	Max	5.5	5.2	6.9	9.7	12.6	15.6	15.8	16.5	14.5	11.8	7.6	7.1	10.7
		Min	0.1	0.2	1.1	2.5	4.7	7.5	8.4	8.6	7.5	6.2	2.5	1.1	4.2
		Mean	2.8	2.7	4.0	6.1	8.7	11.5	12.1	12.5	11.0	9.0	5.1	3.6	7.5

geographical latitude, provides a minimum continentality value of 4.2 at Ballykelly, and a maximum value of 6.7 at Armagh. In comparison with values of more than 60 for continental interiors, it is evident that the degree of continentality in Northern Ireland is very small.

Temperature recording throughout Northern Ireland varies with station type. Dry and wet bulb temperatures are taken hourly at Aldergrove, and at least daily at 09.00 hours at meteorological or climatological stations. These stations also record maximum and minimum temperatures, although the reference period varies with the individual station.

Mean air temperature

Mean annual temperature fluctuates within narrow limits in Northern Ireland. During the period 1941-70, the range of annual temperature at Aldergrove was 1.8° C, with a standard deviation of 0.4° C. On only one occasion, 1949, did the annual temperature deviate more than 0.8° C above the mean (Tout, 1976).

Table 1.7 presents temperature data, uncorrected for altitude, at eight stations selected to give an adequate coverage of Northern Ireland, for the period 1941-70, while Figure 1.4 illustrates the temperature differences between coastal, inland, and upland stations.

Comparison of the temperature data reveals differences between certain inland stations. Castle Archdale, adjacent to Lower Lough Erne, and exposed to the moderating westerly influences from the Atlantic, has a climate more tempered than that of other inland stations. Nearly all the mean monthly winter temperatures at Aldergrove are a little higher than those at Moneydig and Hillsborough principally because of Aldergrove's proximity to the moderating effects of Lough Neagh (Partington, 1970; Stephens, 1963). Moneydig however lies in a hollow between the Sperrins and the Antrim hills, and experiences katabatic winds draining cold air down the hillslopes. These produce minimum temperatures significantly below those attained at Aldergrove. The Hillsborough site is similarly affected by cold air moving down from the uplands to the south.

Seasonal variations of temperature

Consideration of temperature variations throughout the year reveals that highest mean temperatures in winter are found along the coast, reflecting higher mean daily maximum, and more importantly, higher mean daily minimum values. Due to the thermal properties of ocean surfaces, the waters surrounding Northern Ireland do not reach their lowest temperature until February, and for coastal sites fully exposed to maritime influences, such as Kilkeel, the lowest mean temperature is recorded in this month. In contrast, January is the coldest month at most inland stations. Winter also sees the greatest fluctuation in mean temperatures, for temperature contrasts between air masses with westerly and easterly components are at a maximum at this time of year.

By spring the temperature pattern has changed considerably. The highest mean daily maximum temperatures during April are at Armagh (12.7° C). At Kilkeel, during April temperatures average only 11.1° C. Occasionally persistent on-shore winds from the Irish Sea maintain very low temperatures along eastern coasts, and may be accompanied by coastal fog, the "haar", in late spring and early summer. Mean daily

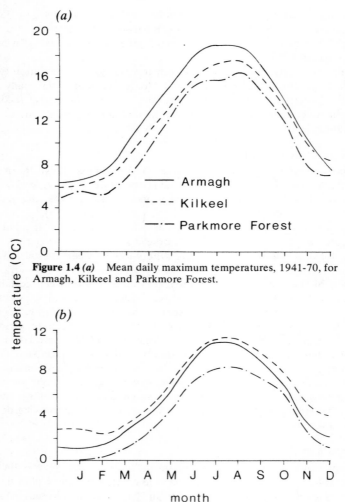

Figure 1.4 (a) Mean daily maximum temperatures, 1941-70, for Armagh, Kilkeel and Parkmore Forest.

Figure 1.4 (b) Mean daily minimum temperatures, 1941-70, for Armagh, Kilkeel and Parkmore Forest.

minimum temperatures, however, are still warmer in coastal areas, as they are in winter, and the daily range of temperature inland may be very large in spring.

Coastal stations are generally cooler than inland sites during the summer months. During spells of anticyclonic weather, the sea breeze effect holds down maximum temperatures along the coast. The effect of a maritime and eastern location upon summer temperatures at Kilkeel is evident from Table 1.7. Indeed, Aldergrove, Armagh and even the less exposed coastal site of Ballykelly have recorded absolute maxima in excess of 27° C in at least 3 months of the year, whereas at Kilkeel, absolute maxima are 22.8° C, 25° C and 22.3° C for June, July and August respectively. The pattern of mean daily minimum temperature, however, is the inverse of the maximum temperature distribution. The mean daily range is therefore at its greatest at this time of year, increasing inland with July values of more than 8° C at Armagh, in comparison with a range of only 6.2° C at Kilkeel.

Whereas July is the month of highest mean temperature at inland stations, August is usually warmer at coastal sites when sea surface temperatures are highest. Kilkeel for example, is 0.2° C warmer in August than in July.

By October the pattern of mean temperature resembles that of January. Coastal areas enjoy higher mean temperatures than inland, due mainly to the significantly higher mean daily minimum temperatures at coastal sites. As at other seasons, the greatest daily range of temperature occurs at inland sites, but by autumn the range has fallen from the summer peak due to the decline in maximum rather than minimum temperatures.

Air temperature in urban areas

The characteristics and causation of the heat-island effect is well documented by Chandler (1961, 1965, 1967, 1976), who reports nocturnal city temperatures often 5° C, and sometimes 10° C warmer than neighbouring rural areas. The effect is produced principally by the gradual release at night of heat stored in the urban fabric during the day. It is most well-developed during anticyclonic weather.

Belfast's thermal environment is distinctive with mean minimum temperatures in the city 2.8° C higher in central Belfast than in the surrounding rural areas. The heat-island over Belfast, however, is not stable, as McPeake (1980) has demonstrated by means of the mobile traverse technique developed by Chandler (1965). Certain familiar features were found: the heat-island follows the margins of built-up areas, the spacing of isotherms reflects building density, and steep thermal gradients occur near to the junction of dense and more open urban development. On calm nights a very highly significant correlation was found between the heat-island intensity and building density. On windy occasions however, the advection of cool air into windward suburbs, displaced the zone of highest temperature a short distance downwind of the peak of highest building densities. Two notable features of the isothermal maps of Belfast were the prominent cold cell over Ormeau Park, and the distinctive tongue of cool air extending well in towards the central districts up the River Lagan.

Extremes of temperature

Table 1.8 presents the extreme maximum and minimum temperatures recorded for each calendar month at Armagh over the period 1901-81. Armagh was selected since it possesses the longest complete temperature record in Northern Ireland. Furthermore, having the maximum continentality index value, Armagh should provide representative examples of the temperature extremes experienced this century.

At Armagh, extreme maximum values have exceeded 30° C in only one month. This contrasts with stations in central and southern England, some of which have experienced temperatures exceeding 35° C in June, July and August. Such high temperatures are usually associated with an inflow of tropical continental air accompanying anticyclonic conditions.

Temperatures below 0° C have been experienced at Armagh in all months other than July and August. Moneydig, in a well-defined frost hollow, has one of the lowest

TABLE 1.8

Extreme maximum and minimum temperatures (°C) at Armagh,
1901-81. (Data from Meteorological Office, Belfast)

	J	F	M	A	M	J
Extreme max. temp.	13.9	14.4	21.7	22.7	25.6	29.0
Year of most recent						
occurrence	1957	1953	1965	1975	1952	1976
Extreme min. temp.	−11.1	−10.6	−12.2	−7.2	−1.8	−0.6
Year of most recent						
occurrence	1963	1969	1947	1917	1979	1930

	J	A	S	O	N	D
Extreme max. temp.	30.6	29.0	27.8	22.8	16.7	15.0
Year of most recent						
occurrence	1934	1975	1906	1908	1948	1948
Extreme min. temp.	3.9	2.2	−4.4	−4.4	−8.3	−10.0
Year of most recent						
occurrence	1918	1944	1919	1926	1919	1909

temperatures recorded (−13.9°C). Temperatures of this severity, particularly at lowland stations, are usually associated with a blocking anticyclone accompanied by a persistent easterly airflow.

In Northern Ireland, periods of extreme temperature are generally short-lived, but occasionally, persistence of certain circulation patterns may lend a particular character to an individual winter or summer. Apart from the winter of 1962-63 and the record-making winter of 1981-82, the winter of 1978-79 was the most severe of recent years, although incursions of mild Atlantic air associated with the remnants of Atlantic depressions periodically interacted with easterly and north-easterly airflows – a situation that did not occur in 1962-63 (Jones, 1979). Figure 1.5 shows the pattern of daily maximum and minimum temperatures from December 1978 to March 1979, and for comparison, those of one of the warmest winters, 1974-75. The repercussions upon temperature of persistence of continental or maritime airflow are clearly evident.

In summer, anticyclonic circulation, particularly if accompanied by a continuous inflow of continental air from the south or south-east, will produce a hot, dry season. Enhanced anticyclonic activity over the British Isles during the well documented drought of 1975-76 (Doornkamp, Gregory and Burn, 1980; Miles, 1977; Murray, 1977; Ratcliffe, 1977; Royal Society, 1978), produced a remarkable persistence of above average daily maximum temperatures between June and August 1976 (Figure 1.6).

Frost

Frost is recorded as 'air frost' when the air temperature falls below 0°C. Since 1961, 'ground frost' statistics have been referred to as the "number of days with grass minimum temperature below 0°C". Ground frost is so much influenced by topography, soils and vegetation cover, that statistics of this element are indicative only of the site at which the recordings are taken.

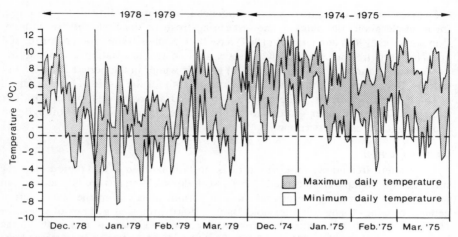

Figure 1.5 Daily maximum and minimum temperatures at Armagh during the winters of 1974/75 and 1978/79.

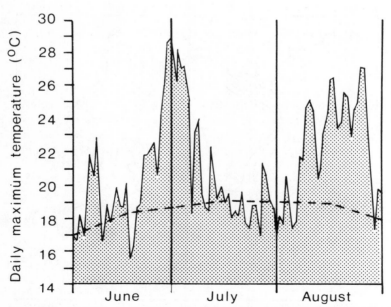

Figure 1.6 Daily maximum temperatures at Armagh, June-August 1976. The dotted line represents mean daily maximum temperatures.

Spatial variation of air frost is less pronounced, but it is still difficult to generalize, for example about the dates of the last spring frost, or the first frost, in autumn. Connaughton (1969) and Glassey (1967) have both examined this problem for Ireland and Northern Ireland respectively. Glassey showed that no station in his selected network was entirely frost-free throughout any one winter in the period 1936-65, but dates of December 31st for the first, and January 10th for the last frost have occurred at some coastal locations. Aldergrove has recorded a screen frost in June on four occasions. The only other stations to record a June air frost are Hillsborough and Moneydig, each on one occasion.

Growing season

In Northern Ireland the growing season is most often taken as that period when the mean daily air temperature exceeds 5.6° C. Such threshold means are not perfect, but are useful in comparing the effectiveness of various places from the standpoint of general farming. Using this threshold Bailie (1980) produced a series of maps for Northern Ireland illustrating the average duration and changes in length of the growing season between 1941 and 1970. Excluding local factors, it is apparent from Figure 1.7a that length of growing season is governed principally by altitudinal and maritime influences. In general the length of the growing season decreases by about 4 days with every 30 metres of altitude. Under 235 days a year (late March to early November) are available over the uplands and fewer than 210 days in the highest areas. The season lengthens to between 250 and 265 days (mid-March to late November) in the central lowlands. Values in excess of 280 days (early March to late

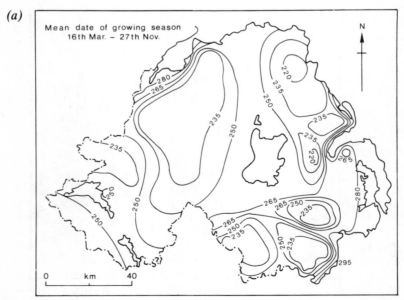

Figure 1.7 The average duration of the growing season in Northern Ireland: *(a)* 1941-70; *(b)* 1951-60; *(c)* 1961-70. (Derived from Bailie, 1980).

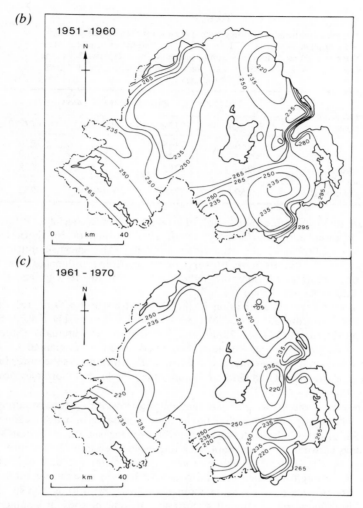

(b)

1951 - 1960

(c)

1961 - 1970

December) are found along the coastal strips of the Foyle estuary, Belfast Lough, east Down and the Ards peninsula, with a maximum growing season of 300 days in the Kilkeel area of the Mourne coastal plain.

Figures 1.7*b* and 1.7*c* show the effect of climatic fluctuations upon the average length of the growing season throughout Northern Ireland, with the 1961-70 decade having much shorter growing seasons than the preceding decade. This was principally due to the cold Decembers of the 1960s which caused the growing seasons to end relatively early. December mildness, particularly in the early 1970s, is reflected in the recovery of the average length of growing season for the period 1971-80 (Table 1.9). These changes in growing season length are responses to changes of temperature, precipitation and atmospheric circulation as outlined by Lamb (1977), and to be considered later.

TABLE 1.9

The average duration of the growing season for the periods, 1941-50, 1951-60, 1961-70 and 1971-80 at the five stations used to calculate Northern Ireland monthly temperature values. (Derived by the author from Bailie, 1980, and data from Meteorological Office, Belfast)

Meteorological Station	Average growing season in days			
	1941-50	1951-60	1961-70	1971-80
Aldergrove	266	266	244	259
Armagh	277	276	252	260
Castle Archdale	268	262	242	258
Hillsborough	268	257	237	251
Moneydig (Garvagh)	259	256	244	257

To measure intensity rather than length of growing season, a special unit, termed a degree-day, is often adopted (Gregory, 1954, 1964). Much of Northern Ireland receives between 2,000 and 2,500 degree-days annually. The highest summits receive only about 1,000–1,500. Because of very strong maritime influences the 2,000 degree-day line occurs at considerably higher altitudes in Northern Ireland than in comparable latitudes over Britain.

With the limit for cereal cultivation in the British Isles at 1,500 degree-days of accumulated temperature each year, Northern Ireland is favourably placed, for all stations under 150 m O.D. have 2,000 to 2,500 degree-days annually (Stephens, 1963). Increased precipitation, humidity and wind speed accompanied by lower temperatures, limit cultivation much above 210 m O.D. which marks the lower limit of rough grazing, although isolated field crops under favourable conditions may occur up to 300 m O.D..

Certain indices of the growing season may emphasize soil moisture requirements. Pasture production is particularly dependent upon a suitable moisture regime, and Hurst and Smith (1967) have defined the grass growing season in Britain as the number of days between April and September inclusive when the soil moisture deficit does not exceed 50.8 mm. This value represents the estimated division between unhindered and drought-retarded growth. Northern Ireland experiences on average about 170 grass-growing days a year, in comparison with only 130 days in south-east England. This reflects the infrequent occurrence of long periods in summer with moisture deficit in Northern Ireland, to be discussed later.

Precipitation

In Northern Ireland, the last 20 years have seen the development of a dense precipitation recording network (Table 1.2). A number of stations also have rainfall observations dating into the nineteenth century, and precipitation is therefore perhaps the best documented of climatic elements in Northern Ireland. (see Plate 1.2).

Precipitation in Northern Ireland is principally in the form of rain or drizzle. Snowfall and hail are infrequent. Precipitation is caused by three principal mechanisms: frontal activity within extra-tropical cyclones, convection, and orographic ascent of moist air. These three mechanisms often interact though the cyclonic component contributes most rainfall, particularly in the west.

Annual and monthly amounts

Figure 1.8 shows the mean annual rainfall over Northern Ireland for the standard period 1941-70. A general decrease in rainfall totals from west to east is apparent, although upland areas with their heavier rainfall complicate this pattern. Furthermore, Perry (1972) and Logue (1978) have suggested the existence of north-south contrasts of rainfall regime under different synoptic patterns, for Ireland as a whole. Rainfall in the highest parts of the Sperrins, Mournes and Antrim plateau exceeds 1,600 mm. This increase of rainfall with altitude is the result of complex processes, produced not simply by the upland acting as a barrier to moist airstreams, but by the hills functioning as high level heat sources on clear days, thereby encouraging the development of convective clouds and the shower activity associated with them. Even with the exclusion of upland areas, Northern Ireland has a wet climate. The driest areas are the Bann-Lough Neagh lowlands, the drumlin country of east Down, and the Ards peninsula.

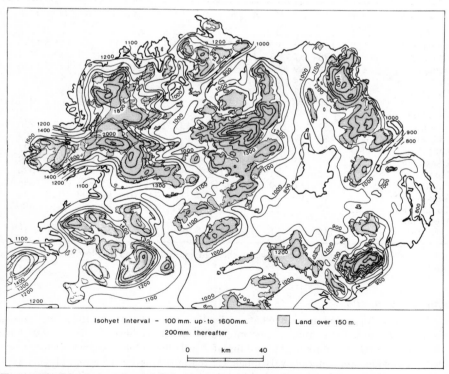

Isohyet Interval – 100 mm. up · to 1600mm. 200mm. thereafter

Land over 150 m.

0   km   40

Figure 1.8 Mean annual rainfall in mm, 1941-70. (Derived from Meteorological Office, Bracknell, 1976*a*).

Table 1.10 presents for the period 1941-70 monthly and annual averages of rainfall for the eleven stations network used by the Meteorological Office to calculate the monthly rainfall for Northern Ireland as a whole, together with data for a number of upland stations. A period of marked minimum rainfall is evident between February and June, when the westerly circulation is less pronounced. A fairly marked rise in precipitation is apparent in July and August everywhere, with stations in the central lowlands experiencing summer rainfall equal to or even exceeding winter values, the result of convective processes. Over the last decade, however, this summer wetness has not been so apparent, for reasons to be discussed later. Away from the lowlands, particularly in the west, a winter maximum of rainfall is more pronounced, associated with the most intense depressions at this season. Upland stations have in excess of 100 mm in each month between August and January, and some sites especially in the west, experience this amount in all months.

With few exceptions, December is the wettest month, although within the period August to January, few of the months are significantly wetter or drier than the others.

TABLE 1.10

Monthly and annual averages of rainfall (mm.) for selected
stations 1941-70. (Data from Meteorological Office, Belfast)

Station	Altitude m O.D.	J	F	M	A	M	J	J	A	S	O	N	D	Yr
Annalong*	130	124	84	93	80	87	81	97	116	119	115	119	125	1240
Armagh*	62	78	57	53	58	61	68	75	87	80	83	77	87	864
Banagher*	111	128	99	84	83	83	80	98	105	118	122	123	147	1270
Belfast P. S.*	5	95	64	63	58	62	62	74	87	92	88	94	99	938
Carrigans	113	105	77	71	66	77	85	90	106	113	115	103	122	1130
Crom*	58	100	70	68	63	74	75	87	97	100	101	89	109	1033
Glenderg Forest	180	161	118	109	100	118	130	137	163	176	174	157	187	1730
Hillsborough*	116	84	57	57	55	60	66	79	96	90	87	84	89	904
Labbyheige	347	150	114	100	96	99	101	127	130	147	148	140	170	1522
Lisnafillan*	38	95	65	58	59	63	73	88	97	97	99	94	105	993
Moneydig*	34	102	72	61	61	70	75	91	94	101	102	94	111	1034
Parkmore	235	155	111	100	102	102	118	143	163	163	161	166	171	1655
Stoneyford*	135	97	68	67	64	69	75	94	104	101	98	94	103	1034
Toomebridge*	15	82	57	52	52	60	64	82	87	90	87	76	91	880
Woodburn North*	217	115	79	78	76	83	85	104	119	120	119	113	119	1210

* denotes station is part of network used to calculate monthly rainfall for Northern Ireland as a whole.

Rainfall variability

The 1941-70 period is somewhat misleading in terms of monthly and annual averages of rainfall, for atmospheric circulation patterns since the late 1960s have produced rainfall amounts in the months of April, June, July, August, October and December which are generally very much less than the long-term average (Figure 1.9). Annual rainfall over the same period has also been below average. This variability is contrary to the popular belief in the reliability of Northern Ireland's rainfall. Examination of rainfall amounts in individual years reveals that an exceptional number of Atlantic depressions crossed the country in 1954 and produced annual rainfall totals 115% of the 1941-70 average, with 9 months having above average amounts. February (149%), March (130%), May (153%), October (164%) and November (142%) were the wettest months relative to long-term average conditions.

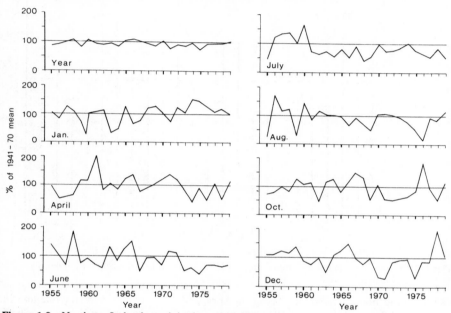

Figure 1.9 Northern Ireland precipitation 1955-79; annual and selected monthly values expressed as percentages of their respective 1941-70 averages.

In contrast, the anomalous high surface pressure during much of 1975 and 1976 mentioned earlier, produced a prolonged rainfall deficiency in Northern Ireland, and the monthly rainfall sequence is shown in Figure 1.10. Rainfall during 1975 was 75% of the 1941-70 annual average, with only January and September experiencing above average amounts, and May, June and December receiving below 40% of their mean. Rainfall was more variable during the winter and spring of 1976, when January, March and May were wet months, but the 3 month period June to August received only 48% of the 1941-70 standard. The drought ended with the heavy rains of September and October 1976.

Droughts of the intensity of 1975-76 are exceedingly rare, but dry periods are not unusual in Northern Ireland. 'Absolute droughts' and 'dry spells' are defined as periods of at least 15 consecutive days, none of which is credited 0.2 mm or more, and 1 mm or more of rainfall respectively.

Between 1931 and 1979 at Armagh, a period of absolute drought has occurred in 24 years, but in only 4 of these years did two spells of drought occur. Dry spells have occurred in all but 7 years, and 1972 experienced four, the greatest number in any one year on record. Since 1931, an absolute drought has occurred in all months apart from

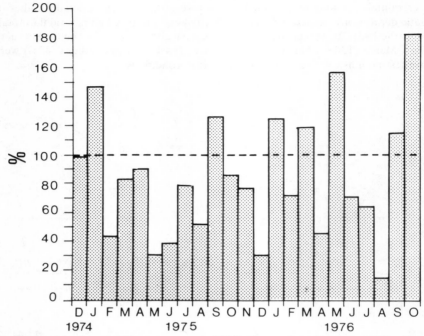

Figure 1.10 Monthly rainfall as a percentage of 1941-70 mean from December 1974 to October 1976 over Northern Ireland.

October, the highest incidence being in April and May, with secondary maxima in August and September. Dry spells also show a spring maximum. This distribution of dryness reflects the annual atmospheric circulation regime outlined earlier, and has been studied by Lamb (1950, 1972*b*). Furthermore, the annual variation in the frequency of droughts and dry spells reflects fluctuations of the atmospheric circulation from year to year.

Daily rainfall

The character of rainfall is not fully revealed by annual and monthly totals, but consideration of daily amounts affords more detail. Two indices of daily rainfall commonly used in this connection are 'rain days' with falls of 0.2 mm or more, and 'wet days' with falls of 1 mm or more. The average number of rain days increases from about 195 on the east Down coast, to over 250 days in the west, north-west and upland areas. Wet days range from 150 in the east to 200 days in the west and uplands.

Disadvantages of the rainfall-day as the arbitrary period for studies of heavy rainfalls have been stressed by Bleasdale (1963, 1970), but it is a convenient time unit. Amounts in excess of 100 mm in one rainfall-day have occurred on a number of occasions at stations in the Mournes, Sperrins and Antrim hills, but falls in excess of 125 mm are rare in upland areas, and absent altogether from lowland stations. The infrequent occurrence of heavy falls is due to relatively low relief and the low frequency of severe convectional activity in summer. It is not possible to present a comprehensive list of heavy rainfall occurrences, although Woodley (1968) has listed amounts for selected stations. Prior and Betts (1974) and Houghton and Ó Cinnéide (1977) have discussed individual events.

Rainfall duration and intensity

To appreciate rainfall duration and intensity characteristics in Northern Ireland, it is useful to compare values at Aldergrove with those elsewhere in Britain. Aldergrove, for example, has 722 hours rainfall per annum in comparison with 506 hours at Camden Square, London. Consistently higher rainfall duration throughout the year reflects the closer proximity of Aldergrove, than London, to depression tracks. Aldergrove also has a mean rainfall intensity of only 1.12 mm per hour in comparison with a national average of 1.3 mm per hour (Atkinson and Smithson, 1976) a figure which supports the general perception that Ireland's rainfall is of low intensity and of long duration.

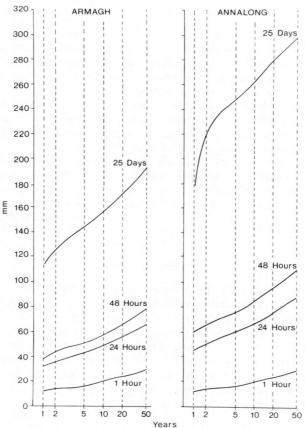

Figure 1.11 Rainfall in mm for a range of durations and return periods at Annalong and Armagh. (Data from Meteorological Office, Belfast).

Important in connection with water management and drainage schemes is the relationship between depth, duration and frequency of heavy rainfall. The Flood Studies Report (Meteorological Office, 1975) provides data to allow the calculation of rainfall amounts for a range of duration and return periods, at any location in Northern Ireland (see also Jackson, 1977a). Figure 1.11 presents this information at Annalong (130 m) and Armagh (62 m) for durations of 1 hour, 24 hours, 48 hours and 25 days, with return periods of up to 50 years. The similarity of values of 1-hour falls over various return periods at the two sites suggests that during short-period heavy falls, often localized in character, the orographic effect is not as significant as convective uplift. In contrast, with longer durations, rainfall amounts are markedly greater at the upland site of Annalong. This is in accordance with the fact that areas experiencing large annual precipitation, receive a great proportion of these amounts from prolonged heavy events associated with large-scale weather systems, and these falls usually occur over uplands for the reasons given earlier.

Snowfall

Although heavy falls of snow are relatively rare in Northern Ireland, the economic consequences of such occurrences can be great. The synoptic patterns most often associated with snowfalls are those producing cold airstreams from northerly or easterly quadrants. Westerly and south-westerly airflows in winter give temperatures well above 0° C even on the highest ground. Snowfalls in the form of instability showers occur over the north and east coasts exposed to onshore winds, although rarely is any great depth of cover attained. The heaviest snowfalls occur with 'polar lows' and with slow moving warm fronts, but with the passage of the frontal system across the area, and the influx of warmer air, a rapid thaw often results.

The average number of days with snow lying on the ground is lowest on the East Down coast, the Lough Foyle lowlands, and the valleys of the Roe and Lower Bann, all having less than 10 days. Inland stations under 150 m O.D. experience between 20–30 days of snow each year, although the Armagh region averages only 18 days. In the Antrim hills, Sperrins and Mournes, snowfall frequency exceeds 30 days per year (Jackson, 1977b).

Evapotranspiration

Water vapour, the source of precipitation, is received by the atmosphere through evaporation from the oceans, inland water bodies, and most land surfaces, and through transpiration from plants. These processes are described by the term evapotranspiration, and together with precipitation form part of a continuous transfer of moisture and heat energy between the atmosphere and the earth's surface. Globally, there exists a balance between these transfer processes, but locally, imbalance between precipitation and evapotranspiration results in periods of water deficit when the latter exceeds the former, and surplus when the reverse occurs. Prolonged deficit or surplus can have severe repercussions for water resource management, even in Northern Ireland (Betts, 1978a, 1978b).

A distinction is made between potential evapotranspiration (PE) and actual evapotranspiration (AE). PE is the maximum quantity of water loss that will occur from a moist surface under given climatological conditions. In contrast, water loss in the form of AE has a lower value, for this term allows for the occasional drying out of the soil surface, and under such conditions little or no evapotranspiration occurs. PE is a somewhat artificial concept, but being influenced by fewer factors that AE, it is less difficult to estimate. Data on PE are therefore easier to collect, and consideration will be restricted to this measure of evapotranspiration.

Instrumental measurements of evapotranspiration in the United Kingdom and Ireland have often proved inconsistent, and few have been undertaken in Northern Ireland (see Chapter 2). In the estimation of PE by the Meteorological Office, an amended version of Penman's formula (1962) is adopted (Grindley, 1970). The meteorological variables used in the Penman estimates of PE, (which Penman terms PT to distinguish his estimates from those based on Thornthwaite's formula), are mean air temperatures, mean deficit from the saturation vapour pressure, mean wind speed and mean sunshine duration. In Northern Ireland only five stations record any two of these elements continuously. The seventeen other stations for which PT estimates are made, rely on one or two daily observations of temperature, vapour pressure and wind speed. Sunshine is recorded continuously at all twenty-two stations, the distribution of which is shown in Chapter 2 (Figure 2.2). Only five stations have PT data for fifteen years or more.

The influence of solar radiation and temperature upon evapotranspiration is reflected in the seasonal variation of PT rates at Aldergrove, an inland site, Kilkeel, a coastal site and Lough Bradan, an upland site (Figure 1.12). At all three stations PT is

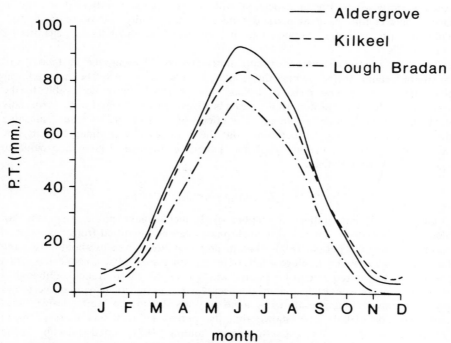

Figure 1.12 Mean monthly PT at Aldergrove, Kilkeel and Lough Bradan, 1964-79.

35

considerably greater during summer than winter, with a maximum in June and a minimum in December. A smaller seasonal range is found at Kilkeel on the coast, with lower summer and higher winter values than at Aldergrove, a low lying inland station, although Lough Bradan, an upland station, has the smallest seasonal variation of the three. Annual PT values exceeding 460 mm along coasts decrease inland to less than 350 mm in upland areas. This spatial pattern reflects the longer duration of sunshine and higher wind speeds of coastal areas.

Fog and mist

Despite recent developments of instrumentation, precise visibility data are comparatively rare throughout Northern Ireland. Fog describes a reduction of visibility to less than 1 km, and mist to over 1 km. Both are due to the presence of suspended water droplets, smoke or solid particles in the atmosphere.

In urban areas, fog polluted by solid particles and industrial gases is often referred to as smog. Clean air controls were first enforced over a limited area of Belfast in 1964, and smokeless zones were extended during succeeding years. Measurements of smoke, grit, dust, lead and sulphur dioxide concentrations are made at numerous sites throughout the city. The consequent improvements of air quality and visibility in Belfast are in line with similar trends in other British cities, although the improvements cannot be solely attributed to the Clean Air Act (Lawrence, 1971). The alignment of the Lagan valley allows a natural corridor for pollution dispersal by prevailing south-westerly winds. It is in association with easterly and southerly airflows, and/or anticyclonic conditions, that marked reductions in visibility still occur in Belfast. Pollutants often become trapped beneath an inversion, and bank up against the Antrim hills.

The haar mentioned earlier, occurs fairly frequently along the east coasts of Northern Ireland. Surface temperatures in the Irish Sea and North Channel are lower than those off the west coast of Ireland, and therefore more favourable to the formation of fog as a warm moist airstream is advected over the cold water, especially in the late spring and early summer. The effects of the haar are to reduce sunshine duration and maximum temperatures, but these are usually confined to a narrow coastal strip, although the fog itself may penetrate the coastal glens and bank up against the Antrim plateau.

Climatic change

Lamb (1977) has outlined a number of distinct climatic phases since the last glaciation. One of the more recent such phases can be identified from the Armagh records. During this period, 1880–1940, mean temperatures rose by about 0.6° C, and have fallen since by 0.3° C. Recent falls of temperature are probably connected with a reduction in the frequency of westerly winds over Northern Ireland, although a time-lag appears to exist in this mechanism, for the period of maximum westerlies preceded maximum temperatures by some 20 years (Lamb and Mörth, 1978). Perry and Fearnside (1980) have shown that the period 1951-70 was marked by an intensification of blocking, and in contrast, Painting (1977) noted a decline in the winter occurrence of blocking anticyclones during the early 1970s, and a northward enhancement of the Atlantic sub-tropical anticyclone, giving positive pressure anomalies near the British Isles. This was accompanied by a fall of pressure over much of the Arctic, producing an increase of Atlantic zonal flow north of 50° N, a diversion of depressions to more northern latitudes, and a succession of mild winters in Northern Ireland. The circulation patterns over Northern Ireland during the 1970s have resulted in long spells of various weather types, the character of which was dependent upon the longitudinal position of the upper waves.

Climatic trends are usually of relatively small magnitude in comparison with the annual variability of climatic elements, and their study must be based upon a complete and homogeneous series of data. Conclusions concerning climatic change require evidence from a number of stations. In Northern Ireland, stations possessing complete and lengthy records of climatic elements are few, and the following discussion of recent climatic trends is therefore restricted to a consideration of temperature and precipitation.

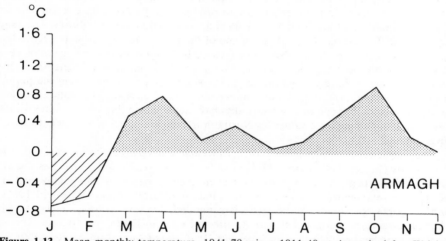

Figure 1.13   Mean monthly temperature, 1941-70 minus 1911-40 at Armagh. (after Wright, 1976).

Wright (1976), discussing recent climatic change in the British Isles, selected Armagh to represent Northern Ireland in an examination of mean temperature changes for each month between the periods 1911-40 and 1941-70, which respectively represent strong zonal and weak zonal epochs of the general atmospheric circulation in the mid-latitudes (Figure 1.13). The marked cooling in January and February reflects this change well, together with the corresponding increase of northerly airflow in those months during the period 1941-70. November and December experienced similar but smaller changes in circulation and correspondingly little change of temperature. A higher frequency of southerly winds during the period 1941-70 brought increased warmth to March, June and September. This increase of southerly circulation was also apparent in April and October although increased warmth in these two months was enhanced by a greater frequency of anticyclonic conditions. May, July and August showed only a small temperature increase. Unfortunately, no station other than

Armagh has complete temperature records of sufficient length to support these findings, although stations in mainland Britain show similar trends.

The uneven distribution of precipitation over a region during the course of a month presents great difficulties in the analysis of temporal variations in precipitation. Following Wright's analysis, the author investigated the monthly changes of precipitation amount from 1911-40 to 1941-70 for Northern Ireland, using an evenly spaced network of stations with complete long-term records. A great variation in the pattern of precipitation between the individual stations was evident, and a marked increase of September wetness was the only feature common to all. Amalgamation of the stations to form a Northern Ireland regional value, revealed a similar pattern to that found by Wright for mainland Britain, namely, an increased summer wetness with the exception of July, and a drier winter half-year in the second of the two epochs. These results agree quite well with what might be expected from increased summer cyclonicity (except in July) and a decreased westerly frequency in winter between 1911-40 and 1941-70 (Wright, 1976). The great variation in temporal pattern between individual stations in Northern Ireland requires these results to be viewed with caution.

Any comparison of the periods 1911-40 and 1941-70 necessarily fails to reflect fully the climatic fluctuation of recent years, and of the last decade in particular. Since the late 1960s, as stated earlier, Northern Ireland has experienced long spells of very diverse weather, and it is necessary to examine how precipitation and temperature during this period have changed from those average values derived from the period 1941-70. The regional precipitation values prior to 1977 were derived from a network of thirty stations, but computational studies have since shown that only eleven stations are required. Temperature values for Northern Ireland are obtained from a network of five stations.

The characteristic variability of Northern Ireland annual precipitation ceased in the late-1960s (Figure 1.9). Since 1967, in only 2 years, 1970 and 1979, has annual precipitation been above average, and even then it was only marginally higher. Successive years with below average precipitation occurred in the 1950s and 1960s, but the persistent dryness of the 1970s is unparalleled in this century. The consistent dryness of certain months each year is also apparent in Figure 1.9. Below average precipitation has been a feature of July since 1960, and of August since 1964. With the exceptions of 1976, 1979 and 1980, relatively low precipitation in recent Octobers contrasts strongly with the wetness in earlier years. A tendency towards April and June dryness is also apparent. More importantly in terms of precipitation effectiveness and water supply replenishment, December between 1967 and 1978 experienced continually below-average rainfall. On several occasions during this period December precipitation was extremely low. The wetness of November and January during the 1970s has not always been sufficient to alleviate the dryness of December, and this has resulted in frequent local water supply problems throughout Northern Ireland during recent summers.

Temperature variations in recent years do not display as distinct a pattern as those for precipitation. Annual temperatures show no overall trend, but Figure 1.14 shows the tendency towards a recent cooling of March, April, May, September and November. Also illustrated is the remarkable warmth of January between 1967 and 1976, and in contrast the run of cold Decembers in the 1960s.

These fluctuations of precipitation and temperature are not of statistical significance

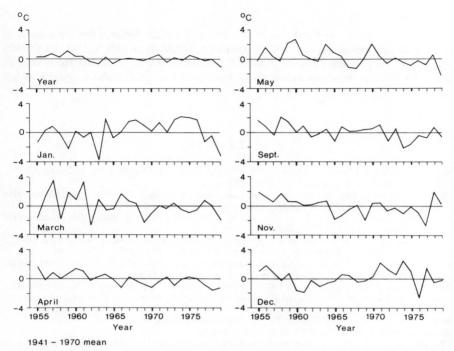

1941 – 1970 mean

Figure 1.14 Northern Ireland temperatures 1955-79; annual and selected monthly values expressed as differences from their respective 1941-70 averages.

in the context of long-period climatic changes. Indeed, the wet June of 1980 abruptly terminating a sequence of dry Junes, clearly demonstrates the hazards of prediction from trends. Of course, monthly averages are somewhat artificial, for synoptic conditions controlling climatic elements do not hold to calendar periods. Furthermore, until a full understanding of the processes of climatic fluctuation has been formulated and the various time scales on which they operate have been determined, reliable predictions of the continuation or change of present trends cannot be made.

ADDENDUM

Subsequent to the writing of this chapter, Northern Ireland experienced some of the most severe winter cold on record during December 1981 and January 1982. A number of stations attained new absolute minimum temperatures. Edenfel, Omagh, for example, recorded −15.9° C on 12 December 1981. At Armagh, between 7-12 January 1982, 130 consecutive hours of sub-zero temperature were recorded, a period of frost which was unrivalled in duration since 1881.

39

Acknowledgements

The author wishes to thank the Meteorological Office, Belfast, for permission to consult climatological records, and in particular, is grateful to Mr S. J. G. Partington and Mr E. N. Lawrence for their helpful comments and suggestions. He wishes to thank Mr V. C. R. Ford, The Queen's University of Belfast, for advice and discussion during the preparation of the script.

REFERENCES

Atkinson, B. W. and Smithson, P. A., 1976. Precipitation. T. J. Chandler and S. Gregory *(eds.)*, *The Climate of the British Isles*. Longman, 129–182.

Bailie, S., 1980. *About the growing season in Northern Ireland 1941-70*. Unpublished BSc dissertation, Department of Geography, Queen's University of Belfast.

Barrett, E. C., 1976. Cloud and Thunder, T. J. Chandler and S. Gregory *(eds.)*, *The Climate of the British Isles*. Longman, 199–210.

Betts, N. L., 1978*a*. The problem of water supply in Northern Ireland. *Water Services*, 82, 10–16.

Betts, N. L., 1978*b*. Water supply in Northern Ireland. *Irish Geography*, 11, 161–66.

Bleasdale, A., 1963. The distribution of exceptionally heavy daily falls of rain in the United Kingdom, 1863 to 1960. *Journal of the Institution of Water Engineers*, 17, 45–55.

Bleasdale, A., 1970. The rainfall of 14th and 15th September 1968 in comparison with previous exceptional rainfalls in the United Kingdom, *Journal of the Institution of Water Engineers*, 24, 181–9.

Boucher, K., 1975. *Global Climate*. English Universities Press.

British Rainfall, (1959-60), 1963. H.M.S.O., 99/100.

Chandler, T. J., 1961. Surface breeze effects of Leicester's heat island. *East Midland Geographer*, 15, 32–8.

Chandler, T. J., 1965. *The Climate of London*. Hutchinson.

Chandler, T. J., 1967. Night-time temperatures in relation to Leicester's urban form. *Meteorological Magazine*, 96, 244–50.

Chandler, T. J., 1976. The Climate of Towns. T. J. Chandler and S. Gregory *(eds.)*, *The Climate of the British Isles*. Longman, 307–29.

Clark, B. J., 1979. An investigation into recent October temperature trends over central England. *Weather*, 34, 374–83.

Connaughton, M. J., 1969. *Air Frosts in Late Spring and Early Summer*. Meteorological Service, Dublin, (Agrometeorological Memorandum No. 2).

Conrad, V., 1946. Usual formulas of continentality and their limits of validity. *Transactions of the American Geophysical Union*, 27, 663–4.

De la Mothe, P. D., 1968. Middle latitude wavelength variation at 500 mb. *Meteorological Magazine*, 97, 333–9.

Dixon, F. E., 1959. An Irish weather diary of 1711-25. *Quarterly Journal of the Royal Meteorological Society*, 85, 371–85.

Doornkamp, J. C., Gregory, K. J. and Burn, A. S. *(eds.)*, 1980. *Atlas of Drought in Britain 1975-76*. Institute of British Geographers.

Glassey, S. D., 1967. *Average and extreme dates of first and last screen frosts in Northern Ireland*. Meteorological Office, Belfast, (Climatological Memorandum No. 61).

Glassey, S. D. and Durbin, W. G., 1971. *Wind at Ballykelly*. Meteorological Office, Bracknell. (Climatological Memorandum No. 68).

Gregory, S., 1954. Accumulated temperature maps of the British Isles. *Transactions of the Institute of British Geographers*, 20, 59–73.

Gregory, S., 1964. Climate. J. W. Watson and J. B. Sissons, *(eds.)*, *The British Isles: A Systematic Geography*, Nelson, 53–73.

Grindley, J., 1970. Estimation and mapping of evaporation. *Symposium on World Water Balance*. International Association of Scientific Hydrology Publ. No. 92, 200–213.

Hardman, C. E. *et al.*, 1973. *Extreme Wind Speeds Over the United Kingdom for Periods Ending 1971.* Meteorological Office, Bracknell, (Climatological Memorandum, No. 50A).
Houghton, J. G. and Ó Cinnéide, M. S., 1977. Distribution and synoptic origin of selected heavy precipitation storms over Ireland. *Irish Geography,* 10, 1–17.
Hurst, G. W. and Smith, L. P., 1967. Grass growing days. J. A. Taylor *(ed.), Weather and Agriculture.* Pergaman, 147–55.
Jackson, M. C., 1977*a.* Evaluating the probability of heavy rain. *Meteorological Magazine,* 106, 185–92.
Jackson, M. C., 1977*b.* The occurrence of falling snow over the United Kingdom. *Meteorological Magazine,* 106, 26–38.
Jones, P. D., 1979. *Climate Monitor,* 8, 4, University of East Anglia (Climatic Research Unit).
Lamb, H. H., 1950. Types and spells of weather around the year in the British Isles: annual trends, seasonal structure of the year, singularities. *Quarterly Journal of the Royal Meteorological Society,* 76, 393–429.
Lamb, H. H., 1972*a. Climate: Present, Past and Future, Vol. 1: I Fundamentals and II Climate Now.* Methuen.
Lamb, H. H., 1972*b. British Isles Weather Types and a Register of the Daily Sequence of Circulation Patterns 1861–1971.* H.M.S.O. (Meteorological Office, Geophysical Memorandum No. 116).
Lamb, H. H., 1977. *Climate: Present, Past and Future, Vol. 2: III Climatic History and IV The Future.* Methuen.
Lamb, H. H. and Mörth, H. T., 1978. Arctic ice, atmospheric circulation and world climate, *Geographical Journal,* 144, 1–22.
Lawrence, E. N., 1971. Consequences of the Clean Air Act: not as simple as they seem. *Nature,* 229, 334–335.
Logue, J. J., 1978. *The Annual Cycle of Rainfall in Ireland.* Meteorological Service, Dublin, (Technical Note No. 43).
McPeake, J. W. R., 1980. *Belfast as an urban heat island.* Unpublished BA dissertation, Department of Geography, The Queen's University of Belfast.
Meteorological Office, 1975. *Flood Studies Report,* Vol. II, *Meteorological Studies,* N.E.R.C.
Meteorological Office, 1976. *Average Annual Rainfall (mm) International Standard Period 1941-70,* Meteorological Office, Met. 0.866 (Northern Ireland), accompanying *Averages of Rainfall over United Kingdom 1941-70,* H.M.S.O.
Miles, M. K., 1977. Atmospheric circulation during the severe drought of 1975-76, *Meteorological Magazine,* 106, 154–164.
Murray, R., 1977. The 1975-76 drought over the United Kingdom – hydrometeorological aspects, *Meteorological Magazine,* 106, 129–145.
Painting, D. J., 1977. *A study of some aspects of the climate of the Northern Hemisphere in recent years,* H.M.S.O. Meteorological Office, Scientific Paper, No. 35.
Partington, S. J. G., 1970. *Water Temperature of Eastern Lough Neagh.* Meteorological Office, Belfast.
Penman, H. L., 1962. Woburn irrigation, 1951–1959; I Purpose, design and weather; II Results for grass; III Results for rotation crops, *Journal of Agricultural Science,* 58, 343–79.
Perry, A. H., 1972. Spatial and temporal characteristics of Irish precipitation. *Irish Geography,* 6, 428–42.
Perry, A. H., 1976. Synoptic Climatology, T. J. Chandler and S. Gregory, *(eds.), The Climate of the British Isles.* Longman, 8–38.
Perry, A. H. and Fearnside, T., 1980. *Northern Hemisphere pentad (5 day) mean sea level pressure values for the period 1951-70, and comparison with earlier epochs.* University of East Anglia. Climatic Research Unit Report No. 7.
Perry, A. H. and Walker, J. M., 1977. *The Ocean-Atmosphere System.* Longman.
Prior, D. B. and Betts, N. L., 1974. Flooding in Belfast, *Irish Geography,* 7, 1–18.
Ratcliffe, R. A. S., 1977. A synoptic climatologist's viewpoint of the 1975-76 drought. *Meteorological Magazine,* 106, 145–154.
Rohan, P. K., 1968. *The Climate of North Munster.* Meteorological Service, Dublin.
Rohan, P. K., 1975. *The Climate of Ireland.* Meteorological Service, Dublin.

Royal Society, 1978. Scientific aspects of the 1975-76 Drought in England and Wales. Summary of discussion meeting held at Royal Society, London, 28 October 1977, on behalf of British National Committee on Hydrological Sciences. *Proceedings of the Royal Society, London,* A 363, 3–137.

Shellard, H. C., 1962. Extreme wind speeds over the United Kingdom for periods ending 1959. *Meteorological Magazine,* 91, 39–47.

Shellard, H. C., 1965. *Extreme Wind Speeds over the United Kingdom for Periods ending 1963.* Meteorological Office, Bracknell, (Climatological Memorandum, No. 50).

Stephens, N., 1963. Climate, L. Symons *(ed.), Land Use in Northern Ireland,* University of London Press, 75–92.

Tout, D., 1976. Temperature, T. J. Chandler and S. Gregory, *(eds.), The Climate of the British Isles,* Longman, 96–128.

Water Service (N.I.) 1980. *Northern Ireland Water Statistics, 1979.* Department of the Environment for Northern Ireland.

Woodley, K. E., 1968. *Frequency of Daily Rainfall Amounts in Northern Ireland.* Meteorological Office, Belfast. (Hydrological Memorandum No. 6).

Wright, P. B., 1976. Recent Climatic Change. T. J. Chandler and S. Gregory *(eds.), The Climate of the British Isles,* Longman, 224–47.

CHAPTER II

Rivers

DAVID N. WILCOCK,
Senior Lecturer in Environmental Science, New University of Ulster

Introduction

From a resource management point of view, Northern Ireland is overendowed with water, and only a small proportion of total streamflow is used for industrial, agricultural or domestic purposes. Management of surface waters is therefore principally concerned with disposal of excess water from the land, with maintenance of river water quality in the face of recent but widespread changes in agricultural and industrial technology, and with safeguarding traditionally excellent fish stocks. Land drainage, fertilizer use, and effluent disposal constitute the major management practices affecting quantity and quality of river water, and it is with these topics that this chapter is principally concerned.

Northern Ireland's water balance

An *approximate* water balance for Northern Ireland, showing the large excess of available supply over demand, is presented in Figure 2.1. Equivalent figures for England and Wales are presented in Table 2.1. With a slightly higher average annual rainfall and lower evapotranspiration losses, each km² of Northern Ireland has to discharge 1.35 times the amount of water discharged from the same area in England and Wales. With a much lower population density, 106 km² as opposed to 328 km² in England and Wales, the demand for water in Northern Ireland is correspondingly lower and public supplies account for only 2.4% of the average annual runoff. This is to be compared with a corresponding figure of 21% for England and Wales. Even considering the once-in-fifty year drought condition, the lowest extreme with which water managers normally concern themselves, the position in Northern Ireland is not critical. The once-in-fifty year low flow can be taken as approximately 10% of average runoff (Rydz in Funnell and Hey, 1974, p. 2), i.e. 65 mm in Northern Ireland. Even this figure is four times the annual average consumption of water in Northern Ireland whereas in England and Wales the corresponding once-in-fifty year flow is only half the annual total consumption. Clearly the basic natural resource equation in Northern Ireland is adequate. Notwithstanding this happy state of affairs from a water supply point of view, Northern Ireland has recently experienced prolonged dry periods in

TABLE 2.1

Northern Ireland's annual water balance data in comparison with those for England and Wales. All data in mm/year.

	Northern Ireland[1]	England and Wales[2]
Precipitation	1095	966
Evapotranspiration	441	483
Stream Flow	647	466
Domestic and Industrial Freshwater consumption	16	102
Saline cooling	97	128
Estuarine and coastal discharges	7.3	17.3
Discharge to Rivers	8.7	82.1
Evaporative losses	0.03	2.9

[1]Data from Water Service and private survey of Northern Ireland industry (1979).
[2]Data from Funnell and Hey, 1974, p. 7.

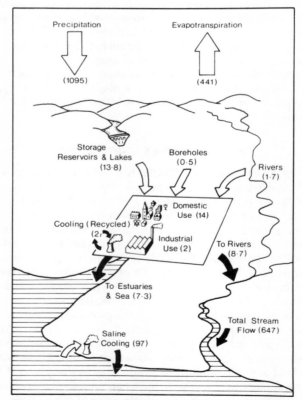

Figure 2.1 Northern Ireland's Water Balance. Units of measurement are millimetres/year.

summer which have created serious water supply problems (Betts, 1978). An inflexible water supply system in which water transfers between areas of temporary surplus and shortage are difficult is the principal cause of these shortages. The piecemeal way in which the regional storage and delivery systems has evolved is outlined by Common (Chapter 3).

Because the demands for water are lower in Northern Ireland than in England and Wales, so are the pressures on water quality brought about by the discharge of this water after it has been used. Thus the discharge of treated water to the rivers of Northern Ireland is only 10.5% of the equivalent figure in England and Wales. Similarily the discharge of treated water to estuaries is lower in Northern Ireland, although at 42% of the England and Wales figure, it is clear that official discharge into estuaries in Northern Ireland constitutes a potential threat to our aquatic environment and should be monitored with great care.

If there are obvious differences in water supply and use between England and Wales and Northern Ireland there is at least one interesting similarity, and that concerns the use of saline water, which is used almost as intensively in Northern Ireland as in England and Wales. In both areas the use of saline water exceeds the use of fresh water, by a factor of 6 in Northern Ireland and a factor of 1.26 in England and Wales. In Northern Ireland the principal users are coal-fired power stations.

Hydrological measurement and research

A very important aspect of environmental management is the continuous monitoring of resources. To produce a regional water balance statement of the type made in the preceding section requires adequate data on all components of the hydrological cycle, and it is now proposed briefly to outline the history and extent of water resource monitoring and principal areas of inquiry by research workers.

Precipitation

The extent and evolution of Northern Ireland's raingauge network have already been described by Betts in Chapter 1. One point worth emphasizing is the poor information about rainfall intensity and duration received from the upland areas. Only 13.5% of daily-read raingauges and 33% of continuous rainfall recorders are situated above 150 m O.D. The respective figure for monthly-read raingauges is very high (83%). The low number of daily-read raingauges results, of course, from the practical difficulty of obtaining observers in these less densely populated areas. What is therefore required are more automatic rainfall recorders. It is in these higher, steeper and more remote parts of the uplands that flood runoff is generated and automatic recorders provide the continuous information about rainfall that is required for flood analyses.

Evapotranspiration and soil moisture

Monthly potential evapotranspiration (PE) rates are calculated as potential transpiration (PT) by the U.K. Meteorological Office for twenty-two stations in Northern Ireland (Figure 2.2). Potential transpiration is the term used to distinguish Penman's techniques of estimating PE from that devised earlier by Thornthwaite. Thornthwaite's formula is not generally thought to be applicable in the British Isles whereas Penman's was devised for British conditions. The Meteorological Office calculations are based on Penman's (1963) formula and are used to estimate soil moisture deficits (Grindley, 1970).

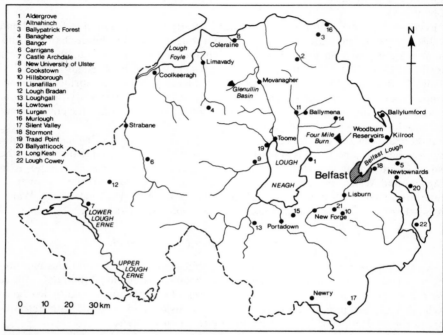

Figure 2.2 Stations in Northern Ireland for which monthly estimates of PT are made. Locations referred to elsewhere in the Chapter are also included.

Mean annual PT in Northern Ireland ranges from 502 mm at Aldergrove (68 m O.D.) to 346 mm at Lowtown (271 m O.D.). PT tends to be greatest in the east and on exposed coasts and lower in the west and upland areas.

When PT exceeds rainfall, vegetation is forced to draw on reserves of water stored in the soil. As soon as this occurs, a soil moisture deficit (SMD) is said to exist. SMDs, accumulated annually from January 1st each year, build up to an average July value of 50 mm for the whole of Northern Ireland although values of 95–105 mm occur at certain localities such as Aldergrove, Hillsborough, and Portrush in dry summer months. Soils normally return to field capacity in September and remain at field capacity or wetter until the following April or May when SMDs again begin to develop. Mean monthly SMD values at selected sites are shown in Figure 2.3.

The practical application of SMD information to Northern Ireland agriculture is still in its infancy and dates from the very dry summers of 1975, 1976 and 1977 when peak SMDs were recorded. At Aldergrove in August 1975 SMD reached 118.7 mm and at Hillsborough 107.4 mm. In the west, at Castle Archdale SMDs reached peak values of 94.2 mm and 81.1 mm in 1975 and 1977 respectively. Before this sequence of very dry summers commercial irrigation was not practised anywhere in Northern Ireland, but

46

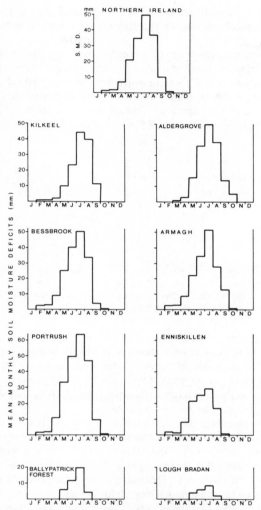

Figure 2.3 Monthly build-up of average SMD values (1961-1968) at 9 selected stations. Figures for each month represent the accumulated SMD total from the beginning of the year. (Data from Northern Ireland Meteorological Office).

investment in irrigation is now slowly developing particularly in the Newtownards, Lisburn and North Armagh areas. The Meteorological Office provides a weekly printout of SMD values and this is used by the Department of Agriculture to advise farmers when to irrigate (MAFF, 1970). The principal benefits of irrigation in Northern Ireland appear to lie in improved seed germination and fruit crop improvement. Other uses of SMD information are in the application of fertilizers and the prediction of surface runoff. Accordingly, both fertilizer manufacturers and the Departments of Agriculture and of the Environment take a continuous interest in SMD values.

Research into the measurement of evapotranspiration in Northern Ireland is of relatively recent origin. Wilcock *et al.* (1978) describe the evapotranspirometer they established at Coleraine, and the way in which annual measured values of PE exceeded Meteorological Office PT estimates by up to 26%. Subsequent calculations of the magnitude and duration of SMD at Coleraine consequently differ depending on whether they are based on estimated PT or measured PE (Figure 2.4).

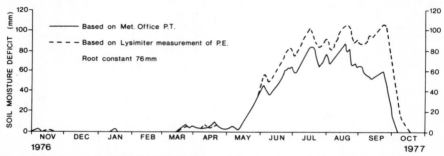

Figure 2.4 Accumulated SMDs (1976-77) at Coleraine derived from Meteorological Office estimates of PT and lysimeter PE measurement.

Groundwater

Groundwater is of increasing importance in Northern Ireland's water supply system both for industry and domestic purposes in rural areas, and a comprehensive survey of groundwater is currently in progress. One measure of its growing importance is that over 35 production wells have been sunk since 1961. Before that date only 8 were in use.

Groundwater is important to water managers because it determines river flow in times of low rainfall. In turn, low river flows determine the ability of a river to dilute effluent and to support fishlife, and river management techniques are therefore directed at ways to maintain or augment these flows. There have already been plans to augment low flows on the Lagan (Manning, 1971) by groundwater pumping, and similar proposals exist for the upper River Main. In view of these growing pressures on groundwater it is desirable that the effects of these changes are monitored in the future more closely than they are today.

Streamflow

The natural drainage network is divided into seven principal areas (Figure 2.5) each of which is internationally regarded as a hydrometric unit for purposes of streamflow measurement. With a drainage area of some 5,300 km² the Bann is the largest basin in Northern Ireland. The Foyle system, with 2,090 km² in Northern Ireland, is the next largest drainage unit followed by the Erne system in the south-west. The Bush (344 km²) and the Lagan (562 km²) are the largest individual basins in the east. Altogether some 61% of Northern Ireland drains to the north coast, 25% to the east coast and 14% through the Erne system.

48

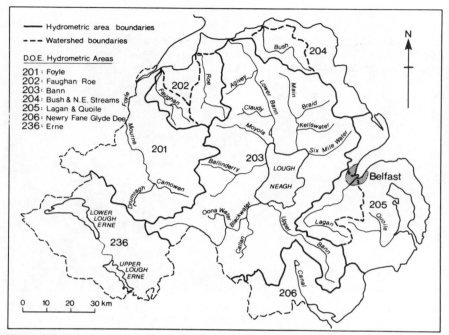

Figure 2.5 Principal Northern Ireland rivers and internationally agreed hydrometric areas.

Although continuous measurements of streamflow in Northern Ireland have been made only during the last decade (Wilcock, 1971, 1977b) there are now 45 stream-gauging stations for which stage-discharge rating curves have been established and 3 stations at which flow-measuring structures have been installed (Plate 2.1). There are a further 19 stations at which water-level is continuously monitored but for which no rating curves have yet been derived, and 2 sites on Lough Neagh and 4 on Lough Erne at which lake levels are similarly observed. The DoA is responsible for stream gauge installation and data collection, while the Department of the Environment for Northern Ireland has responsibility for analysing and publishing data collected from the stations.

Catchment studies

Catchment research projects designed to investigate specific water management problems can be distinguished from the monitoring activities of DoA and DoE, and several such studies have recently been undertaken. Savill and Weatherup (1974) examined rainfall and runoff records from two small catchments tributary to the Woodburn reservoirs north of Belfast. One was a 112 ha forested area planted in the late-1950s and the other was a 26 ha grassland area. The study was designed to examine whether or not afforestation could be shown to significantly reduce runoff as Law (1958), and more recently the Institute of Hydrology (1976), suggest. The authors concluded that although certain differences in runoff behaviour between the two catchments did exist none could unequivocably be attributed to afforestation.

Plate 2.1 *Top:* A flat V weir gauging structure on the Ravernet River, County Down. The tributary drainage area is 70 km². The gauge is part of the DoE hydrometric network.

Plate 2.1 *Bottom:* A cableway for measuring streamflow on the Kellswater River, County Antrim. This station is part of the DoE hydrometric network. The tributary drainage area is 127 km². Staff gauges and housing for water-level recorder can be seen to the right of the picture.

In the upper Agivey valley, Wilcock (1977*a*, 1979*a*) attempted to identify the effects of a small arterial drainage scheme on the hydrology of a small catchment predominantly covered by peat and gley soils. A withdrawal of water from groundwater and soil moisture storage appeared to take place during the first two years after drainage followed by a period of replenishment lasting up to ten years.

Plate 2.2 A parallel trapezoidal flume for streamflow measurement in The Queen's University of Belfast catchment study on the Four Mile Burn in County Antrim.

In catchment studies the possibility of instrumental error is considerable and it is desirable that all components of the water balance be measured very carefully and independently of one another preferably over a long period. Perhaps the most promising such study in Northern Ireland is that jointly set up by the Civil Engineering Branch at the Department of Finance for Northern Ireland and the Civil Engineering Department of The Queen's University Belfast on the Four Mile Burn, 32 km north-west of Belfast (Wright, 1978). Designed to examine the low flow regime of the 20 km² catchment the instrumentation includes 2 autographic rainfall recorders, 27 groundwater observation wells, a weir and 4 flumes (Plate 2.2).

Streamflow characteristics in Northern Ireland

Water resource management is principally concerned with the extreme flows in any catchment rather than with average flows. High flows may overtop channel walls, causing structural damage, bank erosion and flooding. Low flows determine the effluent concentration a river can comfortably sustain. The 8th Report of the Royal Commission on Sewage Disposal (1912), recognising the importance of low flows, suggested that effluent discharge should not exceed one eighth of river discharge, and proposed effluent standards of 30 mg/1 for suspended solids and 20 mg/1 for biochemical oxygen demand (BOD). Low flows also determine the quantities of water available for continuous abstraction by any industries which abstract river water without the aid of impounding reservoirs.

The flow duration curve is one way of describing flow regime and expresses the percentage of time a given flow is equalled or exceeded. Because of the short period in which streamflow gauges have been operated in Northern Ireland, and the complicated field and office work required to produce good flow duration curves, it is not yet possible to produce a complete set of such curves for all drainage basins. In the early 1970s the Drainage Design Data Unit therefore selected for further study 8 well-rated basins, (the Agivey, Blackwater, Bush, Callan, Drumragh, Lagan, Main and Six Mile Water) representing a wide range of hydrological conditions. Duration curves for six of these are shown in Figure 2.6.

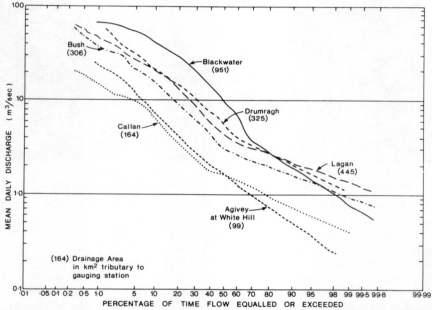

Figure 2.6   Flow duration curves for selected rivers (1973-74). Data from the Drainage Design Data Unit (DoF).

When examining available streamflow records in Northern Ireland, it has to be remembered that the 1970s have experienced remarkable climatic extremes (see Chapter 1) which makes generalization about normal hydrological behaviour very difficult. It is with these reservations in mind that the following generalizations are presented.

Figure 2.7 shows streamflow/km² for flows experienced 5%, 50% and 95% of the time on 11 rivers in Northern Ireland and, for rough comparison, on 3 in southern England, one in Scotland and one in Wales. Although the time-base of the two data sets is not coincidental, the diagram demonstrates the relatively wide range of flows experienced on Northern Ireland rivers. The Q_5/Q_{95} values for Northern Ireland, derived from Figure 2.7 and presented in Table 2.2, are in general two or three times the range of the other British rivers. (The Northern Ireland figures are not much affected by excluding data from the very dry years 1975 and 1976 which might be thought to have greatly depressed the Q_{95} figures). As Ineson and Downing (1965) have shown, the ratio between winter and summer flows is an important indicator of how much seasonal groundwater transfer might take place. In rivers like the Itchen in southern England where 83% of total annual flow is provided from groundwater the Q_5/Q_{95} ratio is 3.5, whereas on the River Ter in Essex, which has a groundwater contribution to annual streamflow of only 39%, the Q_5/Q_{95} ratio is 25. In Northern Ireland, groundwater contributes about 52% of total streamflow (Department of Finance, 1975) but on the basis of the Q_5/Q_{95} ratios seasonal groundwater transfer would appear to be small (Table 2.2).

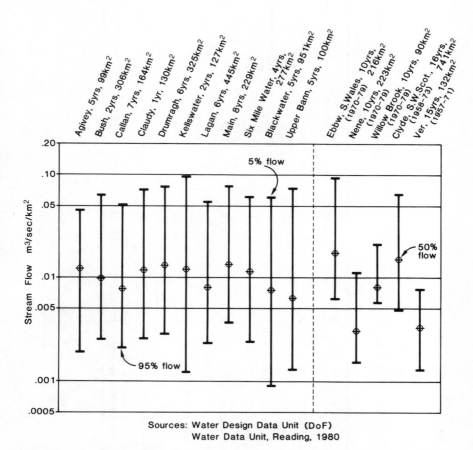

Sources: Water Design Data Unit (DoF)
Water Data Unit, Reading, 1980

Figure 2.7 Median, 5% and 95% flows for 11 rivers in Northern Ireland, and 5 in Great Britain. Data from the N.I. Drainage Design Data Unit (DoF) and from the Water Data Unit Reading.

TABLE 2.2

Q_5/Q_{95} ratios for selected rivers in Northern Ireland and Great Britain.

	Northern Ireland[1]			Great Britain[2]		
River	Length of Record (Years)	Q_5/Q_{95}	Q_5/Q_{95} excluding 1974 and 1975	River	Length of Record (Years)	Q_5/Q_{95}
Agivey	5	23.95	43.86	Nene	10	7.44
Bush	2	25.36	24.73	Willow Brook	10	3.62
Callan	7	24.00	21.00	River Ver	15	6.00
Claudy	1	27.65	27.65	River Ebbw	10	14.96
Drumragh	6	26.92	25.03	River Clyde	16	13.06
Kells Water	2	79.17	79.17			
Lagan	6	23.87	22.85			
Main	8	20.94	20.13			
Six Mile Water	4	25.75	25.72			
Blackwater	5	60.26	24.65			
Upper Bann	5	55.38	53.36			
Mean		53.36	35.75			9.02

[1]Figures provided privately from Drainage Design Data Unit (DoF)
[2]Figures provided privately from Water Data Unit, Reading

Closer examination of Figure 2.7 shows that the greatest variability between the rivers of Northern Ireland occurs at low flow. The Main for example, with a Q_{95} flow of .0037 m³/sec/km² sustains a low flow some four times greater than the Blackwater. Clearly the groundwater flows on the Main are controlled by relatively high permeabilities. In contrast, the low groundwater flows on the Blackwater, Upper Bann and Kells Water indicate low permeabilities. They also indicate potential pollution hazards should the summer effluent load on these streams become excessive. In comparison with the Q_{95} flows, the Q_5 and Q_{50} flows are less variable, the 5% flow on the Kells Water being only twice the magnitude of that on the Agivey. Clearly those factors affecting surface runoff, principally rainfall, topography, vegetation and surface geology are distributed relatively uniformly throughout Northern Ireland, and are in general conducive to fairly high values of discharge/unit area, the Q_5 flows for Northern Ireland appearing to be very comparable to those on the Ebbw and Clyde (Figure 2.7).

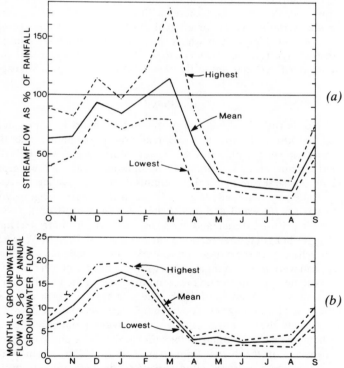

Figure 2.8   Mean monthly variations of streamflow and groundwater flow in four river basins 1973-74. Data from the Drainage Design Data Unit (DoF).

Monthly variations of streamflow in relation to precipitation and of baseflow, throughout any particular year (Figure 2.8), throw further light on the important question of perennial transfers of groundwater between winter and summer. The mean, highest and lowest monthly values from each of four basins, the Bush, Callan, Drumragh and Six Mile Water are shown in Figure 2.8 in order to present the range of conditions as well as the average picture throughout Northern Ireland.

As might be expected, streamflow as a percentage of precipitation in 1973-74 was marginally higher in the north and west, streamflow on the Bush and Drumragh respectively being 64% and 66% of precipitation. In the south and east, the equivalent figures fell to 61% and 59% on the Six Mile Water and Callan. These figures are all very similar and reflect uniformity of runoff behaviour throughout Northern Ireland rather than marked regional differences.

It can be seen from Figure 2.8*a* that nearly all the winter precipitation in December, January, February and March immediately becomes streamflow. At this time of year water-tables are very high, soils are very wet and sub-surface storage is limited. In summer, streamflow is principally maintained by groundwater flow which during April and June of 1974 accounted for more than 87% of total streamflow in all four basins. Although this proportion is quite high, the absolute volume of groundwater flow in summer is quite small, and again there is little evidence that large amounts of groundwater are stored in winter for gradual release into the rivers during summer. This can be seen from Figure 2.8*b* which shows that the greatest volume of annual groundwater discharge (during 1973-74) took place in winter and that only 17% of annual groundwater flow occurred in the five month period April-August.

Drainage

Given that Northern Ireland has one of the largest runoff/unit area figures in the British Isles, that the soils are of widespread low permeability and that stream gradients are often very gentle in their lower courses (e.g. the Bann), it is not surprising that land drainage and flood alleviation have been such widespread problems for so long. These severe physical constraints on natural drainage have often been further compounded by man-made hazards in the form of weirs, originally introduced by rural industrialists for water and power supplies (Gribbon, 1969).

The recent history of arterial and land drainage in Northern Ireland, and the associated changes in agricultural economy, have been described by Wilcock (1979*b*). Early drainage schemes, in the nineteenth century, were installed under a landlord and tenant system and were too piecemeal to have any lasting effect. The first comprehensive drainage scheme implemented in modern times was on the lower Bann. Started in 1930, the scheme was completed in 1942. The strategy was to increase streamflow capacity in the lower Bann between Toome and Coleraine, to draw down lough water levels to 16.32 m and thus to lower outfalls on all rivers draining into Lough Neagh. Under the scheme which gave drainage benefit to 57,000 ha and cost £1 million, the discharging capacity of the lower Bann was increased 29%, from 330 m³/sec to 425 m³/sec. The scheme was financed principally by the Government, providing 80% of the cost. Other schemes, dependent under pre-war legislation on finance from county councils, fared less successfully. Of 13 schemes submitted to county councils between 1930 and 1938, ten were rejected on grounds of excessive cost.

The Second World War saw a new attitude toward drainage. A Drainage Commission was appointed to consider ways of immediately implementing drainage schemes in order to increase agricultural output during the war. Its main recommendation, implemented in the 1942 Drainage Act, was that arterial drainage schemes should receive a 75% state grant. A second recommendation was that drainage requirements throughout Northern Ireland required centralized planning which existing county councils were unable to provide. The Commission recommended the creation of an eleven member Drainage Board as a new administrative body overseeing drainage throughout Northern Ireland.

After the war, the 1947 Drainage Act set up a Drainage Council whose principal task was to determine the "main" arterial rivers in Northern Ireland which were to be improved as the Bann had been. The strategy under which the Council worked was to commence improvement on the major rivers, working from the sea progressively inland along the trunk streams, thus providing an efficient outlet for runoff. By 1977 some 1,250 km of main river had been improved. In 1964 another Drainage Act initiated a second phase of arterial drainage on the tributaries of the trunk streams, the so-called "minor" streams, and by 1976 3,250 km of streams in this category had been improved.

Urban drainage, like arterial drainage, is the ultimate responsibility of DoA under the terms of the 1973 Drainage Order, and although local in character, the problem of flooding in urban areas is sometimes an acute one. Prior and Betts (1974) have documented the history of flooding in Belfast and point out that despite remedial work on the Lagan tributaries and on sewer lines the problem of flooding in Belfast still remains. Elsewhere the problem appears less acute principally because of the 70 urban drainage schemes completed between 1957 and 1976.

There can be little doubt that improvements to arterial drainage have made possible extensive improvements in field drainage. Over 75% of the area now benefitting from efficient field drainage was improved between 1950 and 1976, and the total area under field drainage is now over half the total area in agriculture (see Cruickshank, Chapter 8). Other effects of this massive change to the drainage network on the physical environment of the rivers themselves are more difficult to assess owing to the very recent origin of regular streamflow and water quality monitoring. By how much water-tables have been drawn down, streamflow regimes altered, flood plain soil moisture conditions improved, water quality transformed and fish stocks impaired with regard to quantity and composition, are all questions to most of which definitive answers are as yet unavailable, although respective interests often have their own points of view.

Water quality in rivers

In 1972 the Water Act (N.I.) made the then Ministry of Development responsible for promoting "the conservation of the water resources of Northern Ireland (and) the cleanliness of water in waterways" (The Water Act (N.I.) 1972, Sections 1(a) and 1(b)). In response to its new obligations under the Act, a Conservation Division was created within the Ministry to deal with water supply, sewerage, and other environmental matters. In 1974 the DoE took over the water management function of the former Ministry of Development, and now maintains the river water quality monitoring programme initiated by the Ministry in 1973.

At 35 stations throughout Northern Ireland water is now sampled fortnightly by staff of the Foyle Fisheries Commission and the Fisheries Conservancy Board on

57

behalf of DoE, and at a further 72 stations samples are taken every three months. The samples are analysed, by the Industrial Science Division of the Department of Commerce, for conductivity, pH, dissolved oxygen, biochemical oxygen demand (BOD), ammoniacal nitrogen, chloride, nitrites, nitrates, total phosphorus and suspended solids. Similar surveys in Great Britain are made by the DoE in England and by the Welsh Office and Scottish Development Department.

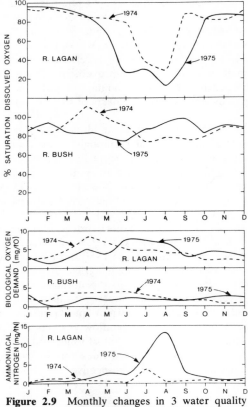

Figure 2.9 Monthly changes in 3 water quality variables at Shaw's Bridge on the River Lagan and at Seneirl Bridge on the River Bush in 1974 and 1975. Data from the Water Service (DoE).

Figure 2.9 illustrates the wide range of conditions which can exist on Northern Ireland's rivers. At one extreme is the Lagan at Shaw's Bridge where in the summer of 1975 water quality was far from satisfactory with a pronounced depression in the dissolved oxygen curve, high BOD counts and a well-defined summer peak in ammoniacal nitrogen. The Bush in contrast, like most of Northern Ireland's rivers, maintains high levels of dissolved oxygen and low BOD counts throughout the year. Ammoniacal nitrogen values, which principally reflect the amount of organic matter in the form of sewage, were so close to zero on the Bush throughout 1974 and 1975 that they have been excluded from Figure 2.9.

Because the Lagan's drainage basin is quite small, one tenth the size of the Bann catchment, its summer streamflow can be quite low, lower indeed on some occasions than the effluent discharge from domestic and industrial sources in Belfast. The average ratio between natural low freshwater flow and effluent volume is 1.09:1 (DoE, 1978). However, while natural streamflow fluctuates from year to year, effluent loadings tend to remain constant. This makes the Lagan a particularly difficult river to manage, and in a dry year such as 1975, the deterioration in water quality on the lower Lagan tends to be very pronounced indeed, because in such years the dilution of effluent by natural streamflow is very low.

Since 1976 water quality at Shaw's Bridge has shown some improvement although it remains uncertain just how much this reflects more favourable hydrological conditions as opposed to marked reductions or improvement in effluent loadings. It is still a legitimate fear that the return of a particularly dry period such as those of 1975 and 1976 might herald a return to the extremely poor water quality conditions shown on Figure 2.9.

TABLE 2.3

Selected characteristics of the National Water Council's classification of river quality.

				Uses		
Class	*Description*	*DO*	*BOD*	*Drinking Water*	*Fish*	*Amenity Value*
1A	Unpolluted rivers	>80%	<3	Yes	Game	High
1B	High quality	>60%	<5	Yes	Game	High
2	Doubtful quality	>40%	<9	After treatment	Coarse	Moderate
3	Poor quality	>10%	<17	No	Rare or absent	Low
4	Grossly polluted	Likely to be anaerobic at times		No	No	Nuisance

DO – Dissolved oxygen as a percentage of saturation exceeded 95% of the time
BOD – Biochemical oxygen demand (mg/1) exceeded 95% of the time

Based on the biochemical parameters outlined above, Northern Ireland rivers, like those in Great Britain, are now classified into five categories (Table 2.3). Comparative figures for river water quality in England and Wales, Scotland, Northern Ireland and the Republic of Ireland are presented in Table 2.4. The overall position in Northern Ireland is clearly good, probably better than in England and Wales although not quite so good as in Scotland or the Republic of Ireland. Until 1978 average values of biochemical analyses were used to classify Northern Ireland's rivers. In 1979, when 95 percentile values were used for the first time, the percentage total lengths in Classes 1*a* and 1*b* were 12.5% and 78%. By 1980, the five respective values were 41.2%, 48.3%, 8.4%, 2.1% and zero!

TABLE 2.4

Water quality in tidal and non-tidal rivers of the British Isles.

Country	Year	Total		Class 1		Class 2		Class 3		Class 4	
		km	%	km	%	km	%	km	%	km	%
England and Wales[1]	1973	38,815	100	29,550	76.1	5,705	14.6	1,925	5.0	1,635	4.2
Scotland[1]	1974	47,772	100	45,407	95.0	1,728	3.6	438	0.9	199	0.4
Northern Ireland[1]	1974	994	100	858	86.2	101	10.1	19	2.0	16	1.7
Northern Ireland[2]	1977	994	100	879	88.5	56	5.6	48	4.8	11	1.1
Republic of Ireland[3]	1971	12,000	100	11,500	96.0	300	2.5			200	1.5

Sources 1. Water Data Unit, 1975, p. 39.
2. Northern Ireland Water Statistics 1977, Water Service, DoE, 1978, Map 9.
3. Toner and O'Sullivan, 1977.

Under the 1977 classification the worst rivers in Northern Ireland (Category 4) were stretches of the Lagan and the Rhone in the Blackwater basin. Under the 1980 classification, there are no Class 4 rivers and only three short stretches, including one on the Lagan upstream of Lisburn in Class 3. Of doubtful quality and in need of improvement are twelve stretches of river including the whole of the Lagan downstream of Moira and parts of the lower Blackwater, upper Bann, and lower Quoile.

The regional classification of river water quality is a great step forward in the environmental management of Northern Ireland's rivers since it enables specific problem areas to be identified and long-term trends to be monitored. There are some reservations among biologists however about the sampling procedure on which the classification is based. An effluent discharge for example might pollute a river for twenty-four hours and decimate a fish population without being traced in the sampling procedure. Because riparian owners might be led to believe that a Class 1 stream can tolerate such isolated effluent discharges, the classification has to be used and interpreted with great care.

Under the 1972 Water Act (N.I.) DoE has power to control all discharges into rivers, lakes, tidal waters and underground strata. This it does through a system of consents which the Department issues to or withholds from all dischargers of effluent. During 1980 for example DoE issued 28 trade effluent consents and refused one. In the same year the Department issued 3,648 domestic effluent consents and refused twenty. Included in the consents were conditions designed to prevent pollution in the receiving rivers or groundwater. The high ratio of consents to refusals privately disturbs some people in view of the high proportion of unsatisfactory effluent samples monitored. Of 261 effluent discharges monitored by DoE in 1980, 136 were unsatisfactory (i.e. failed to comply with at least one consent condition). Warning letters were sent by DoE to 66 of these offenders. During the year 6 successful prosecutions were taken against dischargers of trade effluent.

As well as administering the system of consents the DoE is also responsible through its agents for investigating all reported incidents of pollution. A substantial proportion of these originate on farms. During 1980 a total of 1,427 pollution incidents were investigated, 588 (41%) of them agricultural in origin. Sewage disposal, with 380 incidents in 1980, is the second most frequent source of pollution and industry, with 211 incidents, is third. The figure relating to pollution from sewage disposal highlights one of the anomalies of the present water management system. Under the 1973 Water and Sewerage Services Order the Ministry of Development was made responsible for "the provision and maintenance of facilities for draining and dealing with domestic sewage and trade effluents" (Water and Sewerage Services Order (N.I.), 1973, Article 3). When the DoE took over these obligations after the re-organization of local government in 1973, it inherited a system of sewage disposal facilities in which many improvements were required. Improvements have been carried out since then within the limitations of available finance and this is an ongoing task. Nevertheless, because of its role under the 1973 Order, the Department is nominally one of the principal water polluters as well as being the principal custodian of water quality.

The principal causes of agricultural pollution in Northern Ireland are slurry and silage discharges. So long as traditional farming depended on manure spreading to recycle nutrients, pollution was not a problem. When new intensive farming methods, using fertilizers to produce high grass yields, replaced older methods it became necessary to collect and store wastes in the form of slurry before spreading on the land. The slurries have high BOD values, often in excess of 4,000 mg/1, ten times that of domestic sewage. Silage BOD values are even higher ranging from 12,000–61,000 mg/1. Since the BOD of a river has to be maintained at less than 4 mg/1 in order to maintain fish life, it is apparent that slurries and silage cannot be discharged directly into rivers. Occasionally of course they are, sometimes deliberately but more often by accident. Accidents happen when inadequately sealed slurry tanks leak into small watercourses or when slurry is spread on saturated or frozen ground. In a survey of the Castle River valley east of Limavady, 8% of farms were found to have no waste storage facilities (Oliphant *et al.* 1974). The minimum period for which storage facilities are required was considered by these authors to be four months so that slurry need not be applied to the land between mid-November and mid-March when water-tables are high or the ground may be frozen.

Effluent discharge by industry into the non-tidal portions of rivers is a relatively small problem and principally involves raw material processing. Sand washing plant and meat processing factories have been culprits over the years in the Foyle system.

Domestic sewage and fertilizers are two other principal sources of water pollution in Northern Ireland, and this problem has been extensively studied in the Lough Neagh basin (Wood and Gibson, 1973; Smith, 1976, 1977; Gibson, 1976). The two principal nutrients which enhance algal blooms and hence lead to de-oxygenation of surface waters are phosphorus (P) and nitrogen (N). Although the use of both as fertilizers in Northern Ireland has been substantial since 1960, the use of nitrogen has shown a marked increase in this period (Wilcock, 1979*b*). From an analysis of water quality and streamflow records on six rivers in the Lough Neagh basin, Smith (1977) concluded that sewage is the principal source of phosphorus and agriculture the principal source of nitrogen. The nutrient loading ratio of N to P appears to be important. When this is low nitrogen-fixing blue-green algae can be expected to predominate. This occurred during the dry summer of 1975 when runoff was low. It was the first occasion since 1967 when blooms of blue-green algae appeared in Lough Neagh (Smith, 1977).

Fisheries

Detailed accounts of freshwater and marine fishery resources appear elsewhere in this volume (Chapters 4 and 5) but it would be inappropriate to conclude the present chapter without brief reference to this important rural industry and recreational resource.

The conservation, protection and improvement of inland fisheries in Northern Ireland is the responsibility of the Foyle Fisheries Commission (FFC) established in 1952, and the Fisheries Conservancy Board (FCB) established in 1966. The FCB is responsible for all rivers outside the Foyle system. Ultimate responsibility for fisheries management rests with the Department of Agriculture. Examination of FFC and FCB annual reports shows a deteriorating situation in the state of salmon populations on all Northern Ireland's rivers, 1,062 km of which are officially designated salmonoid waters under EEC regulations. This deterioration is illustrated for the Foyle system in Figure 2.10 which shows an increase in the popularity of angling over the decade up to 1976 and a decline in the angling catch. In the last three years for which data are available, catches have averaged 25% of the long-term average. Over the same period spawning counts for salmon, admittedly imprecise however, have declined from 23,000 per year in 1965 to a little over 3,000 per year in 1974, 1975 and 1976. The Foyle system was quite recently reputed to enjoy the largest run of salmon and grilse in Europe (Morgan, 1969), and it would be an economic tragedy to the western region of Northern Ireland if current trends in salmon stocks proved irreversible.

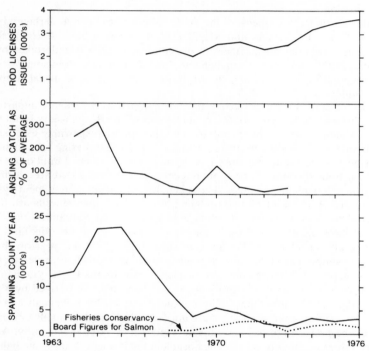

Figure 2.10 Recent changes in angling and salmon spawning rates on Northern Ireland's rivers. Data are from Annual Reports of the Foyle Fisheries Commission (solid lines) and the Fisheries Conservancy Board.

The reasons for the disturbing decline in salmon stocks, which is reflected equally clearly in figures for commercial catches, (see Wood, Chapter 4) are not well understood. Arterial drainage, popularly believed to be a root cause of the problem, may produce short-term deterioration in the biomass of fish stocks but is not believed to have any long-term effects (Vickers, 1969). A recent investigation into changes of fish and invertebrate populations on the River Camowen by the Fisheries Research Laboratory showed that five years after an arterial drainage scheme had been completed, densities of trout under one year old were the highest on record. The authors concluded that "the river has now reverted to its stable pre-drainage condition" (Fisheries Conservancy Board, 1977, p. 122).

UDN disease (ulcerative dermal necrosis), present since 1967 on most rivers, has certainly affected the quality of fish stocks and may have reduced the numbers of juveniles. It has also been pointed out (Elson and Tuomi, 1975) that the first reported incidence of UDN disease in the Foyle system in 1967 coincided with the sudden drop in redd counts. Incidence of this disease now appears to be on the decline. Illegal fishing and offshore commercial fishing are certainly responsible for part of the decline and agricultural pollution is another factor still responsible locally for large fish kills. Most probably an inauspicious combination of all these factors has brought about the present situation.

Research on biological aspects of the Foyle fisheries has been undertaken by Went (1965–1977) and by Vickers and Magill (1970) among others. A comprehensive investigation of fisheries management throughout the Foyle was undertaken by Elson and Tuomi, (1975) and a new management plan has now been drawn up by the FFC aimed at increasing the spawning stocks, reducing the extent of illegal fishing, and reducing pollution.

Fisheries research on rivers outside the Foyle system is principally undertaken by the DoA Fisheries Research Laboratory at Coleraine. The Bush Fishery is run by DoA as an experimental salmon river to determine the optimum spawning escapement of adult salmon and to investigate the economics of artifically rearing salmon smolts.

One aspect of freshwater fisheries management not researched until quite recently in Northern Ireland concerns the economic and social benefits that are, or might be, derived from good angling facilities. These benefits arise from money spent by tourists visiting an area because of its good angling. Other economic benefits are to sports manufacturers, to local owners of fishing rights and to licencing authorities. Various techniques have been devised by economists to assess these benefits and Hadoke (1973) was able to place a 1968 amenity value of £58,600 per year on the Foyle Fisheries by simply calculating the average cost to an individual angler of a year's fishing and multiplying by the number of anglers fishing on the Foyle system in a given year. Hadoke's derived value is probably lower than might be derived by a method incorporating the consumer surplus technique described by Kavanagh and Gibson (1971). This method attempts to measure not only what people actually pay, but what they would be prepared to pay and thus how much they value the amenity. Ascribing monetary values to amenity is a complex problem but it might throw some light on the vexed question of whether greater total economic benefit would accrue to the community as a whole by allowing more game fish to escape from the estuaries into angling waters.

Following the Bledislow Committee report (1961) on the salmon and freshwater fisheries of England and Wales and a similar study for Scotland by the Hunter Committee (1965), a Committee was set up in 1979 to enquire into freshwater fisheries on rivers in Northern Ireland under the control of the FCB. The Committee reviewed the effectiveness of the 1966 Northern Ireland Fisheries Act in developing, improving and conserving salmon and inland fisheries. Among its 43 recommendations were the following:– (i) A new Inland Fisheries Board, to replace the FCB, should be set up, its membership of 12 to be predominantly drawn from bodies interested in the use of inland waters for sport, recreation and commercial fisheries. (ii) Over a period of 3 years rod licences and permits should be increased by 60% in real terms. (iii) A stronger prosecution policy against polluters should be introduced by the DoE. (Black, 1981).

The River Main Public Inquiry

The present chapter is concluded with a brief summary of the issues raised at a public inquiry into an arterial drainage scheme on the upper River Main in 1971. The Inquiry provides excellent specific examples of the conflicts between agricultural, industrial, recreational and environmental interests over the use of rivers and of the difficulties facing the water management industry in the face of these conflicts.

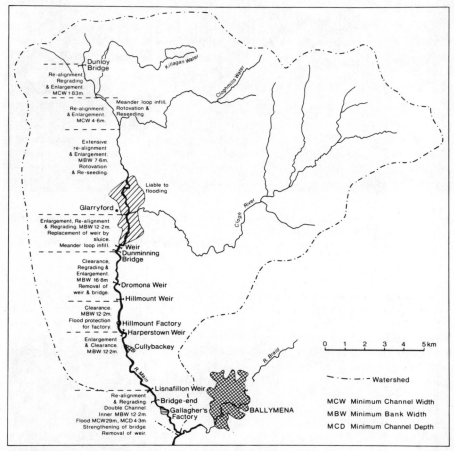

Figure 2.11 Anatomy of the River Main arterial drainage scheme. Details from Hutton (1972).

The drainage scheme, proposed in 1969, was an extension of an earlier scheme on the lower Main completed in 1958. It was designed to give drainage benefit to 4,300 ha of the upper Main and its tributaries (Figure 2.11) and flood relief to 728 ha near Glarryford. The scheme was to involve the removal of several weirs, the removal or reconstruction of four old bridges, the straightening of meanders and the widening and deepening of the existing channel (Plate 2.3). To be carried out by the then Ministry

Plate 2.3 *Top:* Bridge End Bridge near Galgorm on the River Main. This bridge is to be replaced at part of the drainage scheme.

Plate 2.3 *Bottom:* The new drainage channel on the River Main at Gracehill, west of Ballymena.

Plate 2.4 *Top:* Dunminning weir, to be removed and replaced by sluice gates as part of the River Main Drainage scheme.

Plate 2.4 *Bottom:* Flooding at Glarryford, October 1980. Flooding is frequent in this part of the Main valley. This particularly extensive flood followed a rainfall of 38.5 mm on the previous day.

(now Department) of Agriculture at a cost of £1 million the scheme was to be implemented with due regard to the protection of fisheries as far as possible.

Principal areas of contention during the Inquiry focussed on the most appropriate methods of cost-benefit analysis for such an undertaking, the effects of the scheme on flooding, drought flows, and water quality downstream of the main works, and the impact on fisheries and environmental quality. The Ministry's case on the economics of the scheme stated that the net agricultural benefit of the scheme would be £44/ha or £178,676 per year for the 4,063 ha affected. The net agricultural benefits would thus equal the capital investment within five years of the scheme starting. Specific agricultural benefits would include a growing season extended by 6 weeks, lower incidence of certain cattle diseases, and more effective use of fertilizers. Objections to the scheme were raised by witnesses for the FCB who argued that the Ministry's gross margin method of calculating economic benefits excluded real economic losses to the area consequent upon the deterioration of recreational and angling activities.

Hydrological impacts of the scheme were discussed at length. The crux of the scheme's proposals surround Dunminning weir (Plate 2.4) which is to be removed and replaced by sluice gates. The channel at this point would be lowered by about 3 metres. In the Ministry's view this lowering of the channel would draw down the water-table around Glarryford, increase the capacity for sub-surface water storage at times of heavy rainfall, and reduce flooding in the Glarryford area (Plate 2.4). The increased capacity for soil and groundwater storage would further result in the maintenance, or even augmentation, of summer base flows.

Downstream users were concerned that high discharges after drainage might exceed those calculated by the Ministry. It is important to realize in this particular aspect of the Inquiry that no regular monitoring of streamflow had been undertaken on the Main or on any of the rivers of Northern Ireland at the time of this Inquiry, and that streamflows were calculated from empirical formulae not developed specifically for Northern Ireland conditions. The debate consequently focussed on which of the alternative formulae was the most appropriate one for the River Main.

On the subject of low flows there was "strong conflict of opinion between the expert witnesses" (Hutton, 1972, p. 7). The Ministry argued that low flows would be maintained or augmented under the new conditions, a view contested by several witnesses who variously claimed that most soil permeabilities in the area affected were too low to transmit groundwater, and that steepening of the water-table gradient consequent upon channel excavations would increase rather than delay groundwater depletion. If any augmentation were therefore to occur, it would be short-lived. Permanent perennial transfer of water from winter to summer was ruled out by three witnesses.

The low flow issue was important for local industry, pollution control, and fisheries. One small industrial company on the reach of river affected was concerned that low summer flows might be reduced by the scheme and result in a loss of turbine-generated electrical power. The FCB gave evidence about the existing doubtful quality of water in the lower Main and Braid quoting summer BOD values of 4.7 mg/l O_2 and 13.8 mg/l O_2 on the two rivers respectively. Any reduction of dry weather flow would tend to raise these values on a river which the FCB identified as the principal salmon river of the Lough Neagh system. The Board also described the possible effects on fisheries of changes in the natural channel geometry. Removal of runs and holding pools, and the reduction of mean flow depth would remove resting places with spawning sites and would make fish movement up and down the river more difficult.

Recreational, architectural, ecological and economic aspects of the drainage scheme were discussed in a document submitted by the Ulster Countryside Committee and the Nature Reserves Committee. Altogether the Inquiry was the first and most comprehensive public examination of river management problems in Northern Ireland and highlighted problems that result from a lack of hard data and from a partial view of the role of rivers in a modern society.

Acknowledgements

The author wishes to thank staff of the Water Service (DoE), the Drainage Design Data Unit (DoF), and the Fisheries Research Laboratory for their help in providing data for this chapter. In particular I would like to thank Mr P. G. Holland and Dr R. J. Ramsey of the Water Service, Mr J. Hanna of the Drainage Design Data Unit, and Dr G. Kennedy and Mr C. Strange of the Fisheries Research Laboratory for comments on the original draft of the paper. I am also very grateful to the Water Charges Section (DoE) for providing figures of industrial and domestic water consumption and to the 15 major industrial water consumers who provided breakdown figures of their own water use.

REFERENCES

Belfast Meteorological Office, 1979. *Index of Northern Ireland Meteorological Stations.*
Betts, N., 1978. The problem of water supply in Northern Ireland. *Water Services,* 82, 10–16.
Black, R. D. C. (Chairman), 1981. *Angling in Northern Ireland.* Report of the Committee of Inquiry.
Bledisloe, B. L. Viscount (Chairman), 1961. *Report of Committee on Salmon and Freshwater Fisheries,* H.M.S.O. Cmnd. 1350.
Department of the Environment for Northern Ireland, 1978. *River Lagan – Report of a Working Party.*
Department of Finance (N.I.), 1975. *Report of the Design Data Unit for Water Year 1974-75.*
Department of Finance (N.I.), 1976. *Report of the Design Data Unit for Water Year 1975-76.*
Elson, P. F. and Tuomi, A. L. W., 1975. *The Foyle Fisheries: New basis for rational management.* Private report to the Foyle Fisheries Commission.
Fisheries Conservancy Board, *Annual Reports 1969 et seq.*
Foyle Fisheries Commission, *Annual Reports 1966 et seq.* L.M. Press, Lurgan.
Funnell, B. M. and Hey, R. D., 1974. *The management of water resources in England and Wales.* Saxon House.
Gibson, C. E., 1976. An investigation into the effects of forestry plantations on the water quality of upland reservoirs in Northern Ireland. *Water Research,* 10, 995–998.
Gribbon, H. D., 1969. *The history of water power in Ulster.* David and Charles.
Grindley, J., 1970. Estimation and mapping of evaporation. *Symposium on World Water Balance.* International Association of Scientific Hydrology, Publ. No. 92, 200–213.

Hadoke, G. D. F., 1973. *The Salmon Fisheries of the Foyle Area.* Foyle Fisheries Commission.

Hutton, J. B., 1972. *River Main Drainage Scheme, report of a Public Inquiry.* H.M.S.O.

Hunter, J. O. M. Lord (Chairman), 1965. *2nd Report on Scottish Salmon and Trout Fisheries.* H.M.S.O., Cmnd. 2691.

Ineson, J. and Downing, R. A., 1965. Some hydrogeological factors in permeable catchment studies. *Journal of the Institution of Water Engineers,* 19(1), 59–86.

Institute of Hydrology, 1976. *Water balance of the headwater catchments of the Wye and Severn 1970-74.* Natural Environment Research Council.

Kavanagh, N. J. and Gibson, J. G., 1971. Measurement of Fishing benefits on the River Trent. *Proceedings of a Symposium on the Trent Research Programme.* Institution of Water Pollution Control.

Law, F., 1958. Measurement of rainfall, interception and evaporation losses in a plantation of Sitka spruce. *International Association of Scientific Hydrology,* General Assembly of Toronto, 397–411.

Manning, P. I., 1971. The development of the water resources of Northern Ireland. *Quarterly Journal of Engineering Geology,* 4, 335–352.

Ministry of Agriculture, Food and Fisheries, 1970. *Irrigation Guide.* Short-term Leaflet 71.

Ministry of Housing and Local Government, 1964. *Surface Water Year Book of Great Britain 1962-63.* H.M.S.O.

Morgan, J. F., 1969. Surveys of the Water Quality of the River Foyle, *17th Annual Report,* Foyle Fisheries Commission, 51–82. L.M. Press, Lurgan.

Northern Ireland Parliament, 1942, *The Drainage Act (N.I.).* H.M.S.O.

Northern Ireland Parliament, 1947, *The Drainage Act (N.I.).* H.M.S.O.

Northern Ireland Parliament, 1964, *The Drainage Act (N.I.).* H.M.S.O.

Northern Ireland Parliament, 1972, *The Water Act (N.I.).* H.M.S.O.

Northern Ireland Parliament, 1973, *The Drainage Order (N.I.).* H.M.S.O.

Northern Ireland Parliament, 1973, *The Water and Sewerage Services Order (N.I.).* H.M.S.O.

Oliphant, W. B., Hadoke, G. D. F. and Johnston, J. G., 1974. A report on practical problems associated with the management of farm wastes in the catchment area of the Castle River, *23rd Annual Report,* Foyle Fisheries Commission, 75–102. L.M. Press, Lurgan.

Penman, H. L., 1963. Woburn Irrigation 1951-59: Purpose, design and weather. *Journal of Agricultural Science,* 58, 343–348.

Prior, D. B. and Betts, N. L., 1974. Flooding in Belfast. *Irish Geography,* 7, 1–18.

Rodda, J. C., 1967. The rainfall measurement problem. *International Association of Scientific Hydrology.* Pub. No. 78, 215–231.

Royal Commission on Sewage Disposal, 1912. *Standards and tests for sewage and sewage effluents discharging into rivers and streams.* 8th Report, 1, H.M.S.O.

Rydz, B., 1974. Water needs and resources, B. M. Funnell and R. D. Hey, *The management of water resources in England and Wales.* Saxon House, 1–22.

Savill, P. S. and Weatherup, S. T. C., 1974. The effect of afforestation on water runoff in the Woodburn Catchment area. *Forestry,* 47, 45–56.

Smith, R. V., 1976. Nutrient budget of the River Main, Co. Antrim. *Technical Bull. MAFF, London No. 32, 315–339.*

Smith, R. V., 1977. Domestic and Agricultural contributions to the inputs of phosphorus and nitrogen to Lough Neagh. *Water Research* II, 453–459.

Toner, P. F. and O'Sullivan, A. J., *(eds),* 1977. *Water Pollution in Ireland.* National Science Council.

Vickers, K. U., 1969. Salmonid populations of Lough Erne tributaries. *Journal of Fish Biology,* 1, 297–309.

Vickers, K. U. and Magill, V., 1970. Does removal of trout improve salmon production? *18th Annual Report,* Foyle Fisheries Commission, 46–55. L.M. Press, Lurgan.

Went, A. E. J., 1956–1977. A series of papers on the salmon and sea trout of the Foyle system in *Annual Reports* of the Foyle Fisheries Commission. L.M. Press, Lurgan.

Water Service, *Northern Ireland Water Statistics,* Department of the Environment for Northern Ireland, An annual publication since 1974.

Water Data Unit, 1975. *Water Data 1974.* Department of the Environment, (U.K.).

Wilcock, D. N., 1971. Hydrometric Practice in Ireland. *Irish Geography,* 6, 324–328.

Wilcock, D. N., 1977*a*. The effects of channel clearance and peat drainage on the water balance of the Glenullin basin, Co. Londonderry. *Proceedings Royal Irish Academy* 77B, 253–267.

Wilcock, D. N., 1977*b*. Water Resource Management in Northern Ireland. *Irish Geography,* 10, 1–13.

Wilcock, D. N., 1979*a*. The hydrology of a peatland catchment in Northern Ireland following channel clearance and land drainage, G. E. Hollis (ed) *Man's Impact on the Hydrological Cycle in the United Kingdom,* 93–107.

Wilcock, D. N., 1979*b*. Post-war land drainage fertilizer use, and environmental impact in Northern Ireland. *Journal of Environmental management,* 8, 137–149.

Wilcock, D. N., Berry, J. S. and Hasan, M. A., 1978. An experimental measurement of potential evapotranspiration at Coleraine, Co. Londonderry. *Journal of Earth Sciences, Royal Dublin Society,* 1, 195–204.

Wood, R. B. and Gibson, C. E., 1973. Eutrophication and Lough Neagh. *Water Research* 7, 173–187.

Wright, G. D., 1978. The Four Mile Burn Experimental catchment. *Department of Civil Engineering, The Queen's University of Belfast.*

CHAPTER III

Water Supply and Demand

ROBERT COMMON,
Reader in Geography, The Queen's University of Belfast

Introduction

Some twenty years ago the quickening pace of social and economic developments within Northern Ireland raised a number of important questions about the availability of water resources to meet foreseeable demands, and the capability of distribution arrangements to supply diverse consumers. As a member of the Water Resources Committee (N.I.), which functioned between 1961 and 1964, I was bold enough to make some qualitative and quantitative assessments of these matters (Common, 1963). If I was then conscious of the unavoidable shortcomings in those assessments, I am now equally aware of the improvements which have occurred in the water services since that time.

Change and continuity

The present organization of water services in Northern Ireland is based on three principal pieces of legislation passed in 1972 and 1973. These are the Water Act (N.I.), 1972, the Drainage Order, 1973, and the Water and Sewerage Services Order, 1973. The legislative and administrative changes surrounding this legislation have been reviewed by Wilcock (1977) and need not be considered here at great length. Some historical perspective and some particular aspects of present legislation and its evolution are however appropriate.

Permissive legislation allowing local authorities to construct waterworks and sink wells for the supply of water was not available until 1878 when The Public Health (Ireland) Act was accepted. Only limited progress was then made with piped supplies to urban consumers until World War II, although the Belfast City and District Water Commissioners were supplying water on a large scale to Belfast during this period. Most rural districts however remained reliant upon well supplies.

Blatant shortcomings eventually resulted in the Water Supplies and Sewerage Act (N.I.) 1945, which offered considerable scope for the development of domestic and industrial water supply and disposal services. Subject to satisfactory economic and technical considerations, the local authorities became eligible for financial contributions from the Government to provide a water supply, to improve existing supplies and

73

to meet the needs for sewage disposal. Responsibility was laid upon the local authorities to deal with the existing and the estimated water needs of their districts through the vesting of land, the provision of installations and the laying of pipelines.

The contents of this Act wisely drew attention to the operational advantages of Joint Supply Boards. They also provided for consumer complaints and clearly indicated public liabilities over the pollution of water used for supply purposes. Unfortunately political and administrative infrastructures at this time favoured small scale working units, supplying districts rather than regions. Within this framework surface drainage problems and agricultural water needs could not be resolved and separate legislation gave responsibility for these particular problems to the Minsitry of Agriculture, under the terms of the Drainage Act (N.I.) 1947 and the Agriculture Act (N.I.) 1949. The latter Act included the terms of the Agricultural Development Scheme by which financial grants were made available for the reclamation of land and the provision of farm water supplies, as in the Land Improvement Scheme which it superceded.

By 1972, therefore, responsibility for different aspects of water management was shared between several Government Ministries and all the local authorities, research into hydrological and water management problems was limited and the scientific measurement and assessment of water resources were virtually non-existent! Lough Neagh became the focus of initial interest in the study of water management problems during the late 1960s, principally because of growing awareness about the effects of declining oxygen levels in such a large lake. A Lough Neagh Working Group was set up to study the problems of the Lough and its tributary basins. The work of this multi-disciplinary group was very important for it examined a wide range of interconnected problems relating to water supply, water quality, flood protection, fisheries, recreation, tourism, and management structures. Indeed, some of the recommendations put forward by the Group for the Lough Neagh basin were later incorporated into the Water Act (N.I.) 1972.

The Water Act of 1972 gave the Ministries of Development and Agriculture joint responsibility for promoting water conservation and detailed instructions on the prerequisites and the publication of water management programmes. Surface and groundwater pollution was dealt with at some length in terms of the official measures designed to prevent, monitor and punish. Cover statements to deal with the controls, charges and engineering works that might be required for water abstractions were included, as were regulations providing for the inspection or sampling of water and the collection of information on water uses. The Act encouraged the promotion of aquatic recreation, the collection of streamflow data and it also established an advisory Water Council. This Council is composed of professional and lay people (currently numbering fourteen) whose responsibility is to advise the two Ministries of their responsibilities under the Act.

The Drainage Order of 1973 redefined the Ministry of Agriculture's responsibility under earlier Drainage Acts, (for a discussion of which see Chapter 2) and transferred to the Ministry a responsibility for all those drainage matters which previously had resided with local authorities. In a similar way the Water and Sewerage Services Order removed responsibility for water supply and sewerage from local authorities to the Ministry of Development. Prior to 1973, the Counties, County Boroughs, Urban and Rural Districts shared responsibility for these matters, but when these administrative units were abolished in 1972, the opportunity was taken to centralize water and sewerage services within the Ministry of Development. With this new Order, the Government accepted the responsibility to provide water supply and sewage disposal facilities throughout Northern Ireland, and at a reasonable cost. In meeting these obligations, Government officials may consult with representatives from the 26 new District Councils and, if the need arises, they may also receive advice from the Water Council. Provision is made for the Department of the Environment to acquire land, personnel and equipment to meet its commitments and to deal with matters of complaint, appeal and compensation. Since this Order repealed much of the 1945 Act, it necessarily restates, at some length, the rights and duties of owners and occupiers in relation to water supply, sewerage, trade effluents and pollution.

On examining these three pieces of legislation in the context of contemporary and subsequent developments, one wonders why it took almost a decade before the majority of the Water Resources Committee's recommendations were implemented. Water conservation problems were certainly raised by the Ulster Countryside Committee, the Nature Reserves Committee and the Fisheries Conservancy Board, after they had been established as government advisory groups during 1965 and 1966. By the time the Lough Neagh Working Group was established, the neglected condition of many water bodies was both known and worrying. When the legislation finally was approved, however, the Water Council was not provided with any executive powers and the artificial division of water management responsibility between the Ministries of Agriculture and Development was maintained. These two aspects of the legislation, unfortunately, have reduced its effectiveness in subsequent years.

Another development worth noting is that neither of the two Departments responsible for water services, i.e. the Departments of Agriculture and Environmment, has been accountable to publicly-elected representatives at Stormont or at local authority level since 1972. In 1962 no less than 31 rural, 36 urban and 10 joint authorities had been responsible for water supply services. Paradoxically, a third of the total population was served by only one of them at that time, the Belfast City and District Water Commission.

It is also worth recalling that Supply and Sewerage Schemes cost £100 millions in the years between 1945 and 1973, with 50% of this outlay coming from Northern Ireland government grants. This figure represents a small percentage of the public finance budget and has fluctuated between only 1.1% and 1.7% over the last twenty years. Nevertheless inflation, ongoing work and increased total expenditures have now produced outlays which, at first sight, tend to be startling. New water supply works cost £11.8 millions in 1978, with another £10.8 millions going to operations and maintenance costs and a further £2.9 millions being required for wages. At the same time the expenditure on new sewerage works amounted to £7 millions, sewerage operations and maintenance cost £5.1 millions and another wages bill amounted to £2.4 millions.

Approximately 3,300 people are engaged in the Water Service of the DoE. Apart from the relatively small number at Stormont, this work force is based upon 27 offices – 8 in the Western, 7 in the Northern, 7 in the Eastern, and 5 in the Southern Division (Water Service, 1978). Such a labour force together with its offices, workshops, stores, laboratories and engineering equipment certainly seems to be adequate for operating the inherited system and improving it by the implementation of official proposals for the 1975–1995 period (DoE, 1977).

It has been officially stated that almost 90% of Northern Ireland's households are now provided with a piped water supply and that about 85% of them are also served by public sewerage. Most of the least expensive sources of surface water, however, have now been tapped and it is therefore probable that additional supplies will be costlier to provide. The extraction rates of water from Lough Neagh, especially for domestic and industrial purposes in Belfast and Craigavon, may or may not change significantly in the near future (Presho, 1975). Much will depend upon the effectiveness of the new treatment works upon those streams discharging excessive amounts of phosphate and nitrate into the Lough, which Wood refers to in Chapter 4. Eutrophication in Lough Neagh, unfortunately, is also accompanied by water pollution in streams like the Blackwater, Upper Bann and Lagan, in scattered minor burns and at a few coastal sites. And so, in spite of official intentions to improve the supply and disposal of water, debates and disputes continue to indicate that new water problems replace the old ones. These debates often involve a wide range of hydrological, economic, political and social issues and often set rural against urban interests. (Two such clashes of interest have recently figured prominently in the local Press, and will be described in more detail later).

The rural scene

Less than three decades have passed since improvements in water supply and changing conditions in agriculture promoted rural demands. Turner (1963), for example, writing about a rural district near Drumquin, west Tyrone observed that in 1952 some 81% of the households relied upon shallow wells, 15% used deep wells and only 4% drew water from private, piped supplies. With the coming of a public supply from the Lough Bradan pipeline in 1956, the pattern of supply and demand soon changed. By 1962, 53% of the households relied on shallow wells and 9% used deep wells, whereas private piped supplies served 12% and public supplies 26% of the dwellings.

The laying of private and public piped supplies in rural districts only became widespread after 1945, at which time 87% of all rural houses lacked piped water or flush toilet facilities. The provision of piped water was encouraged by Stormont legislation in 1945, but it was an innovation that was to be first adopted by the affluent country dwellers. Economic factors still continue to influence rural supply and even now only 33% of the households mentioned in the west Tyrone example receive a public water supply. Ubiquitous in the countryside, therefore, are the roadside and field wells as well as the disused pumps of the farmyard, cottage garden and village street (Common 1976a). As for the incoming public supply, it came and spread by way of the country road network, in much the same way as did the rural electricity and telephone lines (Figure 3.1).

In many districts it was possible for trunk supply pipelines to be tapped so that more water quickly became available for rural consumption. Such adventitious growth occurred frequently and so contributed to significant changes in overall demand. Rising demands, in their turn, required the catchment areas of supply reservoirs to be extended or additional supply and service reservoirs to be inserted into an evolving system as at Woodburn in South Antrim and throughout the Mournes of South Down. Such improvisation has its limits, however, because of the nature of catchment resources.

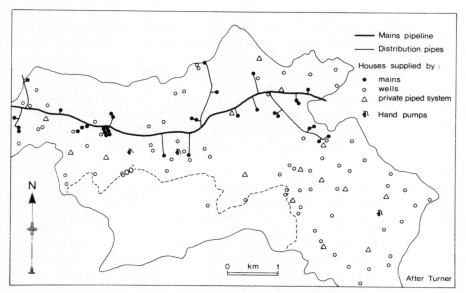

Figure 3.1 Water supply of a west Tyrone district in 1962. The main pipeline picks out the alignment of the Drumquin to Omagh road.

As long ago as 1967, for example, there was the growing probability of a clash of interests between South Down people and the urban dwellers of Belfast Lough over the use of Mourne water. Not surprisingly, therefore, the 1974 proposal to extract and pump from the White Water river into the Silent Valley reservoir was received with considerable and vociferous objections. This official project, it was argued, did not solve the basic supply problems in Belfast and Bangor, it ignored the wisdom of the Nature Conservancy Committee and it raised serious doubts about the meaning of an "Area of Outstanding Natural Beauty". The surface water estimates upon which the extraction proposals were based did not convince local people with riparian rights or naturalists with ecological interests in the catchment. Many of these people, and the local anglers, already knew that new erosional and depositional readjustments were taking place in the system between White Water Bridge and lower White Water Bridge. Inevitably these extraction proposals merely added more uncertainty about the future behaviour of a river in which fresh problems had already been identified.

Four years later another official proposal was made to collect and extract Mourne water for the Belfast area, by means of a dam at Kinnahalla below the existing Spelga dam. This project again raised passions to the extent that another pressure group (K.O.M.R.A.D.E.) was formed to marshall arguments against the scheme. Three important matters were repeatedly stressed by this new group.

Attention was drawn to the consistently low priority placed on the conservation and distribution of Lough Neagh water since the mid-1960s. This, it was asserted, has been an underlying cause of the urban supply problem for which the small capacity dams in the Mournes provide only temporary relief – and at the cost of environmental deterioration. A warning of the ecological damage likely to be incurred by the removal

77

of more water from the Mourne rivers for the new scheme, was also provided by suitably qualified objectors. Most important of all, however, was the non-acceptance of official estimates of the available water and supply costs to the consumer i.e. that the new scheme could not justify the claims of its sponsors.

The dispute over the Kinnahalla proposals took two years to settle, in favour of the objectors. It involved a considerable amount of public money for preparatory work and a truncated public inquiry i.e. £750,000. The affair also proved to be costly for the objectors in terms of money, time and effort, but it did highlight the growth of public disenchantment with bureaucratic decision taking, in which advisory committees rather than informed public representatives were involved.

The urban scene

It would be less than fair, however, not to mention the designation of growth centres by the planning authorities and the incoming of water thirsty industries during the last 20 years. These have all added extra burdens to a water service which had only begun to expand after 1945 (Common, 1964). About one third of the water now consumed is accounted for by demands in the Belfast urban area, but the volume involved is already one third greater than in 1961. The dominant water consumption of this area is such that it requires twice the combined supply of Londonderry, Craigavon, Antrim, Ballymena, Coleraine, Bangor, Carrickfergus and Newtownards.

Artificial fibre plants at Carrickfergus, Antrim, Coleraine, Kilroot (near Carrickfergus), Maydown (near Londonderry) and Limavady as well as rubber tyre factories at Ballymena, Hydepark (N.W. Belfast) and Craigavon have also affected district demands and priorities of supply, for varying periods of time. The Goodyear factory at Craigavon, for example, draws 9–18 Ml/day from Lough Neagh. Woodburn, near Carrickfergus, supplies 22 Ml/day and Carnmoney, near Londonderry, provides 17 Ml/day specifically to local industries.

At Limavady the decision to purchase water from an upland reservoir at Altnaheglish, which belonged initially to Londonderry, was an important factor in the establishment of the Hoechst synthetic fibre plant in 1969 (Patton, 1979). Prior to 1965 the scale of water provision in the Roe valley had been limited by the reliance upon piped spring supplies, which offered only 1.8 Ml/day. Once a trunk pipeline had been laid the length of the valley (Figure 3.2) it became possible to extend the supply system and to install additional service reservoirs. When the reorganisation of the water services occurred in 1973, local fears about the availability of Altnaheglish water being subordinated to the demands of Londonderry were removed, and 75% of the Roe households are now linked to the public supply. Local demands range from 9 Ml/day to 1.4 Ml/day within the system, because of socio-economic differences within the valley. Near Limavady itself, however, a number of wells have recently been established as a tangible insurance against any unforeseen or long term needs which could not be immediately satisfied from the present sources of supply.

Present conditions

Between 1961 and 1977 the Northern Ireland population increased by 119,626 to an estimated total of 1,545,726 persons and the percentage provided with a public water supply gradually grew from 78% to 89%. The consumption of water rose rapidly

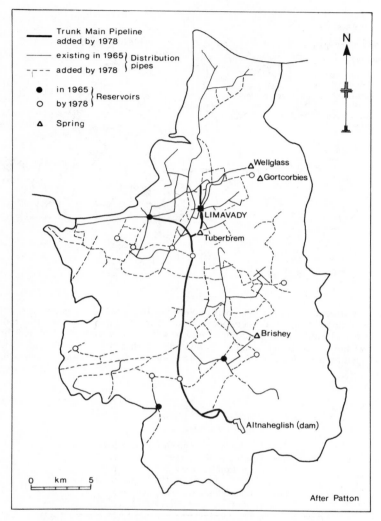

Figure 3.2 Changes in the Roe valley's water supply 1965-78.

in this period so that the rate of supply reached 636 Ml/day by 1977, when the annual volume consumed was 27% greater than 10 years earlier.

As in 1963, water is still drawn from a variety of sources (Figure 3.3), but in combinations which are distinctively different in the Northern and Western Divisions. 94.5% of water requirements in the Eastern and 88% of water needs in the Southern Division come from lakes and reservoirs, compared with 53% and 66% from these sources in the Western and Northern Divisions. Reliance upon river intakes is still a feature of the West and the North, where 36% and 12% of the supply is thus derived.

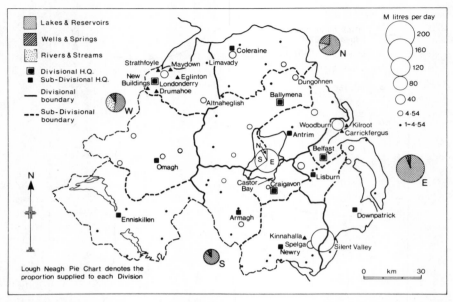

Figure 3.3 Principal water supply sources in Northern Ireland, 1977. The proportional circles indicate the location of supply and service reservoirs. The pie-graphs for each of the four Water Service divisions identify the relative importance of water supply sources, while that for Lough Neagh shows how much Lough water is distributed to each division. Also included are place-names referred to in the text, but not shown on any of the other text-figures in this Chapter.

TABLE 3.1

Public water supply and storage comparisons (by the author). 1961 estimates of storage in Londonderry and Down published by the author in 1963 appear to have been too high, since storage capacity is unlikely to have decreased since.

	A		B	
County	1961	1977	1961	1977
Londonderry	19	18	4,489	3,933
Tyrone	30	27	144	2,924
Fermanagh	42	39	389	1,165
Armagh	13	20	3,971	4,068
Down	8	12	40,008	37,060
Antrim	17	16	893	1,420

A. Estimated percentages of population without piped supplies.

B. Estimates of artificial storage in Megalitres (Ml)

80

Wells and springs also continue to be important sources for 11% of needs in the West and 22% of requirements in the North.

Artificial storage facilities have been improved over the years (Table 3.1), but if the total storage capacity in Northern Ireland is divided by the present daily average rate of delivery, then slightly less than 100 days supply would appear to be available. Behind this oversimplification, however, is the considerable potential for extraction and pumping of water from Lough Neagh at its north-east, south-east and south-west corners. There is also a noteworthy spread in the capacity of reservoirs within Antrim, Down, Armagh and Londonderry, so that actual supply capacity to consumers in these areas ranges from 40 to 250 days. In Tyrone and Fermanagh, the storage installations have a supply capacity of 128 to 216 days. The most significant reservoir to be constructed in recent years is at Dungonnell in the Upper Clogh basin and approximately half its daily drawoff goes to the town of Ballymena. A commendable effort has also recently gone into the exploration of groundwater possibilities. Since reorganisation 4 new wells in the West, 2 in the South, 3 in the North and 2 in the Eastern Division have provided an extra supply of 14.5 Ml/day. The groundwater programme is now continuing in selected parts of the western counties, where traditional methods of supply no longer suffice but a mains supply would be too costly to provide for the dispersed households.

The variety of environmental influences and the rising expectations of the public have ensured that the treatment of water and the monitoring of water quality are now standard practices (Figure 3.4). All treatment plants chlorinate water and many of

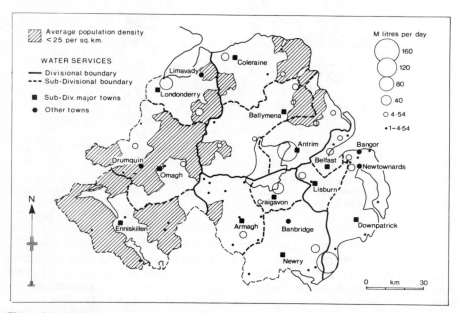

Figure 3.4 Major water treatment facilities in Northern Ireland, 1977. The concentration of larger plants in the east is noteworthy.

them in the Northern and Western Divisions also have to correct pH values. A scrutiny of data, collected between 1963 and 1973, indicates that most water coming into the treatment plants is soft, but occasionally of medium total hardness. Chemical analyses show acceptable traces of manganese, zinc and aluminium in water samples of west and central Londonderry. Aluminium is a feature of water in west Tyrone, copper and aluminium characterize north Antrim and north-east Londonderry, and lead and iron are found in pre-treated water of the Ards Peninsula (Figure 3.5). The results of a systematic analysis of selected fluvial sediments which were published in 1973 (Applied Geochemistry Research Group) are relevant to these particular observations, because they offer explanations for the occurrence of differing trace materials in water samples. They also endorse the practice of chemically analysing all water going into public supplies.

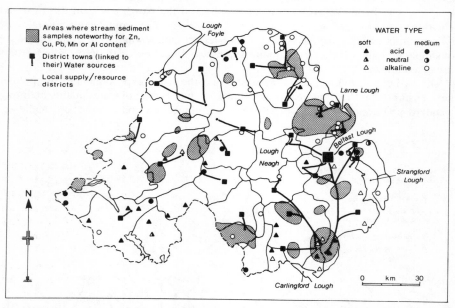

Figure 3.5 Water distribution and water quality characteristics 1977. Note the large number of transfers across District Council boundaries and the large distances between supply reservoirs and urban consumption in the south-east.

Figure 3.6 provides only a general impression of the availability of public sewers and septic tanks in Northern Ireland. A more detailed picture of divisional and district council variations would reveal a breakdown very similar to that shown for public water supplies. The disposal of sludge and waste into the sea is now considerable and deserving of conservationists' attention in several localities. Belfast Lough is reminiscent of the lower Lagan in places, with its smelly and colourful contents coming from nearby industries and urban dwellers. Waters in the nearby Larne Lough also suffer

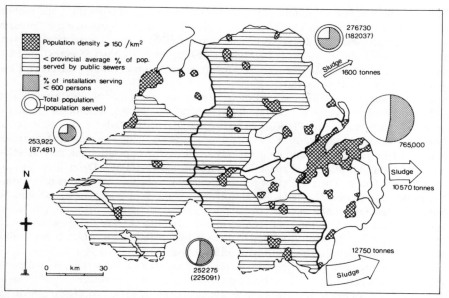

Figure 3.6 Public sewerage availability and sludge disposal, 1977. The piegraphs relate to Department of the Environment Water Service Divisions and indicate the reliance upon installations of limited capacity.

degradation of quality, because of indecision to deal effectively with the competing interests of its users. Pressures upon the biological environment of Strangford Lough mount steadily, to merit action as well as concern. These problems are more extensively reviewed in Chapter 5, but there can be little doubt that the continuing decline in the quality of surface water in parts of Northern Ireland suggests a need for many more water treatment plants to maintain minimum acceptable water quality standards in the major rivers and lakes.

Inland there has been an understandable proliferation of small scale sewerage plants and a considerable reliance upon biological filtration methods of treatment. In the Western Division, however, about 50% of the waste sludge is disposed in an undigested state. The possible application of dewatered sludge as a fertilizer to agricultural land presupposes that harmful parasites and bacteria would not be present and this is a risk which so far has been deliberately avoided.

The supply and waste disposal problems of Craigavon, in the Southern Division, have called forth considerable ingenuity from the water engineers. Growth proposals for the new city necessitated improvements to pumping and treatment facilities at Castor Bay, on Lough Neagh. Lake water has now to be pumped into installations above the city (100 m – 150 m O.D.) for gravity supply purposes. Low stream gradients, proximity to the local lake base level and difficult rainfall/discharge relationships during the year posed one set of disposal problems. Housing built before the Second World War depends upon a combined system of sewers whereas post 1945 developments employ separate sewerage. This difference adds further complications,

83

because the older system permitted foul water and storm water to overflow and pollute local water courses in periods of heavy rainfall. The solution to existing and foreseeable sewerage needs for the area has therefore involved the construction of extra treatment plant, the provision of balancing lakes, covering 64 ha (158 acres), on land designated for amenity purposes, and the formulation of conservation measures for the Bann valley above Portadown.

Diverse supply and disposal problems are also presented by the growth and redevelopment problems of Londonderry, where the terrain conditions are more varied. Some urban renewal is possible adjacent to the old walled city, but the greatest potential for development, on the left bank of the Foyle, is downvalley at Ballyarnett and Shantallow. Limited building prospects occur on the opposite bank at Waterside and Kilfinnan, but additional space is available at Newbuildings, Drumahoe, Strathfoyle and Eglinton. The settlement is now spreading outwards, so that its neighbourhoods become more detached, and although its sources of water supply should be adequate for foreseeable needs, the service reservoirs within the borough lie at comparatively low elevations between 65 m and 100 m O.D. New buildings to be fed by gravity flow are therefore confined to areas below these heights, which considerably restricts development to the south-west and south-east of the city.

In the older property a combined sewerage system used to discharge a considerable volume of untreated waste into the Foyle, but changed circumstances have brought different attitudes to this former practice. Downstream the various post-war industries at Maydown also produce considerable volumes of trade waste, the treatment of which requires careful monitoring to protect the Foyle. For both public health and amenity reasons, both the lower Foyle and adjacent Faughan need effective treatment and control of foul water.

Within the Belfast urban area a somewhat different set of problems has emerged. Here the recent civil disturbances and an interrupted programme for the renewal of the inner city have complicated the tasks of maintaining supply and sewerage systems, which are composed of variously aged segments. Most of the largest sewerage treatment plants in Northern Ireland are to be found in this city or within 48 km of it. Here the treatment facilities have to deal with the widest range of domestic, industrial and agricultural waste loads in a working day and here, too, the need for trade effluent standards to be respected is most pressing.

Conclusions

Careful examination of the Water Service's seven year record is illuminating. Among its many achievements is the very useful data bank of general information on Northern Ireland's water resources that has been built up. Interdepartmental consultation also appears satisfactory especially with the DoA and the possibility of overlapping responsibilities with the Drainage Authority appears to have been avoided.

One criticism however would be the Service's failure to embark on those major improvements and extensions to facilities which are necessary to provide a sufficiently large and flexible water service able to cope with those supply problems that will be with us at the end of the century. Specifically this involves making more parts of Northern Ireland accessible to Lough Neagh or Lough Erne water (Betts, 1978).

A second criticism would be the dearth of information on particular biological and hydrological matters and the need for ongoing research on both practical and theoretical problems. Shortcomings of data frequently are exposed either in confrontations with pressure groups or on those occasions when convincing or thorough estimates about water projects are required. The informed members of society have become more actively involved in matters affecting the quality of life and their preference is for reasoned choice rather than for bureaucratic dictation. The Government might again consider the recommendation made by the Water Resources Committee to provide research grants for suitably qualified persons who are prepared to enquire into problems and hydrological topics relevant to the work of several government departments. And as the water shortages of recent dry summers have demonstrated, there is a growing need for the public to be better informed about the use and the abuse of water as a finite resource.

A brief comment on the role of the Water Council, since its inception in 1972, is also appropriate. Membership of the Council involves the appointment of persons, who are considered to be suitable by Government Departments. This is most unfortunate because it serves to weaken the limited potential of what is at its best a mere advisory body. A truly representative cross section of elected members from the main groups, associations and councils with special water interests would have been much more acceptable to the public.

Nevertheless it is commendable that this Council has, in recent years, drawn attention to the need for realistic charges to be made on water consumed, and to the need for reduction in the amount of water wasted in the supply systems. This can amount to between 30% and 43% of all water used. The Council's call for a long term strategy to deal with Northern Ireland's water services is also timely and justifiable. It became abundantly clear in the Kinnahalla Inquiry that the Department of the Environment has yet to devise a realistic philosophy concerning water resources and their management which is based upon sound ecological and economic principles. It is equally obvious that there is still a clash of interests to be resolved over fishing, water amenities and water supply on the one hand, drainage and flood protection work on the other.

One might have expected the Council to have been more forthright and determined about its views on environmental deterioration and its obvious role as mediator between District Councils and Government Departments has been sidestepped. It is also difficult to see how this Council can be adequately informed and equipped for its "watchdog role", if it forms part of an official closed system on matters involving the use and the abuse of water throughout Northern Ireland.

With regard to the future, present trends suggest that population numbers will continue to increase till the end of this century, but by only 2% (Common, 1976b). It would also seem that urban populations will increase by between 1% and 13% in the Water Service Divisions, to produce an average rise of 5% throughout Northern Ireland. The present prospects for population increase appear to be most favourable from a supply point of view in the Northern and Southern Divisions. Increased state participation and changing economic circumstances have already diversified the economy so that the relative importance of the primary, secondary and tertiary sectors has been altered considerably since 1945. As the modernisation of society proceeds, further changes in the infra-structure might be expected but the official proposals for

85

the next twenty years suggest that they will occur gradually and less dramatically than previously. Even though the activities of the local textile industries and the large water-consuming factories began to decline seriously in 1980 the general trends in the population and the economy suggest that a realistic target for Northern Ireland's water services should be a 95% public supply by 1995.

Although these suggested modifications to the numbers, occupations and distributions of people appear to be slight, the future demands for water could still be disproportionately increased by changes in domestic habits, agricultural and industrial practices. Indeed, the adult population of Northern Ireland has already witnessed a quiet revolution in the collection, distribution and utilization of water since 1945. Future conditions, however, will probably demand the acceptance of new and more frugal attitudes to the use of water resources, as in the rest of West European Society.

Acknowledgements

The author wishes to acknowledge the active co-operation of conservationists in South Down, South Antrim, east- and mid-Tyrone, financial grants for fieldwork from The Queen's University of Belfast, and the assistance of P. G. Holland (Department of the Environment for Northern Ireland) in discussions of hydrological matters.

REFERENCES

Applied Geochemistry Group, 1973. *Provincial Geochemical Atlas of Northern Ireland.* Imperial College, London.
Betts, N., 1978. Water Supply in Northern Ireland. *Irish Geography,* 11, 161-66.
Betts, N. and Prior, D., 1973. Belfast fights for water. *Geographical Magazine,* 45 (12), 844–850.
Common, R., 1963. Water Resources in Northern Ireland. *Journal of the British Association,* 45, 778–807.
Common, R., 1964. (editor) *Northern Ireland from the Air.* The Queen's University, Belfast.
Common, R., 1976a. Water and Society in Ulster. J. House (*Edit.*) *Northern Geographical Essays,* Newcastle University.
Common, R., 1976b. Regional development prospects in Northern Ireland. *Area,* 8(1), 4–9.
Common, R., 1977. *The relevance of the International Hydrological decade to Ulster.* Geography Department Research paper No. 2, Queen's University Belfast, 160 pp. See in particular "The White Water controversy in south Down, 1974", pp. 23–28.
Department of the Environment for Northern Ireland, 1977. *Regional physical Development strategy 1975–95.* H.M.S.O., Belfast.
Northern Ireland Parliament, 1945. *The Water Supplies and Sewerage Act (N.I.).* H.M.S.O.
Northern Ireland Parliament, 1947. *The Drainage Act (N.I.).* H.M.S.O.
Northern Ireland Parliament, 1949. *The Agriculture Act (N.I.).* H.M.S.O.
Northern Ireland Parliament, 1973. *The Drainage Order (N.I.).* H.M.S.O.
Northern Ireland Parliament, 1972. *The Water Act (N.I.).* H.M.S.O.
Northern Ireland Parliament, 1973. *The Water and Sewerage Services Order (N.I.).* H.M.S.O.
Patton, S., 1979. *Limavady's water supply.* Unpublished BA thesis, Queen's University, Belfast.
Presho, N., 1975. A dying lake, *Geographical Magazine,* 48(1), 8–16.
Turner, R. H., 1963. *The changing pattern of water supply in a rural area (of west Tyrone).* Unpublished BA thesis, Queen's University, Belfast.
Water Service, 1978. *Northern Ireland Water Statistics, 1977.* Department of the Environment for Northern Ireland.
Wilcock, D., 1977. Water resource management in Northern Ireland. *Irish Geography,* 10, 1–13.

CHAPTER IV

Lakes

R. BRIAN WOOD,
Professor of Biology and Director of the Limnology Laboratory,
New University of Ulster

Introduction

Although the distinction between ponds, lakes, and widened stretches of rivers is highly arbitrary, a quick scanning of Northern Ireland's Ordnance Survey maps reveals something over 1,100 bodies of water which might fall within the scope of this chapter. They range from disused quarries and artificial mill ponds to the largest body of water in the British Isles, and name 635 loughs including twelve "Black Loughs" and only two "Blue". Let us hope this indicates the underlying dark peaty nature of the water rather than an index of pollution! The vast majority of the water bodies are small, and only 119 exceed ten hectares in area. It follows that Lough Neagh, and Upper and Lower Lough Erne, with surface areas of 383, 34.5 and 109.5 km², respectively, dominate our inland waters. Bathymetric data are not readily available, but local tales of 'bottomless' lakes can safely be discounted. Lower Lough Erne reaches 69 m depth and Lough Neagh 34 m, while many others are deep enough to exhibit summer stratification, though this obviously depends partly on exposure.

The loughs are fairly evenly distributed, although Fermanagh and West Tyrone – with about 360 loughs, including the enormously extensive Upper and Lower Lough Erne system, – is clearly Northern Ireland's lake land. County Londonderry, with fewer than 50 loughs is relatively poorly endowed.

Northern Ireland's loughs exhibit a fairly wide range of gross chemical composition reflecting the geochemistry of their catchments. In Table 4.1, chemical analyses from various sources have been gathered together and a broad four-fold regional classification is presented, although it must be remembered that chemical composition varies from time to time. Water chemistry on the Antrim plateau is principally determined by the combination of peat overlying basalt. Water in the Mournes is soft, much influenced by the underlying hard, granite rock, and the Erne system is significantly influenced by limestone. As shown in Table 4.1, the chemistry of all lakes is essentially a variation on a calcium bicarbonate theme with some loughs near the coast, e.g. Lough Doo, near Fairhead (Figure 4.1), much influenced by the sea. Questions of nutrient chemistry will be discussed later.

The optical properties of lough water vary considerably. Jewson and Taylor (1978), reporting on turbidity in 20 different water bodies throughout Northern Ireland, showed that 1% of the light received at the surface may penetrate to depths ranging from less than 1 m to more than 20 m. While much of this variation was due to light absorption by different algal crops, other factors are also involved, for filtered samples showed a 100-fold variation in their absorbance of ultra-violet light (wavelength, 350 nanometers). Such large variation indicates the great range in light absorbance capacity between clear limestone water at one extreme and dark peaty water at the other.

Northern Ireland's loughs can be considered as natural resources under three main headings:
1. The water industry
2. Fisheries
3. Amenity

It is obvious however, that many facets of sensible freshwater exploitation have common requirements, and that much of what applies to loughs may be equally appropriate to rivers.

TABLE 4.1

Some chemical constituents of selected loughs in Northern Ireland

	Ca	Mg	Na	K	Cl	SO$_4$	Bicarb.	Conductivity μS at 25°C	pH
				(mg/l)					
Antrim Plateau									
Lough Naroon	2.3	1.2	7.9	0.5	9.8	12.2		23	—
Lough Doo	4.8	0.7	25.0	1.5	37.7	24.3	3.0	82	—
Lough Nabrick	5.5	4.8	8.3	0.8	10.0	12.4	27.0	44	—
Bann System									
Ballinrees Reservoir	21.6	8.8	13.0	2.1	—	—	121	254	7.7
Lough Beg	27.3	9.2	13.5	2.6	18.1	23.0	112	290	7.8
Lough Neagh	26.0	9.0	13.5	2.8	17.8	22.6	112	290	7.8
Lough Fea	6.1	2.3	7.8	0.8	—	—	—	80	7.1
Erne System									
Lough Erne	26.9	4.8	10.5	4.6	—	—	198	161	—
Ross Lough	27.4	5.3	10.0	2.1	14.2	18.2	168	145	—
Spectacle Lough	19.5	3.1	9.3	0.7	8.6	11.5	78	77	—
Loughnamaddy	1.6	0.7	5.3	1.0	8.9	11.0	3.0	23	—
Lough Navar	3.4	1.9	14.1	0.4	16.3	3.0	—	104	—
Mournes									
Skillyscolban	18.9	6.2	9.9	0.8	10.3	12.0	102	92	—
Silent Valley	1.8	1.1	7.0	0.5	—	—	—	51	5.6
Spelga	3.3	1.3	8.2	1.0	—	—	—	84	7.6
Others									
Lough Gall	39.1	9.6	13.9	4.3	—	—	—	420	8.6
Augher Lough	49.0	6.3	10.0	2.2	17.4	—	62-170	—	—

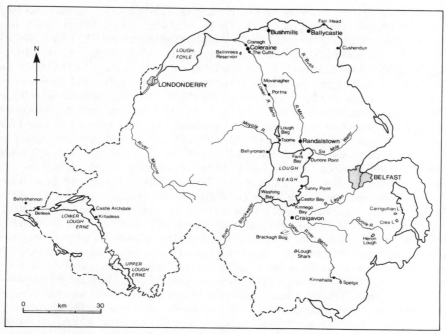

Figure 4.1   Place-names mentioned in the text of Chapter 4.

The Water Industry

Water supply throughout Northern Ireland in 1980 equalled 686 Ml/day (Water Service, 1980). Of this, 555 Ml/day came from impounding reservoirs and loughs, with boreholes, wells and springs providing some 49 Ml/day. The rest (82 Ml/day) came from direct river abstraction. Silent Valley, with its excellent water quality and advantages of gravity feed provides 137 Ml/day, but now no longer dominates supply to the heavily populated Eastern Division. Lough Neagh, through the Dunore Point works, now provides 105 Ml/day to the Eastern Division as well as 19 Ml/day to the Northern Division. Supplies from Lough Neagh to Belfast, of course, suffer from two major disadvantages, the cost of pumping water up out of the Lough Neagh basin and the difficulty of treating the poor quality water.

Reference has been made elsewhere (Wood and Gibson, 1973) to the eutrophication problem of Lough Neagh, in which dense populations of algae regularly develop. In 1979 levels of chlorophyll *a* for the first time exceeded 130 μg/1 when the Lough was well mixed. While such concentrations bring enormous ecological problems, especially of transient oxygen depletion, the algae also present major problems of filtration to the water engineer. Because of these problems, Dunore Point is rarely able to meet its design capacity of 140 Ml/day during the summer months, and one of the reasons given in 1978-79 for the proposed Kinnahalla abstraction in the Mournes (see Common, Chapter 3), as opposed to the Tunny Point scheme from Lough Neagh, was the unreliability of the Lough Neagh source. Properly managed, Lough Neagh represents a bountiful quantity of water and the Lough Neagh Working Group (1973) suggested that 348 Ml/day might be directly extracted by 1980, rising to 716 Ml/day by 2000 A.D. without significant change in water management policy and detriment to other users. As no new major impoundments in the Mournes or elsewhere seem likely without serious conservation drawbacks it is doubly important that the quality of Lough Neagh water be improved, so that this source can be exploited. Demand for water in Northern Ireland is rising steadily although the 1980-81 economic recession levelled-out the demand, the average daily supply for the years 1973 to 1980 being 539, 581, 584, 595, 636, 655, 685 and 686 Ml, respectively. In 1980 Lough Neagh, directly through Dunore Point, Castor Bay, Washing Bay and indirectly through the River Moyola and the Lower Bann (to Ballinrees Reservoir), was providing 200-250 Ml/day. Local industrial abstractions probably increase that figure by 10 to 20%.

Altogether the DoE abstracts water from only 27 loughs and 29 impounding reservoirs, so that only some 5% of our standing water bodies are involved in water supply. Even so, this represents a significant part of our natural water resources which are under strict and sensible control. To these water bodies under controlled management must be added the many loughs, including Lough Erne, which are the responsibility of the DoA. There are numerous other private abstractors of water but details are often considered of commercial value and are therefore not readily available.

The other side of the water industry is the disposal of wastes. Rivers and coastal waters obviously suffer, and with them, any loughs which are downstream of effluent discharges. In this respect Northern Ireland is somewhat different from Scotland, Wales and England where lochs, llyns and lakes have a predominantly upland distribution and escape many problems except perhaps those produced by aggregations of tourists, as for example at Windermere. Both Lough Erne and Lough Neagh are essentially lowland loughs draining some 4,265 km² and 5,700 km², respectively. Effluent from approximately 110,000 people could theoretically drain into Lower Lough Erne and from 330,000 into Lough Neagh. With estimated animal stocks of over one million dairy cows, cattle, sheep and pigs in the Lough Neagh catchment and probably 0.3 million in the Lough Erne basin, the potential for pollution and enrichment of these loughs is obviously great even allowing for their size, the large proportion of agricultural waste returned to the land, and the considerable efforts being made to reduce the organic loading from sewage.

The monitoring techniques and effects of pollution control are outlined in Chapter 2 and the broadly satisfactory state of the rivers is described. Pollution problems in Northern Ireland's loughs however, are great, especially in the two largest. Both show excessive growth of algae, an associated tendency towards a critical lack of oxygen for living organisms, and increasing numbers of more pollution-tolerant fauna (see Wood and Gibson, 1973; Battarbee, 1978; Carter, 1978; Wood, 1980; Gibson, et al., 1980). It is reassuring to know that some 10 years after phosphate was clearly indicated as the cause of the problem, phosphate-removal at 18 sewage works in the Lough Neagh catchment is now economically feasible, and the scheme was completed early in 1982. Associated with this are government directives on the siting of domestic septic tanks, and building requirements for the storage of slurry and silage when subsidies are sought. Education, public willingness to respond to entreaty or prosecution, and responsible circumvention of the anomaly, whereby DoE is both public watch dog and one of the principal polluters, will be the best and perhaps only safeguards of water quality in Northern Ireland.

Fisheries

One of the most obvious beneficiaries of good water quality are fish, and Northern Ireland is rightly renowned for its fishing resources, both commercial and sporting. Again it is impossible to separate rivers from loughs, but an estimate of sport fishing in Department of Agriculture trout waters, which is certainly an underestimate, can be obtained from the 1976 fishing census (DoA, 1978*a*) which calculated 65,000 angling visits lasting 325,000 hours and taking 39,000 fish. When to this is added coarse fishing, private club fishing, the very liberal policy which does not require under 16 year old trout fishermen to obtain a rod licence, and the inevitable illegal fishing, the scale becomes huge indeed. The Fisheries Conservancy Board (1977) for example, whose area of responsibility excludes the Foyle system, tabulate 42,407 licences issued, over 40,000 of them for game fish for the season. Even these figures must be way below the potential for Northern Ireland. Fifteen-day licences sold to non-Northern Ireland residents for example, numbered 284 for game fishing and 266 for coarse fishing in 1969. By 1972, these had fallen to 52 and 23 respectively, but by 1977 had recovered to 68 and 243. The figures for 1978 were 62 and 348, for 1979 were 181 and 1,902, and for 1980 were 205 and 1,936 (Fisheries Conservancy Board, 1980). What the demand would be in the absence of civil unrest is clearly conjectural, but almost certainly very large. There are some 3 million registered coarse anglers in Great Britain and roughly as many again in Europe, of whom about 2,500 visited Lough Erne in 1979-80 on organised package trips (Belford, personal communication).

The reversal of the mid-1970s slump in the exploitation of coarse fishing resources, especially those on Lough Erne, stems from many factors including excellent provision of angling facilities (stands, jetties, etc.) by the amenity branch of DoA and the activities of the Department of Commerce for Northern Ireland and the Northern Ireland Tourist Board among others. Perhaps the most spectacular advertisement for Lough Erne angling was a 1971 competition in which 250 anglers took 2 tons 3 cwt 42 lb of roach and bream in 5 hours. As a result, since 1976 a Benson and Hedges Fishing Festival has been organised annually by the Tourist Board. In 1977 some 10 tons of fish were taken in 3 days and new records are set almost every year. As pointed out in Chapter 2 (Rivers), costing the value of a resource such as angling is not easy, but the Tourist Board have estimated (Belford, personal communication) that 240 anglers at the Festival in 1978 spent some £20,000 in the locality, and that the 2,500 anglers in 1979-80 spent perhaps £150,000. At £1,000 per ton for the Festival period, coarse fish taken for sport clearly have the economic edge over commercial fishing. And most of the catch is returned live to the waters!

In managing a resource, potential conflict exists between sport and commercial catching, and pike in Lough Erne is an example. Until recently the commercial netting of pike had been actively encouraged in the hope that it was thereby improving the trout fishing. A small but locally important fishery developed, which is now under some criticism as the tourist value of pike becomes recognised. The vigour of the debate is in no way reduced by our fundamental ignorance of the size, distribution, fecundity and prey of the natural populations of pike in Lough Erne although a recent studentship by DoA is permitting the first limited study to be made. The interaction between the Foyle inshore salmon netting and angling in the Roe and Faughan is another obvious example.

This is a point perhaps worth considerable emphasis. Until recently salmon and trout have held dominance in the affections of local anglers, and considerable resources are available, for example through an excellent DoA Fish Farm at Movanagher, on the Lower Bann, and the hatchery at Bushmills, for stocking trout and salmon waters. Salmon runs are also regularly monitored on major rivers. The DoA has acquired 39 trout lakes with a total area of 1,200 ha, 5 mixed coarse and game fish lakes (15,430 ha including Lough Erne) and 10 coarse fish lakes (130 ha) which it manages by clearing, stocking and provision of access etc. Some £2.8 million has been spent on these lakes since 1966 (Kerr, 1979). We are much less well informed and equipped to deal with demands on our coarse fish, the excellence of which is not restricted to Lough Erne. Rudd on the Quoile for example, provides excellent coarse fishing. Some work on the roach invasion of the Erne and its crossing with, and apparent exclusion of, rudd is in hand and some aspects of Lough Neagh perch have been studied, but huge amounts of fundamental work remain to be done on natural populations and the 'lesser' life and conditions which sustain them. It seems impracticable, and indeed ought to be unnecessary, to set up rearing and stocking facilities for coarse fish i.e. to have an artificial 'put and take' management. It ought to be possible to live in balance with the superb resources with which all of Northern Ireland is endowed.

Commercial fisheries

Northern Ireland has a long history of the exploitation of fish for food. Bronze Age sites near Toome on the Lower Bann, for example, seem clearly to have had a close relationship with fishing, and Mitchel (1965) reports that in medieval times Lough Neagh eels were marketed in many Irish towns. Again the boundary between lakes, rivers and the sea proves less than satisfactory in considering commercial fish, with migrating salmon and eels in particular being caught in each of these environments.

Lough Foyle: Although not related to a freshwater lough, the Foyle salmon fishery is obviously of major commercial importance with a peak catch in 1963 of nearly 160,000 fish. This figure had fallen to under 40,000 (130,000 kg) by 1977 (Foyle Fisheries Commission 1978). The commercial catch of salmon in the rest of Northern Ireland in 1979 was some 46,000 kg. Many factors including water flows, the after effects of UDN disease (see Chapter 2) and over-fishing at sea are variously invoked to explain the long term changes in the commercial catch. A glance at a Foyle Fisheries Commission Annual Report will immediately highlight the complex interactions of pollution, drainage, fish counting, stocking, disease, tagging, commercial over-exploitation, and other factors as well, which necessarily influence the successful management of such a fishery. For other details of this particular fishery see Chapter 5.

Lough Neagh: Lough Neagh supports four principal commercial fisheries. Salmon are taken near Coleraine at the Cranagh by nets and at the Cutts by traps. As with the Foyle, it is hard to know whether recent declining catches result from natural fluctuations or from other causes. The overall fishing practice appears to allow some 50% of salmon to escape into the Lough Neagh system, so perhaps some salmon grilse provide the potential breeding stock. However, the pattern of catching is highly dependent on water flows as shown in tagging studies undertaken by the DoA Fisheries Research Laboratory at the Cutts. Within stipulated limits, the discharge of water from Lough Neagh is controlled by the sluice gates at Toome, and we see here an interesting example of the interaction between different facets of Lough resource management such as water storage, land drainage and fish migration. In the case of Lough Neagh discharge, the problem is enhanced by the different timing and quantities of discharge required by eels.

Eels, in almost exact reversal of salmon behaviour, migrate from the sea as elvers, feed and grow as brown eels in freshwater and at incipient sexual maturity return as silver eels to the sea. Just as mature salmon need to feel the current at the Cranagh before they move upstream, so the mature eel needs to sense the current of the lower Bann before it will move out of Toome Bay and into the traps at Toome and Portna. Migration is even more subtly controlled as eels migrate only at night and at the dark of the moon. The interplay between salmon and eel migrations and water discharge are summarised in Table 4.2 compiled from the recommendations of the Lough Neagh Working Group (1973).

TABLE 4.2

Fish migrations and desirble flows in the River Lower Bann

Fish	Period	Flow required
Salmon – smolts to sea	April – May	Moderately high. Never less than 1590 Ml/day with freshets
Salmon – adults upstream	May – August	as required
Eels – elvers upstream	Mid-March to mid-May	Low flows near to 1590 Ml/day minimum
Silver eels to sea	September to November	Gradual increase above 1590 Ml/day minimum, with freshets at appropriate times of the lunar cycle

The eel fishery on Lough Neagh and the Bann has a long and colourful history and is now run through the Lough Neagh Fishermen's Co-operative. Some 500 men work for the Co-operative, most of them on long-line fishing for brown eels. The present arrangement whereby the fishermen share in the profit of the total catch of eels has done much to reduce trawling, over-fishing and poaching. A missed brown eel probably later contributes to the profit as a silver. The Co-operative's self-control of bonuses probably does more to bring mavericks into line than did bailiffs and court fines in the past. The law and the management of the Co-operative make valuable provision for the conservation of eel stocks. Young elver for example are transported upstream (see later). The Queen's gap, a break in the nets which allows silver eels to escape downstream to the breeding grounds, is maintained at twice the legal limit. Nominally the gap should equal $^1/_{10}$ of channel width, but in practice at Toome and Portna it is $^1/_5$ of channel width. A further management practice is to stipulate a minimum hook size, No. 4, permitted in brown eel long-lining, while in 1978 a maximum permitted daily catch was introduced equal to 8 stones (=50 kg) per day per boat of brown eels.

Northern Ireland's total catch of eels in 1978 (including the small Lough Erne catch) was 732,000 kg and was valued at £968,000 (DoA, 1978b). By 1980, the respective figures had risen to an estimated 1,000,000 kg with a sale value of £2,200,000. Of the 1978 catch, the Lough Neagh Co-operative contributed some 500 tons of brown eels and 175 tons of silver eels worth approximately £817,000. The Lough Neagh eel fishery is, as far as is known, the largest in Europe. Much of the catch is sold in Holland and the quality is such that it is economically worthwhile to ship eels live to the European markets by aerated road tanker and by air freight. The eel fishery is one of British Airway's principal clients in Northern Ireland.

Although total populations of Lough Neagh eels are hard to quantify, a rough estimate based on annual elver runs, on the approximately 9-10 year stay of the average silver, and on fishing and other mortality of browns, suggests that perhaps 200,000,000 are present at any one time. As there appears to be plentiful food (eels are bottom feeders, midge larvae are bottom dwellers and the nuisance swarms of adult midges around Lough Neagh argue that by no means all are taken), it has been the annual practice to catch elvers at the Cutts and to release them after transport to Lough Neagh. Normally between 7 and 10 million are annually moved in this way, although the number sometimes reaches 20 million, a figure which can be compared with an annual total elver recruitment of 0.4 million to Lough Erne. As a management policy the capture of elvers at the Cutts and their subsequent release in Lough Neagh is obviously well intentioned, but there is little scientific basis for it. One interesting facet of elver transport is that, since 1932, it has been carried out for three periods of time and discontinued for two. Each transition has been followed, some 8-10 years later, by a dramatic change in the sex ratio of the silver eel catch with elver transport apparently increasing the frequency of males which are much smaller than females. The mechanisms of this change in population structure remain obscure, although Parsons, Vickers and Warden (1977) have explored and found wanting various explanations. Certainly wild claims that 'pollution' has caused a dramatic reduction in growth rate cannot be sustained.

The pollan fishery on Lough Neagh has rapidly declined in importance relative to eels since 1900, when it was the more important of the two fisheries on the Lough. At the turn of the century, 500 fishermen were directly employed in the fishery, and perhaps as many again in boat-making and other allied services. The annual value of the pollan fishery exceeded £7,000 from the sale of 449 tons. Although catch records are not complete, the volume transported by rail and marketed in Belfast, London, Liverpool and other British ports clearly shows a thriving pollan fishery. In 1849 a brief fall in the harvest was blamed on pollution from flax-retting and pollan are known to be highly susceptible to pollution. In 1924 *Gammarus* was invoked as eating huge numbers of pollan eggs although there is no scientific evidence to confirm this. The pollan fishery was of but very local significance by 1938 when Northern Ireland

Railways carried only 3 tons. The food shortages of the war years raised this to 269 tons in 1944, but this figure fell to 105 tons by 1947, to 13 tons by 1950 and 2 tons by 1953.

The sales figures presented above may be a bad guide to the size of the pollan crop today, for virtually all of the harvest is now sold locally, and Wilson (1979) suggests from conversations with the principal local dealer that perhaps up to 200 tons were taken annually until 1976. In his own studies however, Wilson found progressively increasing difficulty in catching pollan up to 1978, when commercial fishing for pollan was virtually abandoned. He identifies a particular feature of pollan populations, namely the frequent and inexplicable elimination of all the fish in a particular age class. In a species reaching maturity at 3+ years and not normally surviving to 6+, mortalities of whole generations on this scale quite naturally produce wild oscillation in the fishing yield from year to year. Based on admittedly inadequate fishing data, he estimated the 1976 population to be about 14 million fish. The 1977 population was nearer 3 million, the 1977 recruitment having failed. From detailed analyses of population structures, he concludes that gill netting with 30 mm bar meshes would prevent over-fishing, permit the optimum sustainable yield and allow pollan to survive bad recruitment years. The size of the sustainable yield would clearly depend on recruitment and the cause of the noted recent failures is clearly an area over-ripe for study. Even so, returning to crops of between 150 and 400 tons per annum seems possible, pollution and other factors permitting.

If pollution is the real cause of the declining pollan crop, specific explanations could be the low oxygen levels or the silting up of breeding gounds. Overfishing could also be a factor, although Wilson personally discounts this, or there could well have been a recently bad recruitment year. Other possible factors are administrative. Recently, the legal taking of perch in December, January and February may have facilitated the accidental taking of gravid pollan in this, their close season. Whatever the reasons for the recent decline, and a combination of several of the above factors cannot be ruled out, the fact remains that former levels of fishing could not at the present time be sustained. Most fishermen have been earning a secondary income by taking perch which have come to dominate the pelagic fish of Lough Neagh. Perch have long existed in Lough Neagh, and in the 1970s, they became so common as to be commercially exploitable with a ready market in Switzerland for perch fillets, and offal used as fish meal. Figures are difficult to confirm, but three local dealers have provided data which show that, by 1980, the perch catch was worth over £1,000,000 at the lough side. Alas, the fishery has virtually disappeared, possibly through over-fishing and possibly through the explosive population of roach, for which there is no known market. Those who carelessly introduced roach (as discarded live-bait?) may have much to answer for, as may those who advocate the introduction of any new species before basic research is done. The doubtful wisdom of introducing new species – perch were introduced in the late 18th Century by Viscount O'Neil (Doyle 1854) – will be dealt with under the heading of Amenity below.

Lough Erne: The pike fishery on Lough Erne has already been mentioned. About twenty commercial licences are issued and although details are not available and some fish are marketed in the Republic, the recorded catch was 13 tons in 1976. Some eels are also taken but the number is very small in comparison with the Lough Neagh catch.

Amenity

Many would consider a supply of potable water or unrivalled sport fishing to be amenities of great merit, but these having already been dealt with, we shall consider other amenities such as boating and nature conservation.

The closeness of the sea to even the most inland parts of Northern Ireland tended to lessen the use of inland waters for sailing and cruising. Incredible as it may seem to Londoners or Mancunians, Lough Neagh's 383 sq. km support only three sailing clubs. One is at Antrim, on the Shane's Castle Estate, at the mouth of The Six Mile Water, a second is at Ballyronan's new marina on the Tyrone/Derry shore, and a third is the Lough Neagh Sailing Club, serving the Craigavon Area from its base in Kinnego Bay. These clubs have a total membership of between 500 and 600, though family and other group memberships make accurate estimates difficult. Lough Erne Sailing Club is long established at Killadeas and boasts one of the few boathouses where sailing boats can be put away still fully rigged, a useful by-product of the flying boat stations based on Lough Erne during the Second World War. Not restricted merely to boating, the sheer size of our two largest loughs permits many activities with conflicting needs to co-exist. Power-boating and water-skiing co-exist with dinghy sailing, for example, and bird conservation co-exists with gun clubs.

Although by most standards Lough Neagh and the Lower Bann represent superb inland cruising waters, they undoubtedly fall a long way behind the Erne in extent and scenic appeal. On the lower Bann navigation is maintained largely by the efforts of the Lough Neagh and River Bann Association. On Lough Erne six commercial operators hire out craft, in excess of 100 boats. Again, the Tourist Board has made estimates of the economic return on this resource. Public and private development investment is valued at about £1.3 million, with 1978 income to the Fermanagh area reckoned as some £600,000. Nearly 60% of bookings in 1978 came from outside Northern Ireland. Several times that number of privately owned (i.e. non-commercial) boats must use Lough Erne and a significant personal hiring system may well operate. The Erne system must represent one of the finest stretches of inland cruising water in the world, and although it is as yet underexploited it is good to see that bodies such as the Tourist Board are already aware of the dangers of over-development and the destruction of its greatest asset, quiet uncrowded beauty. Many facilities are needed to sustain a hire cruiser fleet and few would criticise the developments so far. Navigable channels on the Erne have recently been re-marked and a major bathymetric survey is in hand. The DoA, since 1973, has spent £1.4 million on water recreation facilities at 70 sites and twelve more sites are currently being developed (Kerr, 1979). Jetties and fishing stands, car parks and paths have been provided. Local and district councils, as well as the DoE through its responsibilities for nature conservation, have also done much and the tasteful developments for example at Castle Archdale and Belleek are to be applauded. The dispersal of holiday boat traffic must surely remain a major goal if the essential remoteness of the Erne is not to be abused and many, fairly small, harbourings will be required (See Plates 4.1 and 4.2 opposite).

Much of Lough Erne is fairly shallow and the successful development of its boating potential must depend on the maintenance of relatively high Lough water levels. High water levels of course hinder land drainage on the shores of the Lough and herein lies a management conflict. Another such conflict arises when lough levels are drawn down

Plate 4.1   The marina at Castle Archdale, on Lower Lough Erne, is regarded as a very successful example of its type. The development blends very well with the surrounding environment.

Plate 4.2   Cruising on the waters of Lower Lough Erne, County Fermanagh, illustrates the recreational development of such lakes during the 1970s. In the background, new growth of trees along the lake shore marks the new land area that has emerged since the lowering of the lake level.

by hydro-electricity generation at Ballyshannon. Even though Ballyshannon's demands are greatest in winter, water input to Lough Erne in summer may be very low and careful manipulations of water level are necesary to avoid conflict. In passing, large winter draw-down might conceivably have a significant effect on angling. If insect larvae, laid as eggs during summer in inshore areas, are left exposed in the winter, the food chains of fish may well be disrupted.

From the point of view of wildlife conservation, loughs obviously provide important foci for nature reserves and areas of scientific interest because of their fringing vegetation, their wildfowl populations, and the rarer creatures they contain. Examples of such areas are Randalstown Forest on the shores of Lough Neagh containing wildfowl and mixed woodland below former shore lines; Quoile Pondage, rich in wildfowl which feed on the marshes and transition area between salt marsh and fresh water created by the construction of the barrage; and Brackagh Bog which contains pools in cut-over peat bog, rare plants and breeding wildfowl. Other examples are Farrs Bay on Lough Neagh, an area of unspoilt carr and fen below successive shore lines; Loughaveema, the "vanishing" lake between Cushendun and Ballycastle; Lough Beg, internationally important for its breeding populations of wildfowl and waders as well as for macrophytes and rare shore plants; and Lough Neagh itself, containing very large populations of tufted duck and pochard, which at their peaks perhaps equal the wintering populations in the rest of the British Isles. Lough Neagh also contains important flocks of swans, great crested grebes and widgeon. All these areas together with Lough Shark (reedswamp), Carrigullian, Heron and Clea Loughs (freshwater vegetation, wildfowl and passerines), large areas of the Ernes and numerous water-based bird sanctuaries, are listed by the DoE.

In a less spectacularly obvious way, some loughs contain rare species and many more may be found to do so when we find time to study them. Mention has already been made of the decline in the pollan populations of Lough Neagh. Although of considerable commercial value, it also has an exceptional biological interest. Ferguson et al. (1978) by elegant electrophoretic studies of blood proteins, have shown that it belongs to the species Coregonus autumnalis whose nearest location outside Ireland is Siberia and Alaska. There it migrates between salt and freshwater and tolerates very cold water. Geographically near neighbours in Scotland, Wales, England and the rest of Europe are a quite different species. Lough Neagh and Lough Erne pollan surely represent an unusual glacial relict. How dreadful if carelessness or greed should render them extinct for, although conspecific with their Siberian branch, they have clearly evolved a separate pattern of behaviour and temperature tolerance. A better known, though until recently even more poorly studied, glacial relict is Mysis relicta, the so-called freshwater fairy shrimp of Lough Neagh. Elsewhere it tolerates brackish water and ultra-pure conditions.

It seems highly likely that other exotic rarities will turn up in our loughs in the fullness of time and study. In any case, even if new species do not turn up, there is ample evidence from other studies that long-isolated populations of the same species develop very subtle genetic differences which may prove to be highly valuable in achieving self-sustaining fish populations after stocking. In this connection it is perhaps worth noting that only two "wild" populations of the ubiquitously introduced rainbow trout successfully breed in Ireland. At present Ireland contains the last refuge in the British Isles of many, long-isolated fish populations. While clearing and re-stocking policy by anglers is obviously well intentioned, it seems right to ask whether it would be completely well advised throughout Northern Ireland. Much the same argument applies to unthinking introductions of new species. The roach introduced into Lough Erne, and more recently into Lough Neagh, are clearly changing the coarse fishing quite dramatically, and the 18th and 20th century sowings of perch and roach in Lough Neagh could reap a very debatable harvest if – and what follows is highly speculative – it proves to be at the expense of the pollan and, conceivably of the char which died out in Lough Neagh between 1815 and 1825.

Conclusion

Clearly Northern Ireland has a resource of immense value in its loughs. Even in drought we are not short of water, merely the means of supplying it. We have locally very important inland fisheries which ought to do much to sustain rural communities. In angling and cruising, we have potential resources which could naturally provide the basis of a vigorous tourist trade, in exactly those areas least likely to be industrially developed. Developing this resource rather late, we can learn from and avoid the dreadful mistakes made elsewhere. But we are still woefully ignorant of the ecological and environmental bases on which sensible resource management must depend and some of our practices, well intentioned no doubt, have been questioned above. Other practices, such as sewage disposal into lowland lakes, have undoubtedly been wrong and even where enormous amounts of careful work have been done, as for example on Lough Neagh, response by management has been slow. Surely also the fish stocks of Lough Erne and Lough Neagh, with their supporting water conditions, deserve a major resource study.

Acknowledgements

I very gratefully acknowledge the considerable help given by many people in providing information and data used. Especially my thanks are due to Shane Belford (Northern Ireland Tourist Board), J. M. Kerr (DoA), B. Rippey (New University of Ulster), C. E. Gibson (Freshwater Biological Investigation Unit), G. Kennedy (DoA Fisheries Laboratory) and K. Vickers (DoA). Clare Carter helped gather up the final bits and pieces when I was abroad.

REFERENCES

Battarbee, R. W., 1978. Observations on the recent history of Lough Neagh and its drainage basin. *Philosophical Transactions of the Royal Society, London,* Series B. *281,* 303–345.

Carter, C. E., 1978. The fauna of the muddy sediments of Lough Neagh, with particular reference to eutrophication. *Freshwater Biology, 8* (6), 547–560.

Department of Agriculture for Northern Ireland, 1978a. *Angling Guide.* Stormont.

Department of Agriculture for Northern Ireland, 1978b. *Report on the Sea and Inland Fisheries of Northern Ireland 1977.* H.M.S.O. Belfast.

Doyle, J. B., 1854. *Tours in Ulster.* Dublin.

Ferguson, A., Himberg, K-J. M. and Swardson, G., 1978. Systematics of the Irish pollan (*Coregonus pollan* Thompson): an electrophoretic comparison with other Holarctic Coregoninae. *Journal of Fish Biology, 12,* 221–233.

Fisheries Conservancy Board for Northern Ireland, 1977. *Annual Report.*

Fisheries Conservancy Board for Northern Ireland, 1980. *Annual Report.*

Foyle Fisheries Commission, 1978. *Twenty-sixth Annual Report for 1977.* L.M. Press, Lurgan.

Gibson, C. E., Foy, R. H. and Fitzsimons, A. G., 1980. A limnological reconnaissance of the Lough Erne system, Ireland. *Internationale Revue der Gestamten Hydrobiologie, 65,* 49-84.

Jewson, D. H. & Taylor, J. A., 1978. The influence of turbidity on net phytoplankton photosynthesis in some Irish lakes. *Freshwater Biology, 8,* 573–584.

Kerr, J. A. M., 1979. *Water Recreation. The role of the Department of Agriculture.* Report to Northern Ireland Water Council. 7pp. mimeograph.

Lough Neagh Working Group, 1973. *Advisory Report Vols. I and II and Appendices.* Ministries of Development (=Environment) and Agriculture. Stormont.

Mitchel, N. C., 1965. The Lower Bann Fisheries. *Ulster Folklife,* Vol. II.

Parsons, J., Vickers, K. U. and Warden, Y., 1977. Relationships between elver recruitment and changes in the sex ratio of silver eels, *Anguilla anguilla* L., migrating from Lough Neagh, Northern Ireland. *Journal of Fish Biology, 10,* 211–229.

Water Service, 1980. *Northern Ireland Water Statistics, 1980,* Department of the Environment for Northern Ireland.

Wilson, J., 1979. *A preliminary study of the biology and exploitation of the pollan (Coregonus pollan,* Thompson). Unpublished D.Phil. Thesis, New University of Ulster.

Wood, R. B., 1980. Pollution of Lough Neagh: a multi-disciplinary approach. *Analytical Proceedings, 17,* 369-374.

Wood, R. B. & Gibson, C. E., 1973. Eutrophication and Lough Neagh. *Water Research, 7,* 173–187.

CHAPTER V

Estuarine and Inshore Waters

PATRICK J. S. BOADEN,
*Director, The Queen's University of Belfast,
Marine Biology Station, Portaferry, County Down.*

Historical background

The resources of Northern Ireland's inshore and estuarine waters have, for the most part, been ignored, mismanaged or abused during the past fifty years. This statement may need some qualification and explanation; for example, it must be said that similar statements would be true for much of the sea around the European coast. However, there is now considerable knowledge about such problems as pollution and overfishing which face European waters and considerable information about the scientific and social aspects which must be taken into account when planning the use of inshore areas. There are even signs that this information is being transferred into positive action in some areas such as the Dutch Wadden Sea. Unfortunately the situation in Northern Ireland remains largely in the early information gathering stage.

Neglect of our marine resources can be attributed, in time, to the second decade of this century. Prior to this, the whole of Ireland had been well served by amateur and professional marine scientists and natural historians. There are for example extensive records of dredging expeditions to explore the marine life off the Down and Antrim coasts dating from the 1850s when G. C. Hyndman, G. Dickie, J. G. Jeffreys and others were active. It is obvious from William Thompson's *Natural History of Ireland* published in 1856, four years after his death, that there was an extensive supply of fish to the Belfast Market from the County Down ports. Peoples' taste ranged somewhat wider than today; one wonders what today's reaction to the bright green bones of cooked garfish would be.

Three activities at the turn of the century are worth special mention. Members of the Belfast Naturalists' Field Club had continued to be active in study of marine life, and several including R. Welch, J. Wright and R. Patterson contributed accounts of their work to the 1902 Guide for the British Association meeting in Belfast. In 1903, representatives of the Belfast Field Club, the Belfast Natural History and Philosophical Society and the Queen's College (now Queen's University) formed the Ulster Fisheries and Biology Association. A fisherman's house at Larne Harbour was converted to a Marine Laboratory, a steam launch purchased and a resident naturalist and a boatman employed. Various publications resulting from work at the Larne

Laboratory included both pure and applied aspects of marine science. One of these was a study of bacterial content of the common mussel which was at that time being carted from Belfast Lough to be relaid in Larne Lough for natural purification before being marketed as far afield as London. So, concern over the condition of Belfast Lough is not an entirely modern phenomenon! The first decade of the century also saw publication of recommendations by Professor Letts of Queen's College to help solve various problems arising from inadequate sewage disposal in Belfast Lough; these led to some of the early reclamation schemes in the inner Lough area. The Larne Laboratory closed in 1908 owing to financial and logistic difficulties.

The early years of the twentieth century were thus a period of considerable activity and concern over marine life in the region. At this time the Fisheries Branch of the Department of Agriculture and Technical Instruction for Ireland was producing some very fine work, much of which was published in their "Scientific Investigations" from 1901 onwards, when E. W. L. Holt was Scientific Adviser to the Branch. Under his leadership the Branch made considerable contributions to the advance of marine science. These included work on oyster culture and quality, salmon tagging and artificial propagation, plankton and water movement and reports of fishing grounds including the area lying off the Mournes and Dundrum Bay (Figure 5.1). The period of the First World War and the political division of Ireland brought investigation of marine resources nearly to a stand-still.

For the succeeding thirty years or so, public interest in the habitats, resources and management of our inshore waters is probably best described as desultory. This is not

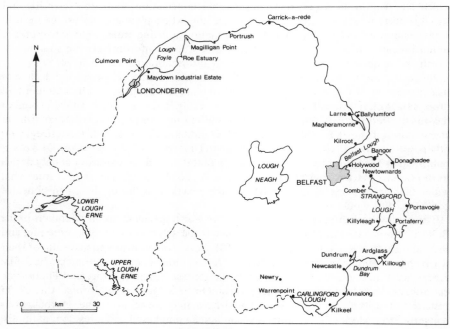

Figure 5.1 Place-names used in the text of Chapter 5

to say that there was no work. Administration and regulation of sea fisheries continued through the Ministry of Agriculture for Northern Ireland, empowered under various Acts of Parliament, and also later through the Foyle Fisheries Commission which was established as a cross-border body in 1952. R. MacDonald and Nora F. McMillan published occasional papers on marine fauna and flora of the Antrim and Down coastline and in 1951 a joint paper on the natural history of Lough Foyle. Other aspects of the marine environment continued under jurisdiction of appropriate authorities such as the Belfast Harbour Commissioners and the Board of Trade.

Interest in the marine environment increased in the 1950s. This had been heralded by the establishment of a marine biology field station at Portaferry by The Queen's University of Belfast in 1945, following use of temporary premises in the Fish Market at Ardglass and in Portaferry. Fisheries Branch activity increased and although little original research was undertaken more effort was devoted to collection and collation of catch statistics as well as to funding and regulation of the fisheries.

The Fisheries Act (Northern Ireland) 1966 can be taken to mark the advent of more active fisheries work both in freshwater and marine environments. The study of economic aspects of the Northern Ireland sea fishery by P. H. Hughes (1970) gives an excellent picture of the status of the industry at this time. Expansion of Queen's University activity in marine biology, in particular during the late-1960s, led to the appointment of permanent academic staff at Portaferry in the early 1970s. Such events were related to the growing economic importance of the fishing industry and to the growing environmental awareness of the general public. The need for both increased exploitation and increased conservation of marine resources had become apparent.

At this point it is worthwhile to reiterate the definition of conservation as "the wise use of resources" and to explore some of the biological resources in more detail before considering their use and management in specific environments around the Northern Ireland coast.

Fisheries

It is customary to consider the fish upon which our fisheries are based under three main headings. These are pelagic fish, demersal fish and shellfish. The first two of these categories relate to the general life style of the species concerned. Pelagic fish are actively swimming and usually shoal-forming fish living near the sea surface. Salmon and trout are also considered with this group. Demersal fish are bottom, or near-bottom, living fish which are often slower and more solitary species. Shellfish includes all crustacean and molluscan catches.

Pelagic Fish

HERRING – *Clupea harengus* (L.): The herring has been the subject of a local fishery for many hundred years and there is little doubt that both fish and fishery were formerly more prosperous. There are, for example, remarkable early photographs of the Ardglass Herring Fishery in the R. J. Welch Collection in the Ulster Museum. The reader is referred to Wheeler (1969) for biological details of the life history of herring and other fish species. Imposition of Northern Ireland and EEC regulations since 1977 has restricted local activity in this fishery severely, the catch being approximately halved after the 1976 season. Herring is landed by Northern Ireland boats at the County Down ports, and also in the Isle of Man and Great Britain.

Recent investigations of the Mourne herring have stressed the overfished nature of this stock: the fish are not being allowed to grow or reproduce sufficiently to give a sustainable high yield. To add to the problems of this fishery, recruitment (the addition of young to the stock) is naturally very variable and rather unpredictable. It appears that local weather and current conditions may have a very large influence on distribution within the Irish Sea. Although the weight of catch has fluctuated considerably over recent years, figures show a great increase in commercial value (Figure 5.2). This emphasizes that, although obviously important to the industry and its employees, monetary return is no guide to rational exploitation of fish stocks. The catch values for 1978 represent a particularly high value per weight of approximately £436 per tonne. Although the catch rose to 5,200 tonnes in 1980, the value dropped to £1,394,818 or about £268 per tonne.

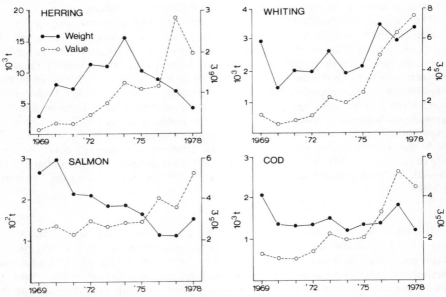

Figure 5.2 Weight and quayside value of the most important Northern Ireland demersal and pelagic fish catches 1969-78. The herring, whiting and cod figures are for all landings in the British Isles by Northern Ireland boats. The salmon data include half of the catch within the Foyle Fisheries Commission area.

MACKEREL – *Scomber scombrus* (L.): The mackerel, although a pelagic species, is not closely related to the herring and a higher proportion of its diet consists of the young stages of other pelagic fish. It has become more heavily exploited internationally and is of increasing importance to the Northern Ireland fleet although at present representing a small proportion of the total catch. This increase is due mainly to boats participating in the south-west England fishery rather than to local catches.

SALMON – *Salmo salmar* (L.): Stocks of the North Atlantic salmon have been in decline for a number of years. In Northern Ireland there is an important local fishery in

Lough Foyle and along the Antrim coast, that at Carrick-a-rede being an important tourist attraction (as indeed is salmon fly fishing in freshwater). Decline in the fishery (Figure 5.2) has been ascribed to many causes the most likely being overfishing both locally and off the coast of Greenland; pollution of fresh and inshore waters has also been a contributory factor. Fortunately the incidence of salmon disease 'UDN' (ulcerative dermal necrosis) declined considerably during the late-1970s and no longer seems a major factor.

SEA OR BROWN TROUT – *Salmo trutta* (L.):   The variability of this species in colour, shape and behaviour has caused a certain amount of confusion but the sea and brown trout are really races of the same fish. The brown trout may be migratory or non-migratory depending to a large extent on whether it inhabits large or small bodies of water. The sea trout migrates downstream after hatching and then spends about three years at sea, sometimes travelling over considerable distances, before upstream spawning migration. The commercial fishery is really a side line of the salmon catch and until 1971 catch statistics were included with the Northern Ireland salmon figures.

RAINBOW TROUT – *Salmo gairdneri* Richardson.:   This species has been introduced from north-western America. It is more tolerant of high temperatures than the brown trout and has been used for stocking many European lakes and reservoirs. It has become a commercially important species because of its relative ease of culture. In particular it can be acclimatized to seawater where its growth is more rapid and the flesh takes on a pink colour which is held to be gastronomically desirable. The species is being raised in Northern Ireland chiefly in freshwater but to some extent in sea loughs. Since 1972 when this activity began, there has been rapid development, 225 tonnes production being achieved in 1976 when the value reached over £325,000. Annual production has been maintained at about this level, but market price has dropped. In 1980, freshwater fish farms in Northern Ireland produced 210 tonnes of rainbow trout valued at £291,900.

Demersal Fish

This fishery comprises many species, about twenty of which are listed in the annual statistics of the Department of Agriculture for Northern Ireland. In rough order of total catch weight the seven most important species are whiting, cod, coalfish (saithe), monk (angler), place, hake and the group comprising rays and skates. However, in terms of quayside value the sole displaces the hake as sixth in importance and the value of brill nears and occasionally exceeds that of the ray group. The demersal fishery, like the pelagic, has for many years been concentrated in the Irish Sea (International Council for Exploration of the Seas' area VIIa) with much less effort being expended off the North Coast (VIa). As stated, whiting and cod are the most important species and dominate the fishery by contribution of about three-quarters of the total catch.

WHITING – *Merlangius merlangus* (L.):   This is a shallow water member of the cod family and is relatively common on sandy to muddy grounds around most of Europe. Adults are important predators of sand-eels, sprats, shrimps and crabs which form a large part of their diet. Young whiting tend to live close inshore and until about 3 cm long often associate with the stinging lion's mane jelly fish *(Cyanea)* and compass jelly fish *(Chrysaora)* presumably deriving protection from them.

In recent years the County Down boats have been particularly successful in the whiting fishery (Figure 5.2) to the extent that under EEC regulations some of the catch has had to be withdrawn from the market. Whiting are also a by-catch of the 'Dublin Bay Prawn' fishery and, since the latter has a lower legal mesh size (70 mm compared with 90 mm), immature whiting are at times caught in large quantities. Over half the *landed* whiting catch has come from the prawn fishery in some years even though between 45% and 95% of the fish has had to be thrown overboard as undersized.

COD – *Gadus morrhua* (L.): The cod extends into deeper water than the whiting, but is nevertheless often common on the same grounds. Adult fish take a wide range of food which varies seasonally but in winter usually includes herring and sand eels as well as brittle stars and other invertebrates.

The catch landed by Northern Ireland boats in recent years has ranged between 1 and 2 thousand tonnes and whereas this is equivalent to only about half the whiting catch by weight it has close to the same quayside value (Figure 5.2).

Shellfish

Seven or eight species are recorded in the annual fishery statistics. The weight and value of the catch varies from year to year, but the value of landings at Northern Ireland ports forms an unusually high proportion in comparison with other European fisheries. The relative importance of the various species fluctuates but taken over a number of years (1973–1978) the order in terms of quayside value is Dublin Bay prawn, scallop, lobster, squid, queenie and winkle; crab and shrimp are a very small proportion. Recent years have seen the re-establishment of an oyster industry and renewed interest in mussel production.

DUBLIN BAY PRAWN – *Nephrops norvegicus* (L.): This fishery has increased considerably since mid-century when the species was hardly sought after. By 1960–1962 the landed value equalled or exceeded that of whiting. By 1969 it dominated the Northern Ireland fishery being worth more than the total of all other fish and shellfish landings and accounting for about a quarter of the total catch by weight. The sharpest increase in value was in 1976 when, although the actual *Nephrops* catch fell, the value rose by over 70% to reach £1 m sterling for the first time (Figure 5.3).

In general appearance and biology the "prawn" or Norway Lobster is more akin to a small burrowing lobster than a true prawn or shrimp. It is found in muddy grounds where it constructs chambered burrows in the sediment. The species tends toward nocturnal activity and the best catches are often made at dawn and dusk. A detailed account of the species can be found in Figueiredo and Thomas (1967).

The problem of whiting mortality on *Nephrops* grounds has already been mentioned, but in recent years it has become clear that the prawn is itself being over-exploited and in danger of severe decline. This is apparent partly from the fishing effort necessary to maintain catch levels, but chiefly from measurement of the average size of the prawns caught. For several years this has been within a few millimetres of the size considered necessary for survival of the fishery. Indeed, during the 1970s, at least half the prawns netted were below the size considered marketable (i.e. the mean carapace length was below 27 mm). Changes in permitted mesh size of nets (and banning use of the cod-end) in 1979 led to complaints of catch reduction to a half or third of previous levels; if such estimates were true, they emphasize the dangerously large proportion of the population which is close to the critical size and the need for imposition of these or stronger measures to ensure the long term survival of the fishery. Statistics for 1979 show a landed liveweight of 4,706 tonnes with a quayside value of £4,396,766, but in 1980 record a fall to 3,149 tonnes valued at £2,324,556.

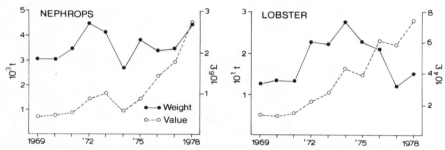

Figure 5.3 Weight and quayside value of Dublin Bay prawn and lobster landings by Northern Ireland boats 1969-78. The prawn figures are for all landings in the British Isles, lobster for landings at Northern Ireland ports.

LOBSTER – *Homarus gammarus* (L.):   Our other crustacean fishery is only worth a small fraction (one tenth to a fortieth) of the *Nephrops* catch (Figure 5.3). However, it is more in the nature of a longshore fishery and, as along the Antrim coast, it may make a valuable contribution to the local economy. Unfortunately the lobster has declined from considerable overfishing, and published statistics are confusing because of various conversions from numbers of lobsters to whole weight or to meat weight. Conversation with local fishermen and examination of catch records indicate that although the number of pots fished and the frequency of fishing has increased considerably over the past two to three generations, the number and size of lobsters being caught has fallen drastically. It is difficult however, to know the number being taken by 'weekend' fishermen and by divers, which do not appear in official records. The lobster catch rose in 1979 and 1980 to 18 and 16 tonnes respectively, but the market value fell to approximately £71,300 and £52,700 in those years.

SCALLOPS AND QUEENIES: Two bivalve shellfish are dredged commercially by Northern Ireland boats. These fairly closely related forms are *Pecten maximumus* (L.) the scallop or clam, and *Chlamys opercularis* (L.) the queenie. Occasionally other species of *Chlamys* e.g. *C. varia* (L.) from Strangford Lough have been sold under the latter name. It is thought that the scallop may be locally overfished in inshore waters and there has been conflict regarding the effects of collection by diving rather than by traditional methods. The latter certainly have far more general impact both on the stock and the habitat of the species although diving certainly has helped deplete some grounds which otherwise might have acted as a reserve stock for recruitment onto dredged grounds. The queenie catch variability probably reflects changes in fishing effort rather than other factors (Figure 5.4).

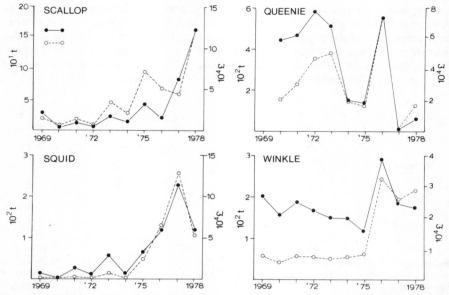

Figure 5.4 Weight and quayside value of the other important Northern Ireland shellfish catches 1969-78. The scallop, queenie and squid figures are for landings into Northern Ireland ports. No 1969 data for queenies are available.

SQUID AND WINKLE: To the layman the value of these two very different molluscan species may be the most surprising feature of the Northern Ireland fisheries. Quantities and values are shown in Figure 5.4.

The squid – *Loligo forbesi* Steenstrup is sold to the European market where its value has risen steeply since the early 1970s. It is mainly caught as a by-product of the demersal fisheries and its total value now approaches that of the hake.

The edible periwinkle *Littorina littorea* (L.) is hand collected from the shore chiefly on the County Down coastline, despite contrary bye-laws in some places. Fairly large quantities are exported to France via the Republic of Ireland. The species is now hard to find in commercial quantities in many areas where it was formerly abundant. In 1980 about 390 tonnes were collected, and the sale value of £55,198 actually exceeded that of lobsters.

OYSTERS: There were formerly extensive beds of the native, flat or Whitstable oyster *Ostrea edulis* L. in Lough Foyle, Strangford Lough and elsewhere. These declined to near extinction in the 19th century. However, experiments initiated by the Department (then Ministry) of Agriculture Fisheries Branch in 1970 have led to the successful re-establishment of oyster culture particularly using the Pacific oyster *Crassostrea gigas* Thunberg. This has been mainly through raft and lantern culture in which growing oysters are suspended in the water column. In 1974 a mere forty dozen oysters were marketed from commercial beds in Northern Ireland; three years later this quantity had increased over five-hundred fold, about half being sold for direct human consumption and the rest for 'growing-on' elsewhere. Since 1980, there has been a tendency to lay oysters on the sea bed in the lowest part of the intertidal zone. The proportion of oysters sold for growing-on has increased to over 60%, and the total number sold in 1981 reached over 1,250,000.

Seaweed

Various types of seaweed have been harvested from the shore and shallow water around the Down and Antrim coast. At present there is a small local market for the red seaweed *Rhodymenia palmata* (L.), usually sold in the dried form as dulse. It is harvested by cutting from the stipes (that is the stem-like portion) of the large brown seaweeds (kelps) that grow at and beyond low water. Formerly kelps and other brown intertidal seaweeds were harvested for agricultural manure. Boulders set out in grid patterns for settlement and growth of seaweed, particularly the knotted, boxy or egg wrack *Ascophyllum nodosum* (L.), can still be seen in Carlingford and Strangford Loughs. Details of the fierce conflicts which sometimes arose over seaweed rights can be found by referring to Estyn Evans (1967). The brown seaweeds were also formerly used in glass manufacturing processes and in production of iodine although it is doubtful that any seaweed rights of tenants extended to commercial exploitation.

At present some seaweed is harvested in the Larne area. It is dried at a plant in County Mayo and thence exported to a processing plant in Scotland. The fairly extensive beds in Strangford Lough and on the outer County Down coast have attracted attention recently as a possible additional source of seaweed for the alginate industry. It has been estimated that the total wet weight of knotted wrack in Strangford Lough is about 12,000 tonnes which might mean 3–4,000 tonnes annual growth available for harvesting. Cutting on this scale would have a considerable detrimental effect on the overall ecology of the Lough (Boaden and Dring, 1980) which would have to be considered when assessing possible economic benefit.

Prospects

The value to Northern Ireland of exploiting marine biological resources should be clear from the various figures presented. Totalled catch weights and value of all fish landed in Northern Ireland and by Northern Ireland boats operating elsewhere are given in Figure 5.5. Outside Northern Ireland the principal landings are at Whitehaven, Campbelltown and Peel by boats operating from the north Irish Sea.

Setting aside the possibility that catches could be increased by a change in allocation from the fisheries quota system, since this does not in itself increase the actual resource, what are the prospects for increased exploitation? At present they seem very poor. The Irish Sea is grossly overfished. The stock of most commercial species has fallen by factors of up to two-thirds since the mid-1950s and it is thought that some species, for example the skate, *Raja batis* (L.), are close to extinction from the area (Brander, 1980). It is possible that the fishery would recover and indeed give increased yield if fairly Draconian conservation measures were enforced for a number of years.

Prospects for increased yield from fish and shellfish culture seem much brighter. A changing emphasis away from traditional fishing methods (albeit with their near space age location and guidance systems) towards fish-pounds, rafts etc. would mirror the change from hunting to husbandry which on land occurred in prehistoric times. An account of fish farming prospects in Northern Ireland may be found in the symposium report listed (Anon, 1974). The criteria for successful fish-farming include economic factors such as market demand and profitability, but environmental factors such as freedom from parasites, predators and pollution are also of prime importance. The dangers from accidentally introducing parasites, predators and competitors along with imported stock, especially of non-native species, are fairly well documented: the history of the oyster industry in Europe is beset with cautionary tales. Fortunately Northern Ireland has remained free of many of the pest organisms concerned, but close control over introduction must be maintained. There should certainly be no unlicensed introduction.

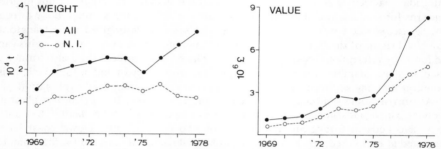

Figure 5.5 Weight and quayside value of Northern Ireland's total sea catch (excluding salmon). The lower graph line shows landings both in Northern Ireland and elsewhere, by the Northern Ireland Fishery.

Pollution

It is not known to what extent the decline of Irish Sea fisheries is also attributable to pollution. The eastern Irish Sea is probably the most polluted sea area in Europe. Unfortunately areas which are particularly suitable for marine fish or shellfish farming, namely shallow inshore high productivity areas, are also particularly susceptible to pollution. Knowledge of levels of possible pollutants such as heavy metals, organochlorides, sewage pathogens and excess nutrients in Northern Ireland waters is rather limited at present. The water circulation patterns relied on for dilution and dispersion are also poorly known.

Monitoring of water quality and/or assessment of concentration of pollutants and pathogens in marine organisms are joint responsibilities of the Department of the Environment (N.I.) under the Water Act (N.I.) 1972 (which unlike its Great Britain counterpart extends to estuarine *and* marine waters), the Department of Agriculture (N.I.) under the Fisheries Act (N.I.) 1966 and the public health authorities. The DoE also administers the Dumping at Sea Act (1974) in relation to Northern Ireland although at the time of writing the appropriate committee has never met because no applications for licences have been made. Measurement of water quality for the DoE is usually carried out by the Industrial and Forensic Science Laboratory of the Department of Commerce. Water quality figures have not been published for the most part but some are available, for example from work conducted by the Fisheries Branch, Queen's University and the Ulster Polytechnic. Maxwell (1978), for instance, gives nutrient and phytoplankton values indicating eutrophication in Belfast Lough.

Effluent disposal and dumping of waste at sea could be listed amongst uses of inshore water which are beneficial but unfortunately the dispersive capacity of the environment is being exceeded in some areas.

Use and management of the inshore environments

Before looking briefly at the use and abuse of various parts of Northern Ireland's inshore waters it will be helpful to describe the various beneficial uses to man of marine and estuarine waters. These have been outlined as follows:

"BENEFICIAL USES OF MARINE AND ESTUARINE WATERS

If it is agreed that a condition of pollution is dependent upon the subsequent beneficial uses of the water, it is well to delineate these uses.

The following list includes most of the uses that are beneficial to mankind (but not necessarily beneficial to every other form of life):

Swimming, surf bathing, and skin diving.

Beach picnicking and aesthetic enjoyment (i.e., just sitting and looking at the water or breathing the salt air).

Boating and navigation.

Water skiing and other marine sports.

Propagation of fish, shellfish, and other animals.

Propagation of kelp and other attached algae.

Sports fishing and commercial fishing (which incidentally are beneficial to man but not to the captured fish).

Industrial water supply, especially for cooling.

Municipal water supply (after demineralization).

The relative importance of the beneficial uses varies with season, with locality, and with the viewpoint of the user. In most situations they are compatible, but in some cases they are antagonistic, such as sports fishing versus commercial fishing, or water skiing versus bathing and skin diving."

(McKee, in Olson & Burges, 1967)

Extraction of chemicals and power generation should also be added to the list, although these and demineralization are not practised in Northern Ireland.

The Northern Ireland coastline, if measured from a 1:63,360 scale map, is approximately 560 km long but it is not all subjected to equal pressure. In terms of real impact man's activities tend to be concentrated in our sea loughs, which is largely the outcome of using the sea as a transport medium and the historic location of towns near fords and ferries.

Lough Foyle

This is basically an estuarine system with a rather low species diversity in the inner reaches. Its most interesting biological features are the Roe estuary and the Magilligan dune system. There are extensive mussel beds and good opportunities for oyster culture. Experimental introduction of the American Hard Shell Clam *Venerupis decussata* L. has already been made by the Fisheries Branch.

The southern end of the Lough near Culmore Point receives most of the domestic and industrial effluent. Surveys undertaken in 1952, 1968 and 1978 by the Department of Industrial and Forensic Science show that there was little change in the measured water quality parameters although this was a period of considerable industrial expansion. Sewage from Londonderry was thought to be the most significant adverse factor. In view of the proposed new outfall for primary treated sewage at Culmore Point and following recommendation from the Foyle Fisheries Commission the DoE has been monitoring Lough Foyle water quality annually since 1975.

Du-Pont Nemours (Anon, 1960) commissioned a general biological survey of the Lough in connection with the establishment of their Maydown factory and have since arranged for occasional monitoring of the marine life. Since movement of the Research Division of the Fisheries Branch to The Cutts, Coleraine, various investigations of the Lough, including the distribution of species in relation to the new Culmore outfall, have begun. The fisheries are administered through the Foyle Fisheries Commission, salmon being the most important fish species.

North and North-East Coast

The coastal waters are not greatly exploited for fishing although the coastline is one of our major tourist assets. There is a locally important lobster fishery but this has declined markedly. Salmon are also caught along the coast. A small proportion (about a twentieth) of the Northern Ireland fish catch is landed at Portrush mainly for local consumption, especially in the summer. Haddock, cod and plaice are the main species. The offshore area may be the best site around Northern Ireland for wave generated electricity.

Larne Lough

Records from the former Larne Marine Biological Station show that the Lough was a biologically rich area at the turn of the century. This richness is now considerably less. The lough is chiefly used as a physical resource for transport, dispersal of heat from the Ballylumford Power Stations and as a source of clay lubricant and a tipping ground by the Magheramorne Cement Works. It is probably the latter two factors, through smothering and sea floor emergence, which have depressed the biological diversity of the Lough which otherwise (especially in view of the raised temperature) might have been particularly suitable for fish/shellfish culture. The coast in the vicinity of Larne has one of the smallest tide ranges in the British Isles.

Belfast Lough

The inner and northern parts of the lough (to Kilroot) have been heavily exploited for dilution of industrial and domestic effluent, or for land reclamation and as a transport route. As a result of the first two activities the biological resources have been depleted or forfeited. Fishing is banned in the Lough, but in any case there may be little to catch. The aesthetic and recreational resources are certainly not what they might be and raw sewage is a fairly common occurrence on the lough shore. Fishing bait (ragworm and lugworm) is dug for on a commercial scale on the inner north shore.

Surveys of the lough have been conducted in recent years by the Industrial and Forensic Science Division (mainly concerned with oxygenation, suspended solids and similar physical and chemical measurements), by the Fisheries Branch (bottom fauna), by the Ulster Polytechnic (plankton and related parameters such as nutrient status, Maxwell, 1978) and by Queen's University (shore life – a survey in part financed by the Northern Ireland Electricity Service in relation to the Kilroot Power Station). The Fisheries Branch have also made some studies of the tidal Lagan. Much of this information has not been published yet but any statement that the lough is not polluted (there have been several in recent years) is blatantly untrue. The general "health" of the lough is described and discussed in the symposium "Belfast Lough – a threatened environment" (Maxwell, 1980).

The main flow of water in and out of the Lough is along the northern shore with a lesser flow past Bangor and Holywood. There is a circular current motion near the central part. The Lough is fortunately rather shallow so that a relatively small amount of turbulence stirs the water which is kept well oxygenated in spite of (or at times because of?) extreme eutrophication of the inner reaches. The latter have extensive diatom blooms. Diversity of bottom and shore life is reduced considerably and this can be ascribed to the general environmental degradation.

In the mid-1970s at least primarily treated sewage from approximately 632,000 people and crude sewage from about 49,000 was being discharged directly to the Lough. Large amounts of phosphates and nitrates are also discharged by industry. It is not known to what extent the ensuing eutrophication is depressed by other factors such as heavy metal discharges. Zinc (Austin and McGrath, 1979), chromium and titanium compounds are known to be amongst these. There are also organic discharges which have included substances such as ethylene glycol and hot dye liquors whose effect, if any, is unknown. Various materials including sewage solids and chemical wastes are barged out of the Lough and dumped offshore.

Outer County Down Coast

This coastline is in general more sheltered and of greater biological diversity than the Londonderry-Antrim North Coast. There are a number of small towns with ports such as Annalong, Donaghadee, Dundrum, Killough and Newcastle which were formerly of much greater importance to fishing and shipping. Such towns (and the numerous caravan sites in parts of the area) provide an important recreational outlet and include some fairly good sailing and boating facilities. Other economic activities on this coast include sand and gravel extraction from the shore; outer Dundrum Bay has been used to off-load oil tankers because of its relative lack of water movement. The main resource use however is the fishery.

The three main fishing-boat harbours in Northern Ireland are Ardglass, Kilkeel and Portavogie. These are administered by the Northern Ireland Fishery Harbour Authority. There was extensive harbour redevelopment at Kilkeel in the early 1970s and the 1980s will see re-development at Portavogie partly funded by the European Regional Development Fund.

In recent years the fishing fleet has consisted of between 250 and 300 boats. The majority of these are under 40 ft. and many operate out of the smaller ports with part-time crews. In 1980 there were 159 boats of over 40 ft. of which 17 were registered in Ardglass, 60 in Portavogie and 82 in Kilkeel. The latter two ports had more large boats including 26 in the 70-80 ft. category at Kilkeel. Boats often land fish at other than their home port principally because of marketing and processing facilities. Since completion of the harbour works the Kilkeel landings have been about twice the value of those at Portavogie, with Ardglass values intermediate between the two.

The general level of pollution in the Irish Sea is rather worrying but, fortunately for Northern Ireland fisheries, the main problem lies in the Liverpool Bay Area. Concern has been expressed over levels of radioactivity since the eastern Irish Sea receives discharges from several nuclear power and processing plants (Hunterston, Chapelcross, Windscale, Calder Hall, Springfields, Capenhurst, Wylfa and Trawsfynydd). Annual reports concerning this problem are published (see Hunt, 1979). Radioactivity levels in the Northern Ireland fisheries grounds and along the East Irish Coast are about a fifth to a tenth of those in Morecambe Bay which are generally held to be negligible.

Strangford Lough

This is undoubtedly Northern Ireland's most complex and diverse inshore area. It is the subject of one of the largest non-government conservation schemes in Europe. The National Trust for Places of Historic Interest or Natural Beauty owns or leases most the intertidal zone and has at least shooting rights over the remainder. It owns part of the bed of the Lough as well as land adjoining the shore. Management is implemented through the Trust's Strangford Lough Scheme. The area includes several important National Nature Reserves established, because of marine biological interest, by the Conservation Branch of the DoE. A working group convened by the Department recently recommended that "Strangford Lough should be conserved as a major recreational, educational and wildlife resource" (Strangford Lough Working Group 1978, p. 10). Appendix I to the report (Boaden and Furphy) should be consulted for more detail of the Lough's wildlife status, general morphology and planning problems and for elaboration of the six quotations and comments that follow.

(i) "Various geographical and biological features make Strangford Lough unique" (p. 3):—

The Lough is highly unusual in occurring in drumlin country and has various interesting geomorphological features including peripheral raised beaches, offshore drumlins, pladdies and diverse sedimentation. "The eelgrass beds and other vegetational features", such as the wrack beds and fringing salt marsh, "are of at least national importance but, because of their role in supporting the invertebrate fish and bird life acquire international significance" (I, p. 6).

(ii) "The northern part is internationally important particularly in terms of bird life, the southern and other parts in terms of marine life" (p. 3):—

Most parts of the Lough are of ornithological interest, and several of the islands provide important tern breeding sites (which need protection from summer picnickers). The northern sand and mud flats however are of particular importance and provide winter habitat for 30-40,000 waders (dunlin, knot etc.) and over 20,000 wildfowl (geese, ducks etc.). On both counts the area qualifies for protection under the international Ramsar Convention. Wildfowling is controlled through the National Trust, there being about 350 permit holders.

In the southern part of the Lough, the high productivity of plankton, microscopic and other algae and the eel-grass produces food for the many invertebrates and in turn, for fish and birds. About one-and-a-half thousand invertebrate species are known from the Lough and its approaches.

(iii) "The Lough is of high national, provincial and local value for recreation and tourism" (p. 3):—

There is specialist angling for large skate and tope and more general sea angling at the southern end of the Lough and immediately outside it. This is an important recreational and tourist resource. There are nine sailing clubs and a cruising club as well as many private boats based in the Lough. There is also extensive use by sub-aqua divers and by ornithologists. The lough is a major summer and weekend tourist attraction and the Northern Ireland Sailing Centre is at Killyleagh.

(iv) "It is equally important as a resource for all levels of education" (p. 3):—

Strangford Lough is visited frequently by natural science classes from many schools. The Queen's University Marine Biology Station at Portaferry has a large number of visiting groups including university, polytechnic and training college students as well as marine research workers. Work conducted from the Station includes various specialized accounts of the wildlife such as those by Williams (1954), Boyd (1973) and Erwin (1977).

(v) "It is the centre of a growing shellfish industry" (p. 3):—

There is little traditional commercial fishing in the Lough and expansion might be prejudicial to other interests (for example long-lining would rapidly deplete angling stocks) and indeed to the whole fishing industry itself, since it is thought that larvae and other young stages of fish and shellfish from the Lough help replenish the heavily exploited County Down fishing grounds. There is an increasing weekend fishery by amateur boatmen and divers chiefly for the already exploited scallop and lobster population. Oyster culture is a much more welcome venture. The 1976 value of oyster stocks in the Lough if grown to maturity was estimated at £70,000-80,000; the total value of other recorded catches of fish and shellfish was £5,626.

(vi) "Care must be taken to protect these uses from over-exploitation, mutual conflict and pollution" (p. 3):—

This should be more or less self evident. The Lough receives various effluents either directly or via the rivers and small streams. There is some eutrophication at the north end from nutrients in the joint Comber/Newtownards sewage works effluent which is otherwise well treated. There have been problems in the Quoile/Killyleagh area where raw sewage and tannery effluent have been discharged close to shore. High levels of chromium and to a lesser extent lead have been found in sediment and organisms including seaweed from the Killyleagh area; the lead may stem from former mine workings close to the Lough. Levels found in shellfish from the Lough have all proved acceptable. The treatment of all discharges into the Lough or its water courses was regarded as unsatisfactory in the 1970s but it was understood that the DoE were to undertake improvement works.

Following from the recommendations of the working group it seems likely that Strangford Lough will move towards National Park or equivalent status. This could not be accomplished under legislation existing at the time of the report but might be brought about for example through extension of the National Trust Scheme with some delegated powers and an appropriately expanded committee. Recently (December 1981), the DoE established a liaison group to help correlate activities in relation to the Lough.

Barraging the Strangford Narrows for generation of electricity has been discussed from time to time, and in August 1981, a feasibility study was published by the Northern Ireland Economic Council (see Newbould Chapter 11). This is an engineering possibility, although costs might be prohibitive: the Narrows are over 30 m deep and Northern Ireland at present has one third spare generating capacity. Tides in the Lough would be reduced to about 1 m instead of the present 2-3.5 m range and most of the intertidal area would be permanently covered, with substantial effects on all interests in the Lough. Possible siting of a power station in the Narrows has been previously dismissed on ecological grounds (Ministry of Commerce for Northern Ireland, 1972).

Carlingford Lough

Little is known about the biology of this area. Blockhouse Island usually supports a tern colony in summer months and the Lough is a favourite haunt of dogfish. The Mill Bay salt marsh is a National Nature Reserve. Seaweed was formerly harvested in large quantities, but the wrack "gardens" have been untended since the 1930s. There was also a shore based late season trammel net fishery for herring. The shore although muddy is fairly rich. There is some collection of common winkles which are exported and the Department of Fisheries (Dublin) have investigated mussel productivity. Sea access to Newry is now disused but replaced by container port facilities at Warrenpoint.

Offshore Developments

Sea bed or sub- sea bed activities have not been discussed above. There is some possibility that oil may be found off Rathlin Island and there may be metal ores, for example of lead, off Carlingford and the Mournes. Extraction of chemicals from seawater by ion exchange or from animal and plants remains a possibility if there is sufficient local industrial demand.

Summary

The natural biological resources of Northern Ireland's inshore and estuarine waters make a valuable contribution to the economy but the fisheries are over-exploited and will continue to decline unless stricter conservation measures than previously taken are enforced. When necessary, as now, fisheries must be managed on the basis of short term restriction for long term benefit rather than the reverse. There is room for harvesting more of the natural productivity of our sea loughs by fish and shellfish culture. Strangford Lough already has major recreational, educational and wildlife resource use but needs greater integration of management if these values are to be maintained. The water quality in Larne and Belfast Loughs leaves much to be desired. In the former case improvement could lead to rapid rehabilitation and use of biological resources. In the latter case it is unlikely to contribute much to fisheries development in the foreseeable future but could lead to much greater amenity value; industrial and domestic effluent disposal and transport will remain the major uses.

The lack of knowledge, for example of the fauna and flora of Carlingford Lough or off the North Coast, of inshore water movements, of the level of pollution and of larval recruitment to our fisheries is considerable. There is therefore a need for much basic information to enable more rational planning of Northern Ireland's inshore and estuarine waters.

REFERENCES

Anon., 1960. Lough Foyle, Northern Ireland. Biological, chemical and physical studies. July 1959. Report to E. I. DuPont and Company. *Academy of Natural Sciences, Philadelphia.*

Anon., 1974. *Fish farming – its problems and applications in Northern Ireland.* Department of Extra Mural Studies, The Queen's University, Belfast.

Belfast Naturalists' Field Club, 1874. *Guide to Belfast and the adjacent counties.* Ward, Belfast.

Boaden, P. J. S. and Dring, M. J., 1980. A quantitative evaluation of the effects of Ascophyllum harvesting on the littoral ecosystem. *Helgoländer wissenschaftliche Meeresuntersuchungen.* (14th European Marine Biology Symposium), 33, 700–710.

Boyd, R. J., 1973. The relation of the plankton to the physical, chemical and biological features of Strangford Lough, County Down. *Proceedings of the Royal Irish Academy, 75B,* 317–352.

Brander, K., 1980. Fisheries management and conservation in the Irish Sea. *Helgoländer wissenschaftliche Meeresuntersuchungen.* (14th European Marine Biology Symposium), 33, 687–699.

British Association, 1902. *A guide to Belfast and the counties of Down and Antrim.* Belfast.

Department of Agriculture and Technical Instruction for Ireland. *Report on the sea and inland fisheries of Ireland. Scientific Investigations (1901–1921).* H.M.S.O. Dublin.

Department of Agriculture, Northern Ireland. *Fisheries research and technical work.* Annual Reports of Research and Technical Work. H.M.S.O. Belfast.

Department of Agriculture, Northern Ireland. *Report on the Sea and Inland Fisheries of Northern Ireland.* Issued annually. H.M.S.O. Belfast.

Erwin, D. G., 1977. A diving survey of Strangford Lough: the benthic communities and their relation to substrate – a preliminary account. *Biology of Benthic Organisms.* B. Keegan, P. O'Ceidigh and P. J. S. Boaden (*eds.*), Pergammon Press, Oxford. pp. 205–214.

Estyn Evans, E., 1967. *Mourne Country. Landscape and Life in South Down.* 2nd edition. Dundalgan Press, Dundalk.

Figueiredo, M. J. and Thomas, H. J., 1967. *Nephrops norvegicus* (L., 1758) Leach. A review. *Oceanography and Marine Biology, Annual Review, 5,* pp. 371–407.

Foyle Fisheries Commission. *Annual Reports.* L.M. Press, Lurgan.

Great Britain & Northern Ireland Parliament, 1974. *Dumping at Sea Act 1974.* H.M.S.O., London.

Hughes, P. H., 1970. *The Sea Fishing Industry of Northern Ireland. An Economic Study.* H.M.S.O., Belfast.

Hunt, G. J., 1979. Radioactivity in surface and coastal waters of the British Isles. *Aquatic Environment Monitoring Report. MAFF Directorate of Fisheries Research, Lowestoft, (3),* pp. 1–36.

Letts, E. A., 1908. *Final report on the scheme of sewage purification for Belfast, and its probable effects on the Lough.* Baird, Belfast.

MacDonald, R. and McMillan, N. F., 1951. The natural history of Lough Foyle, Northern Ireland *Proceedings of the Royal Irish Academy, 54B.*

McGrath, M. S. and Austin, J., 1979. Zinc and copper levels in Belfast Lough. *Marine Pollution Bulletin, 10,* pp. 86–88.

Maxwell, T. H., 1978. The plankton of Belfast Lough. W. K. Downey and G. Ní Uid, (*eds.*), *Coastal Pollution Assessment.* National Board for Science and Technology, Dublin. pp. 103–136.

Maxwell, T. H. (*ed.*), 1980. *Belfast Lough – a threatened environment?* Institute of Biology, N.I. Branch and Ulster Polytechnic, Jordanstown (in press).

Ministry of Commerce, Northern Ireland, 1972. *Kilroot Power Station Scheme Report of the inquiry into scheme No. 19,* Manuscript report.

Northern Ireland Parliament, 1966. *The Fisheries Act (Northern Ireland)*, H.M.S.O.
Northern Ireland Parliament, 1972. *The Water Act (Northern Ireland)*, H.M.S.O.
Olson, T. A. and Burgess, F. J., 1967. *Pollution and Marine Ecology*. Wiley Interscience, New York.
Strangford Lough Working Group, 1978. *Report to the Department of the Environment*. Department of the Environment for Northern Ireland, Belfast.
Thompson, W., 1856. *The Natural History of Ireland. IV Mammalia. Reptiles and Fishes, also Invertebrates*. Reeve & Benham, London.
Wheeler, A., 1969. *The Fishes of the British Isles and North-West Europe*. MacMillan, London.
Williams, G., 1954. Fauna of Strangford Lough and neighbouring coasts. *Proceedings of the Royal Irish Academy, 56B*, pp. 29–133.

CHAPTER VI

The Coast

RICHARD W. G. CARTER,
Senior Lecturer in Environmental Science, New University of Ulster.

Introduction

Northern Ireland has about 560 km of coastline (Figure 6.1*a*) providing wide contrasts of environment and habitat. In common with the coasts of many countries, the Northern Ireland coast has become the scene of conflict as demands for recreation, industry and private development increase and change. Within a British context, the coast of Northern Ireland may be considered unique in that it is both geologically "mature" and largely in equilibrium with the forces of nature, yet also subject to substantial commercial and recreational pressures. Although the coastal system is complex, efforts must be made to balance these pressures against vulnerability. The only logical means of achieving this is through enlightened management. The aim of this chapter is to consider the background against which an integrated management 'plan' for the Northern Ireland coast might be developed. While it is obviously naive to suggest that such a plan can be implemented for the whole coastline, it is nevertheless useful to set broad idealistic objectives to guide management in all planning situations, however specialised.

Physical and biological setting

It is almost impossible to define the term 'coast'; indeed whole texts have been largely devoted to this (e.g. Ketchum, 1972). Physically and biologically, the coast may be considered to include those zones where marine and terrestrial activities interact. Thus, in addition to such obvious features as sand beaches and cliffs, estuaries, marshes and underwater nearshore areas must be included. Within these zones animals and plants have become adapted to the marine environment through varying degrees of tolerance to salt, inundation and exposure. It is not intended to examine in detail the various systematic attributes of the Northern Ireland coast; such information, if required, may be sought elsewhere. However, one simple integrating concept that has been used effectively in other places (e.g. Tanner, 1960) is to consider the average yearly level of wave energy along the coast (Figure 6.1*b*). Wave energy determines many coastal characteristics: for example the magnitude of littoral sediment movement increases with the energy level, so that high cliffs are more likely to form on high energy coasts. Furthermore, where high energy waves break, the upper beach will tend to be wider and therefore more sediment will be available to form dunes. Presence or absence of certain shore organisms is also well-known to be related directly to the ferocity of wave attack and sediment type. The latter is also dependent on wave action, with muds being deposited in areas of relative calm and gravels in more exposed locations. Obviously many other factors, for example the sediment economy, will determine precise conditions at any one site.

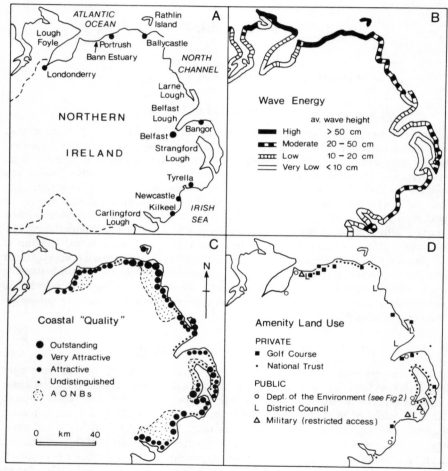

Figure 6.1a Location map.

Figure 6.1b Wave energy levels around the Northern Ireland coast.

Figure 6.1c Coastal 'quality' assessment in Northern Ireland (After Ulster Countryside Committee (H.M.S.O. 1978a).

Figure 6.1d Selected aspects of Northern Ireland conservation.

Figure 6.1*b* has been compiled from both deep-water and shore-based wave records from the Atlantic and Irish Sea. Broadly the coast divides into two sections: one, the high energy north coast with its spectacular, high rock cliffs and intervening sand beach/dune complexes; and two, the moderate energy east coast where topography is more subdued. On both these coasts little sediment is transported along the shore, most being trapped within the enclosed embayments which constitute 'closed' cells. Within these sections there are six estuaries – Carlingford Lough, Strangford Lough, Belfast Lough, Larne Lough, the River Bann estuary and Lough Foyle. Wave activity in the estuaries is low, and in some places like the south-east corner of Lough Foyle almost non-existent as few waves are capable of traversing the shallow shoaling slope without being completely dissipated before breaking. Where energy is low, sediments are usually mixed, fringing marshes and shell banks form, and erosional features are generally absent.

The coast represents a delicately-balanced, physical system. Although sediment does move, there are few instances of progressive erosion or deposition, except in the retreating boulder clay cliffs near Kilkeel (McGreal, 1979). Balance has been achieved by a redistribution and resorting of material left across the natural coastline towards the end of the last ice incursion into Ireland about 13,500 years ago (Stephens *et al.* 1975) – these processes are still occurring at Kilkeel. Subsequent variations of sea level within the last 13,000 years have affected these sediment movements. The biological system is imposed on the physical system and responds to changes in it by maintaining a diversity capable of exploiting and adjusting to varying conditions.

Along the Northern Ireland coast human activities have caused numerous modifications. Some of these, like the construction of harbours and jetties, are immediately obvious. Others are not so apparent – for example the changes in the flora of the sand dunes caused by trampling visitors, or the disturbance caused to breeding birds by opening footpaths in previously inaccessible areas. In some areas objective assessments of human impact on coastal environments are being made quite regularly, but in others perception of potential dangers is only beginning. Some modifications may be considered as progressively detrimental, like the erosion of sand dunes or the disposal of hazardous waste. Alternatively, they may be single finite adjustments following original construction, as with the River Bann training walls (Carter and Rihan, 1976). It is with the problems of imbalance caused by man that coastal environmental management must be pre-occupied, although it must be stressed that man should not be considered an 'intruder' and exclusion is not the preferred solution. Rather, management should adopt a responsive and objective attitude, aimed at early recognition and enlightened guidance of new trends, so that the coastal environment may be enjoyed by the maximum number of people with the minimum detriment.

Legislation relating to the coast of Northern Ireland

There is little direct legislation pertaining to coastal protection, preservation or conservation in Northern Ireland and very little history of any concern over these issues (Rea, 1981). Widespread consternation during the 1930s over unplanned coastal developments in Britain led to numerous surveys, by-laws and some general legislation (Sheail, 1976). A Coastal Preservation Committee was set up by the

Ministry of Health in 1938, and many subsequent investigations and surveys (e.g. Steers 1944), were commissioned during the planning renaissance of the mid- and late-1940s. All of these developments excluded Northern Ireland, then with its autonomous government. Although as Sheail notes, (1976, p. 269) these early surveys 'brought few direct benefits for coastal protection' ("protection" is used in its widest sense), much of the amassed information proved invaluable as a basis for later zoning and scheduling exercises. Again in the 1960s, the need for reconciliation between developers and conservationists on the British coast led to a directive, from the then Ministry of Housing and Local Government to county councils with coastal responsibilities, asking for clear policy statements on future planning in order to alleviate growing conflicts. Northern Ireland did not participate in this review.

In Northern Ireland, the Department of Agriculture is responsible for sea defence, and works are overseen by the Drainage Council. The appropriate legislation is contained in the Drainage Order 1973, which, to quote Article 3, relates to "construction, reconstruction, alteration, improvement, repair, maintenance, demolition, or removal for the purpose of protection against the flooding, including the sowing and planting of vegetation". It is important to note that the word "protection" is here used, somewhat narrowly, to mean defence from wave attack. This Order repealed the Drainage (Sea Defence) Act of 1955 in which many of the 1973 provisions were originally laid down. The 1955 Act, in its turn, was simply an extension of the 1947 Drainage Act to embrace sea defences. Many British Parliamentary Acts do not extend to Northern Ireland: for example, only the inconsequential third section of the Coast Protection Act (1949) applies in Northern Ireland, whereas the important first and second sections, which resolved ambiguities in the existing practical aspects and legal definitions of sea defences, and which set out a framework for protective action against erosion, flooding and avulsion, do not apply. In short the British legislation is far more dynamic.

The position regarding coastal conservation and preservation is much clearer, as the Amenity Lands Act (N.I.) 1965 provides both advisory and statutory guidelines for coastal development. The Act is primarily concerned with public amenity management of the countryside, including the acquisition, disposal, covenanting and scheduling of land. These functions are largely the responsibility of the Conservation Branch of the Department of the Environment, assisted in its tasks by two non-elected statutory committees – the Nature Reserves Committee (NRC) and the Ulster Countryside Committee (UCC).

Finally the coast is subject to a range of non-specific legislation, one of the most important examples being the Caravan Act (N.I) 1963. This Act allows public authorities to own and operate caravan sites, and implements a licensing system for all sites which have to conform to model standards.

Coastal planning and responsibility in Northern Ireland

There is little scope for imaginative and integrated coastal planning in Northern Ireland. Overall, the coastline is subjected to a plethora of controls and restrictions imposed by a range of public and private bodies. Public responsibility is broadly shared at Government level. The Planning Service of the Department of the Environment for Northern Ireland is ultimately in charge of overseeing all private and public development, although small or uncontentious matters are dealt with by District Councils. The DoE also has an important nature conservation function which has been actively pursued since the passing of the Amenity Lands Act. Harbours and coastal engineering aspects are dealt with by the Department of Finance for Northern Ireland, usually on instructions from other Departments, tourism (not necessarily recreation) by the Department of Commerce through the Northern Ireland Tourist Board, commercial fishing and coastal erosion of undeveloped land by the DoA, and sewage disposal by the Water Quality Branch of the DoE. It is therefore quite feasible for interdepartmental conflicts to arise over such common issues as caravans, fishing or conservation. There is as yet no government plan for coastal development in Northern Ireland, although the issue has been raised, for example by Stephens (1957) and in Forsyth and Boyd (1970). To date, lack of an official planning strategy is both surprising and anomalous, as Northern Ireland is the only area in the British Isles, and possibly Western Europe, where no such exercise has been carried out. It is noteworthy that broad development planning strategies have been proposed for the rest of the Irish coast (Martin *et al., 1974; National Coastline Study*, Vols. I-III, 1972-73). While there are obvious advantages and attractions in not having guidelines which may prove inflexible as conditions and attitudes change, a pragmatic evaluation of coastal potential would be of immense benefit to all concerned with the proper use of coastal resources. Some local plans do exist: for example the Limavady Area Plan (1973) covers the north coast of County Londonderry, and other Area Plans include details of coastlines within their boundaries. However no detailed scientific evaluation has been made of available resources, although various systematic attributes have been surveyed on occasions. For example, between 1920 and 1940, Queen's University attempted an inventory of coastal biology in Northern Ireland and a number of reports were published in the *Irish Naturalists' Journal*. In addition, local surveys have been made: in 1959 the Du Pont Corporation financed a detailed ecological and physical study of Lough Foyle, an exercise partly repeated in 1974 by the Water Quality Branch of the Department of Industrial and Forensic Science. Also worth mentioning are a survey of coastal amenities on the North Antrim coast by University College, London in 1970, and an investigation of the Quoile Pondage, County Down by The New University of Ulster in 1973 (Wood and C. E. Carter, 1978). These examples, however, are limited in either scope, objective or area, and no serious attempts have been made to integrate this diffuse, but extensive, body of information.

A sedulous effort to assess coastal "quality" was made by a sub-committee of the Ulster Countryside Committee in the early 1970s. The subsequent Coastal Survey Report (DoE, 1978*a*) attempts to grade the coast according to intrinsic value as a possible aid to future development tactics. Unfortunately the results, upon which Figure 6.1c is based, are somewhat subjective and appear to be biased towards isolated scenic grandeur such as cliffs and wilderness areas. The grading is therefore not a true assessment of quality *per se*. All coastal dunes for example are ranked relatively low, and marshes and other wetlands are considered "undistinguished", whereas in reality a wide range of coastal dune, marsh and wetland environments is to be found, varying markedly in quality from place to place. One result of this, admittedly preliminary, UCC survey is that the DoE is currently engaged in the preparation of an overall strategy for use and development of coastal areas in Northern Ireland. In essence the strategy will be concerned with:—

    (i) coastal areas that need safeguarding for one reason or another,

    (ii) areas in which developments should be concentrated, and

    (iii) the steps required to restore lost amenities and create new ones.

A pilot scheme based on Island Magee, County Antrim, was completed in late 1978, and two local draft reports for the north and north-east coasts have been compiled (RPRT, 1978; DoE, 1979a). These studies go some way to fulfilling the wide ranging objectives outlined in the Northern Ireland Regional Physical Development Strategy 1975–1995, published in 1977 (see pages 86–88).

Much of the Northern Ireland coast falls within Areas of Outstanding Natural Beauty (AONBs) or Areas of Scientific Interest (ASIs) (Figure 6.1c) which were designated following the passing of the Amenity Lands Act. Until the "Cockcroft Report" on rural planning policy and procedures (DoE, 1978b), development (including siting and design) within AONBs was somewhat more strictly controlled than in other rural areas. Under the revised planning procedures (DoE, 1978c; 1978d), developed in the light of the Cockcroft Report proposals, AONB status will become less relevant in planning, and instead some coastal areas will become incorporated into new Areas of Special Control (ASCs) which were designated by the Divisional Planning Officers in 1979. Within ASCs a planning applicant will have to prove "need" for development to be sanctioned. AONB and ASC boundaries are not necessarily contiguous, the latter being apparently based on the criterion of "high visual amenity" and tending to be somewhat smaller than AONBs. Regional variation

Plate 6.1 Site clearance for a caravan site in fragile duneland at Benone, Magilligan, County Londonderry, in February 1979.

in the criteria employed to designate ASCs exists even across an area as small as Northern Ireland, and the effects of this policy change on coastal development cannot, as yet, be assessed, although it may prove difficult to operate. To take one example, the Magilligan area of County Londonderry, one of the most important dune complexes in Ireland, now carries only a limited degree of special planning status as it is outside an ASC zone, although still within both an AONB and an ASI. Recent conflict between the development of a private caravan site in dunes adjacent to the beach (Plate 6.1) and the proposed public development plan do not bode well for this relaxation of planning controls.

Conservation of biological and geological sites is guided by the Nature Reserves Committee (NRC) of the DoE. According to the Committee's first report (Northern Ireland Parliament, 1967) conservation is effected by (i) preserving rare species and important outcrops from excessive interference and general degradation, and (ii) setting aside and maintaining a selection of habitats and sites representative of those existing in Northern Ireland. To achieve these aims, 61 Nature Reserves (NRs) and 44

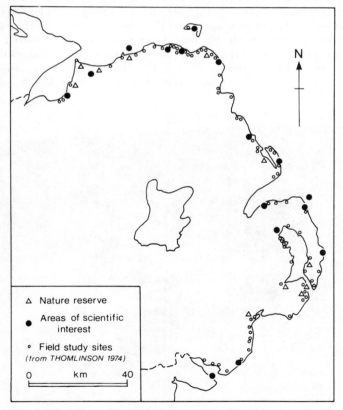

Figure 6.2 Nature Reserves, Areas of Scientific Interest and Field Study sites on the Northern Ireland coast.

Areas of Scientific Interest (ASIs) have been declared or notified, and coastal sites are shown in Figure 6.2. Most were designated between 1965 and 1971 but new sites are still being added. The NRC considers planning applications in ASIs; judging by the rate of applications (*c.* 3 per year) pressure is greatest along the North Antrim coast. A large number, but not all, NRs and ASIs are extensively used for school and university field exercises, a use which in some ways conflicts with strict conservationist tenets by popularising and thus increasing visits to vulnerable sites. However, co-ordination and organisation of fieldwork activities, particularly through the expanding network of field study centres, should help to minimise these risks. A useful handbook of accessible study sites has been produced (Thomlinson, 1974), and those on the coast are mapped in Figure 6.2. Recently, longer-term management objectives for NRs and ASIs have been set out by the NRC (DoE, 1976).

In addition to the work of central government, much local planning and day-to-day maintenance is undertaken by District Councils; for instance, caravan site licensing and the provision and upkeep of recreation facilities. Several local development schemes are currently being undertaken among which are those at Red Bay (Water-foot), County Antrim, Tyrella, County Down and Benone, County Londonderry.

In Northern Ireland private organisations own and manage considerable stretches of coastland (Figure 6.1*d*). In some areas even the foreshore and sea bed is under private control. Most important is the National Trust which owns *c.* 1,400 ha of coastal property, and holds in covenant a further 160 ha. Its properties, which include many of the most scenic and interesting sites – e.g. The Giant's Causeway, County Antrim (Plate 6.2) and Murlough National Nature Reserve, County Down – have been

Plate 6.2 The internationally important Causeway cliffs in County Antrim, owned and managed by the National Trust.

progressively acquired over the last 40 years, although a considerable number were purchased with money either raised as a part of the Enterprise Neptune Appeal, initiated in the 1960s, or provided through the Ulster Land Fund. The National Trust strives to manage its properties to a high standard, but is always conscious of visitor requirements. In addition to maintaining and managing coastal property, the Trust has been active together with co-operating groups and individuals both in developing long distance footpaths (The North Antrim and Mourne Coastal paths as part of the Ulster Way) and in operating the Strangford Lough Wildlife Scheme which is aimed at minimising disturbance to important birdlife while still allowing shooting by authorised gun clubs and riparian owners.

Other significant coastal landowners are the Ministry of Defence, which owns considerable tracts of Magilligan, County Londonderry and Ballykinler, County Down – and golf clubs. In different ways both practise, albeit indirectly, a form of natural preservation by restricting public access. Unfortunately, in both cases management is somewhat unscientific, and aimed simply at maintenance or improvement of such specific aspects as golf course fairways and greens, firing ranges etc. The twelve coastal golf links occupy important recreational land often adjacent to popular holiday resorts like Castlerock, Portstewart, Portrush, Newcastle. Most were founded in the nineteenth or early twentieth centuries, and the courses were fashioned by non-mechanical means over a period of years. Continuous grass cutting and remedial seeding has resulted in a somewhat reduced plant and animal diversity, and an artificial ecology along the fairways, although the "rough" may retain more natural characteristics. The golf clubs give rise to two types of environmental pressure; they confine non-playing visitors to the periphery, thus causing grossly imbalanced stresses over small areas of the coastal zone, and through the social contacts of club members, they can exert sustained political pressure should it be required.

Finally there are a number of other bodies, such as the Royal Society for the Protection of Birds, which may have a local but direct effect on the Northern Ireland coast. Other bodies, such as the Tourist Board, have a more diffuse and indirect effect.

Evaluation and utilization of coastal resources

It is difficult to assess and evaluate coast resources because few have a value which can be easily calculated. Often value arises simply from location with respect to population centres. Broadly the coastal resources of Northern Ireland are of four types:—

(i) *Those resources based on the intrinsic natural character of the coast itself* such as amenity land, recreation zones, preferred seafront development sites or important scientific/education locations. Northern Ireland is embarrassingly rich in these.

(ii) *Mineral resources.* Although many mineral zones have non-coastal locations, some (e.g. beach placers) are restricted to coastal sites by their mode of formation while others are, or were, only worth exploiting near the sea as transport is, or was, easier to organise (e.g. the Ballycastle Coalfield). At present, removal of beach sand is causing concern in Northern Ireland.

(iii) *Agriculture and fishing resources.* Some agricultural enterprises benefit from a coastal location because of ameliorating climate or soil factors. However much of the coast is relatively poor land in the form of sand dunes or marshes and these defy attempts at improvement. A few reclamation or impoundment schemes have been undertaken, but improvement of marginal land away from the coast has usually proved more rewarding. Certain agriculturally-based riparian rights such as wrack removal, fishing, sand extraction and access are still exercised along the shore. There is a small but declining commercial fishing industry at numerous harbours around the Northern Ireland coast, but this is discussed in detail elsewhere (Chapter 5) and will not be considered further. Recreational sea angling is very popular in many places.

(iv) *Use of coastal waters for effluent disposal*. Until recently, many coastal settlements discharged raw or slightly treated sewage into the sea, although standards have markedly improved in the last 20 years. Some industrial waste is also disposed of at sea.

Amenity value

The coast of Northern Ireland is one of the most scenically attractive in Europe. Indeed if the average summer temperatures were a few degrees higher the area would undoubtedly rival more renowned tourist coastlines like the Algarve, or the South of France. Amenity value may be judged in two ways: by relative popularity of an area for recreational or leisure pursuits, and by intrinsic scientific or artistic merit. The former is slightly easier to quantify, as some statistical information has been accumulated by local authorities, hotelier associations and the Tourist Board. Temporal and spatial patterns of development have followed conventional trends, with much of the early growth impetus focussed by the railways, widening out after the Second World War as car ownership became widespread. There are many examples: Portrush became a major tourist centre after the railway arrived in 1855, while the adjacent villages of Portstewart and Portballintrae "suffered" from lack of a rail link. Some towns – Castlerock and Whitehead are examples – were largely founded on railway commercialism.

Two developments have markedly changed tourism in the last 30 years. Firstly, the pervasive twin-factors of increased leisure plus motorised mobility have spread-out effects both in space and time. Secondly, the period of civil unrest since 1968 has re-orientated the holiday industry towards the domestic market. Two consequences of these developments are noteworthy as they have a direct bearing on future coastal management: (i) the increasing domination of day and half-day trippers strongly related to fine weather and (ii) the phenomenal increase in caravans since 1960. Studies of the first trend (Carter, 1975; Wilcock, 1976) have shown not only the increasing popularity of short trips, but also a strong spatial segregation of destinations across Northern Ireland. People from south and east Belfast and the Lagan Valley usually visit County Down, while those from west and north Belfast journey to the north Antrim coast. Similarly it appears, although few confirmatory data have been collected, that residents from Londonderry and other places west of the River Bann tend to favour County Donegal. Not all of this general pattern can be ascribed to accessibility factors: tradition almost certainly plays some part. At the coast many visitors cram into "honeypots" like Portrush (Plate 6.3) or Tyrella. Not all these sites have obvious attractions, yet very high densities (up to 1,000 people per hectare) often occur. Honeypots where large numbers may be catered for *en masse* also relieve pressure on adjacent, perhaps more sensitive areas (see Chapter 6 case study). However there is a considerable art in managing high density recreation areas, so that their "attractiveness" is maintained.

Plate 6.3 Holiday crowds at Portrush, County Antrim. This is one of the major Northern Ireland coastal resorts, attracting up to 20-30,000 people at fine summer weekends.

Rapid development of caravan sites has, somewhat surprisingly, gone uninvestigated, although a few local studies (Craigavon Divisional Planning Office, 1977; Lake, 1975; RPRT, 1978; Mowat, 1978) give insights into the magnitude of the trend. In almost all areas the number of static caravans has risen dramatically over the last 20 years. Along the coastal strip south of Newcastle, County Down, the number has increased from 15 in 1963 – the year of the Northern Ireland Caravan Act – to over 1,000 in 1976 (Figure 6.3). Similarly on the north coast, where the first caravan arrived in 1933 (*Coleraine Chronicle* 30 September 1961), the 170 vans occupied in 1960 had increased to 4,200 by 1976 (**RPRT**, 1978), with permissions outstanding for a further 2,000. Recently, prefabricated chalets have become popular with developers, in lieu of caravans. Comparable trends have taken place around Newcastle and on the Ards Peninsula. Almost all caravans are individually owned and although extensive hiring does take place, site occupancy rates even at peak holiday times rarely exceed 60%. Facilities for the small proportion of short-stay "touring" caravans have been sadly neglected, particularly by private developers, and well-appointed European-style camp sites are almost non-existent. While the massive increase in caravans is largely a reflection of the changing holiday market, the origins of the boom may be traced back to the unplanned chalet "hutments" which sprang up along, and disfigured, the Northern Ireland coast in the 1930s, late-1940s and early-1950s. (Those established before the Planning Acts of 1944 obtained an unwarranted legitimacy, and were eventually difficult to remove because of it). Such developments were particularly extensive around Portrush and Portstewart, and are still visible further west along the coast at Downhill. In the period 1930 to 1960 the local press reported constantly both the "eyesore" complaints of local residents, and grumbles about lack of services from the chalet dwellers themselves – see, for example, the long-running saga about rubbish collection and water supply in the *Coleraine Chronicle* throughout 1946. In 1958, the Londonderry County Council initiated action to remove the makeshift hut community stretched out along the A2 coast road, for health (there were several typhoid outbreaks in 1960) as well as aesthetic reasons. Altogether 63 ha of coastal land were vested, 212 shacks demolished and the Juniper Hill caravan site provided as an alternative (RPRT, 1978). This and other clearance schemes led to the establishment of many coastal caravan sites.

The caravan site "explosion" has a paradoxical nature, for although it represents a major and often sought-after type of tourist development, much of the revenue or benefit frequently does not pass to the local communities. This is particularly true in the larger well-organised sites where "all facilities are provided", and thus most profits

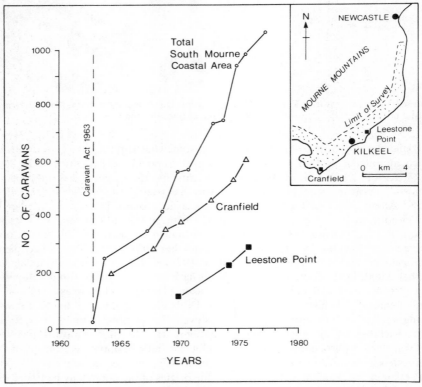

Figure 6.3 Growth of caravan numbers in the Mourne coastal area.
(From Craigavon Divisional Planning Office, 1976).

accrue to the owners. In some cases uncontrolled growth may overwhelm smaller communities. At Annalong, County Down, for example, the summer caravan population is 3 times the local resident population, and thus puts an excessive burden on local services and community structure. Also many sites are visually obtrusive and poorly sited, for example in old sand pits subject to flooding, or too close to vulnerable dunelands. The deleterious impact of caravan development is all too obvious in many places (Plate 6.4). Eventually unchecked growth of caravan sites may deter potential users and other casual visitors. This lesson has been learned the hard way in North Wales (Martin, 1971) and it is difficult not to envisage a similar problem arising in Northern Ireland, as the UCC pointed out in 1969 (DoE, 1970). However, it may also be argued that the undesirable aspects of caravan development in Northern Ireland might have been much worse, but for the former rural development policy.

Plate 6.4   Caravans adjacent to the beach on the Ards peninsula, County Down.

The pressure of visitors is felt most strongly on the beaches and dunes where considerable damage has been caused, often unintentionally, to the extremely fragile ecosystems. Many dunelands have been severely degraded in the last 20 years (Wilcock 1976, 1978a, 1978b). The recent increase over the last two or three years in trail-bike riding on dunelands has already made a significant impact in some areas. Human activities may also disturb sensitive wildlife, particularly breeding birds. Often such disturbance is unrecognised by the perpetrators, and long-term effects are subtle and hard to unravel, as Watson's (1979) study on the birds of the County Antrim coast has shown. The possible conflict between nesting peregrines and the opening up of the County Antrim coastal path is a pertinent example of this problem.

Coastal conservation is important as it preserves and maintains many aesthetic and natural attributes. In Northern Ireland the Conservation Branch of the DoE and the National Trust are the two most active coastal conservation bodies, between them controlling about 90% of the attractive coastlands. A conservation strategy was proposed in 1970 following a conference organised by the Extra-Mural Department of Queen's University (Forsyth and Boyd, 1970), and a similar approach forms the basis of the current Conservation Branch policy in as much as sites are designated or zoned according to their value (aesthetic, educational, scientific, historical etc.) and are then patrolled by field staff, who may be permanent wardens or peripatetic overseers. Increasingly the value of countryside interpretation is being recognised, and in 1978 an interpretative centre – The Portandoo Centre – was opened in Portrush to act as a link between the public and the staff, properties and policies of the Conservation Branch. Management plans are being formulated and implemented for a wide range of sites: from Crawfordsburn Country Park on the shores of Belfast Lough (which purportedly receives one million visits each year) to desolate rarely-visited sites like Carrickhue salt marsh and shell ridge in Lough Foyle. In this way it is hoped that a wide range of habitats and recreation facilities will become available to suit all interests.

The National Trust also maintains a wardening system, for example at the Giant's Causeway and the Murlough National Nature Reserve. As part of the Trust's long-standing commitment to education and interpretation, better visitor centres have been provided recently at both the above-mentioned properties.

Mineral extraction and riparian rights

Historically a number of rights – prescriptive rights – were granted to coastal communities by landlords and landowners which allowed such exploitation of coastal

Plate 6.5 Sand removal from White Park Bay, County Antrim in 1980.

resources as fishing (piscary), wrack collection, grazing (pasturage) of dunes, marram cutting for thatch and the extraction of beach sand. Many of these practices have died-out or become subsumed into commercial operations, but the continuation and acceleration of sand extraction is now causing severe problems. Beach and dune sand should not be viewed as a renewable resource as there are no processes providing major present-day additions to the overall sediment budget. Therefore extracted sand is not replaced, although unfortunately the shoreline processes obligingly cover-up the short-term evidence of loss. However, longer-term adjustments arise from the results of depletion. Exercise of the prescriptive right of sand removal in Northern Ireland had a minimal effect for many generations as the amount that could be removed by hand was negligible. Sadly, the introduction of mechanical excavators, plus a rising demand for construction material and agricultural sand has caused a serious problem on some beaches (Plate 6.5). For example, since 1960 it is estimated that over 20,000 m³ (or 56,000 tonnes) have been removed from White Park Bay, equivalent to almost 2% of the total available sand. However, it is not so much the amount, but the manner and location of the extraction which causes most concern. Sand removal by front-loading tractors from parts of seaward dune faces simply exacerbates wind and sea erosion. Sand removal is a problem at Castlerock, Portstewart, White Park Bay, Cushendun, Cushendall and Tyrella. At Portrush, where the practice has now been stopped, massive removal before 1960 on both the East and West Strands has led to abnormal dune erosion which at one point is threatening the golf links. As the long-term effects of sand removal are almost wholly detrimental to coastal stability, urgent restrictive legislation is needed to curb the practice.

Recently the NRC averted the threat of commercial seaweed harvesting in Strangford Lough, but elsewhere this practice has died out. It was formerly widespread in the eighteenth century – see for example Mullen's description of the kelp industry on Rathlin Island (1974). Some marram cutting for thatch is still undertaken at Magilligan Point.

Land reclamation

Over the years coastal areas (particularly estuaries) have held a great fascination for would-be land reclaimers. In Lough Foyle a number of attempts were made to reclaim slob-land (mud flats) in order to finance the Coleraine and Londonderry Railway (Currie, 1973). Along several stretches of the muddy estuarine coast, cord grass *Spartina anglica* has been planted, ostensibly for protection, but most likely with one eye on eventual reclamation. *Spartina* was planted in Lough Foyle at Ballykelly in 1935 and 1955 (Plate 6.6), in Strangford Lough at Ardmillan in 1930, and in Belfast Lough at Kinnegar in 1932. Unfortunately, *Spartina* rapidly colonises intertidal mud, often ousting *Zostera* (eel grass) and thus replacing valuable wildfowl and wading bird feeding grounds. Although eradication is difficult, as every *Spartina* plant must be removed or killed, persistent attempts have been made, over the last 10 to 15 years, to eliminate the plant. The NRC noted the *Spartina* problem in 1968 (Northern Ireland Parliament, 1969, p. 20) and subsequent NRC reports detail removal activities. Clearing was undertaken in 1972 at Mount Stewart and Gransha Point in Strangford Lough, and at Mill Bay in Carlingford Lough, where Queen's University students painstakingly dug out every visible plant. Despite these measures *Spartina* continues to colonise new sites, and at present a removal programme which involves spraying with

Plate 6.6 Extending *Spartina* marsh at Ballykelly in the low energy environment of Lough Foyle. The original plantings were in 1935.

the herbicide *Dalapon* is being undertaken in Strangford Lough, even though concern exists over the possible effects of sudden widespread sediment release, following die-back and erosion, on the expanding commercial shell-fish beds.

Almost all the Northern Ireland coastal dunes have passed through phases of improvement, reclamation and destruction. The commonest technique is to plant marram grass *Ammophila arenaria* or sea-lyme grass *Elymus arenaria* to trap wind-blown sand. Unfortunately recent damage initiated by visitor pressure is occurring at a significantly faster rate and over a wider area than any earlier deleterious processes and is being caused by a group which collectively has little understanding or interest in maintaining healthy vegetation. Because of these factors many traditional methods of planting and fencing are entirely inappropriate to the present situation and newer approaches have had to be formulated. Wilcock and Carter (1977) chronicle the restoration undertaken at Portrush since 1969, concluding that an engineering and ecological solution based on a thorough scientific assessment of the site is the only valid method of tackling dune degradation in Northern Ireland. On some inland dunes buckthorn *Hippophaë rhamnoides* has been introduced to discourage trespass. Like *Spartina* this plant may cause ecological disturbances and eradication is difficult.

Waste disposal

As in many countries, the coastal waters of Northern Ireland are considered a convenient repository for effluent. While the sea does provide a suitable medium for diffusion, degradation and decomposition of waste, there are many attendant pollution problems. Type and effect of pollutant varies from mildly unpleasant to highly toxic.

There is mounting concern about the long-term build-up of heavy metals, hydrocarbons, organophosphates and nitrates particularly in estuaries, where effluent may be retained for long periods. Poor water quality in Belfast Lough has been reported for some years (Maxwell 1978), and there is concern about Strangford Lough, particularly in the upper reaches near the sewage outfall at Ballyrickard. Major industrial waste disposal occurs in Belfast Lough, Larne Lough, Lough Foyle, the Quoile Pondage, and near Castlerock. While much of this effluent may be "satisfactory" in an immediate sense, longterm effects are often unknown.

Towards an integrated coastal plan?

Despite Stephen's (1957) 'Plea for coastal planning in Northern Ireland' little progress has been made, notwithstanding the considerable volume of disparate research pertaining to the coastal zone that has been undertaken in the interim. In recent years there has been a complete reorganisation of local, regional and European government and considerable legislation relating to the environment is now being, or will be, applied. Overall the need for an assessment of coastal resources and a scheme for their rational use is badly overdue. At a recent seminar in Cork (Downey and Ní Uid, 1978) an attempt was made to bring together scientists studying different aspects of the Irish coast with a view to co-ordinating "base-line" information. From this seminar one unconcealable fact emerged: the great disparity of attitudes and approach not only between the scientific community and the Government on the one hand, but within the scientific community on the other. Despite the present high volume of "coastal" research, little of it seems to be of practical value to environmental managers.

Coastal management is probably a skilled art: at the moment decisions are usually heuristic and intuitive, but as social and financial pressures mount, far greater objectivity will have to be applied to the problems. Consider, for example, the construction of the sea wall at the West Bay in Portrush. This wall was built largely to quell local agitation as the solution to an erosion problem, but instead is likely to be a trigger for more damage. While the position of the high water mark remains fixed by the sea wall, the beach at Portrush is incapable of adjusting to storms and gradually sand is being removed into deeper water. Eventually further remedial work will be required, probably at a far higher cost. A careful assessment followed by realistic management might have alleviated these continuing problems.

A praiseworthy and realistic attempt at providing base-line information on coastal conflicts is contained in the recent Strangford Lough Working Group Report (1978). This document not only defines the present condition of the Lough, but also assesses the present and future trends, identifying conflicts between gun clubs, water skiers, conservation groups etc. Although, somewhat inevitably, the report is unable to produce a consensus opinion, it does provide an admirable framework for the construction of an effective management plan. The importance of routine gathering of such information has become obvious recently, as the basis for the environmental impact statement for the proposed tidal power barrage across Strangford narrows (Newbould and Carter, 1981).

The recent decision of the DoE to undertake production of a coastal plan is a step in the right direction, and the aims of the plan, outlined before, are realistic. It is worth noting, however, that "plan" in the DoE context is used in a somewhat narrow sense and refers largely to the processes of physical planning policy and development. It might be better to take a broader view, advocating that all available data should be synthesised in a "plan" which embodies the concept of environmental diversity, and which can therefore be used as a basis for sound management. The sort of topics with which such a plan might be concerned are:—

1. The physical dynamics or kinetics of the coast: sediment budgets, wave climates etc.
2. The ecology – diversity, stability, productivity, storage, energy flows etc. – of subaqueous and subaerial shore zones.
3. Water and sediment quality and any changes therein: both chemical and biological monitoring techniques can be used.
4. Recognition and definition of hazards and likely adjustments to them. These include, for example, storms, oil spills, and heavy metal pollution.
5. Regional and local trends in long term population movements as they affect the structure of coastal communities.
6. Anticipated future patterns of economic development in tourism, recreation, industry and commerce, and their likely impacts on the coastal environment.
7. The education of public attitudes to, and perceptions of, the coastal zone.
8. Decision-making processes and the role of external pressures on attitudes to coastal matters. Of central interest would be the potential disparity between political and non-political decisions.
9. Present-day management techniques and managers: the origins and effectiveness of common local practices on the coast: the adaptability of personnel etc.

The drawing together of such base-line information is an integral part of management, allowing due emphasis where it is needed. However, data must be gathered, sorted, reduced and analysed if they are to assist in the management process. Eventually it is to be hoped that any effective plan will balance use against value, honeypots against wilderness and ephemeral against established along the entire coast of Northern Ireland.

Two further management aims should be considered. First, management must be an adaptive and continuing process. Several recent initiatives, like the dune restoration at Portrush, have been less than successful simply because the local authorities have not realised that good effective environmental management requires an ongoing commitment of labour, money, and ideas. Second, there is an urgent need for environmental education in Northern Ireland. Many day-to-day irritations (vandalism, litter etc.) might be alleviated if the public were better educated. Some progress, but on a small scale, has been made through the interpretative centres, like Portandoo, and by public lectures. But a visit to Holland or Denmark would soon convince sceptics as to how much more could be done just to raise the level of public appreciation and awareness.

Throughout this chapter it has been emphasised that human activities are the main threat to the coast as they cause imbalance. Often the effects of these activities are not immediately apparent and more than likely they are removed from the point of initial impact, so that perception of problems varies greatly between groups and individuals, leading to politically – or economically – biased solutions. Despite this there is a growing realisation that rates of coastal change have been unnaturally accelerated by man and some form of firm management is essential.

Acknowledgements

I would like to thank Mr R. B. McMullen, Mr J. Furphy, Mr C. Conn, Mr C. McIlwaine and Professor P. J. Newbould for kindly commenting and advising on this chapter. In spite of their kind help all responsibility for the accuracy of the material rests with me.

REFERENCES

Carter, R. W. G., 1975. *Tyrella Beach, Co. Down: an environmental survey*. Department of the Environment for Northern Ireland, Planning Service. Unpublished report.

Carter, R. W. G. and Rihan, C. L., 1976. The River Bann Mouth Bar. *Irish Geography, 9*, 121–123.

Craigavon Divisional Planning Office, 1976. *Mourne coastal area – Caravan/chalet development. A draft policy control statement.*

Currie, J. R. L., 1973. *The Northern Counties Railway*. Volume I: 1845–1903. David and Charles, Newton Abbot.

Department of the Environment for Northern Ireland, 1970. *Fourth Report of the Ulster Countryside Committee.* H.M.S.O.

Department of the Environment for Northern Ireland, 1976. *Tenth Report of the Nature Reserves Committee.* H.M.S.O.

Department of the Environment for Northern Ireland, 1977. *Northern Ireland Regional Physical Development Strategy 1975–1995.* H.M.S.O., 95 pp.

Department of the Environment for Northern Ireland, 1978a Coastal Survey Report. *Eleventh Report of the Ulster Countryside Committee.* H.M.S.O.

Department of the Environment for Northern Ireland, 1978b. *Review of the rural planning policy.* (The Cockcroft Committee) H.M.S.O.

Department of the Environment for Northern Ireland, 1978c. *Policy for the control of development in rural areas I.* H.M.S.O.

Department of the Environment for Northern Ireland, 1978d. *Policy for the control of development in rural areas II.* H.M.S.O.

Department of the Environment for Northern Ireland, 1979a. *East Antrim Coastal Study,* Area Plan Section, County Hall, Ballymena.

Department of the Environment for Northern Ireland, 1979b. *North East Area Plan.* H.M.S.O.

Downey, W. K. and Ní Uid, G., 1978. *Coastal Pollution Assessment.* National Board for Science and Technology, Dublin.

Forsyth, J. and Boyd, D. E. K., (eds.) 1970. *Conservation in the development of Northern Ireland.* Department of Extra-Mural Studies, Queen's University, Belfast.

Great Britain and Northern Ireland Parliament, 1949. *The Coast Protection Act.* H.M.S.O.

Ketchum, B. H., (ed.) 1972. *The Water's Edge: Critical problems of the coastal zone.* MIT Press, Cambridge Mass.

Lake, M., 1975. *Caravanning on the North Ulster Coast.* Unpublished Diploma Thesis, Leeds Polytechnic.

Limavady Area Plan 1973. H.M.S.O., Belfast.

Martin, A., Shipman, P., Brady, H. and Hyde, N., 1974. A conservation strategy for the Irish coastline. *Ekistics, 218,* 74–80.

Martin, J., 1971. *Caravanning in Denbighshire.* Denbighshire County Council. Tourism and Recreation Report No. 1.

Maxwell, T. H., 1978. The plankton of Belfast Lough. *Coastal Pollution Assessment,* W. K. Downey and G. Ni Uid, National Board for Science and Technology, Dublin, 103–136.

McGreal, W. S., 1979. Factors promoting coastal slope instability in south-east County Down, Northern Ireland. *Zeitschrift fuer Geomorphologie,* N.F., 23, 76–90.

Mowat, R. B., 1978. *The Geography of Caravanning in the Ards region.* Unpublished MSc Thesis. The New University of Ulster.

Mullen, J. E., 1974. *The Causeway Coast.* Century Services Ltd., Belfast.
National Coastline Study, Vols. I-III 1972/73. Bord Failte Eireann and An Foras Forbartha, Dublin.
Newbould, P. J. and Carter, R. W. G., 1981. Environmental assessment. *Strangford Lough Tidal Energy.* Northern Ireland Economic Council Report, No. 24, 38–44.
Northern Ireland Parliament, 1947. *The Drainage Act (N.I.)* H.M.S.O.
Northern Ireland Parliament, 1955. *The Drainage (Sea Defences) Act (N.I.).*
Northern Ireland Parliament, 1963. *The Caravans Act (N.I.).*
Northern Ireland Parliament, 1965. *Amenity Lands Act* (N.I.), H.M.S.O..
Northern Ireland Parliament, 1967. *First Report of the Nature Reserves Committee.* H.M.S.O.
Northern Ireland Parliament, 1969. *Third Report of the Nature Reserves Committee.* H.M.S.O.
Northern Ireland Parliament, 1973. *The Drainage (Northern Ireland) Order. S.I. No. 69 (N.I. 1)* H.M.S.O.
Rea, D., 1981. *Decision making in coastal protection in Northern Ireland.* Unpublished MSc thesis, The New University of Ulster.
Regional Plan and Research Team (RPRT) 1978. *Report on the coastline of the Londonderry Planning Division.* Coleraine.
Sheail, J., 1976. Coasts and planning in Great Britain before 1950. *Geographical Journal, 142,* 257–273.
Steers, J. A., 1944. Coastal preservation and planning. *Geographical Journal, 104,* 7–27.
Stephens, N., 1957. A plea for coastal planning. *Irish Naturalists' Journal, 12,* 164–167.
Stephens, N., Creighton, R. and Hannon, M., 1975. The late-Pleistocene period in North-eastern Ireland: An assessment 1975. *Irish Geography, 8,* 1–23.
Strangford Lough Working Group, 1978. *Report:* Northern Ireland Department of the Environment.
Tanner, W. F., 1960. Florida coastal classification. *Transactions Gulf Coast Association of Geological Societies, 10,* 259–266.
Thomlinson, P. M., (ed.) 1974. *Field study sites in Northern Ireland.* Queen's University, Belfast Teachers Centre.
Watson, P., 1979. Bird and man on the coast of County Antrim. *National Trust Studies 1979,* Sotheby-Parke-Bernet, 67–76.
Wilcock, F. A., 1976. *Dune physiography and the impact of recreation on the North Coast of Ireland.* Unpublished DPhil thesis, The New University of Ulster.
Wilcock, F. A., 1978a. Managing beaches and dunes for recreation. *Technology Ireland, 10,* 39–44.
Wilcock, F. A., 1978b. The management of sand dune resources in Northern Ireland. *Coastal pollution assessment,* W. K. Downey and G. Ní Uid, National Board for Science and Technology, Dublin, 100–102.
Wilcock, F. A. and Carter, R. W. G., 1977. An environmental approach to the restoration of badly eroded sand dunes. *Biological Conservation,* 11, 279–291.
Wood, R. B. and Carter, C. E., 1978. Water quality in an Ulster Nature Reserve. *Proceedings Royal Irish Academy, 78B,* 301–311.

COASTAL DUNE AND BEACH CONSERVATION IN COUNTY DOWN – TWO CASE STUDIES

Mrs. JO WHATMOUGH,
*Warden, Murlough National Nature Reserve, National Trust,
Rowallane, Saintfield, County Down*

and

RICHARD W. G. CARTER,
Senior Lecturer in Environmental Science, New University of Ulster.

Introduction

County Down has one of the most varied and scenically attractive coastlines in Ireland with the backdrop of the Mourne mountains contributing to the beauty of the area. Geologically the coastal strip is made up of glacial and fluvioglacial deposits which are still being actively eroded in places to provide sand, gravel and mud for deposition in beaches, estuaries and dunes.

Most of the County Down coast is within an hour's drive of Belfast and other major population centres south of Lough Neagh, making it exceedingly popular for half-day and day excursions. In addition there are numerous sites for static caravans, and more traditional accommodation is available in towns such as Newcastle. Recent increases in demand for recreation facilities have given rise to considerable planning problems.

This short study focuses on two of the most popular beach and dune areas – Tyrella (Grid Reference J 47 35) and Murlough (J 40 33) (Figure 6A.1) – which, despite basic physical and ecological similarities, have exhibited considerable contrasts in use, development and management over recent years. As recreation demands increase, it is likely that considerable reassessment of coastal management in Northern Ireland will have to be undertaken, particularly where fragile environments like sand dunes are at risk. Hopefully, experiences in County Down should assist in future planning.

Tyrella

Tyrella comprises a wide, flat beach 1.3 km in length, backed by 43 ha of mature dunes. Since 1835, the date of the first reliable maps, no major shoreline changes have occurred within the bay, although in recent years dune degradation and localised shoreline retreat have become noticeable. Sequential air photographs taken over the last 30 years show that the extent of bare sand in the dunes has increased fourfold, mostly along the seaward dune line. In 1975, 69% of the foredunes showed signs of severe erosion compared with 13% in 1962. These progressive changes are mainly the result of too many uncontrolled visitors trampling across easily damaged dune vegetation, although both sand extraction and agricultural activities have contributed to a limited extent.

A survey conducted in 1975 showed that about 120,000 people visited Tyrella each year, (Carter, 1980) although the majority arrive on warm summer Sundays when up to 6,000 people and 1,500 cars may be present. (Plate 6A.1). At these times visitor densities of *c.* 700 per 100 m² near access points are among the highest recorded anywhere in Western Europe. Overall recreation demand is strongly dependent on the weather, and in consequence is exceedingly erratic in character.

Almost 90% of visitors pay a private access charge enabling them to drive and park on the public beach. Over 60% come regularly, mostly from Belfast and Craigavon, although the area is particularly popular with people living in towns in central and west County Down. Conversely, significantly few people from South Down (Newcastle, Newry) visit Tyrella. When asked why they visited Tyrella, which has few amenities, most people replied they found it pleasant, convenient and they could park on the beach. Despite general satisfaction most people, somewhat paradoxically, disliked crowds and thought the area dirty. Also, many expressed concern about lack of facilities and general management.

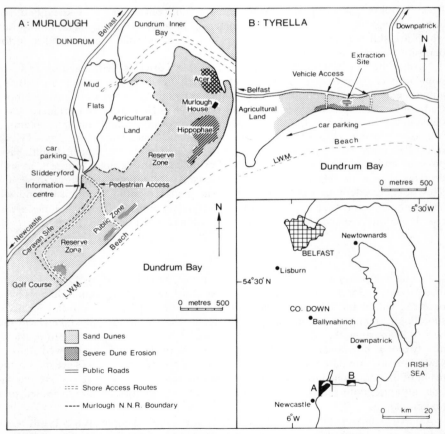

Figure 6A.1 Location of Murlough and Tyrella showing access tracks and other features referred to in the text.

Plate 6A.1 Tyrella Beach, June 1975. Copyright Mr C. F. Newman (Photo ref. 6054 9)

At present the beach and dunes are subjected to no formal management, despite concern at all levels of government. To understand this situation it is necessary to examine the recent history of development proposals, and how they relate to local land-use practices.

In the mid-1960s the then County Surveyor, Mr G. Craig, produced a development plan for Tyrella, which aimed to vest those areas not under public control, and subsequently to level the dune area for hard-standing car parks, a caravan site, shops and a promenade. It was considered that the beach and dunes were of no special scientific interest and that the site should be developed as a 'honeypot' recreation area.

Despite revision in 1968, the Craig Plan ran into considerable practical difficulties. First, it proved extremely difficult to establish who owned what land. (In fact, later investigation (Carter, 1975) listed at least 53 affected landowners, some of whom were absentee.) Second, despite Tourist Board approval, the scheme was not enthusiastically adopted by the existing Northern Ireland Ministry of Development who considered it too expensive. Also, progress was not facilitated by the bureaucratic process, which in six years, directly involved 38 officials, only one of whom participated throughout. Vesting orders were made in 1972 citing implementation of the Craig Plan, but 12 objections were received, and eventually the scheme was dropped when local government reorganisation took place in 1974.

Local interest in Tyrella has been spasmodic; at the outset of the Craig proposals, some residents, particularly those fearing a loss of livelihood formed a short-lived protest association. Individuals expressed concern over loss of riparian and extraction rights and one farmer claimed that the dune pasture was important for over-wintering animals. Non-resident interest was slight, although some, when questioned, felt that 'something ought to be done' to clear-up the area and blamed the local authority for the apparent inactivity.

The background survey by Carter (1975) was followed by more detailed development and management plans (Wilcock, 1977; Hyde, 1980), aimed at conserving the dune areas but without affecting the popularity of the area. These plans, commissioned by Downpatrick District Council, advise that management should be flexible enough to cope with day-to-day variations in demand and able to deal with any emerging problems. Both recommend that facilities be improved, but not made attractive in their own right. Limited car parking would be made available at the rear of the dunes and pedestrian access to the beach carefully regulated along reinforced walkways. On fine days the hard-standing car parks would be augmented by zoned beach parking. Also a limited capacity, transit caravan site would be sited at the western end of the dunes, with a separate access to the beach. Entrance fees etc. would be put towards maintenance costs – remedial ecological work, litter collection and so on – and may possibly allow employment of a part-time warden. With these measures it would be feasible to balance the fragile environment against the recreation demand, and to alleviate future problems.

In 1980, it was intended to issue new vesting orders to bring the dune area under public (District Council) control, thus enabling a phased implementation of management proposals. However, this initiative was unsuccessful, and the beach dune system is in serious danger of complete degradation. Eventually, it will become unattractive to visitors, and the straightforward, relatively inexpensive improvements now advocated will be made impossible.

Tyrella is an important asset to the overall recreation strategy of the County Down coast. At present it absorbs a considerable amount of 'pressure' although at the expense of progressive beach/dune changes, which must soon be tackled.

Murlough

Murlough, north-east of Newcastle, consists of around 350 ha of beach and sand dunes within Dundrum Bay. The area nearest the town is owned and managed by the Royal County Down Golf Club, while the remaining 282 ha are leased in perpetuity by the National Trust. It is the conservation and management of the latter area which concerns us.

In addition to the usual attractions, the dunes are of considerable botanical, zoological and archaeological interest, and the area was designated a National Nature Reserve (NNR) in 1975. A comprehensive survey of the scientific aspects of the NNR has been made by Whatmough and Nairn (1978). For management purposes Murlough is divided into two zones: a "public" zone including most of the beach and portions of the adjacent dunes, within which access is by-and-large unrestricted, and a "restricted zone" comprising the remainder of the dunes.

Unlike Tyrella, Murlough has experienced a far more coherent pattern of ownership. Until 1956 the area was owned and managed by the Downshire estate, principally as a rabbit warren, although after 1909 military training activities prevailed up to 1955. After this, the Forestry Division of the then Ministry of Agriculture took a 20 year lease on 111 ha and proceeded to plant Corsican pine *(Pinus nigra)*. (Plate 6A.2*a*). This prospect of afforestation alarmed local conservationists and galvanised them into demanding a more realistic management plan that would highlight rather than obliterate the natural attractions. Subsequently, the National Trust were invited by the Downshire family to negotiate a lease.

The long period of military presence did little to enhance or protect the area and many unsightly derelict buildings and fortifications were abandoned in 1955. Many of these were further vandalised by an ever-increasing number of trespassers. The establishment of caravan sites around the fringe of Newcastle in the early 1960s, and the general rise in pleasure trips, brought more visitors to Murlough and consequently more pressure. At present there are 30,000 caravan berths in Newcastle alone.

By the time the National Trust had organised the lease much of the area was suffering erosion. This was most severe in the proximity of the expanding caravan sites, especially along paths leading to the sea. The beach/dune line is strengthened by a gravel storm ridge and as a consequence is relatively immune from damage, but the adjacent dunes have deteriorated badly.

Initially it was decided to zone the area and to impose access restriction, people being admitted only through one well-signposted pedestrian entrance at Slidderyford (Figure 6A.1). A small 40 car park was provided, although later the reconstruction of the main Newcastle road provided much additional space along the hard-shoulder. Away from this access, secure boundary fences were erected. (Plate 6A.2*b*). Labour for these projects was supplied from various governmental unemployment relief schemes, particularly the Urban and Rural Improvement Campaign and Enterprise Ulster.

Plate 6A.2a Murlough dunes in 1962 (Reproduced from an Ordnance Survey aerial photograph with the sanction of the Controller of Her Majesty's Stationery Office, Crown Copyright reserved)

Comparison of the aerial photographs in Plates *2a* & *b*

1. Expansion of caravan and camping sites adjacent to Reserve.

2. New main road with hard shoulder parking.

3. Forestry plantation (rectangular dark patch between caravan site and beach).

4. Network of footpaths in public zone, the main paths from road and caravan site being timbered.

5. Dissection of the vegetation on the coastal dunes at the ends of footpaths.

6. General lack of people erosion elsewhere on the Reserve, in fact showing a loss of open sandy areas by the growth of vegetation.

7. Spread of sea buckthorn over dunes to right, invading the younger coastal dunes. Also greater evidence of trees scattered over the duneland.

Plate 6A.2b Murlough dunes in 1975 (Reproduced from an Ordnance Survey aerial photograph with the sanction of the Controller of Her Majesty's Stationery Office, Crown Copyright reserved)

The general public are now directed along a well-signposted 1.5 km path from the car park to the beach. There are few opportunities to encourage the more peripatetic-minded visitor, but it is possible to visit the reserve area by obtaining a permit. Similarly horse riding is allowed by permit along way-marked bridle paths.

A number of conservation techniques have been tested. For example two-year field trials were undertaken using gravel, duckboards, wire netting and threaded beams in order to ascertain the best type of durable path surface. These showed that threaded fir beams were the most effective on slopes but that cheaper wire netting performed equally well on low gradients. Off the main paths simple fertilizer applications proved sufficient to maintain an erosion-resistant vegetation cover. As well as paths many bare areas have been reseeded and thatched using brushwood to promote natural revegetation and deter trespass.

Despite intensive management a number of serious problems remain at Murlough. The coastal dunes remain badly scarred and attempts at remedial action have tended only to slow down rather than reverse physiographic changes. Earlier efforts, between 1880 and 1900 and in the 1930s, to stabilize bare sand surfaces using Sea Buckthorn *(Hippophaë rhamnoides)* resulted in inpenetrable thickets over wide areas and presaged extensive ecological changes. Similar ecological problems have arisen through the introduction of Sycamore *Acer pseudoplatanus* near the channel leading to Dundrum Inner Bay. A persistent problem is posed by rabbits *(Oryctolagus cuniculus)* which exert severe grazing pressure. Their burrowing activity also leads to slope instability. Occasional fluctuations in the rabbit population, as for example the decline due to myxomatosis in 1955, are often mirrored by vegetation changes. Kelly (1977) thinks that the recent invasive spread of buckthorn is in inverse proportion to the density of rabbits.

A major development objective at Murlough is to encourage education use at all levels. Since 1968, over 10,000 students have visited the site, and to cater for them a variety of guides and interpreted trails are provided. Recently a permanent visitor information and interpretation centre has been opened.

Conclusions

Tyrella and Murlough are two similar coastal sites a few kilometres apart that have developed in different ways due largely to the vagaries of ownership and management. Both attract large numbers of visitors, although at Tyrella arrivals are concentrated into only a few days each summer while Murlough has a far more even distribution through the year. It would appear from questionnaire surveys at the two sites (Carter, 1975; Brown, 1977) that many visitors find Tyrella unsatisfying, while at Murlough there is general consumer approval of the environment. It is fairly obvious that the judicious combination of short and long-term management has significantly raised the "quality" of Murlough, and it is somewhat paradoxical that visitor satisfaction – measured in terms of return visits – simply amplifies recreational pressure, so stretching management resources still further. At Murlough what began as a necessary exercise in dune conservation has become a full-blown recreational operation, catering for primary (day trippers), secondary (active outdoor pursuit enthusiasts) and tertiary (educational) visitors. The transition is one penalty of running a successful operation. At Tyrella, on the other hand, progressive degradation is causing concern, and the inability of authorities to even react, let alone adapt, to such changes has serious implications for coastal conservation in County Down.

It is obvious that until some integrated coastal planning strategy is available, even the best managed sites can do little more than 'stem the tide' against mounting pressures.

REFERENCES

Brown, S., 1977. *Two studies of visitors to Murlough Nature Reserve.* Unpublished BSc Dissertation, The New University of Ulster.

Carter, R. W. G., 1975. *Tyrella Beach: an environmental survey.* Unpublished report to the Department of the Environment for Northern Ireland.

Carter, R. W. G., 1980. Recreation pressure on environmental change in a small beach/dune complex at Tyrella, County Down. *Irish Journal of Environmental Studies, 1* (2), 62–70.

Hyde, N., 1980. *Tyrella Beach plan.* Unpublished report to Down District Council.

Kelly, J. J., 1977. *An autecological study of Hippophaë rhamnoides at Murlough Nature Reserve, Dundrum, County Down.* Unpublished MSc Thesis, Queen's University, Belfast.

Whatmough, J., 1977. Murlough Nature Reserve – conservation of a sand dune system. *National Trust Year Book, 2,* 61–72.

Whatmough, J. and Nairn, R. G. W., 1978 *Murlough National Nature Reserve — Management Plan.* The National Trust.

Wilcock, F. A., 1977. *Tyrella Beach Management plan.* Unpublished report to Down District Council.

CHAPTER VII

Rocks and Minerals

JOHN C. ROBERTS,
Senior Lecturer in Environmental Science, New University of Ulster

Introduction

It is difficult at the present to envisage the fundamental changes the landscape of what is now Northern Ireland has undergone in the geological past. Today, topographic features assume a degree of permanence to the short-lived human eye, but a brief study of the rocks of Northern Ireland quickly disabuses such a viewpoint. The rocks present abundant evidence that ancient seas inundated this region on at least six occasions. Following these, severe crustal movements rearranged the ancient landmasses and oceans, and threw up mighty mountain chains (today planed down to their roots), which in turn modified climate to produce desert conditions. On yet a later occasion, the region witnessed protracted volcanic activity and finally, in the most recent past, deep cover by ice sheets. Indeed, it is the passing of such events, the progress of sedimentation in a variety of different sedimentary environments, the effects of deformation and fracturing of rocks, the extrusion and emplacement of melted rock and recession of ice sheets which were responsible for the mineral heritage of today. Therefore, it is apposite to consider these changing geological environments in more detail before discussing mineral resources.

The changing geological environment

(a) Pre-Cambrian rocks

The oldest rock sequence in Northern Ireland comprises a great thickness of muds, sands and lime-rich oozes, now indurated into rock, which were deposited in a continental shelf environment some 600-700 million years ago. These strata were very much altered by metamorphic action having been deeply buried in the earth's crust, and now appear as a succession of slates, schists and metamorphic limestones. Today, these outcrop in the Sperrin Mountains and over much of County Londonderry, and as a small inlier in north-east Antrim (Figure 7.1). These are the oldest rocks of Northern Ireland, and, as such, form the basement series upon which younger strata have been laid, and in Counties Londonderry, Tyrone and Fermanagh, it is calculated that they underlie 2,500 km^2 (Wilson, 1972). Another feature to note is that this sequence of

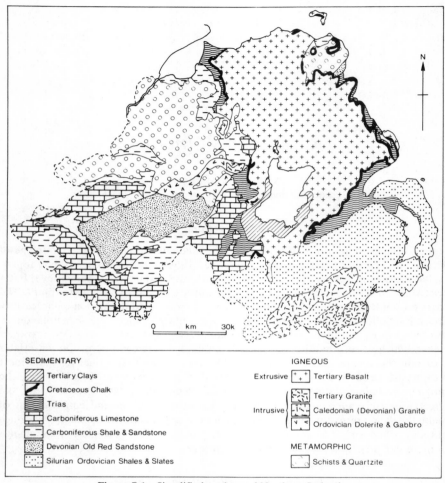

Figure 7.1 Simplified geology of Northern Ireland.

Pre-Cambrian rocks can be correlated with similar strata in Donegal and the south-west Highlands of Scotland, indicating that in Pre-Cambrian times sedimentation took place within a single marine sedimentary basin. Also, in both Scotland and Northern Ireland the southern limit of outcrop of these old rocks is defined by a strong fracture or fault line, the Highland Boundary Fault.

(b) Lower Palaeozoic rocks

Strata of this age crop-out in many parts of Northern Ireland, but predominantly in Counties Down and Armagh. These rocks contain the first convincing fossil remains –

again of a marine nature, and constitute the Ordovician and Silurian systems of Northern Ireland. From Table 7.1, it is evident that no Cambrian strata have been found and this might indicate non-submergence of the crust until Ordovician times. The rocks and fossils indicate at least two different marine environments (1) shallow, shelf-sea conditions with sandstones, conglomerates, mudstones and a shelly fauna, formerly well exposed at Pomeroy in County Tyrone, and (2) interbedded sandstones and shales attributed to deeper-water sedimentation under conditions of turbid flow. In addition, in County Tyrone, an igneous complex was emplaced in Ordovician times, and associated sediments included black shales, cherts and submarine pillow lavas (Wilson, 1972).

These Ordovician and Silurian strata crop-out mainly in Counties Down and Armagh where they form part of the Longford-Down Massif. The Silurian strata mainly comprise alternations of sandstones and shales, now highly deformed by folding and faulting so that the muddy or shaly strata have acquired a slaty cleavage. The sandstones are of a particular variety called greywacke and indicate deposition in fairly deep water on the flanks of a rapidly subsiding basin. These rocks can be correlated with similar strata in the Southern Uplands of Scotland. At the close of Silurian times, marine conditions had persisted intermittently for approximately 140 million years.

Marine sedimentation was terminated by the Caledonian Orogeny. This was the culminating phase of a protracted process of crustal deformation which had started back in Pre-Cambrian times. The main metamorphism of the Caledonian had occurred in early Ordovician times, and this, the later culmination, produced less metamorphism, but did cause severe folding, faulting and uplift of the former marine sediments. Associated with the Caledonian movements was the emplacement of the Newry Granodiorite.

(c) Upper Palaeozoic rocks

Old Red Sandstone: The reality of Caledonian earth movements is manifest in the striking colour change of the overlying Old Red Sandstone rocks. This sequence, in places at least 1,000 m thick, comprised of sandstones, shales, very coarse conglomerates and contemporary andesitic lava flows with the emphasis on red, brown and yellow pigmentation of strata. The stratigraphic sequence, rock character and primary sedimentary structures all point to non-marine sedimentation, possibly in alluvial environments representing the rapid accumulation of huge volumes of detritus derived from the recently emerged Caledonian mountain chain.

The Carboniferous System: This period saw the progressive invasion of Ireland by encroaching seas. Accordingly, in most areas the oldest Carboniferous deposits are a sequence of coarse conglomerates, sandstones and shales indicative of shallow water sedimentation of deltaic character. These basal deposits vary in thickness at around 200 m. As Carboniferous times proceeded, true marine conditions set in and sediment type changed to lime-rich muds which eventually lithified into limestones; the limestone sequence varies in thickness from about 300 m at Omagh to over 2,000 m on the eastern shores of Lough Erne. Such thickness variations indicate that the crust subsided at differential rates in the different basins of sedimentation.

Era	Epochs	Period	Radiometric Age (M.a. = millions of years)	Principal Rock Types
Cainozoic	Epochs	Holocene	10,000 years	Glacial and post-glacial sedimentation
		Pleistocene	1.8 M.a.	
		Pliocene		
		Miocene	5 M.a.	Evolution of landforms
		Oligocene	22.5 M.a.	Lough Neagh Clays and Lignites
		Eocene	53.5 M.a.	Downwarping of Lough Neagh basin
		Palaeocene	65 M.a.	Basaltic volcanicity and Granite intrusions
Mesozoic		Cretaceous	133 M.a.	Sandstones, Conglomerates and White Limestones (Chalk)
		Jurassic	195 M.a.	Liassic, Limestones and Mudstones
		Triassic	235 M.a.	Sandstones, Siltstones and Salt deposits
Upper Palaeozoic		Permian	280 M.a.	Sandstones, Marls, Magnesian Limestones and Salts
		Carboniferous	360 M.a.	Upper – Sandstones, Shales and Coals. Lower – Conglomerates, Sandstones, Shales and Limestones, Basaltic Lavas.
		Devonian (Old Red Sandstone)	430 M.a.	Conglomerates, Sandstones and Shales. Lavas. Granites.
Lower Palaeozoic		Silurian	460 M.a.	Greywackes, Siltstones. Granites and Slates. Lavas and Ashes.
		Ordovician	530 M.a.	
		Cambrian	570 M.a.	Not represented
Precambrian				Metamorphic rocks. Schists, Quartzites and Slates.

Crustal instability is even more clearly indicated by the rock successions of the coal-bearing measures. These sequences display a repetition of rock types in a more or less regular pattern indicating oscillatory crustal movements; such patterns are called cyclothems. A typical cyclothem might begin with a fireclay or seat earth indicating a terrestrial environment. A coal seam follows – again terrestrial, then the coal passes upwards into dark-coloured shales with a marine fauna showing subsidence had occurred. There follows a succession of shales and sandstones with a freshwater fauna which passes upwards into the next fireclay, completing the cycle of sedimentation. Therefore, Carboniferous times in this part of Ireland were characterized by the onset of a marine transgression, a truly marine phase with abundant limestones, and finally, a time of oscillating sea levels.

Carboniferous sedimentation was halted by strong earth movements of the Hercynian or Armorican Orogeny. The effects of this deformation in the north of Ireland were slight, with minor folding, but with much faulting the effects of which largely determine the present day outcrop pattern of the upper Palaeozoic strata (Wilson, 1972). These faults are also very important in that they acted as controls on directions of mineralization.

(d) Mesozoic rocks

Permo-Triassic strata: Many aspects of the Permo-Triassic strata strongly resemble the much older Old Red Sandstone. Both sequences were produced after orogenic culmination and are brightly coloured sediments. Their successions are mainly sandstones and shales (marls), although the Permian does contain one marine horizon, the Magnesian Limestone. Much of the sedimentation seems to be of a non-marine character, occurring in a terrestrial environment under conditions of high evapotranspiration, e.g. the thick deposits of rock salt owe their origin to such conditions. It is ironic that strata formed under such conditions are nowadays the source of supply of abundant groundwater! Towards the close of Triassic times the sedimentary environment became increasingly humid, shown by the accumulation of the Tea Green Marls, culminating in true marine sedimentation of the Rhaetic beds. The Permo-Triassic varies in thickness and is poorly exposed, but boreholes at Portmore and Longford Lodge reveal thicknesses of 1,200 m and 700 m respectively. The marine nature of the Rhaetic beds is evidenced by abundant marine fossils, fish teeth and concentrated bone beds.

The succeeding Jurassic strata were also deposited in a marine environment. Their dominant rock type is dark blue mudstone, with thin limestone layers, which crops-out around the edge of the Antrim plateau. At their outcrop, sequence thickness rarely exceeds 30 m, but boreholes have proved a greater thickness, e.g. Portmore has 269 m of Lower Lias (Wilson, 1972), and stratigraphic evidence suggests that only lower Jurassic sedimentation occurred in Ireland providing an attenuated succession in comparison to the much thicker sequences of England.

The final sedimentary episode of Mesozoic times again represents marine conditions. Shallow-water, pebbly sandstones – the Hibernian Greensand – indicate a marine transgression and pass quickly upwards into lithified calcareous oozes, or chalk. The chalk is a very pure white limestone of Cretaceous age containing marine fossils of both micro and macroscopic nature. Another interesting characteristic is its mineralogical purity of almost 100% calcium carbonate. The absence of any appreciable amount of other clastic detritus, e.g. sand grains or rock fragments has provoked speculation about the depositional environment of the chalk sea. At the close of Cretaceous times, slight earth movements caused uplift with folding and faulting.

(e) Tertiary times

The start of the Cenozoic saw drastic changes in the geological environment of the north of Ireland. No longer was the area one of marine sedimentation, but now a landmass already quite deeply eroded and destined to be covered by thick lava flows of Eocene age. Volcanism is the keynote of Tertiary times in the north of Ireland with lava fields, dyke swarms, deep-seated granites and explosive volcanic vents – all manifestations of the Britto-Arctic Volcanic Province. Lavas are best seen in County Antrim where two chemically different basalts are widespread. The Lower Basalts are olivine-rich, but the Middle Basalts (Causeway Basalts) are olivine-free tholeiites, a much more even textured rock with the characteristic columnar jointing. Today, a maximum thickness of 800 m of lavas remains, but estimates put the original thickness close to 1,800 m (Wilson, 1972). Eruption was completely subaerial, but not continuous as the red-weathered tops of successive lava flows indicate. There is evidence of one longer interval of quiescence when the Interbasaltic Horizon formed by deep weathering of the Lower Basalts to produce laterites and iron-rich bauxites.

Slieve Gullion and the Mourne Mountains were the major centres of intrusive volcanicity and represent the injection of granitic magmas within the earth's crust, slow cooling leading to formation of granitic rocks. The Mourne Granite is not a simple entity but a complex of five different granites resulting from multiple injection over a long time interval.

The other records of Tertiary volcanism can be found in the dyke swarms of north-east Ireland, the thick sills, e.g. Fair Head, the volcanic plugs of Slemish and Tievebulliagh and the explosive vents of north-east Antrim, e.g. Kenbane Head and Carrick-a-Rede.

The principal sedimentary event of Tertiary times was the deposition of the Lough Neagh Clays. Prior to this the plateau basalts were faulted and warped so that the clays were deposited in a structurally controlled depression – ultimately to become Lough Neagh. The clay is derived from the breakdown of Carboniferous rocks to the west of the Lough plus contributions of clay minerals from other sources. The greatest recorded thickness of the clays is 349 m in the Washing Bay Borehole (Wilson, 1972) where a succession of iron bearing clays (sideritic clays), lignites and sand occur having accumulated in a lacustrine environment.

(f) Quaternary period

In the very recent past, i.e. approximately 2 million years ago, continental ice sheets covered most of Ireland, and depending upon expansion or contraction of the ice sheet, laid down sediments of appropriate character. Deep deposits of ice-moved boulder clay occur, and are covered by or associated with accumulations of sand and gravel – laid down by meltwater. In late- to post-glacial times, climate fluctuated considerably and during some of the warmer interludes conditions were favourable for micro-organisms to flourish in lakes. Such lake deposits in the Bann Valley include extensive accumulations of diatomite, while in cooler wetter times peat growth proceeded.

Rocks as economic resources

Before considering the mineral wealth of Northern Ireland, it is best to define the meaning of mineral deposits. In the present context, the term mineral is applied to any naturally occurring substance of economic importance, irrespective of its chemical (mineralogical) composition or physical appearance; accordingly basalt (an igneous rock) is as important a mineral resource as is rock salt, a chemically discrete entity, i.e. a mineral *sensu stricto*. The wide variation in rock type within Northern Ireland provides excellent potential for mineral resources, and those discussed are only those which have or are being exploited. Most of the factual material for this section was derived from a series of excellent open file reports produced by the Geological Survey of Northern Ireland.

(a) Sand resources

The economic importance of sand is immense. Before discussing the economic geology of sand, it is worth recalling that sand, i.e. the product of natural mechanical breakdown of rocks, is the essential constituent for man-made constructional rocks, i.e. concrete.

Within Northern Ireland, sand resources fall into two categories i.e. consolidated sandstones of varying ages, or unconsolidated sands and gravels of post-glacial or

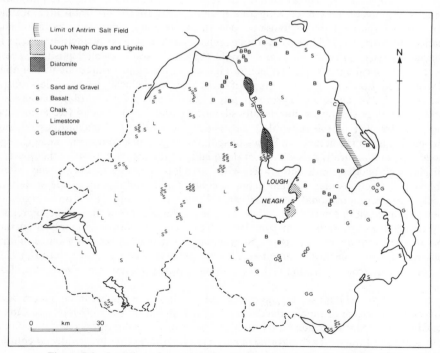

Figure 7.2 Location of quarries of various rock types in Northern Ireland.

recent origin. The economic relevance of the two sources has changed greatly, the days of extensive quarrying of sandstones for building and architectural purpose are past, the emphasis has shifted now to sources of aggregate for modern constructional materials. However, much evidence still remains of the building stone resource in many older public buildings, churches and railway parapets. The sources were either the basal sandstones of the Carboniferous, or Bunter sandstones of Triassic age, both produced beautifully coloured freestones, ideal for stonemasonry.

Aggregates: The prime sources of sandstone for aggregate purposes are in the lower Palaeozoic gritstones of Counties Down and Armagh (Figure 7.2). Here, Silurian greywackes and slates are mined at some 26 localities to produce some 2,676,000 tonnes in 1974 (Cameron, 1977). Both rocks are mined together and separated later. Some of the shales, although useless for wearing aggregate, are capable of bloating to produce light-weight aggregates for special constructional purposes. The gritstones (greywackes) provide the highest quality material for creating coarse aggregates with a very high polished stone value (PSV). However, care has to be taken to ensure no contamination of the grit by basaltic dyke material or slaty mudstone. Indeed, the grit itself is frequently cleaved and necessitates special crushing techniques to ensure good fragment shape. Therefore, it must be appreciated from the geology map (Figure 7.1) that a considerable potential of gritstone sources exists in Northern Ireland.

Unconsolidated sands: The availability of sand and gravel is now a major requirement in most regions of the United Kingdom. Such deposits are the natural source of sand for the construction industry to use in cement, concrete aggregate and general fill and ballast. In Northern Ireland, sand sources relate to three geological environments: (1) glacial deposits, (2) beach sands and gravels, (3) alluvial sources – all deposits of a very recent geological age. As can be seen in Figure 7.2, the major sources lie in Counties Tyrone and Londonderry, the areas of most extensive glacial outwash deposits, a resource which accumulated approximately 13,000 years ago. The geology of the sand and gravel deposits varies, but usually they occur as sheet or mound-like accumulations. Extraction of the mineral is easy since the material is unconsolidated, but depending upon the actual conditions of sedimentation, rock composition can change suddenly, and naturally this will affect the quality of the product. Usually the quarries display well-bedded sands and gravels with varying proportions of silt and clay, while the coarse fractions may contain pebbles, cobbles and boulders of a wide variety of rock types. Compositional variation can be troublesome since high proportions of pebbles of basalt or schist drastically affect the mechanical properties of the aggregate by reducing its strength (Cameron, 1977). However, the most commonly occurring pebbles are vein quartz, quartzite and granite, i.e. "strong" rocks. As a single mining enterprise, sand quarries outnumber all other quarrying activities; Cameron (1977) records 81 quarries operating in 1974 with an annual production of almost 4 million tonnes.

Sand and gravel deposits on the dunes and beaches of Northern Ireland have been an attractive source of supply; the dangers of such exploitation are obvious (see Carter in Chapter 6). Marine beach sand is useless for constructional purposes, but the littoral sands around Lough Neagh have been extracted on a scale that has produced conflict between the fish farmer and sand producer (Common, 1978).

One important aspect of the husbandry of the resource derives from the careful mapping around urban areas by the Geological Survey of Northern Ireland. The maps indicate the areas underlain by sand and gravel and also comments upon their suitability as aggregate sources (Manning, 1972). This approach is basic to planning and development in that building development should be directed away from sites of mineral potential.

Special purpose sands: Frequently sand is required for specialized technical purposes, e.g. glass making and the construction of foundry moulds. The chemical composition and physical texture of such sands is critical to their usefulness, and resources are usually of a limited character. Glass sands need to be exceptionally pure with a low percentage of iron oxide, and also well size sorted; such sands occur near Cookstown at Kildress (Cameron, 1969) in strata of Lower Carboniferous age. The useful sands occur in two units 12 m and 7.5 m in thickness, but exploitation is prevented by the depth of overburden and unfavourable groundwater conditions. Robbie (1950) described high quality glass sands from the Marble Arch area of County Fermanagh, but again the deposits were very localized and not economic to mine. Strata of Carboniferous age at Ballycastle also yielded sandstones of glass making quality, and at the same locality dune sands proved equally useful.

The casting of metals requires sand for mould preparation. The principal requirements are that the sand is clean, well-sorted but none-the-less contains a small amount of clay which acts as a natural bond to prevent collapse of the mould when the pattern is withdrawn. Also, the sand obviously must be of a refractory grade and permeable to permit exit of hot gases. In Northern Ireland, all such sands are found in superficial deposits i.e., either dune, beach or fluvioglacial environments (Old, 1972), and are mined to meet local requirements only.

(b) Limestone resources

Limestones are worked from strata which range in age from Pre-Cambrian and Carboniferous to Creteaceous for use as aggregate, agricultural purposes and cement manufacture. Cameron (1977) recorded 38 working limestone quarries with the greatest proportion of mining carried out in Lower Carboniferous strata. Chalk has been quarried in a haphazard fashion along most of its outcrop to provide either lime or crushed rock for soil treatment, while recently, crushed chalk has become important as a special white architectural finish. In 1974 limestone extraction totalled about 1,824,000 tonnes (Cameron, 1977).

(c) Basalts and other igneous rocks

Tertiary basaltic lavas provide a rich source of stone for aggregate and ballast purposes being mined mainly in County Antrim and parts of County Londonderry. In 1974, 60 quarries worked basalts or basaltic rocks with a yield of 8,173,000 tonnes (Cameron, 1977). However, although present in vast quantities not all basalt is suitable for economic purposes in that texture and wearing qualities are extremely variable, and this necessitates careful re-selection of materials. Most of the lava flows have vesicular tops and bottoms, some are laterized and deeply weathered, and such physical conditions render the rock unsuitable for engineering purposes. The best quality basalt is quarried in north Antrim from the Middle Basalts. These homogenous flows have fine, even-grained textures, few vesicles and a fresh appearance. However, even this rock does not provide a perfect aggregate because certain flows are closely jointed and this in turn affects crushed fragment shape (too bladed) making it unsuitable for creating coarse aggregates of motorway standard.

Other sources of igneous rocks also provide aggregate and ornamental stone. High quality aggregate is provided by the thick dolerite dykes of County Fermanagh, while small-scale quarrying in the Mournes produces granite for ornamental purposes.

(c) Clay resources

The north of Ireland is rich in different kinds of clay deposit. They include clays which result from direct sedimentation processes, e.g. Lough Neagh Clays, i.e. weathered and transported clay minerals, or *in situ* weathering of Tertiary basalts, e.g. the bauxites and laterites of County Antrim. Also, brick-making clays are produced by the mechanical crushing of Carboniferous shales and mudstones, e.g. the Coalisland brick industry.

Brick clays: Such clays have been worked in several parts of Northern Ireland from Carboniferous rocks to post-glacial sediments. The chemical composition of the clay determines its economic processing, e.g. high quartz clays usually provide refractory material – fire bricks – while the more aluminous clays are used for manufacturing house or building bricks. Fire bricks are made from quartz-rich seat earth deposits in the Carboniferous, e.g. the Magpie Clay at Coalisland (Fowler, *et al.*, 1961), but house bricks are made from clays of quite diverse geological age. The Carboniferous shales of Coalisland, when crushed, produce good quality clay (Fowler, *et al.*, 1961), and in the Belfast area, Keuper Marls of Triassic age were extensively dug for brick clays. However, with the passage of time much of the evidence of former Keuper excavation has vanished, pits having been back-filled or built over, and recently only one working pit remained at Collin Glen (Manning *et al.*, 1970). The great value of clays of post-glacial age is evidenced by the long activity and late closure of the Lagan Vale Brick Co. in 1958.

Pipe and ceramic clays: Clays suitable for the production of earthenware pipes occur near Coalisland in the Lough Neagh Clay formation. These are known as ball clays and are capable of rough glazing and are used mainly for sanitary piping. Ball clay deposits may also be present to the south of Lough Neagh but their economic potential is doubtful owing to a thick cover of glacial drift (Bazley, 1976).

Bloating Clays: Another important resource is shale and clay which expands, or bloats when heated. Such clays expand and emit gas, which imparts lightness to the aggregate, and become sealed with a glassy coating. The main sources of such shales have been discussed by Arthurs *et al.* (1974) who list 14 localities which display excellent bloating characteristics, the majority of which occur in the Lower Palaeozoic mudstones of County Down and are derived from gritstone quarries.

Diatomite: Deposits of diatomite clay occur along the Bann Valley from Lough Neagh northwards to Ballymoney. They are approximately 1-2 m thick and have been extensively worked by a small private company in the Toomebridge area for several years. Industrially, diatomite is important as a general purpose filler and as insulation material (Old, 1971).

Bauxites and bauxitic clays: Laterite is a natural weathering product of basaltic lavas, and if climatic conditions permit, can be further chemically differentiated to form bauxite (Eyles, 1952). Bauxite, an ore of aluminium is developed usually above the bauxite clay or lithomarge of the Interbasaltic Horizon and is associated with lignite accumulations. The bauxite ore occurs as a thin layer, approximately 1 m in thickness with aluminium oxide content of about 40%, i.e. sufficiently rich to justify mining as an aluminium source during the Second World War (Turner, 1969). However, two varieties of bauxite occur – a red ferruginous rock containing up to 30% iron oxide, and a paler, grey-coloured bauxite with up to 40% silica, mined formerly to produce alum (Turner, *op. cit.*). Reserves of the ore are vast, but away from the coastal sites of County Antrim a basaltic cover of as much as 760 m obviously precludes extraction. Since 1980, bauxite has been used as a filter to remove phosphate in tertiary sewage treatment in Northern Ireland.

(d) Carbonaceous deposits

Carbonaceous minerals were obtained from 3 stratigraphic horizons; (1) Coal beds in Carboniferous strata, (2) Lignites associated with weathered horizons in the Tertiary basalts, (3) thick, lignite interbeds within the Lough Neagh Clays. Both coal and lignite represent the coalification of vegetable matter with a progressive decrease in the percentage of volatiles towards the coal end of the spectrum.

Carboniferous coals: Coal was worked from about 1672 in the Coalisland area of County Tyrone (Fowler *et al.,* 1961) from strata of Millstone Grit and Coal Measure age. Eight coal seams are present, but only the Main Coal which varies in thickness from 2.8-3.5 m is a real economic proposition, and stratigraphic thinning, seam splitting and faulting all render large scale extraction difficult. Recently in response to the energy crisis, interest in the potential of the coalfield was revived with a drilling programme carried out in 1978, to prove reserves and also the quality of the coal (see Newbould, Chapter 11).

The only other coalfield of note within Northern Ireland occurs in a faulted, synclinal structure at Ballycastle in north Antrim. Two seams, the Main Coal and the Hawk's Nest, provided the bulk of the coal, but due to intensive mining both are now worked out, and only reserves of poor quality coal remain below the Fair Head Sill (Wilson, 1972).

Lignite: Lignites, or lignitic coals, are associated with the Interbasaltic Horizon and Lough Neagh Clays. A comprehensive survey of lignite resources was carried out by Bazley (1976) in the area east of Lough Neagh; reserves are estimated at about 20 million tonnes, but again adverse geology, of thick overburden and high water tables discourage mining. However, a recent proposal to opencast mine lignite for power station fuel is being considered by the Government. There are two seams of lignite with differing calorific values, and seam thicknesses of up to 22 m are known. Interbasaltic lignites are much thinner and so have been exploited on a local basis only and cannot be regarded as a potential economic resource.

(e) Iron ore

Iron-rich sediments can be found in rocks of almost any geological age, but the main source of iron minerals has been the Interbasaltic Horizon of the basalts, with some 5 million tons of ore extracted over a 70 year period (Wilson, 1972). Also, in the Ballycastle area, blackband ironstones occur in the Carboniferous rocks and were exported to Scotland (Wilson, 1966).

(f) Natural salts

Massive accumulations of natural salts occur in Triassic strata between Carrickfergus and Larne (Wilson, 1974). The main salt, halite or rock salt, is interbedded with red Triassic mudstones, and the total thickness of salt in the Larne borehole is approximately 500 m.

Oil and gas potential

Up to the present, little attention has been focussed on the oil and gas potential of Northern Ireland. However, recently it was decided to begin drilling offshore close to Rathlin Island, where natural gas is the main prospect (see Newbould, Chapter 11). The geology of Northern Ireland is such that potential oil and gas producing strata exist at depth, and it is hoped that suitable geologic structures may be discovered which permit the entrapment of these resources.

The production of hydrocarbons requires abundant organic activity at the time of sedimentation of the rocks, and in lower Carboniferous times dark-coloured limestones, bituminous in places, with a distinctive oily smell occur quite abundantly. Higher up in the rock sequence the presence of coal seams again indicates an abundant production of hydrocarbons; and again in the lower Jurassic strata, suitable organic-rich black shales occur.

Production of oil and gas is obviously an essential part of the process, but equally important is the presence of suitable reservoir rocks to permit accumulation of the resource. Such rocks have to be permeable to the flow of fluids and gases and require quite a large amount of pore space between the mineral grains which comprise the rock; many suitable reservoir rocks occur in the abundant sandstones of the Carboniferous, and especially so in the Permo-Triassic sequence. The third requirement of an oil or gas field is also fulfilled, namely that impermeable strata are present to cap and prevent leakage of the oil or gas upwards. Many thick beds of shale and mudstone occur, also very thick deposits of rock salt in the Triassic, all of which – if bed attitudes are suitable, would act as good cap or trapping layers and assist in the formation of oil and gas fields.

A further hopeful sign of the oil and gas potential of Northern Ireland is seen in the results of deep boreholes drilled during the last twenty years. The deep bores at Magilligan, Portmore and Ahoghill all reveal exceptionally thick sequences of Permo-Triassic rocks, in some cases floored by deposits of Carboniferous age, i.e. successions of rocks which are potential hydrocarbon sources and reservoirs. To date the only actual gas yields were recorded in a deep borehole drilled by the Marathon Petroleum Co. Ltd., near Derrygonnelly, County Fermanagh. However, the gas potential of the Irish Sea received a further boost by the discovery of offshore gas reserves in Morecambe Bay. Indeed, the prospects of hydrocarbon production in Northern Ireland are very favourable, especially when the extent of potential producing strata is appreciated, and also the strong possibility of discovering more Mesozoic sedimentary basins in our shallow seas.

Rocks as a water resource

Not only are rocks valuable as mineral sources, but they also act as reservoirs and conduits for groundwater. Indeed, in the context of Northern Ireland, groundwater resources are critical for planning and development in many areas, since the surficial storage capacity – with the exception of Lough Neagh – is very low. The ability of a rock to allow water to permeate and then flow within it depends upon the physical properties of porosity and permeability. Porosity is the volume of pore space available, while the ease of water flow through a stratum is permeability, and is itself a function of void space, degree of cementation and intensity of fracture systems. When strata are both porous and permeable, they assume the status of potential aquifers. Manning (1971, 1972) produced a comprehensive report on the groundwater resources of Northern Ireland, and his work forms the basis for the following discussion.

Consolidated rocks and groundwater potential

Strata of Pre-Cambrian and Lower Palaeozoic age are usually poor aquifers. This results from the degree of compaction, cementation and recrystallization the rocks have undergone, e.g. the metamorphic sequences are almost impermeable, with water derived only from shallow wells in the weathered zone, and the same poor yielding capacity is true for the older igneous rock in Northern Ireland. The Devonian rocks are poor aquifers also, since they are very well indurated; they supply only private requirements, e.g. creameries or farms. The greatest water bearing capacity of the older rocks is found in the Lower Carboniferous succession. The basal clastics, i.e. sands and conglomerates, have been little investigated, and the main aquifers are limestones. It is interesting to note that the limestones possess a low porosity, but because they are closely jointed they are very permeable. Numerous wells in Tyrone and Armagh draw upon this water source (Manning, 1971); yields are quite good, e.g. the Cabragh borehole produces 109 m³/hour.

Permo-Triassic rocks

The Permian succession is mainly impervious in character and forms a good water seal to the overlying Bunter Sandstone of Triassic age. The Bunter Sandstones are red and brown in colour with well-developed joint systems and form an excellent aquifer especially in the Lagan Valley, Belfast-Newtownards area with wells yielding up to 13 m³/hour. Bunter Sandstones in the Limavady area have produced flows of up to 38-53 m³/hour (Benfield and Price, 1971). It is interesting to note how local variations in geology affect water bearing potential of such a good aquifer as the Bunter Sandstone. In the Belfast area the presence of igneous dykes or minor changes in lithology produce drastic reductions in flow rates, e.g. 5 deep wells in close proximity to a dyke yielded only 8 m³/hour, but a new deep well sited away from the dyke produced flows of 87 m³/hour; it is estimated that dykes reduce flows to a level of 20% potential yield and demonstrate clearly the need for careful geologic investigation prior to well siting.

Jurassic rocks

These strata have little water bearing capacity but form an important impervious seal to the overlying Cretaceous Chalk, and herein lie most of the engineering problems created along the Antrim coast road and in parts of Belfast.

Cretaceous rocks

The Hibernian Greensand and Chalk display low porosity of 2-5%, but large volumes of water are transmitted through joints and faults, so that the formation produces copious spring sources e.g. at Ballycastle, Carrickfergus and Belfast.

Tertiary rocks

The basalts are, in general, poor bearers of water. Water may be obtained from the slaggy tops of lava flows or from intensely fissured horizons, but in general terms the basalts are regarded as potentially poor water sources. The Lough Neagh Clays are far too impervious for water movement, and so contribute nothing to groundwater supply.

Quaternary unconsolidated deposits

Glacial drifts and recent valley fillings provide very rich groundwater sources in Northern Ireland. The glacial deposits are usually of two types (1) unstratified boulder clays and (2) current-sorted accumulations of sand and gravel. The boulder clays yield little water, but act as a good upper seal for bedrock aquifers. On the other hand the sand and gravel deposits, especially some river gravels are profuse sources of groundwater. To date 12 detailed surveys have been made of glacial and alluvial gravels, e.g. the Enler Gravels of County Down, and the Braid gravels between Ballymena and Broughshane, the latter being of great importance since industrial developments in the area require daily supplies in excess of $11,360 m^3$ (3 million gallons).

Therefore, it is clear that rocks are important contributors to water supply in Northern Ireland. Far too little is still known about groundwater movements, but the setting up of gauging sites (Wilcock, Chapter 2) to monitor precipitation, percolation and evaporation will improve our understanding of the problems.

Environmental impact of the mineral industry

In Northern Ireland little detailed assessment has been made of the effects of mineral extraction upon the quality of the environment. Wallwork (1973) discussed dereliction attendant upon mine abandonment, and concluded that there was little cause for concern regarding sand and gravel mining, but hard rock quarrying presented different problems. Common (1978) also cites examples of sand pit abandonment and dereliction, and raises the question as to the level of prior investigation of the mineral resources before quarrying begins. However, in the case of unconsolidated rock deposits few environmental problems should arise, since regrading the land surface and backfilling worked out pits is not difficult, and restored land can be returned to an appropriate usage. A far greater problem derives from the reluctance of quarry owners to remove derelict plant, and the persistence of this in turn encourages local dwellers to contribute further additions of domestic waste, unwanted furniture, car bodies and indestructable polythene objects. It is quite understandable why such indiscriminate dumping occurs in rural areas, but the opportunity to do so would be removed if legislation required backfilling of sand quarries when mining ceased.

Hard rock quarries present a different problem. Usually they persist for longer time intervals as working concerns, and greater volumes of rock are removed. When such quarries are abandoned they could well become legitimate dumping sites for all manner of wastes, provided bed rock is fairly impermeable, and also if local groundwater conditions are known. If a careful record is kept of the nature of the waste fill (which should be kept as uniform as possible) there is no reason why such areas could not be redeveloped after a relatively short time span.

In many parts of the United Kingdom the principal impact of quarrying is to produce obvious scars in the countryside. In Northern Ireland, topography usually prevents this happening. Large areas of County Antrim, and parts of County Londonderry constitute plateau land, where rock extraction is only possible by "sinking" quarries. Genuine outcrop quarrying is confined to some river valleys, or to the coastal outcrop of basalt and chalk; in the coastal setting, chalk quarrying has frequently enhanced the scenic vista. The sinking of quarries inland means that the excavation is hidden, and indeed in many cases quarry presence is detected mainly by noise, dust and cracked road surfaces, rather than by topographic scars and huge spoil heaps.

Other aspects of mineral extraction have produced little effect on the environment. The quantities extracted were usually small, and in many cases mining ceased a long time ago. Around the rim of the Antrim plateau and in the coalfield areas, grassed-over mounds of former spoil heaps remain, but are insignificant to the mountainous deposits in other parts of the United Kingdom.

Conclusions

The principal aim of this chapter has been to describe the geology of the exploited mineral wealth of Northern Ireland. However, it could be misleading to suggest that no other mineral resources exist, since numerous records of minor occurrences of base metals occur, whilst the recent comprehensive geochemical survey of the Sperrin Mountains produced encouraging results (Arthurs, 1976). The geochemical analysis of stream waters and subsequent computer mapping of the results indicates many high anomalies of a wide range of metallic elements, with copper, lead and zinc particularly prominent.

The geological evolution of Northern Ireland produced rock successions which are rich in natural mineral reources. As stated above the resources range from vast accumulations of sand and gravel, ore deposits of various kinds to natural underground freshwater reservoirs. Already much economic usage has been made of these resources, but in the present economic climate their relevance is diminished. Perhaps the most exciting aspects of the geological heritage are yet to unfold. If, as seems highly likely, reserves of natural gas are discovered then a short-term alleviation of our energy problems is possible. Nonetheless it is reassuring to remember the range and abundance of mineral resources which Northern Ireland possesses, and that from time to time as the economic climate dictates they may be utilised.

REFERENCES

Arthurs, J. W., Mitchell, W. I. and Spence, R., 1973. Preliminary investigation into sources of expandable shale in Northern Ireland. *Geological Survey of Northern Ireland, Open File Report,* No. 39.

Arthurs, J. W., 1976. Mineral potential survey. Sperrin Mountains Area. *Geological Survey of Northern Ireland.*

Benfield, A. C., and Price, D., 1971. Groundwater investigation at Bolea, County Londonderry. *Institute of Geological Science Hydrogeological Department,* Interim Report WD/72/2.

Bazley, R. A. B., 1976. The Tertiary and Quaternary sediments of Lough Neagh – a consideration of the economic potential of the clays, lignites and ironstones. *Geological Survey of Northern Ireland.* Open File Report No. 55.

Cameron, I. B., 1969. The glass sand at Kildress, Cookstown. *Geological Survey of Northern Ireland.* Open File Report No. 18.

Cameron, I. B., 1977. Sources of aggregate in Northern Ireland. *I.G.S. Geological Survey of Northern Ireland.* Report 77/1.

Common, R., 1978. Sand and gravel in Northern Ireland. *Yearbook of the Royal Society of Ulster Architects.*

Eyles, V. A., 1952. The composition and origin of the Antrim Laterites. *Government of Northern Ireland. Memoir of the Geological Survey.*

Fowler, A. and Robbie, J. A., 1961. Geology of the country around Dungannon. *Government of Northern Ireland, Memoir of the Geological Survey 2nd Edition.*

Manning, P. I., Robbie, J. A. and Wilson, H. E., 1970. Geology of Belfast and the Lagan Valley. *Government of Northern Ireland. Memoir of the Geological Survey.*

Manning, P. I., 1971. The development of the water resources of Northern Ireland; progress towards integration. *Quarterly Journal of Engineering Geology,* Vol. 4, 335–352.

Manning, P. I., 1972. The development of groundwater resources of Northern Ireland. *Geological Survey of Northern Ireland.* Association Session Report.

Old, R. A., 1971. Notes on Diatomite. *Geological Survey of Northern Ireland.* Open File Report No. 52.

Old, R. A., 1972. The use and resources of moulding sand in Northern Ireland. *I.G.S. Geological Survey of Northern Ireland.* Report No. 72/8.

Robbie, J. A., 1950. High-grade silica sand near Marble Arch, County Fermanagh. *Geological Survey of Northern Ireland.* Open File Report No. 51.

Turner, D. C., 1969. Bauxite and bauxitic clay in Northern Ireland. *Geological Survey of Northern Ireland.* Open File Report, No. 40.

Wallwork, K. L., 1973. Mining, quarrying and derelict land: an aspect of land use in Northern Ireland. *Irish Geography,* VI, No. 5. 570–578.

Wilson, H. E. and Robbie, J. A., 1966. Geology of the country round Ballycastle. *Government of Northern Ireland. Memoir of Geological Survey.*

Wilson, H. E., 1972. Regional Geology of Northern Ireland. *Geological Survey of Northern Ireland.*

Wilson, H. E., 1974. The south Antrim saltfield. *Geological Survey of Northern Ireland.* Open File Report No. 48.

CHAPTER VIII

Soil

JAMES G. CRUICKSHANK
Senior Lecturer in Geography,
The Queen's University of Belfast

Introduction

Soil is difficult to evaluate as a natural resource, mainly because its resource value for agriculture, or for forestry, is qualified by an interaction with other environmental factors, such as climate and topography, as well as by the way the soil is used and managed by man. This problem exists wherever soil is considered as a medium for plant growth, which is the approach adopted here, and its resolution involves regarding soil as part of 'site', recognising all the properties of the land surface itself as well as those of the atmosphere above and the soil below – that is, all the variables that might affect and limit the growth of plants, recognising that some of these physical conditions can be changed or modified by man. Soil is only one of this complex of interconnected 'site' factors, and only an attempt can be made in this chapter to assess the value of soil as a resource being used for agriculture and forestry in Northern Ireland.

Evaluation of soil as a resource demands a context of place and time, in this case Northern Ireland in the 1980s. Resource value can only be understood in the framework of certain socio-economic conditions and a stage in technological development of a society, including techniques by which man can and has altered the character of the natural resource. This applies particularly to soil, as the management techniques of drainage, cultivation and fertilization, can change some features of soil over time. In a few important cases, man-made changes to soil can be long lasting and nearly permanent, notably in the example of soil drainage. Soil also evolves naturally, meaning that its relationship with the rest of the natural environment is also a dynamic one. The natural condition and stage of development of a soil should be recognised, but its value as a medium for plant growth must be assessed within the total physical and non-physical environment in which it exists. Its value is not absolute, but relative and continuously changing.

It is possible to adopt an entirely different view of this resource by considering soil, such as in the form of a peat or a sand/mineral deposit, as a material. Water-laid deposits of clay, sand, gravel, or organo-mineral deposits of diatomite (Plate 8.1), or peat as an organic growth system, can all be regarded as soil because they can support plant growth. They may or may not have developed soil profiles depending on their

Plate 8.1 Cultivated diatomite (see Chapter 7) in fields at Toomebridge, on the River Lower Bann. Diatomite is an unusual soil, which behaves as a loamy, slightly acid soil, suitable for potatoes.

age and local conditions, but they are all soil materials and are widely exploited in Northern Ireland for brick-making, road-building materials, insulation products, and as a source of domestic fuel. Some of these kinds of exploitation of soil materials as natural resources will be examined in other chapters, but it is not the approach followed here.

Soil formation

Soil is a three-dimensional medium, a cover of unconsolidated mineral and organic materials that makes-up most of the land surface. It is highly variable in thickness and internal character, a variability which reflects local conditions of formation and re-organisation within the soil body. Because of its complex internal character and dimensions, the soil cover is normally sampled or examined by taking a vertical section, called a soil profile or soil pedon, through all its layers. In such a unit of study of manageable size, the internal layers or "soil horizons" can be examined, measured and sampled for subsequent analysis. These soil horizons are not depositional, but have been formed by the re-organisation and re-arrangement of mineral and organic materials. The formation of soil takes place in two stages, certain "primary" processes like the weathering of minerals and the decay of organic litter producing the fine mineral and organic products, which are then re-arranged by "secondary" processes involving sorting transfers by soil solutions. This sorting creates distinctive horizons within the soil.

In Northern Ireland, soil formation was interrupted by the Pleistocene glaciations so that the current cycle of soil profile formation, or pedogenesis, dates from approximately the start of the post-glacial period, about 10,000 years ago. However, our soils have formed in mineral material, much of which was physically and chemically altered much earlier, during inter- and pre-glacial phases of weathering. The time scale of the primary process of weathering to produce the mineral matrix of soil, stretches far back in time into the Tertiary geological period, long before the Pleistocene glaciations. These glaciations re-worked the weathered material by ice action into glacial till, or boulder clay, and meltwater re-deposited some of it in sand and gravel formations. Organic decay, or humification, operates on a much shorter time scale of a few years, unless the process is inhibited by wet local conditions causing the accumulation of organic deposits, such as peat.

It is not necessary in this review to investigate the environmental conditions of pre- and inter-glacial phases that have controlled the early stages of weathering, as in this chapter, the assessment is concerned with the products of weathering as found *now* in Northern Ireland soils. Even in the post-glacial period, precision is not necessary in trying to establish the environmental conditions controlling the secondary processes of pedogenesis. At the best, only an indirect impression could be attained by interpretation of pollen evidence and the reconstruction of past vegetation. From the accepted ideas about vegetation history based on pollen records, it is known that the north of Ireland has had a mild, humid climate, conducive to soil processes like gleying and leaching for most of the last 10,000 years. Notable have been periods such as the Atlantic starting about 7,000 B.P., and Sub-Atlantic c. 2,500 B.P. (Smith *et al.,* 1971) when the climate is thought to have become wetter than before, and when soil leaching leading to acidification in freely draining soils was markedly accelerated. These phases changed the rate of processes currently and continuously affecting soil formation in the north of Ireland, rather than being new or different processes. It can be said that our local soils are developed in weathered mineral material, identified now in the form of glacial drift, that has been inherited from possibly over a million years of slow rates of physical and chemical weathering. Subsequently, soil profiles have been formed in this weathered material, by processes such as gleying and leaching, operating at variable rates over the past few thousand years (Cruickshank and Cruickshank, 1981). The soil landscape of Northern Ireland is a mosaic of soil materials and soil profiles of different ages, representing different stages in essentially the same soil-forming processes.

The wetness of climate, in particular the fact that precipitation exceeds evapotranspiration in almost every month of the year everywhere in Northern Ireland (exceptions being found only in the central and eastern lowlands from May to July), means that the excess of moisture from the atmosphere enters freely draining soil and passes vertically downwards as a "leaching" soil solution, known as the "leachate". This is a weak, organic acid, and at freely draining sites, has the effect of leaching or removing certain chemical and bio-chemical compounds from the surface horizons into subsoil horizons, or even out of the soil system altogether. Under more alkaline conditions on lime-rich materials, leaching can take only a physical form and results in the movement of fine clay particles into lower soil horizons in profiles called grey-brown podsolics, but usually it involves chemical changes resulting in increasing acidity in the surface horizons. Leached, freely draining soils include the sequence from brown earths, acid brown earths, to brown podsolics as transitional soils, and ultimately to the most

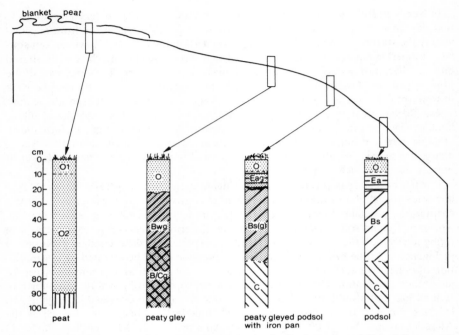

Figure 8.1a The probable altitudinal sequence of upland soils, from about 150 m O.D. up to the edge of blanket peat, at 300 m O.D. in the east and 200 m O.D. in the west.
O=organic horizon
E=eluviated, leached horizon, which is acid *(a)*.
B=middle horizon with deposition of sesquioxides (s), or with signs of gleying (g).
C=soil parent material

leached, extremely acid podsols. If freely draining site conditions were found every-where in Northern Ireland, leached soil profiles would also be found everywhere. The fact that only about 45% of soils are leached is because the majority of our soils are imperfectly or poorly drained, preventing the free movement of soil solutions required for leaching. It is estimated that approximately 54-55% of our soils are imperfectly drained, possibly 40% gleyed mineral soils and 13-14% peat (and up to 18% if all peaty soils are included).

Soil groups or soil associations

The main soil profile types found in Northern Ireland are illustrated and described in Figure 8.1a and 8.1b. The distribution of these soil profile types is shown in Figure 8.2 (Map of Northern Ireland soils), and it can be seen that the distribution is complicated by the occurrence of organic soils or peat, and by a geological influence involving the grouping of soil profile types by soil parent materials associated with particular rocks. The full range of soil profile types does not necessarily appear on each rock formation, as these in turn exert an influence on soil profile development. The

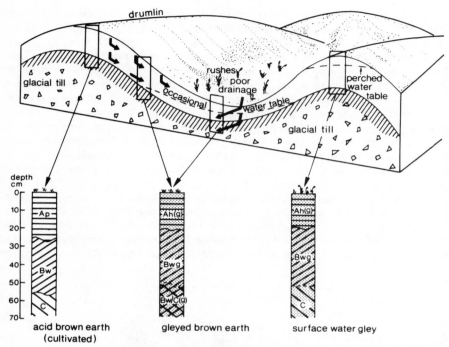

Figure 8.1b The probable slope sequence of soils on a lowland drumlin, indicating gleying (g) in soils of lower positions.
A=surface soil horizon with humus (h) or gleying (g), or both.
B=middle horizon with weathering (w) dominant, and little deposition from leaching.
C=soil parent material
Cultivated or ploughed soils have a surface Ap horizon.

geological grouping of soils, sometimes known as 'soil associations', allows a systematic description of soils to be given. Each main rock formation will be considered, and in a way, this approach also divides the soils into regional or geographical arrangements. The approximate areas and percentage areas for each unit are shown in Table 8.1.

Basalt

Tertiary basalt lavas cover 4,009 sq. km (1,548 sq. miles) and comprise almost one-third (30%) of the landscape of Northern Ireland. They form the most extensive soil parent material in the region, and represent the largest continuous unit of basic igneous rock in the British Isles. Where they occur elsewhere, such as in Mull or Skye in the west of Scotland, the derived soils are of less agricultural significance because of elevation, exposure or peat cover. In Northern Ireland, basalt does extend over a wide altitudinal range from sea level to over 500 m O.D., but more than three-quarters of the area of basalt soil is within the agriculturally improved land below 300 m O.D. Basalt landscapes occur mostly in County Antrim, except for its north-east corner, but also extend short distances westward and south-westward into neighbouring counties. The 'basalt soils' are most commonly developed on clay-rich glacial till, and are usually gleys or gleyed brown earths of medium to high base status. As such, they are very fertile soils, highly suitable for grassland farming, especially in the north, central and southern parts of County Antrim (McAllister and McConaghy, 1968).

The basalt soils in Northern Ireland can be subdivided into three types, which also have a distinct geographical separation. About one quarter of the basalt area lies above 300 m O.D. in the uplands of east and west Antrim, and here the soils are peaty gleys or peat. These soils have only limited agricultural value for hill sheep or cattle, but many of the State forests are to be found here. About half the basalt area supports mineral gleys on clay-rich till on middle and lower slopes in County Antrim, and the remaining quarter has a mixture of slightly gleyed and freely draining brown earths on sand deposits or loamy till around towns such as Coleraine, Kilrea, Ballymena, Antrim and Lurgan. This last group of soils has the widest range of use and the highest potential productivity of the basalt soils.

Although highly valued for grassland-cattle farming, basalt soils have some distinctive properties which are not always advantages for agricultural usage. They are usually first identified by a characteristic chocolate-brown colour, with gleying expressed by ferric orange and purple-brown mottling. Soil structure is usually strongly and clearly developed on drying-out, in crumb or blocky peds. Chemically, basalt soils are

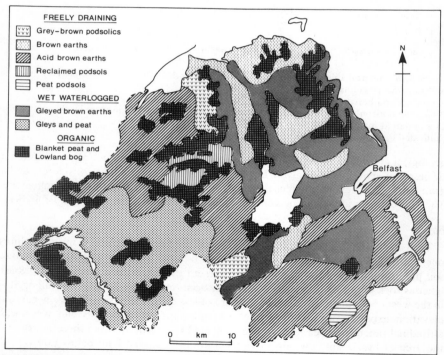

Figure 8.2 Simplified soil map of Northern Ireland.
Gleyed or waterlogged soils predominate in the west and in the uplands of the north-east. Well-drained soils predominate in County Londonderry and in County Down.

known for large and normally base-saturated cation exchange capacities (McAleese and McConaghy, 1957 and 1958). They tend to be rich in exchangeable calcium and magnesium, and also in oxides of iron and aluminium, weathered from ferro-magnesian minerals. This iron-aluminium complex is responsible for fixing, and making unavailable to plants, both natural and applied phosphate; in other circumstances, it may contribute to cementing of subsoil horizons where leaching has taken place. Liming is often necessary to increase the availability of phosphate, rather than to compensate for excessive leaching and acidification.

TABLE 8.1

Northern Ireland soils arranged by rock type parent materials

Soil parent rock	Soil profile type	Approx. area hectares	% area of N.I.	
BASALT	Peat and peaty soils over 300 m O.D.	100,000	7.4	
	Gleys on middle slopes	180,000	13.3	30.3
	Brown earths and some gleys on loam till	130,000	9.6	
MICA-SCHIST	Peat and peaty gleys	90,000	6.6	
	Acid brown earths and brown podsolics	110,000	8.0	17.6
	Podsols and peat podsols on gravel in County Tyrone	40,000	3.0	
CARBONIFEROUS LIMESTONE	Gleys and peat gleys of Fermanagh and Tyrone	170,000	12.6	
	Grey-brown podsolics in Armagh and Londonderry	20,000	1.5	14.1
SILURIAN SHALE AND GREYWACKE	Gleys and acid brown earths on drumlins	140,000	10.4	
	Acid brown earths and gleys on sloping ground	160,000	11.8	26.0
	Acid brown earths in east coastal County Down	50,000	3.8	
GRANITES AND TRIASSIC SANDSTONE	Acid brown earths and brown podsolics	140,000	10.4	
OLD RED SANDSTONE	Gleys and gleyed acid brown earths in Counties Tyrone-Fermanagh	20,000	1.5	

Shale and Greywacke

The second most common soil parent material in Northern Ireland is that derived from rocks of the ancient Lower Palaeozoic, namely the Ordovician and Silurian systems, found mainly in County Down and County Armagh. These are greywackes, shales and slate rocks, comprising about 25-26% of the total land area, and which are weathered to produce predominantly loam and silt-loam textured soil material. The soil profiles developed are spatially inter-mixed because they are mainly associated with variable local topography of the drumlin landscape (Figure 8.1*b*) in the south-east. About half the shale-greywacke derived soils are gleys and gleyed acid brown earths of the drumlins, while the other half is mostly composed of acid brown earths, with some leaching on steeper slopes and sandy textures in east or west-central County

Down. These soils are not of high base status, and do not have large reserves of exchangeable cations. Consequently, they become acid where sandy textures and site conditions allow leaching. Generous liming and the application of manures and fertilizers are necessary to maintain fertility on the shale-greywacke soils; the high level of farm management in this part of Northern Ireland guarantees that this is found almost everywhere. There is little need usually for artificial drainage on these loamy and sandy soils (Cruickshank, 1975).

Mica-schist

Ancient and much altered sediments of Pre-Cambrian times, the foundation of the geological sequence in the local area, are found in the mica-schists of the Sperrins, in Counties Londonderry and Tyrone, and in north-east Antrim. If the fluvio-glacial sand deposits of County Tyrone are included, these metamorphosed sediments provide parent material for about 18% of the soils in Northern Ireland. These are found mainly in the west or north-west, and at higher elevation between 100 and 600 m O.D. in the Sperrin Mountains and their outliers. Climatic extremes of high rainfall and cool temperature regimes, combined with coarse sandy textures, encourage leaching and acidification. Approximately half the schist soils are peaty gleys or peat, due to site wetness in locations above 200 m O.D. The rest are leached to some degree, either as brown podsolics or acid brown earths in the Sperrin valleys (Plate 8.2), or as podsols on the schist-derived sand and gravel deposits around Pomeroy in County Tyrone.

The schist soils are sandy in texture and naturally acid. With leaching, they can become extremely acid, and almost all such soils require frequent and heavy liming. Sandy textures do not always ensure free drainage, because these soils often suffer from compacted, cemented subsoil horizons which contribute to surface water gleying. The soils are deficient in iron and potash, but respond remarkably after potash application. Farm size tends to be small in the Sperrins and management poor, after years of declining returns (Cruickshank, 1978). Net farm incomes are derived almost entirely from grants and subsidies in the hill areas, but well-managed profitable farms can be found in lowland areas like the Roe valley in County Londonderry. With high levels of fertilizer inputs, schistose soils can be productive and versatile, and for example, have always enjoyed a reputation as good potato soils in the lowlands.

Carboniferous Limestone

In County Fermanagh, and parts of County Tyrone and County Armagh, sedimentary series of the Carboniferous provide parent materials for a variety of soil types, covering about 14-15% of the land area of Northern Ireland. The rocks are calcareous sediments, limestones, shales and sandstones, mainly from the Middle and Lower Carboniferous. Most of the soils are gleyed to some degree, and in certain areas like the lowlands around Upper Lough Erne in County Fermanagh, the tenacious clay loam till of the 'Calp' series is very strongly gleyed (Cruickshank, 1961). Such soils may be base-rich and chemically fertile, but their physical properties adversely affect their agricultural potential. In extreme cases, where clay content is over 40% and is combined with a high silt content, it can be very difficult to make any artificial drainage effective. Mole drains are often found, but usually stone-filled ditches at close spacing are necessary to improve soil drainage and the problems of management mean that the agricultural value of these soils is low. Adams, Jack and Dickson (1970) have also

Plate 8.2 19th century cultivation or lazy beds in the Sperrins, County Tyrone, which have been abandoned for about eighty years and on which peat is forming again.

reported severe problems with the growth of Sitka spruce trees on some of these soils, probably because lack of aeration inhibits decay of needle litter. However, where loam textures occur and drainage is good, such as in west Armagh and on the east side of the Roe valley in County Londonderry, grey-brown podsolic profiles are associated with highly valued agricultural land that has a wide range of potential uses.

Old Red Sandstone

Apart from a small unit in north-east Antrim, there is a single extensive area of Old Red Sandstone series, extending from mid-Tyrone to the east shore of Lower Lough Erne, deeply covered in drumlinised glacial till. Around the towns of Dromore and Trillick in west Tyrone, the till has a clay loam texture and is difficult to drain. In the extension westward into County Fermanagh, textures change to sandy loam and drainage conditions improve slightly. However, these soils are deficient in phosphate, low in potash and require frequent liming. Under intensive management, grass production is high, but usage of the land can be difficult.

Granite and Triassic Sandstone

Soils developed on different parent materials, but sharing a common characteristic of sandy textures, are found on the upland granite of Slieve Croob and the Mournes, and on the much less resistant Triassic sandstone of the Lagan valley and the Cookstown-Dungannon area of east Tyrone. In the granite marginal hill land of County Down, soils are usually well drained and leached to the stage of acid brown podsolics or podsols. Climatic conditions may be limiting for agriculture on higher ground, and steep slopes make fields difficult to cultivate. In the sandstone lowland areas, soils are acid brown earths or brown podsolics with good physical properties, but requiring heavy fertilizer application. Collectively these sandy soils comprise about 10% of the land area of Northern Ireland. At higher elevations, soil compaction can lead to surface gleying and poorly drained profiles.

Agricultural land classification

The evaluation or rating of land for its agricultural potential has been widely undertaken in the past by landowners, such as the Church and State, usually for taxation purposes. This would appear to be one of the main purposes for establishing the resource value of soil, at least in its agricultural use. But even in this respect, it is not possible to isolate completely the soil from other variables which collectively comprise 'site' or 'land' for agricultural use. However, as this is the most common exercise involving the evaluation of the whole soil as a natural body, rather than soil as material, it is worth reviewing the history of land classification for agriculture in Northern Ireland.

The first official classification of the value of land for agriculture, presented in a numerical style and undertaken throughout Ireland, was the survey directed for the Government by geologist Sir Richard John Griffith (1784–1878), and repeated again about twenty years later. The first 'General Valuation' took place from 1826 to 1836 under several Irish Valuation Acts, and concurrently with the preparation of the first Ordnance Survey six-inch maps (1:10,560). The usefulness of this survey was limited by the fact that land was subdivided into arbitrary units of less than 10 hectares, called 'convenient lots', which do not coincide with present land subdivisions. In the second 'General Survey and Valuation' from 1852 to 1858, the mapping units were subdivisions of farms and townlands, coinciding with many present field boundaries. The instructions given to surveyors were more specific so that a standard approach was almost achieved throughout Ireland. Greater recognition was given to soil conditions in this survey, although the interest was limited to the most obvious properties of the top soil (stoniness, texture, wetness and organic matter). Land was cultivated in small plots, spade-dug into ridges (lazy beds) to improve drainage. Inherent chemical fertility was the most highly valued of soil properties. In particular, soil fertility was assessed by the natural lime content or nearness to a source of lime, such as limestone or even beach sand. Apart from lime, seaweed and animal manure, fertilizers were not available in the mid-nineteenth century. Labour was plentiful and could be used to locally improve soil drainage within cultivated plots, which were then used mainly to grow potatoes or cereals. The Griffith Valuation was based on criteria that reflected the interaction between agriculture and environment of more than a century ago (Cruickshank, 1972). It was abandoned as a basis for land taxation in Northern Ireland in 1922, but curiously, is still used for that purpose in the Republic of Ireland.

A revision of agricultural land classification was not undertaken again in Northern Ireland until the 1950s, and published in "Land Use in Northern Ireland" in 1963 (Symons, 1963). The scheme was still based largely on the physical conditions of land, but the criteria subjectively selected as important were different from those of Griffith in the 1850s. Location was no longer regarded as important because of the revolution in transport, and the advent of artificial fertilizers meant that inherent chemical fertility was not of prime consideration. The need for and the high cost of all kinds of drainage improvement have raised such physical factors to a much higher position in the ranking of variables limiting agricultural practice and productivity. However, even field and arterial drainage can be improved by man, albeit at some cost, so the most permanent physical properties of land are ultimately the most important and limiting in any scheme to evaluate its agricultural potential. This is the assumption in the land classification scheme of 1963, in which the main classes reflect altitude and aspect with related climatic conditions, slope, depth of free drainage in soil, and other physical properties of soil such as thickness, stoniness, texture and unevenness of physical characteristics. In some cases, individual classes of land were based on distinctive landscapes of Northern Ireland such as the class B3 for drumlin areas, and class B4 for rocky and peaty marginal hill land (Plate 8.4). A simplified map of this agricultural land classification scheme is shown in Figure 8.3, and a key to the main classes, their percentage areas and soils in Northern Ireland is in Table 8.2.

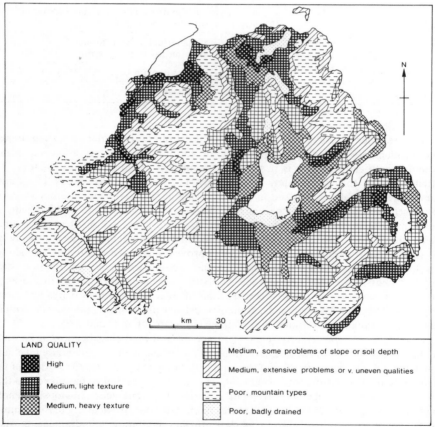

LAND QUALITY

▓ High

▤ Medium, light texture

▨ Medium, heavy texture

▥ Medium, some problems of slope or soil depth

▧ Medium, extensive problems or v. uneven qualities

⬚ Poor, mountain types

⬚ Poor, badly drained

Figure 8.3 Simplified map of agricultural land classification in Northern Ireland, adapted from Cruickshank and Symons (1963) in *Land Use in Northern Ireland*. The best quality land for agriculture is found in the lowlands around Lough Neagh, and in the valley lands of the Lagan, Lower Bann, Roe and Foyle.

TABLE 8.2

Land quality for agriculture in Northern Ireland (Symons, 1963)

Class	% area of N.I.	Soils and main locations
A	4	Acid brown earths and brown earths on basalt drift, around Limavady, Coleraine, Ballyclare. Also Lagan valley and Omagh area
B1	14	Brown earths of basalt loam drift. Acid brown earths on sandy drift in lowlands of County Londonderry and County Down
B2	10	Gleys of clay-rich till of lowlands around Lough Neagh
B3	17	Drumlin landscapes, variable soils but most gleyed. Some brown earths and grey-brown podsolics in County Down
B4	24	Hill margins and middle slopes, variable soils often gleyed and variable topography
C1	17	Peaty soils of higher hill margins around 240–300 m O.D. mostly in the Sperrins
D1	9	Blanket peat and mountain land over 300 m O.D.
C2+D2	5	Gleys and basin peat, lowland bog

In these schemes, soil is recognised as one of the physical variables affecting the use and productivity of land for agriculture or for forestry, but its influence is not quantitatively assessed nor is it separated from that of other physical factors. An attempt to do this came later, in the early 1970s with a case study in County Londonderry which is discussed in the next section. Neither is any attempt made in these schemes to establish how current physical conditions have come about, in particular the impact of man in improving drainage. This is consistent with other agricultural land classification schemes used in other countries, as far away as Australia and New Zealand, where the 'unimproved' physical condition of land allows for drainage improvements by man. In the wet environments of Ireland, such improvements have been considerable and started in an organised way in the early nineteenth century with the first construction of river flood control banks and stone drains in fields. The Myroe polder, at the Roe estuary in County Londonderry, with its sea dyke and pumping stations, was constructed at this time (Plate 8.3).

Soil drainage is particularly relevant to agricultural land classification in an environment such as that of the island of Ireland. The island is one of generally level and low-lying topography, with 80% of the land area being below 150 m O.D. Most of the river systems have a slow rate of flow and very little natural fall to base level, so that the many river drainage improvement schemes in recent years obviously benefit surrounding agricultural land. Soil textures in the lowlands, particularly in the drumlin areas, are in the clay or clay loam class, further inhibiting soil drainage in such landscapes of glacial till deposits; almost everywhere climatic wetness further exacerbates the drainage problem. Over the decades and centuries, man has been responsible for installing various forms of artificial underdrainage in the fields of Northern Ireland, but the extent of that has not been fully recorded. In the most recent period from 1949–1976, grants have been available for underdrainage and records indicate that about 18% of the area under crops and grass has benefitted from field drainage schemes. The extent, or indeed the present efficiency, of previously installed under-drainage, prior to 1949 and going back to the first stone drains, is not certain. It is estimated that at least half (Green, 1979) of the agricultural land in Northern Ireland has received underdrainage at some time, and possibly the proportion is much higher in the worst areas. Wilcock (1979) considers the proportion to be much higher if the effect of field ditches is included. Table 8.3 lists the proportions of each county (as % crops and grass) receiving underdrainage in the 1949–1976 period. Little significance can be attached to the geographical variation, except to the much lower proportion in County Down which generally has the least rainfall and best natural soil drainage of any of the counties. The figures are mainly for installation of tile and mole drainage, as stone drains declined in importance throughout this period, ending around 1970.

In recent years, much of the underdrainage has been by plastic pipes where loam textures allow the technique to be effective. Field trials in County Fermanagh (O'Neill, 1980) have shown that gravel-filled tunnel drains are the most effective in draining clay soils, although mole drains can create a dramatic improvement for a short period in the same clay-rich soils. Trench drains alone do not provide adequate drainage improvement in such soils, and must be supplemented by either mole or gravel-filled tunnel drains.

Plate 8.3 The Myroe polder at the estuary of the River Roe in County Londonderry. The polder was reclaimed from marine deposits in the mid-19th century, and is enclosed by a sea wall with pumping stations. Clearly, this is a case where man has improved the agricultural value of the land, which is now in the top class.

TABLE 8.3

Land benefitting by installation of underdrainage in period 1949–1976, as a percentage proportion of area in crops and grass in each county.

(Statistics from Department of Agriculture for Northern Ireland.)

Antrim	19.67%
Armagh	18.62%
Down	10.86%
Fermanagh	16.86%
Londonderry	21.28%
Tyrone	20.82%

Soil type and its influence in agriculture and forestry

In Northern Ireland, there is a remarkable range of 'soil types' if we define this term as soil series, which is a combination of soil profile and soil parent material. There are at least seven distinctive soil parent materials derived from different rock types (basalt, shale, schist etc.), and many more if peat, alluvium, and sand and gravel formations are added. On each of these parent materials, the complete range of soils is a group, normally called a 'soil association'. In each of these associations, it is possible to make a subdivision into soil series by soil profile, e.g. brown earth, podsol, gley etc., and it is the soil series that is regarded as the basic mapping unit of soils. Although no comprehensive soil survey has been organised in Northern Ireland, it can be confidently stated from the author's field experience that there are at least thirty, and probably about forty, different soil series to be found in the region. The variety would be much greater if these soil series were further subdivided by particular soil properties in surface horizons, into the 'types' and 'phases' of the American classification. It is probably sufficient to repeat that in Northern Ireland there is an exceptional range of soil series, reflecting the variety of geology, topography and climate, but this range is not reflected to the same degree in land use or in the planting of different tree species in forestry.

By the beginning of the 1980s, the agricultural landscape of Northern Ireland had become a monoculture of grass, with about 93% of the improved land being devoted to grass. Gone is the great diversity of land use, including root crops, cereals and flax, that was to be seen up to the time of the Second World War, and even after that. With the dominance of grass in essentially a single crop agriculture, it cannot be claimed that soil has an influence on land use or the selection of particular crops for particular fields. There is only a partial influence from soil on the fields selected for potatoes or market gardening, because although both tend to do well on sandy soils, other factors such as the location of markets and farm organisation are usually stronger controls. Likewise, apart from obvious extremes, there appears to be relatively little influence from soil type on the price paid for farm land or the rent achieved for 11 month conacre rents, because market forces unconnected with the physical environment can determine value or price at the present. With these examples, it can be questioned whether soil has any resource value, or particularly, whether there is any spatial variation in its value. Even in the spatial variation of levels of management, a recent study of the Sperrins area (Cruickshank and Cruickshank, 1977) suggested that altitude, with its climatic limitations, was the most effective control.

The influence of soil type in agriculture may possibly be seen in farm profit margins per unit area and in the productivity of land, although even here there is a complex of other physical and management variables interacting with soil. To investigate this relationship between soil and agricultural profit margins, and also to comply with recent thinking that agricultural land classification should be based on soil property variation rather than on soil series, a research project was established in the Roe valley, County Londonderry, and results published in 1971 (Cruickshank and Armstrong, 1971). The Roe valley was selected because it had, within a small area, six different rock types and eight different soil parent materials. In all, there were fourteen soil series, so the study area was almost a microcosm of Northern Ireland soils, and also one where the most common farm enterprises were to be found. Seven of the soil series were selected for special study; on each soil series, ten farms were selected for an investigation of the relationship between profit margins (gross margin returns) and eight soil properties from the topsoil, and also the same from the subsoil. First, it was found that the seven soil series were not distinctively different in six of the eight soil properties measured on subsoil samples, indicating that the genetic units of soil series are not ideal as mapping units for agricultural land evaluation. The eight soil properties measured on subsoil samples did account for up to 43% of the spatial variation in gross margin returns, and were all shown to be limiting on several farm enterprises examined. The conclusion drawn was that individual soil properties and groups of soil properties can be significant in explaining some of the difference in farm profitability from place to place.

The amount of the range in farm profit margins established in the Roe valley soil series is interesting as a measure of the variation throughout Northern Ireland, and does provide a quantitative index of the resource value of soil in grassland farm enterprises. For mixed farming enterprises based on grass, the gross margin profits per unit area of the worst soil series (acid and gleyed schist-derived soil) were 65% of those of the best soil series (slightly acid, well-drained sand). It should be remembered that gross margin profits are calculated after the subtraction of variable costs of labour, machinery and seeds etc., and also that these figures came from only seven selected series in the Roe valley. These soils did not represent the full spectrum of soil series over all of Northern Ireland, so that the regional variation would almost certainly be greater, and gross margins per unit area of the worst soils very much less than 65% of the best in agricultural use. Some of such differences might be overcome to some extent by greater management efficiency (Plates 8.4 and 8.5). It has also been demonstrated elsewhere that a great change in relative soil values in the Roe valley had taken place since 1850 (Cruickshank, 1972), which re-inforces the need for regular revision of soil-land valuation systems, as technology and economic conditions change.

In forestry, soil differences are also recognised as important, requiring different tree planting and management practices, and influencing different yield levels in tree crops (as reported in publications by D. A. Dickson and P. S. Savill, 1974 and 1975). General qualitative differences in the problems encountered with the main soil types during the growth cycle of tree crops are well known, and could be expressed as cost differences. However, quantitative estimates of such costs would only be speculative, because the growth cycle of tree crops is so long that management practices may change, and it is very difficult to forecast economic conditions throughout the cycle.

Plate 8.4 Evidence of variable land management in marginal agricultural land at about 150 m OD in the Sperrins. In such cases, better management and higher levels of input can compensate to some extent for poor physical conditions. This is Class B4 land, which forms a quarter of the land area of Northern Ireland.

Plate 8.5 Class 1 agricultural land near Newtownards, County Down, and used here for arable crops. Such land forms only 4% of the land area of Northern Ireland. It is well-drained, loam textured soil, found in lowland sites.

The risk of windthrow may be of major economic consequence, but the part played by soil is difficult to separate from climatic factors, slope, altitude and aspect. MacKenzie (1974) did find a satisfactory significant relationship between windthrow and soil type, mainly controlled by the rooting depth available to trees. Rooting depth is limited either by permanently waterlogged horizons or compacted-cemented horizons, where field bulk density is more than 1.6 (mass: volume ratio). MacKenzie reported that in soils like brown earths or podsols, where rooting depth could be up to 1 m, the risk of windthrow for Sitka spruce was negligible or very low. In blanket peat, the risk was only moderate, possibly due to the relatively young age of many of the plantations and possibly to the interlocking organic structures within the peat, but on gleys and peaty gleys, with less than 35 cm rooting depth, the risk of windthrow was high. In this highest category of risk, 1.27 to 1.74% of the trees were damaged compared with 0.05% on brown earths at the time of the study.

TABLE 8.4

Tree growth in Northern Ireland forests on various soil types

Soil profile types	% forest land	Average yield class for:		
		Sitka spruce	Lodgepole pine	Norway spruce
1. Leached soils, brown earths and podsols	17	16.8 (90.3)	9.2 (100)	17.0 (99.4)
2. Leached soils with surface peat (mor)	10	14.9 (80.1)	7.4 (80.4)	12.9 (75.4)
3. Surface water gleys	18	18.6 (100)	7.7 (83.6)	17.1 (100)
4. Peaty gleys	16	15.2 (81.7)	6.3 (68.5)	14.7 (85.9)
5. Shallow peat (< 1 m)	12	13.2 (70.9)	8.4 (91.3)	13.8 (80.7)
6. Deep peat	27	12.9 (63.3)	7.3 (79.3)	11.6 (67.8)
Area planted in hectares		19913	3068	2629
% of total area planted		62	10	8

These figures were provided by the Forest Service, DoA, and are based on the area planted up to end of 1969 (32,170 ha.), and not the area planted by end of 1977 (51,168 ha.).

Table 8.4 provides quantitative data on yield class for the three most common planted tree species on six soil types, as recorded by the Forest Service, Department of Agriculture for Northern Ireland. For both Sitka spruce, by far the dominant species in our forestry plantations, and Norway spruce, the highest yield class is found on surface water gleys. These soils have moderately good chemical fertility and usually only minor drainage problems. Deep and shallow peat together comprise 39% of the planted area, and yield classes are quite low for Sitka spruce despite considerable fertilizer application, but current management and fertilizer practice may increase yield in future. The yield class data makes no allowance for costs of preparation and fertilization of the soil, and commonly the soils with lowest yield will be the most expensive to manage, but cheapest to buy or rent.

In this Northern Ireland case study, yield class recorded on deep peat is only around 67 to 69% of the highest yields for the two spruce species. In similar soil productivity data for Sitka spruce in west central Wales (Jones, 1972), yield class on upland deep peat was between 45 and 65% of the highest yields, found on brown earths. The difference in profitability would be much greater between these soil types planted in spruce, although this could be reduced by the difference in the original buying price of the land. In Northern Ireland, as elsewhere in the British Isles, recent afforestation schemes have been largely limited to sub-marginal agricultural land such as upland blanket peat, which is usually extremely acid and infertile, even for coniferous trees. Savill and Dickson have reported from their Northern Ireland field trials (1971, 1974, 1975, 1977) that heavy applications of phosphate are required at planting, and later, to achieve even a modest yield class for Sitka spruce on the most acid peat. Nitrogen fertilization is also necessary for sustained growth on the worst sites.

Conservation of the resource

This chapter has been mainly concerned with inventory and evaluation of soil as a natural resource, and in conclusion, some attention should be given to management and conservation of the resource. As agriculture plays such a large part in the economy of Northern Ireland, both as a producer of food and as an employer, it is of vital importance to the community in this region that soil is maintained in optimum condition for future production of food, fibre and timber. It is probable that dependence on soil for such production may become greater in future decades, with public appeals for local self-sufficiency in food supply.

Conservation of soil must be examined in the context of the local physical environment, as well as the demands of land use and management being made on the soil. The almost universal crop of grass throughout the agricultural area of Northern Ireland means that soil is provided with an almost permanent physical protection from attack by wind or running water. Soil erosion is a negligible hazard because of all-year-round protection. There is reasonable security in the future because the dominance of the grass crop is likely to continue, and may even increase further; the situation would be very different with permanent arable land use under prevailing local conditions of rainfall.

Possible physical damage to the soil must always be considered in the context of grassland land use and ground surface wetness due to local climate. Grass offers surface protection and also is the best natural promoter of soil structure stability, created by the deep penetration of fine rootlets. But acting against soil structure stability is the wetness of the soil surface, found on almost all soils in the winter months and exacerbated on soils with a high clay content. Soil structure is temporarily damaged by saturated conditions, and can be destroyed for longer periods if the soil is subjected to physical pressure when saturated. Trampling by cattle when soil is wet has this effect, called 'poaching' or 'puddling', which can change soil into a 'porridge-like' medium. This is common practice in the pastoral agriculture of Northern Ireland, and clay-rich soils in wet situations and the wettest climate are the most susceptible. Physical damage to the soil caused by agricultural machinery can also be serious.

At the worst, poaching is usually restricted to certain parts of fields and is a medium-term kind of damage that can be cured by controlled grazing. It is a part of the emphasis on cattle in local agriculture which has more serious long term impact on soil through aspects of intensification of production and the high densities of livestock carried on the land. The use of fertilizer has been increasing steadily over the past three decades, and in 1973 the average fertilizer application rate was 294 kg/ha (2.34 cwt/acre) (Wilcock, 1979). The increase primarily reflects the increasing use of nitrogenous fertilizers in grassland management, followed closely by potash (K_2O) and phosphate (P_2O_5). Subsidies encouraged the application of lime in the 1950s, but this has fallen to such an extent that much of the agricultural area is showing a lime requirement again. In areas of intensive management of grassland, very high fertilizer application rates have had extreme effects of producing 'die-back' in the pasture, as well as dangerously high levels of nitrate in soil and drainage water. McAllister (1977) has reported from a survey of 200 farms that the application of P and K fertilizers is at best indiscriminate, and that many farms with pig or poultry enterprises already had surpluses in P and K before buying fertilizer. The very large populations of cattle and pigs produce enormous supplies of liquid manure called slurry, and excessive levels of NPK in Northern Ireland soils are usually correlated with concentrations of pigs and cattle on farms practising intensive management. Production of slurry is often much greater than any available means of disposal or distribution. This is one of the most important and potentially harmful effects of intensive livestock agriculture on soil fertility, which is currently being monitored by agricultural chemists of DoA. Nutrient pollution of the most intensively managed soils and local drainage water is a reality now, and a serious hazard for the future under existing systems of farming.

In contrast, the improving practices in forestry appear to do little harm to the environment and could be regarded as constructive changes for the better in the soils so improved. Forestry usually is restricted to such poor soil that physical improvement by drainage or ploughing-up compacted 'pans' may be necessary before planting surface water and ground water gleys. Blanket peat in the uplands, the most commonly used soil in forestry, is so acid and infertile that intensive drainage and heavy fertilizer applications are necessary before trees will grow at all. These physical and nutrient improvements, made for afforestation schemes, affect such a small proportion of total land area (only about 5-6%), and the degree of change is so much less than in intensive agriculture, that environmental impact is not generally a concern.

The overall conclusion is that grassland pastoral agriculture in the lowlands, and afforestation plantations in the uplands, are suitable and harmonious uses of soil-land in a climatically wet environment, frequently involving moisture-retentive clay soils. Conservation of the resource for future generations is not seriously at risk if the danger of nutrient pollution from intensive livestock enterprises is kept under control.

Acknowledgements

The author wishes to thank Mr D. A. Dickson, Forest Soils Section of DoA, for discussion of the text in preparation, and Mr J. Kerr, Water, Drainage and Conservation, DoA, and Dr P. S. Savill, formerly of the Forest Service of DoA, for supplying data for this chapter. The author alone is responsible for all interpretations and opinions.

REFERENCES

Adams, S. N., Jack, W. H. and Dickson, D. A., 1970. The growth of Sitka spruce on poorly drained soils in Northern Ireland. *Forestry*, 43 (2), 125–133.

Cruickshank, J. G., 1961. A reconnaissance soil survey of County Fermanagh. *Irish Geography*, 4 (3), 190–201.

Cruickshank, J. G., 1970. Soils and pedogenesis in the north of Ireland. *Irish Geographical Studies, Edit.* N. Stephens and R. E. Glasscock, The Queen's University of Belfast, 89–104.

Cruickshank, J. G., 1972. Soils and changing agricultural land values in part of County Londonderry. *Irish Geography*, 6 (4), 462–479.

Cruickshank, J. G., 1975. Soils of the northern and central parts of County Armagh. *Irish Geography*, 8, 63–71.

Cruickshank, J. G., 1978. Soil properties and management levels of marginal hill land in the Sperrin Mountains, Co. Tyrone and Co. Londonderry. *Irish Journal of Agricultural Research*, 17, 303–314.

Cruickshank, J. G. and Armstrong, W. J., 1971. Soil and agricultural land classification in County Londonderry. *Transactions of the Institute of British Geographers*, 53, 79–94.

Cruickshank, J. G. and Cruickshank, M. M., 1977. A survey of neglected agricultural land in the Sperrin Mountains, Northern Ireland. *Irish Geography*, 10, 36–44.

Cruickshank, J. G. and Cruickshank, M. M., 1981. The development of humus-iron podsol profiles, linked by radiocarbon dating and pollen analysis to vegetation history. *Oikos*, 36, 238–253.

Dickson, D. A., 1971. The effect of form, rate and position of phosphatic fertilizers on growth and nutrient uptake of Sitka spruce on deep peat. *Forestry*, 44, 17–26.

Dickson, D. A., 1977. Nutrition of Sitka spruce on peat – problems and speculations. *Irish Forestry*, 34, 31–39.

Dickson, D. A. and Savill, P. S., 1974. Early growth of *Picea sitchensis* on deep oligotrophic peat in Northern Ireland. *Forestry*, 47, 57–88.

Green, F. H. W., 1979. *Field drainage in Europe: a quantitative survey*. Institute of Hydrology, Report No. 57, Wallingford, Oxon.

Griffith Valuation. See Valuation Books and Valuation Maps (e.g. for 1834 and 1858), Public Records Office, Belfast.

Jones, G. E., 1972. *The effects of selected environmental hazards on the growth of Picea sitchensis in three forests in Wales*, Unpublished PhD thesis, Geog. Dept., U.C.W., Aberystwyth.

McAleese, D. M. and McConaghy, S., 1957–1958. Studies on the basaltic soils of Northern Ireland. *Journal of Soil Science*, 8, 127–134, 135–140; 9, 66–75, 76–80, 81–88, 289–297.

McAllister, J. S. V., 1977. Spreading slurry on land. *Soil Science*, 123, 338–343.

McAllister, J. S. V. and McConaghy, S., 1968. Soils of Northern Ireland and their influence upon agriculture. *Record of Agricultural Research*, Ministry of Agriculture, Northern Ireland, 17, 101–108.

MacKenzie, R. F., 1974. Some factors influencing the stability of Sitka spruce in Northern Ireland. *Irish Forestry*, 31 (2), 110–129.

O'Neill, D. G. 1980. An investigation of the gravel tunnel drainage system. *Annual Report on Research and Technical Work for 1980*. Enniskillen Agricultural College, 10–13.

Savill, P. S. and Dickson, D. A., 1975. Early growth of Sitka spruce on gleyed soils in Northern Ireland. *Irish Forestry*, 32 (1), 34–49.

Smith, A. G., Pearson, G. W. and Pilcher, J. R., 1971. Belfast Radiocarbon Dates III, *Radiocarbon*, 13 (1), 103–125.

Symons, L. J., Edit., 1963. *Land Use in Northern Ireland*, U.L.P. London, pp. 288.

Wilcock, D. N., 1979. Post-war land drainage, fertilizer use and environmental impact in Northern Ireland. *Journal of Environmental Management*, 8, 137–149.

CHAPTER IX

Peatland

ALAN C. HAMILTON,
Lecturer in Environmental Science,
New Univeristy of Ulster

Introduction

Peatland forms a conspicuous part of the landscape of Northern Ireland. Characteristic features include permanently high groundwater, the presence of water-loving plants and, of course, the presence of peat. The actual area of peatland depends on the definition of peat used, and on the attitude to reclaimed or partially cut-over land. The peat surveys of Scotland and Wales defined peat as a superficial organic soil horizon, 30 cm or more thick (Robertson, 1968; Taylor, 1968). In a recent peatland survey that includes Northern Ireland (Hammond, 1979), a similar definition is used with the qualification that the 30 cm thickness is of drained peat, and based on this, Northern Ireland has 12.4% of its land area or 171,265 hectares in peatland (see Figure 9.1). An earlier survey (C.S.R.D., 1956) put the figures much higher, 17.8% of land area and 240,000 hectares, but the peatland measured included all peaty soils, some with much less than 30 cm thickness of peat.

As a resource, peatland is a source of organic matter and exploitable land. In the past, a pragmatic approach to exploitation has proved satisfactory for some purposes, but with the recent drive towards more intensive use of peatland, the need for a more fundamental analysis of the nature of the resource has become apparent. This must describe the peatland ecosystems, and also the manner in which peat has accumulated before proceeding to a discussion of peat and peatland as natural resources at the present time.

Past and present peat-forming ecosystems in Northern Ireland

(i) *General characteristics of peat-forming ecosystems*

Peat consists predominantly of the partly decomposed remains of plants derived from wet terrestrial and semi-aquatic habitats. It accumulates when the rate of input of dead organic matter exceeds the rate at which it is lost, i.e.:

Rate of production of organic matter by *in situ* ecosystem	Rate of import + of organic detritus	Rate of > decomposition	Rate of export + of organic detritus

In most situations the main factor favouring peat formation is a low rate of decomposition compared with the rate of production (Kavanagh and Herlihy, 1975). Net primary production varies greatly between different mire types (mire=a peat-producing ecosystem (Moore and Bellamy, 1973)). Some reedswamps are the most productive, and some bog communities the least productive of temperate ecosystem types. There is a general correlation between the rates of production and decomposition in mire ecosystems. Variables which control decomposition rates include nutrient supply, temperature and the height of the groundwater (Clymo, 1965). The last of these influences decomposition by helping to determine the depth of the upper aerobic soil horizon, in which nearly all decomposition occurs. It is not surprising that Ireland, with its cool moist climate, generally subdued topography and extensive areas of clay-rich superficial deposits of low permeability, has large areas of peatland.

Detritus movement contributes substantially to the peat-forming equation, but only in mires with an incomplete vegetational cover. Where lakes and mires abut, a gradation can sometimes be observed from fine-textured mud deposited in deeper water through a transitional zone of coarse detritus mud to reedswamp peat deposited around lake margins (e.g. Smith, 1961). Much of the organic matter contained in lake sediments is frequently detrital or allochthonous in origin, i.e. in-washed.

(ii) Past and present mire types of Northern Ireland

Floristic composition provides a means of classifying the past and present mires of Northern Ireland. There are several reasons for this. First, vegetation forms one of the most important components of mires. Second, many peat deposits contain identifiable remains of the plants which helped to form them, thus allowing comparison between ancient and modern vegetation types. Third, the distribution of species is closely related to the distribution of many other important mire variables. Two problems with using floristic compositions for a general mire classification are the paucity of identifiable fossils in some well decomposed peat types and the fact that at any one time species distributions are determined not only by current environmental characteristics, but also by environmental history. Species often show lags in their responses to environmental change; slow rates of spread can, for example, limit the actual distributions of some species to fractions of their potential ranges.

A wide-ranging survey of mire vegetation in Britain (Daniels, 1978) demonstrated that one of the most important factors determining floristic composition is trophic status. This finding supports the traditional tripartite classification of mires into fen, poor fen and bog (Moore and Bellamy, 1973). Fen ecosystems (used here to include reedswamps) are nutrient-rich, receiving their nutrients from surrounding areas; they may be referred to as rheotrophic (nourished by the flow). Bog ecosystems are nutrient poor, nutrient input being limited to precipitation and dust; they are frequently termed ombrotrophic (nourished by the rain). Poor fen is intermediate.

At the present time small patches of fen are widely distributed over Northern Ireland, but the most extensive and best known fens are to the south of Lough Neagh, in north Armagh. Their plant communities have been described by Duff (1930) and White (1932), both of whom considered that an important determinant of species composition is the height of the groundwater table. At one extreme, fenland communities grade into aquatic communities containing such non-emergent species as

Elodea canadensis*, Myriophyllum spicatum and *Nuphar lutea*; at the other end of the spectrum, fenlands grade into poor fen and bog communities with *Calluna vulgaris, Molinia caerulea, Polytricum commune* and *Sphagnum*.

Fens have been present throughout the post-glacial, and many species have been identified (e.g. Jessen, 1949; Smith, 1958) from fossils in the extensive fenland peat deposits which underlie most raised bogs in Northern Ireland and which began to be overrun by the bog communities after *c.* 7,000 B.P. *Cladium* and *Phragmites* are two of the commonest herbaceous plants and others recorded include *Equisetum, Hydrocotyle, Menyanthes, Osmunda regalis, Polypodium vulgare* (probably epiphytic), *Scirpus lacustris, Thelypteris palustris* and *Typha latifolia*. Among woody plants, *Betula* is particularly common, its presence probably indicating the former occurrence of relatively dry, nutrient-deficient fen. *Frangula alnus* (Smith, 1958), *Pinus sylvestris, Rhamnus, Quercus* and *Salix* are also recorded. There is considerable floristic variation between and within these early post-glacial rheotrophic mires, but as yet there has been no thorough attempt to document this variation or to relate it to environmental influences.

Sphagnum is one of the most important genera of ombrotrophic mires and, of the 24 species known from Ireland, the majority occur in bog habitats (Smith, 1978). Some bog deposits consist largely of *Sphagnum* remains and, although there has been a recent decline in its abundance, *Sphagnum* is still very common. Two characteristics of *Sphagnum* important to its success are the spongy texture of both living and dead *Sphagnum*, giving high water retention and allowing a local water table above the level of the regional water table, and the high ability of living *Sphagnum*, compared with other plants, to exchange internally held hydrogen ions with other cations in the external solution (Clymo, 1963; 1964). By helping to remove the mire surface from the influence of groundwater and by extracting nutrients from the environment, *Sphagnum* creates wet, acidic conditions which few other plants can tolerate.

Large areas of bogland are today administered by the Forest Service, Department of Agriculture for Northern Ireland. The performance of trees planted on bogland is related to the nutrient status of the peat and foresters have devised a classification of peatlands with reference principally to their modern vegetation, here used as an index to nutrient status (Forest Service, 1978). For deep (>1 m) blanket peat, for instance, the four peatland categories recognized are : (1) dystrophic (=very poorly nourished; 5% of total area of deep peat), with abundant *Sphagnum, Narthecium ossifragum, Calluna* and *Erica tetralix; Rhacomitrium* and *Cladonia* also occur and open pools of water are associated only with this class; (2) oligotrophic (=poorly nourished; 48%), with abundant *Calluna, Scirpus caespitosus (Trichophorum caespitosum), Eriophorum* spp.; (3) mesotrophic (=moderately well nourished; 42%), with abundant *Eriophorum vaginatum, Molinia, Deschampsia flexuosa* and *Anthoxanthum odoratum;* (4) eutrophic (=well nourished; 5%), with abundant *Juncus acutiflorus, J. effusus* and *Holcus lanatus*. In terms of the bog/poor fen/fen classification scheme, the presence of abundant *Molinia* would commonly be regarded as indicative of poor fen rather than bog (Daniels, 1978) and the division between bog and fen falls somewhere near the category 2/3 boundary. Mesotrophic and eutrophic blanket mires are found on sites which receive some nutrient input through flushing.

---

* Terminology follows Smith (1978) for mosses and Webb (1967) for vascular plants

Bogs have been extensive in Northern Ireland since *c.* 7,000 B.P. Fossils indicate that there are many similarities between modern and past bog communities, but some species of *Sphagnum*, such as *S. imbricatum,* were much more abundant at some times in the past than now. Modern bog communities are also somewhat unusual in that many sites have witnessed a recent change involving replacement of 'wetter' by 'drier' types of bog communities.

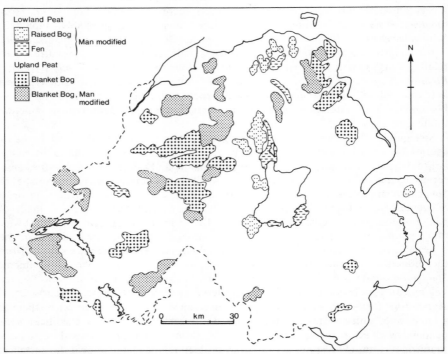

Figure 9.1 Simplified peatland map of Northern Ireland, based on the map by Hammond (1979). Almost all peatland lies in the west and on the uplands of the north-east, usually in close association with wet, gleyed mineral soils.

Peat deposits of Northern Ireland

Almost all the peat in Northern Ireland dates from the post-glacial period which began about 10,000 years ago when the climate became rapidly warmer. Vegetation increased in height and density, with trees spreading into areas previously covered by sparse herbaceous and dwarf shrub (tundra) vegetation, the soil surface became much more stable and organic-rich deposits started to accumulate in wet sites.

Most of the peat deposits of Northern Ireland can be classified in relation to the modern landscape/ecosystem types which overlaps with their floristic classification. The two main landscape types concerned are *blanket mire* and *basin mire*; intermediates between these are quite common. Blanket mire occurs on hills and mountains in all topographical situations except for very steep (>20°) slopes. Basin mire differs in being typically found at relatively low (<200 m O.D.) altitudes in valleys or other depressions; a prominent type of this is the three-layered raised mire. Of the estimated 171,000 hectares acres of peatland in Northern Ireland, *c.* 130,000 ha are blanket mire and the remainder mainly basin mire (Hammond, 1979).

(i) *The peat deposits of blanket mires*

The distribution of blanket mire, or blanket bog, is related to the slow rate of decomposition found in areas with very high effective precipitation (see Figure 9.1). The lower margin of blanket peat is generally correlated with the 1,250 mm mean annual rainfall isohet and lies at *c.* 315 m O.D, in the Mournes, 305 m on the Antrim Plateau (215 m in the north-east), 305 m on the Sperrins (120 m near the Donegal border) and 210 m in County Fermanagh (Cruickshank, 1970). Blanket peat is found at sea level on the west coast of Ireland.

Blanket peat is typically acid, bog peat. On gentle slopes the thickness is generally 2-3 m. Although it is rather homogeneous in appearance, three strata can sometimes be discerned. The lower stratum, which is present from *c.* 150-200 cm below the surface (in a typical 2 m peat profile) is relatively dark coloured and highly humified, with little plant structure preserved. The middle stratum (*c.* 10-150 cm) is relatively light coloured and fresh (before darkening on exposure) and contains more readily recognizable macrofossils, these being chiefly *Sphagnum*, *Eriophorum* and *Calluna*. The upper stratum (*c.* 0-10 cm) can be relatively dark coloured and contains decreased quantities of *Sphagnum* and increased quantities of *Calluna, Eriophorum* and sometimes *Rhacomitrium* (Figure 9.2*b*).

The cause of this change from the lower more humified to the middle less humified peat is generally held to be climatic. A change to wetter conditions is indicated, not only by gross sediment stratigraphy, but also by an increase in the ratio of Cyperaceae to Ericaceae pollen (Jessen, 1949; Morrison, 1959). In the low altitude blanket peat deposits of extreme western Ireland, the same climatic event could have been responsible for a switch over to *Schoenus/Molinia* dominated communities; *Schoenus/Molinia* peat is only present in the upper 60-100 cm of blanket peat profiles (Jessen, 1949). There appears to be little good evidence concerning the date of the change.

Blanket bog peat is developed on a variety of substrates including bare rock, various types of mineral soil, lake mud, herbaceous fen deposits and wood peat (Goddard, 1971; Jessen, 1949; Morrison, 1959; Pilcher, 1973). Tree stumps are very common at the base of the blanket peat (Plate 9.1).

Large areas of blanket peat in Northern Ireland, as in other parts of the British Isles, are currently suffering from erosion. One of the most severely affected hill areas in Northern Ireland is the Mournes, with almost complete removal of peat from the summits of the principal mountains (Armstrong *et al.*, 1930), and similar effects can be seen in the Sperrins and the Antrim plateau. Erosion is both through channel incision and through mass movement of bog bursts. Gully erosion is very widespread in Northern Ireland (Tomlinson, 1981) and, as in the Pennines (Bower, 1962), the gullies tend to assume a dendritic pattern on more level ground and a sub-parallel pattern on slopes. Once established, the rate of gully erosion is likely to have accelerated and the area of exposed unvegetated peat to have increased. Unlike gully incision, bog bursts affect only small areas, and accounts of Irish bog bursts are given by Bishop and Mitchell (1946), Colhoun *et al.*, (1965) and Delap and Mitchell (1939). In general, the factors responsible for their occurrence are not well understood, though it seems that an important trigger may be exceptionally wet weather (Colhoun *et al.*, 1965).

Plate 9.1   Pine stumps revealed after the cutting and removal of peat in blanket mire in the upper valley of the Main in County Antrim.

(ii)   *The peat deposits of raised mires*

Raised mires, also known as raised bogs or red bogs (Praeger, 1934) are usually found at relatively low altitudes, on relatively flat ground and many were originally lakes. They lie mainly in the valley of the Lower Bann, the river basins of west Tyrone, in north Antrim and near the southern shore of Lough Neagh, (see Figure 9.1). Almost all have been affected to some extent by peat cutting and many have been partly reclaimed for agriculture (Plate 9.2). In their undisturbed state they typically possess an inverted-saucer shape, the following three zones being distinguishable: a central part which is slightly convex or nearly flat (the dome), a sloping margin (the rand) and a marginal low-lying area (the lagg).

Figure 9.2*a*, based on Mooney (1978) shows a transect through the peat deposits of a lobe of the Garry Bog near Ballymoney, County Antrim. Due perhaps to a combination of the effects of nearby drainage and forestry operations, the deposits in the region of this section have shrunk by an average of 1.4 m since 1833 (Wishart, 1978). Even so, with a maximum recorded depth of 8.8 m, the organic deposits are thicker than is usually the case with Irish raised mire deposits, but in other respects peat stratigraphy is fairly typical. In many places the organic deposits are developed on a sheet of blue-grey clay deposited in a lake during late Midlandian times, the change to the succeeding more organic sedimentation probably occurring soon after 10,000 B.P. The oldest organic deposit is generally a detritus mud, 60 cm thick (in the case of the 8.8 m profile marked on Figure 9.2*a*) and containing *Phragmites* leaves and *Betula* wood. This is succeeded by a reedswamp peat 2.1 m thick and containing fairly abundant wood. The fen peat is overlain by a well humified *Sphagnum* peat 2.6 m thick and very decayed, so that species are difficult to identify. This stratum is succeeded by less humified *Sphagnum* peat, 3.4 m thick and containing only occasional *Eriophorum* spp. *Sphagnum imbricatum* is abundant. The upper *c.* 10 cm is dark coloured and contains frequent *Calluna* fossils.

This three-fold division of the bulk of the peat body into lower fen peat, middle well-humified *Sphagnum* peat and upper less humified *Sphagnum* peat is the normal sequence recorded from raised mires in Ireland (e.g. Jessen, 1949; Smith, 1958). The boundaries between these horizons are typically fairly sharp, the lower, for instance, occurring within only 10-20 cm of the peat profile (e.g. Hammond, 1968). There is considerable debate concerning the relative importance of successional development and of changes in external environmental factors, particularly climate, as causes of these vegetational changes.

Considering first the change from fen to bog peat, Hammond (1968) has demonstrated for a raised mire on the border between Counties Kildare and Offaly that this change occurred at a successively later date from the centre outwards towards the margins. During early post-glacial time, a fen containing *Phragmites* and fringed by a *Betula* zone gradually spread outwards as the water table rose with the accumulation of peat in a basin. After the Boreal/Atlantic transition, here ^{14}C-dated rather early at 7,540± 125 B.P., the mire continued to expand laterally and vertically, but the fen was

Plate 9.2   A raised bog or raised mire in the upper valley of the Agivey, in County Londonderry.

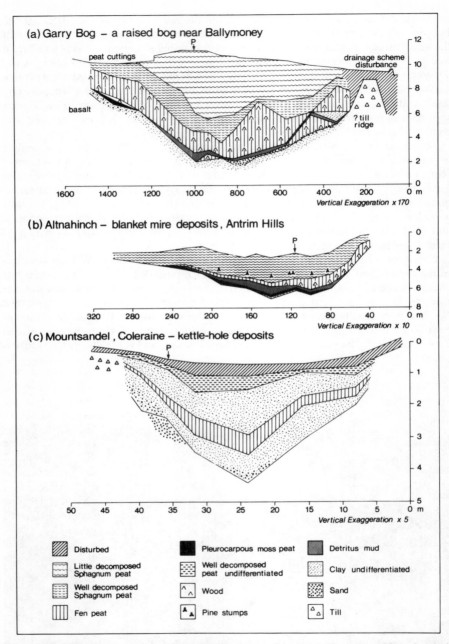

Figure 9.2 Cross-sections through three different types of peatland. The composition of organic layers in each cross-section is used to establish the origin and classify the type of peatland (as discussed in the text of Chapter 9).

replaced by *Sphagnum* bog and a zone of *Alnus* now occurred on the outside of the *Betula* fringe. It seems likely that many other raised mires have followed a similar pattern of development, the fen/bog transition occurring at different times at different places.

As raised mires expanded laterally and vertically, the rates of nutrient input into their central parts are likely to have diminished. For any particular mire, contributing factors would have included (1) a decreased source area for nutrients (with mire expansion), (2) a decreased nutrient output per unit source area, (3) an increased mire area to act as a sink for nutrients and (4) perhaps a progressive canalization of water flow and the development of lagg streams (for the latter, see Bellamy, 1968). These considerations do not, however, rule out climatic change as a possible contributory factor. One argument for the importance of a climatic trigger is that there appears to be a definite lower time limit, for Ireland as a whole, for the fen/bog transition. This lower limit is the Boreal/Atlantic boundary, a level which is traditionally recognized by a marked rise in the concentration of *Alnus* pollen in the peat (Jessen, 1949) and which is dated in lowland parts of Northern Ireland to roughly 7,000 B.P. (Pilcher, 1973; Smith and Pilcher, 1973). Although lacking proper 4-dimensional stratigraphic control, the evidence indicates that bog development commenced at about the Boreal/Atlantic boundary at Ballyscullion (Jessen, 1949; Mitchell, 1956), Cloughmills (Jessen, 1949), Fallahogy (Smith, 1958) and at a slightly later date at Garry (Mooney, 1978).

The climatic change which occurred at the Boreal/Atlantic boundary is believed to have been towards wetter conditions. Various data support this theory. The increase in the *Alnus* population is itself often regarded as evidence of such a change (Moore and Bellamy, 1973). The Boreal/Atlantic boundary approximately marks the onset of peat accumulation in a kettle hole at Mountsandel (Figure 9.2c) and a great increase in the rate of sediment accumulation in a small lake at Kilrea (Smith, 1961). A rise in the level of Lough Neagh by c. 12 m occurred at c. 6,000 B.P., i.e. somewhat later than the Boreal/Atlantic boundary (O'Sullivan *et al.*, 1973). This event may, however, have been related not so much to climatic change as to change in the base-level of the Lower River Bann associated with sea-level rise. The lake level rise submerged some mires previously established around Loughs Neagh and Beg (Jessen, 1949).

The link between increased wetness and a switch from fen to bog probably operated through a reduction in nutrient supply to the mire surface. Perhaps one of the several factors likely to have been involved is that hydrological conditions became such as to cause general water movement away from, rather than towards the centres of well vegetated mires. Variation in the characteristics of different mire systems and of their catchments would have ensured a certain amount of variation in the responses of mires to climatic change. Once bog species of *Sphagnum* had become well established, the accumulation of their dead remains would have tended to raise the central parts of mire surfaces, thus further reducing influxes of groundwater from surrounding areas to the inner parts of mires.

(iii) *Other peat deposits*

In Counties Down and Armagh there is a very large number of peat deposits present in the hollows between drumlins. Peat deposits can also be found in low-lying situations elsewhere. An example is shown in Figure 9.2c, illustrating the stratigraphy of kettlehole deposits at Mountsandel, Coleraine, where Boreal peat deposits are absent, probably because the climate was too dry, and peat accumulation commenced in Atlantic times. As is frequently the case in such small basins, the upper layers of peat have been disturbed by agricultural activities. Indeed, the combined effects of peat removal for fuel and of reclamation for agriculture must have greatly decreased the extent of such small peat deposits in Northern Ireland (Brown, 1968), and the example of County Down is shown in Figure 9.3.

Finally, organic deposits, including peat, dating to the Woodgrange Interstadial Period are known from interdrumlin hollows (Smith, 1970) and other basins. An example is shown in Figure 9.2c. A few earlier organic deposits are known from Northern Ireland (Bazley, 1978).

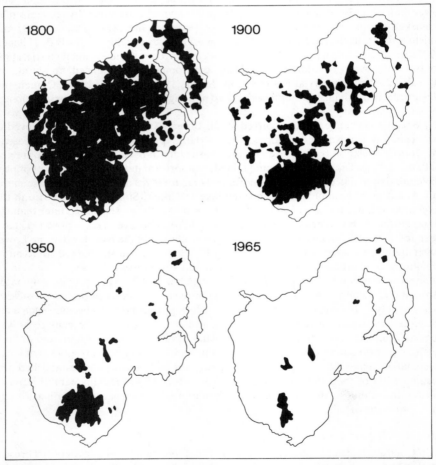

Figure 9.3 Maps of various dates showing the removal of peatland by man, mainly from the lowlands, in County Down (Brown, 1968).

Uses of peat

Present day rates of peat accumulation are negligible in comparison to modern rates of peat removal by such processes as erosion, oxidation and cutting. Therefore, for all practical purposes, peat is a non-renewable and fast disappearing resource. Among the properties of peat exploited in its principle uses are its high energy content, its content of organic compounds, its high water-holding capacity and its high cation exchange capacity.

(i) Use as a fuel

Historically, by far the most important use of peat in Northern Ireland is as a fuel. Almost all of this use has been on a domestic scale, with only infrequent industrial exploitation, including for iron smelting (Coe, 1969). A survey of modern cutting on the Garry and two other County Antrim bogs (Wishart, 1978) has shown that most cutters live close to the bogs which they exploit and that, since turf-winning is time-expensive, most are pensioners or belong to other social groups who can readily spare or make the time available for the job. It is uncertain when turf-winning first became an important part of the rural economy, but it seems likely that wood was the main fuel in most areas until the great forest and scrub destruction of the 17th and 18th centuries. The 1977 rate of peat removal on the Garry Bog was equivalent to a reduction of 1.8 m depth per annum over an area of between 1.05 and 1.7 ha (Wishart, 1978).

Peat is cut with a long-handled spade with a flange set at right angles to the blade. Turf banks may be cut either vertically or horizontally (breasted), the choice depending on the orientation of lines of weakness in the peat. When the peats are dry enough to be handled without breaking, they are placed in small mounds (castles) which may be rebuilt (turncastled) to further assist drying. The peats may then be transported home or, alternatively, if they are to remain on the bog over winter, they are built into large stacks. Turf barrows are used for moving peat on the bog and transportation is by car or tractor and trailer. Ideal weather conditions for working are dry, warm and windy periods of early summer (Plate 9.3).

Although most fuel exploitation has been of bog or relatively fresh fen peat, well decomposed fen peat was also used for fuel around Lough Neagh. In contrast to *Sphagnum* peat, this type of fen peat required kneading and sun baking (White, 1932). It was said to be superior as a fuel to normal peat.

The calorific value of peat depends in part on the extent to which it has been dried. Thus, in comparison with coal which has a calorific value of *c.* 6,000 cal g^{-1} and with fresh *Sphagnum* peat which has a water content of *c.* 90-93% (Dallas, 1967), turf briquettes (water content only 10-12%) give *c.* 4,100 cal g^{-1}, machine-cut turf (25-40%) gives *c.* 3,000 cal g^{-1} and hand-cut turf (*c.* 35%) gives *c.* 2,600 cal g^{-1} (Miller, 1968; Lunny, 1968). Peat has normally been burnt in open fires, an inefficient use of the fuel. A consequence of the cellular structure and consequent high surface/volume ratio of peat is that turf is an extremely reactive fuel (Lunny, 1968). Ignition occurs at about 150-210° C, a temperature at which much of the carbon, representing about half of the potential heating value, volatizes and much of the contained energy is liable to be lost. Methods of improving the value of turf as a fuel are to increase the time of residence in the furnace, to maintain a high furnace temperature and to increase the

Plate 9.3   Peat cutting and drying at a lowland bog in County Antrim.

turbulence of the gas (turf volatiles)/air mixture. Considerable thought has been given to the application of these principles in the design of both domestic (Miller, 1968) and industrial heating units. A modern domestic convector heater can cut down heat loss up the chimney flue from 75%, as is liable to occur with an open fire, to 25-40% and also heats a room more uniformly (Miller, 1968).

A survey of the peat resources of Northern Ireland was carried out in 1952-53 by the Council of Scientific Research and Development in conjunction with The Queen's University (C.S.R.D., 1956). The aim was to locate mires suitable for industrial exploitation as sources of fuel or other raw materials and only mires of over *c.* 200 acres were examined. Total peat reserves (for all mires) were estimated at 300 million tons (at 30% moisture content), but of this only an estimated 7 million tons were believed exploitable by then available industrial methods. This industrially usable peat occurred on six bogs ranging in area between 500 and 1,500 acres. The reserves were judged to be insufficient to support a power station (Howard, 1968).

The level of past and present industrial exploitation of peat for fuel and other products in Northern Ireland (Department of Commerce for Northern Ireland, personal communication; Rural Industries Development Committee, 1963) contrasts with the situation in the Irish Republic, where a combination of imaginative development and more extensive suitable peat deposits in very large raised mires, has led to the establishment of peat-burning power stations and other medium-sized peat-based industries. In 1969-70, 36% of the electricity supply in the Republic was produced by peat-burning units (Freeman, 1972). Some of the turf for electricity generation is hand-won by private producers, but most is mechanically extracted by Bord na Mona, the Irish State Peat Board established in 1946 to develop the country's peat resources

(Lawlor, 1968). Some details of equipment design and operation are given in W.A.R. Green (1968) and Lunny (1968). Bord na Mona supplies milled (fragmented and dried) peat to power stations and large quantities of peat briquettes and moss peat. Peat briquettes consist of milled peat which has been artifically dried to a low water content and pressed into hand-sized chunks (Barron, 1968); they are used as a fuel, both domestically and industrially.

The energy crisis has produced an upsurge in the demand for peat as a fuel. Production by Bord na Mona is insufficient to meet demand and a quota system has been instigated for exports to Northern Ireland. According to the Department of Commerce for Northern Ireland (personal communication), imports from the Irish Republic in 1977 amounted to 5,277 tons of 'peat' (moss peat for horticulture- value £171,788) and 24,642 tons of 'agglomerated peat' (peat turf and peat briquettes; value £426,224). This contrasts with an export of only 120 tons of peat from Northern Ireland (value, £6,033). Imports from Bord na Mona in 1978 by McDowell's of Randalstown, the main importer, amounted to 6,000 tons of briquettes, 15,000 tons of turf and 5,000 tons of peat moss (personal communication). These were annual allocations, and liable to fluctuate or cease in future.

(ii)   *Use as a soil conditioner*

Milled fresh *Sphagnum* peat ('moss peat') is widely employed as a soil conditioner in horticulture. Its value is partly to increase the organic content of soils, aiding water-holding capacity and benefitting soil structure, and partly associated with the very high cation exchange capacity of *Sphagnum* peat. The latter can, of course, only be realized if cations are available in the soil from some other source. In 1952-53 three bogs in Northern Ireland were worked on a commercial scale for moss peat (Howard, 1968), but only very small scale exploitation continues.

Since about 1960, a further development in the horticultural use of peat has been for the production of propagating pots, valuable for seedling transplantation with minimum root disturbance. These pots are manufactured from a mixture of peat, and organic fibre (jute or wool waste) with the addition of nutrients (Rural Industries Development Committee, 1963).

(iii)   *Other uses of peat*

Peat has considerable potential, which has been barely exploited in Northern Ireland, as a raw material for the production of chemicals and other products. Before 1914 there was a plant producing ammonia at Carnlough and a gas plant at Portadown (Rural Industries Development Committee, 1963). Activated charcoal was produced for a short period in the mid-1950s at Londonderry, using peat from the Irish Republic, but the peat proved to be of an unsuitable quality and the plant was closed. The possibility of extracting wax from peat has been the subject of research by the Industrial Division of the Department of Industrial and Forensic Science at Belfast, but there has been no commercial production.

Uses of peatland

Peatland can be regarded not only as a source of peat, but also as an exploitable area. As is the case with the peat itself, there is a long history of exploitation of peatland on a piecemeal individualistic basis, but, in contrast to peat, intervention on an institutional scale has in recent years become of great importance. Once regarded by many as wasteland, the value of peatland is increasing yearly, with ever greater possibilities of conflict or compromise between alternative uses. One manifestation of this is the increasing competition from hill farming faced by forestry in the aquisition of hill peatlands.

(i) Some low input productive uses

Various animals and plants are or could be harvested from peatland with relatively low levels of input of capital or energy.

In the case of fens, *Phragmites* was once widely gathered for thatching, but very few men are still employed in the trade. Flax stems, today imported, constitute another material employed for thatching, but there seems to be no record of *Cladium* being used. The latter makes a very durable thatch and was once widely cut for this purpose on the East Anglian fens (Godwin, 1978). Fens are also important as habitats of various waterfowl.

Cranberries (*Vaccinium oxycoccos*) and bilberries *(V. myrtillus)* are gathered from bogs for food, and wine making. In America cranberries and blueberries (*Vaccinium spp.*) are grown on an industrial scale directly on peat deposits, with little preparation of the ground (Moore and Bellamy, 1973). This might be a possible minor industry for Northern Ireland.

The red grouse (*Lagopus lagopus scoticus*) can be found on many bogs, but intensive management of peatland for grouse, such as is practised on heathland, including peatland, in England and Scotland (Gimingham, 1972), is virtually non-existent (Forest Service, DoA personal communication; Watson and Miller, 1976). Partly because of their now extensive ownership of blanket peatlands, the Forest Service (DoA) has become increasingly aware of the benefits, in terms of increased bags of grouse, of good management of peatland for grouse shooting and, following experimental work at Gortin Glen, more intensive management practices are being slowly introduced. These management practices recommended for grouse production include drainage to increase the amount of *Calluna,* the principal food, and rotational burning to create a patchwork of young and middle-aged *Calluna* stands. Young Calluna is relatively nutritious and older *Calluna* provides cover for the birds.

A few red deer (*Cervus elaphus,* or perhaps the hydrid with sika) are found at Killeter (County Tyrone) and this species is a possible herbivore for upland peatlands. The red deer is indigenous in Ireland and herds in a wild state are present around Killarney, in the Wicklow Mountains and at Glenveagh, Donegal.

(ii) Farming and peatland

Large areas of peatland have been and often still are used as unimproved pastureland. The productive, herbaceous, seasonally-flooded fens of Lough Neagh were, for instance, traditionally grazed in summer or cut for hay (White, 1932). Of much greater general importance, because of their substantial area, are hill peatlands. These are unsuitable for cultivation, principally due to their altitude (Symons, 1963) and they have traditionally been utilized as rough grazing for cattle and sheep at very low stocking densities of perhaps 3-5 acres/ewe (An Foras Taluntais, 1977). In the past, sheep have been the more important animals in terms of numbers, but the use of cattle is today increasing. Sheep graze the hills all year, but have access to lower pastures on mineral soil at certain times, especially when lambing. A traditional method of management has been periodic burning to remove old, woody vegetation and encourage new growth, an activity which has generally been carried out in too haphazard a fashion and at intervals too infrequent for optimum results. Fencing, which at times has also been used by some farmers, helps in the maintenance of correct stocking levels. A common limitation on the numbers of animals which can be kept in the hills during the summer is the quantity of winter grazing available on the improved pastures (inbyes).

Research on methods of improving hill farming has been undertaken at Glenwhirry, County Antrim, the hill farm attached to Greenmount Agricultural College (Hunter, 1968 *a & b*; McClelland, 1968). This work has shown that substantial improvements in production and profit can accrue from good grazing management (using fencing), drainage, liming, fertilizing and reseeding (Hunter, 1968*a*). The poor soils and adverse climatic conditions, reducing potential economic returns, necessitate careful selection of areas which could benefit most fully from applications of fertilizer and reseeding (Reith, 1973). In the Irish Republic, much work on methods of reclaiming low altitude uncut blanket peatland has been undertaken at Glenamoy, County Mayo (e.g. Burke, 1968; O'Hare, 1973; O'Toole, 1968) and of cut-over peat at Lullymore, County Kildare.

Reclamation of lowland peatland dates back several centuries (Walsh *et al.*, 1958) and reference to early methods of bog reclamation can be found in the Memoirs of the first (1833) edition of Ordnance Survey maps (Wishart, 1978). One method was to burn the surface of the flow moss (the name given to the upper fresh *Sphagnum* peat) and to collect the ashes which were then left in pits over the winter, and then mixed with stable dung and spread on marginal boglands. Potatoes, oats and grass were all planted on reclaimed bogland.

Drainage of peatland and of other areas liable to flooding involves both field and arterial drainage (Wilcock, 1979). The latter is carried-out as a central government activity, the aim being to improve the drainage characteristics of major water courses, a prerequisite in many areas for effective field drainage. Field drainage is carried-out by the individual farmer, financially assisted by substantial grant-aid, and involves the installation of underdrainage and surface ditches. Today, underdrainage is usually installed by laying lines of earthenware or plastic pipes at a depth of 100-120 cm. A permeable back-fill such as graded gravel may be used above the drains. There has actually been little research in Northern Ireland on the effects of drainage schemes on other aspects of the environment (Wilcock, 1979).

Reclaimed fenlands, such as those deriving from fen peat exposed after removal of raised bog *Sphagnum* peat, can be naturally productive. Successful reclamation of bog peatland, however, depends not only on satisfactory drainage, but also on the application of suitable quantities of lime, nutrients (potassium, phosphate and nitrogen) and trace elements (especially copper, cobalt and molybdenum) (An Foras Taluntais, 1977; Hunter, 1968*a*; Kavanagh and Herlihy, 1975; O'Toole, 1968). Initial fertilizing and heavy liming followed by annual applications of fertilizers and liming at about 5-yearly intervals are recommended practices. Reserves of nitrogen are actually high in peat (O'Hare, 1973), but usually less than 5% of this is available in forms capable of being utilized by plants (Puustjarvi and Robertson, 1975). Microbiological activity, aiding nitrogen mineralization, is stimulated by drainage, fertilizer application or decreased acidity, and nitrogen is also made available by fixation if clover is planted. The high cation exchange capacity of peat ensures that drainage losses are low and fertilizer utilization efficient. On low level blanket peat at Glenamoy, a grass/clover (*Lolium perenne/Trifolium repens*) sward was established over a 3-year period by surface sowing without initial rotovation (An Foras Taluntais, 1977). The main difficulty in grassland farming on peat at Glenamoy is that of utilization of grasses on soils which have a low load-bearing capacity and are easily poached. This low-altitude reclaimed blanket peatland can probably best be used in conjunction with dry mineral soils and unreclaimed peatland. This contrasts with the reclaimed raised mire peatlands situated further from the coast in drier areas and which can be used for large-scale vegetable production, especially of root crops like carrots and parsnips, and such crops as sugar beet. The risk of frost in low-lying sites somewhat limits the value of reclaimed raised bogs for potatoes (Symons, 1963).

(iii) Forestry and peatland

At one time, for instance during the Atlantic Period, much of Ireland including all but the highest parts of the hills, was forest covered. By 1600 A.D. about one eighth of the land area of Ireland, confined to lowlands, was still forested, but this had been reduced to only 2% by 1800 A.D. and much of the countryside was treeless (McCracken, 1971). State planting commenced in Ireland in 1903, but it has only been during the last 30 years that planting has attained a substantial level in Northern Ireland. Government policy that forestry should not compete with agriculture has helped to ensure that peatland, and particularly blanket peatland, has played a major role in recent afforestation schemes. The first large-scale attempts at tree planting on deep peat were in 1949.

Trials have indicated that Sitka spruce (*Picea sitchensis*) and Lodgepole pine (*Pinus contorta*) are the most promising species for forestry purposes on deep blanket peat in Northern Ireland (Jack, 1973). Both species produce acceptable sawn timber, but if fast grown, Lodgepole wood is liable to be knotty. The wood of Sitka, but not Lodgepole, is a desirable species for chipboard manufacture. When planted on peat, Sitka has a higher yield class than Lodgepole (Forest Service, 1976) and Sitka has become by far the most widely planted tree in Northern Ireland. In spite of the increased nutrient mobilization induced by artificial drainage, there are considerable problems of nutrient deficiency with Sitka on blanket peat (Dickson, 1977; Dickson and Savill, 1974; Parker, 1962).

Dickson (1977) has discussed possible solutions to this problem. In the case of existing plantations these include application of nitrogen in the form of urea at intervals of 3-4 years, improvement of existing drainage, application of lime and removal of the Sitka and replacement by Lodgepole. Lodgepole is less nutrient demanding than Sitka (Dickson, 1977) and has roots which extend deeper into the anaerobic soil layer (Coutts and Philipson, 1978b). The current practice is to plant Lodgepole only on oligotrophic sites, with Sitka on mesotrophic and eutrophic sites (Forest Service, 1978). Recent experiments with Sitka in which lime application and rotovation have preceded the excavation of deep drains have been encouraging (Dickson, 1977). A more detailed account of the extent and problems of forestry in planting peatland is given by R. W. Tomlinson in "Vegetation" Chapter 10.

(iv) Peatlands as catchments

Peatlands, particularly of blanket peat, form substantial components of many river catchments in Northern Ireland. However, very little research into the hydraulic properties of peat or its influence on streamflow has been undertaken in Northern Ireland, and what knowledge exists on this subject has therefore been largely inferred from other areas, principally from the Republic of Ireland, where considerable research into the problems of peat hydrology has been in progress for several years (e.g. Dooge, 1975; Burke, 1975; Galvin, 1976).

Recent research into peat hydrology stresses that the amount of water which any body of peat will store, and the speed with which it will be transmitted, depend very largely on the peat's level of decomposition. Poorly decomposed surface peats for example can hold relatively large volumes of water when saturated but drain very quickly. Well-decomposed peats, in contrast, hold smaller volumes of water when saturated, but retain large proportions of this water even in dry conditions because they transmit water very slowly. It follows that the behaviour of any particular peat body depends on the distribution within it of well- and poorly-decomposed peat.

It is dangerous to generalise about any subject in which the amount of experimental fieldwork is limited, but field data suggest very strongly that in a temperate maritime climate such as Northern Ireland's, undrained peat seldom exerts the beneficial seasonal effects on streamflow that are often attributed to it. It does not seem to act like a long-term sponge holding back water in winter and releasing it in summer. Residence times in peat, where these have been measured, appear to be quite short (Robertson et al., 1968), and flash floods are liable to follow closely on heavy precipitation.

One of the principal users of peatland in Northern Ireland is the Forest Service (DoA), and a considerable research effort has been directed at ways of effectively lowering the water tables in peatlands in order to improve rooting systems, tree stability and crop yield. Surface drains on the blanket peat and peaty gleys of Northern Ireland have generally proved an ineffective method of lowering water tables. (e.g. Savill, Dickson and Wilson, 1974; Savill, 1976). Elsewhere in Ireland the story is the same. In a detailed examination of different ditching techniques in well-decomposed peats at Glenamoy in County Mayo, Burke (1975) found that 1 metre deep ditches were ineffective in lowering water tables at distances from the ditch greater than 1.83 metres. Effective lowering of the water table in such peats therefore requires 1 metre deep ditches every 3.66 metres. This very high density of artificial drainage far exceeds normal ditching practice in the afforested peatlands of Northern Ireland.

In less decomposed peats, a lower water table can be achieved with a wider ditch-spacing. Where ditching was successful in lowering water tables on relatively well-decomposed peats at Glenamoy, the mean summer depth of the water tables in the drained area is about half a metre. This is sufficient however to have an effect on streamflow. Over a twelve month period, streamflow from drained peats at Glenamoy was found to be 79% of precipitation as compared to 47% on neighbouring undrained peats (Burke, 1975). By lowering the water table peat drainage also increases storage capacity and ensures that after heavy rainfall streams coming off a drained catchment will not start to flow as soon as those in undrained areas.

The effects of a small arterial drainage scheme on the streamflow of a catchment containing large proportions of peat and gley soils was investigated by Wilcock (1977,

1979) who concluded that even minor works might be temporarily quite effective in withdrawing water from catchment storage, in reducing high flows and in increasing low summer flows. However there was evidence that these benefits are likely to be short-lived.

(v) Conservation of peatlands

The area of peatland that has been little disturbed by man, and retains vegetation approaching that of 'natural' peatland, is shrinking fast. The area of uncut and unreclaimed land on the Garry Bog has shrunk from c. 2,158 acres in 1833 to 812 acres in 1977 (Wishart, 1978). Although extensive areas of 'natural' blanket peatlands persist, these too are disappearing fast with the recent increase in land under forestry. It has been estimated that man has modified about 31,000 of the 35,000 hectares of lowland peat and about 30,000 of 132,000 hectares of blanket peat in Northern Ireland (Hammond, 1979).

The statutory provision for the establishment of National Nature Reserves and Areas of Scientific Interest, the latter receiving partial protection, is the Amenity Lands Act (Northern Ireland) 1965. In addition to areas managed by the Conservation Branch, Department of the Environment, the government organization which administers the Act, the Forest Service, maintains a supplementary series of sites known as Forest Nature Reserves. The aim of the Conservation Branch is to acquire the best possible sites in each habitat type, a policy which, in the case of peatlands, has to date only been partly realized. The best intact bogs lie in the Fairy Water valley, County Tyrone, but no examples of these or other low altitude raised mires have yet been designated reserves. Three high altitude raised bogs within general blanket peat areas have been acquired: these are Lough Naman (County Fermanagh), Killeter (County Tyrone; two areas) and Meenadoan (County Tyrone). Three small Reserves within Slieveanorra Forest (County Antrim) are examples of blanket peatland, two showing active peat erosion. The Garron Plateau (County Antrim), an extensive blanket bog, is proposed as an Area of Scientific Interest. To the south of Lough Neagh, Brackagh Bog (County Armagh) has been acquired as an example of cut-over bog and fen (cf. White, 1930; 1932) and the Birches (near Washing Bay, Lough Neagh), which was bought from the Irish Peat Development Company, is to be managed partly as a recreational/educational area (Peatlands Park). At the Birches it is intended to establish a Countryside Centre, thematically based on the history of peat utilization.

In the case of raised and blanket peatland, the only active management practice is prevention of excessive grazing; to this end, it has proved necessary to fence Naman. Management of Brackagh and the Birches presents additional problems. Both are liable to encroachment by shrubs and trees, and pollution, for instance by dumping, needs to be eliminated. Public access to the Birches may need to be restricted in view of the hazardous terrain caused by the existence of numerous old peat cuttings. The continued existence of extensive areas of fenland vegetation on Brackagh Bog is endangered by lowering of the regional water-table associated with the lowering of the level of Lough Neagh and drainage improvement works on the Upper River Bann. This bog, once regularly flooded, is only very rarely inundated today and a system of sluices, with active management, will have to be installed to ensure the continued existence of the rich fenland fauna and flora.

In a broad sense the aim of peatland conservation is not only to maintain areas of relatively undisturbed mires and peat deposits for the edification of future generations. It is also to ensure that peatland resources are used for the best long-term interests of mankind and not squandered for immediate returns. In a country and, indeed, in a world of limited natural resources the pressures on peatlands are bound to increase. Rapid transformation of even remote areas of peatland are quite feasible in an economic and political climate in which such transformation using large injections of energy and capital are considered desirable. Different usages of peatland are often reconcilable and it is vital that channels of communication between people working in institutions concerned with peatland management remain open (Allen, 1974). In this context the unofficial policy of the Forest Service to devote about 10% of forest areas to amenity and conservation is to be applauded and it is hoped that such enlightened attitudes will persist and spread, thus helping to ensure the conservation of one of Northern Ireland's most valuable resources.

REFERENCES

Allen, J., 1974. Landscape conservation and exploitation. *Marginal land: integration or competition?* The Potassium Institute. Colloquium Proceedings, No. 4, 107–123.

An Foras Taluntais, 1977. *The future of Glenamoy.* Report of a working group.

Armstrong, J. I., Calvert, J. and Ingold, C. T., 1930. The ecology of the Mountains of Mourne with special reference to Slieve Donard. *Proceedings of Royal Irish Academy,* 39, B, 440–452.

Barron, F., 1968. Briquetting of milled peat in Ireland. *Transactions of the Second International Peat Congress, Leningrad, U.S.S.R.: Edit.* R. A. Robertson. H.M.S.O., Edinburgh, Vol. 1, 483–497.

Barry, T. A., 1969. Origins and distribution of peat types in the bogs of Ireland. *Irish Forestry,* 26, 40–52.

Bazley, R. A. B., 1978. Interglacial and interstadial deposits in Northern Ireland. *Geological Survey of Northern Ireland.* Report 77/16.

Bellamy, D. J., 1968. An ecological approach to the classification of European mires. *Proceedings of the Third International Peat Congress, Quebec, Canada, Edit.* C. Lafleur & J. Butler. Runge Press Ltd., Ottawa, Canada, 74–79.

Bellamy, D. J. and Bellamy, S. R., 1967. An ecological approach to the classification of the lowland mires of Ireland. *Proceedings of the Royal Irish Academy* 65, B, 237–251.

Bishop, D. W. and Mitchell, G. F., 1946. On a recent bog-flow in Meenacharvy Townland, Co. Donegal. *Scientific Proceedings of the Royal Dublin Society,* 24, 151–156.

Bower, M. M., 1962. The cause of erosion in blanket peat bogs. *Scottish Geographical Magazine,* 78, 33–43.

Brown, L. T., 1968. *A survey of turf working in County Down.* Unpublished M.Sc. thesis. The Queen's University of Belfast.

Burke, W., 1968. Drainage of blanket peat at Glenamoy. *Transactions of the Second International Peat Congress, Leningrad, U.S.S.R., Edit.* R. A. Robertson. H.M.S.O., Edinburgh, Vol. 2, 809–817.

Burke, W., 1975. Aspects of the hydrology of blanket peat in Ireland. *Hydrology of marsh-ridden areas,* Studies and Reports in Hydrology, 19, UNESCO – International Association of Hydrological Sciences, 171–182.

Clymo, R. S., 1963. Ion exchange in *Sphagnum* and its relation to bog ecology. *Annals of Botany,* 27, 309–324.

Clymo, R. S., 1964. The origin of acidity in *Sphagnum* bogs. *The Bryologist,* 67, 427–431.

Clymo, R. S., 1965. Experiments on the breakdown of *Sphagnum* in two bogs. *Journal of Ecology,* 53, 747–758.

Coe, W. E., 1969. *The engineering industry of the North of Ireland*. David & Charles.

Colhoun, E. A., Common, R. and Cruickshank, M. M., 1965. Recent bog flows and debris slides in the north of Ireland. *Scientific Proceedings of the Royal Dublin Society*, 2A, 163–174.

Cruickshank, J. G., 1970. Soils and pedogensis in the North of Ireland. *Irish Geographical Studies, Edit.* N. Stephens and R. E. Glasscock, Department of Geography, The Queen's University, Belfast, 89–104.

C.S.R.D. (Council of Scientific Research and Development), 1956. *The Northern Ireland Peat Bog Survey*. Final report of the preliminary survey. H.M.S.O., Belfast.

Coutts, M. P. and Philipson, J. J., 1978*a*. Tolerance of tree roots to waterlogging. 1. Survival of Sitka spruce and Lodgepole pine. *New Phytologist*, 80, 63–69.

Coutts, M. P. and Philipson, J. J., 1978*b*. Tolerance of tree roots to waterlogging. 2. Tolerance of Sitka spruce and Lodgepole pine to waterlogged soil. *New Phytologist*, 80, 71–77.

Dallas, W. G., 1962. The progress of peatland afforestation in Northern Ireland. *Irish Forestry*, 19, 84–93.

Dallas, W. G., 1967. Irish peats and their drainage for afforestation. *Irish Forestry*, 24, 8–23.

Daniels, R. E., 1978. Floristic analyses of British mires and mire communities. *Journal of Ecology*, 66, 773–802.

Delap, A. D. and Mitchell, G. F., 1939. On a recent bog-flow in Powerscourt Mountain Townland, Co. Wicklow. *Scientific Proceedings of the Royal Dublin Society*, 22, 195–198.

Department of the Environment (Northern Ireland) Conservation Branch, 1977. Guide to the National Nature Reserves, Forest Nature Reserves, Areas of Scientific Interest and Bird Sanctuaries in Northern Ireland. Nature Reserves Committee & Wild Birds Advisory Committee. 3rd Edition.

Dickson, D. A., 1977. Nutrition of Sitka spruce on peat – problems and speculations. *Irish Forestry*, 34, 31–39.

Dickson, D. A. and Savill, P. S., 1974. Early growth of *Picea sitchensis* (Bong.) Carr. on deep oligotrophic peat in Northern Ireland. *Forestry*, 47, 57–88.

Dooge, J., 1975. The water balance of bogs and fens. *Hydrology of marsh-ridden areas*, Studies and Reports in Hydrology 19, UNESCO – International Association of Hydrological Sciences, 233–271.

Duff, M., 1930. The ecology of the Moss Lane Region, Lough Neagh. *Proceedings of the Royal Irish Academy*, 39B, 477–496.

Forest Service, 1976. Inventory of State Forests 1974-75. Department of Agriculture, Northern Ireland. Unpublished.

Forest Service, 1978. Forest Service Code. Department of Agriculture, Northern Ireland.

Freeman, T. W., 1972. *Ireland*, Methuen.

Galvin, L. F., 1976. Physical properties of Irish peats. *Irish Journal of Agricultural Research*, 15, 207–221.

Gimingham, C. H., 1972. *Ecology of heathlands*. Chapman & Hall, London.

Goddard, A., 1971. *Studies of the vegetational changes associated with initiation of blanket peat accumulation in north-east Ireland*. Unpublished Ph.D. thesis, Queen's University, Belfast.

Godwin, H., 1978. *Fenland: its ancient past and uncertain future*. Cambridge University Press.

Green, W. A. R., 1968. Mechanical design features of bog development and production machinery. *Transactions of the Second International Peat Conference, Leningrad, U.S.S.R., Edit.* R. A. Robertson. H.M.S.O., Edinburgh, 291–315.

Hammond, R. F., 1968. Studies in the development of a raised bog in central Ireland. *Proceedings of the Third International Peat Congress, Quebec, Canada, Edit.* C. Lafleur & J. Butler. Runge Press Ltd., Ottawa, Canada, 109–115.

Hammond, R. F., 1979. *The Peatlands of Ireland*. Soil Survey Bulletin. 35, An Foras Taluntais, Dublin.

Howard, A. J., 1968. Peat resources and development in Northern Ireland. *Transactions of the Second International Peat Congress, Leningrad, U.S.S.R., Edit.* R. A. Robertson. H.M.S.O., Edinburgh, Vol. 1, 27–28.

Hunter, A. A., 1968*a*. Improvement of hill land. *Agriculture in Northern Ireland*, 42, 402–404.

Hunter, A. A., 1968*b*. Hill cow management. *Agriculture in Northern Ireland*, 43, 273–276.

Jack, W. H., 1973. The growth of trees on peat in Northern Ireland. *Peatland Forestry*. Natural Environment Research Council, 27–50.

Jessen, K., 1949. Studies in late Quaternary deposits and flora-history of Ireland. *Proceedings of Royal Irish Academy,* 52B, 85–290.

Kavanagh, T. and Herlihy, M., 1975. Microbiological aspects. *Peat in horticulture, Edit.* D. W. Robinson & J. G. D. Lamb. Academic Press, 40–49.

Lawlor, D. C., 1968. Operation of Bord na Mona, the Irish State Peat Board. *Transactions of the Second International Peat Congress, Leningrad, U.S.S.R., Edit.* R. A. Robertson. H.M.S.O., Edinburgh, Vol. 1, 321–325.

Lunny, F., 1968. Design and operation of medium-sized steam boiler installations for turf-firing. *Transactions of the Second International Peat Congress, Leningrad, U.S.S.R., Edit.* R. A. Robertson. H.M.S.O., Edinburgh, Vol. 1, 401–423.

McClelland, T. H., 1968. Hill farming – can it pay? *Agriculture in Northern Ireland,* 43, 45–49.

McCracken, E., 1971. *The Irish woods since Tudor times.* David and Charles, Newton Abbot.

Miller, H. M. S., 1968. Use of peat as a domestic fuel in Ireland. *Transactions of the Second International Peat Congress, Leningrad, U.S.S.R., Edit.* R. A. Robertson. H.M.S.O., Edinburgh, Vol. 1, 471–482.

Mitchell, G. F., 1956. Post-Boreal pollen-diagrams from Irish raised bogs. *Proceedings of Royal Irish Academy,* 57B, 185–251.

Mitchell, G. F., 1976. *The Irish landscape.* Collins, London.

Mooney, C. T., 1978. *The Garry Bog, stratigraphy and pollen analysis.* Undergraduate dissertation, Department of Environmental Science, New University of Ulster.

Moore, J. J., 1972. Report of the Glenamoy (Ireland) ecosystem study for 1971. *Proceedings of the Fourth International Meeting on the Biological Productivity of Tundra, Leningrad, U.S.S.R., 1971, Edit.* F. E. Wielgolaski & T. Rosswall. Published by the Tundra Biome Steering Committee, International Biological Programme, Wenner-Gren Center, Sweden, 281–282.

Moore, P. D. and Bellamy, D. J., 1973. *Peatlands.* Elek Science, London.

Morrison, M. E. S., 1959. Evidence and interpretation of "Landname" in the north-east of Ireland. *Botaniska Notiser,* 112, 185–204.

O'Hare, P. J., 1973. The integrated use of peatlands. *Peatland Forestry.* Natural Environment Research Council, 51–62.

O'Sullivan, P. E., Oldfield, F. and Battarbee, R. W., 1973. Preliminary studies of Lough Neagh sediments, 1. Stratigraphy, chronology and pollen analysis. *Quaternary plant ecology, Edit.* H. J. B. Birks & R. G. West. Blackwell, Oxford, 267–278.

O'Toole, M. A. 1968. Lime requirements for pasture establishment on blanket peat. *Transactions of the Second International Peat Congress, Leningrad, U.S.S.R., Edit.* R. A. Robertson. H.M.S.O., Edinburgh, Vol. 2, 743–753.

Parker, R. E., 1962. The problems of peatland forestry. *Irish Forestry,* 19, 4–14.

Pilcher, J. R., 1973. Pollen analysis and radiocarbon dating of a peat on Slieve Gallion, County Tyrone, Northern Ireland. *New Phytologist,* 72, 681–689.

Praeger, R. L., 1934. *The botanist in Ireland.* Republished in 1974 by EP Publishing Ltd., England.

Puustjarvi, V. and Robertson, R. A., 1975. Physical and chemical properties. *Peat in horticulture, ed.* D. W. Robinson & J. G. D. Lamb. Academic Press, 23–38.

Reith, J. W. S., 1973. Soil conditions and nutrient status in hill land. *Hill pasture improvement and its economic utilisation.* The Potassium Institute, Colloquium Proceedings No. 3, 5–12.

Robertson, R. A., 1968. Scottish peat resources. *Transactions of the Second International Peat Congress, Leningrad, U.S.S.R., Edit.* R. A. Robertson. H.M.S.O., Edinburgh, Vol. 1, 29–35.

Robertson, R. A. and Jowsey, P. S., 1968. Peat resources and development in the United Kingdom. *Proceedings of the Third International Peat Congress, Quebec, Canada, Edit.* C. Lafleur & J. Butler. Runge Press Ltd., Ottawa, Canada, 13–14.

Robertson, R. A., Nicholson, I. A. and Hughes, R., 1968. Runoff studies on a peat catchment. *Transactions of the Second International Peat Congress, Leningrad, U.S.S.R., Edit.* R. A. Robertson, H.M.S.O., Edinburgh, Vol. 1, 161–168.

Rural Industries Development Committee, 1963. *Increasing employment in rural areas in Northern Ireland – a report on the past, present and future use of peatlands.* Northern Ireland Council of Social Services.

Rycroft, D. W., Williams, D. J. A. and Ingram, H. A. P., 1975a. The transmission of water through peat, I. *Journal of Ecology,* 63, 535–556

Rycroft, D. W., Williams, D. J. A. and Ingram, H. A. P., 1975b. The transmission of water through peat, II. Field experiments. *Journal of Ecology*, 63, 557–568.

Savill, P. S., Dickson, D. A. and Wilson, W. T., 1974. Effects of ploughing and drainage on growth and root development of Sitka spruce on deep peat in Northern Ireland. *Proceedings of the International Symposium on Forest Draining*, 2-6 September 1974, Finland, 241–252.

Savill, P. S., 1976. The effects of drainage and ploughing of surface water gleys on rooting and windthrow of Sitka spruce in Northern Ireland. *Forestry*, XLIX, 2, 133–141.

Savill, P. S. and McEwen, J. A., 1978. Timber production from Northern Ireland 1980–2004. *Irish Forestry*, 35, 115–123.

Smith, A. E. J., 1978. *The moss flora of Britain and Ireland*. Cambridge University Press.

Smith, A. G., 1958. Pollen analytical investigations of the mire at Fallahogy Townland, County Londonderry. *Proceedings of the Royal Irish Academy*, 59B, 329–343.

Smith, A. G., 1961. Cannons Lough, Kilrea, Co. Derry: stratigraphy and pollen analysis. *Proceedings of the Royal Irish Academy*, 61B, 369–383.

Smith, A. G., 1970. Late- and post-glacial vegetation and climatic history of Ireland: a review. *Irish Geographical Studies, Edit.* N. Stephens and R. E. Glasscock, Geography Department, The Queen's University, Belfast, 65–88.

Smith, A. G. and Pilcher, J. R., 1973. Radiocarbon dates and vegetational history of the British Isles. *New Phytologist*, 72, 903, 914.

Symons, L., 1963. Rough grazing, peat bog and woodland. *Land use in Northern Ireland, Edit.* L. Symons. University of London Press Ltd., 143–151.

Taylor, J. A., 1968. Peat deposits of Wales. *Transactions of the Second International Peat Congress, Leningrad, U.S.S.R., Edit.* R. A. Robertson. H.M.S.O., Edinburgh, Vol. 1, 37–48.

Tomlinson, R. W., 1981. The erosion of peat in the uplands of Northern Ireland. *Irish Geography*, 14, 51–64.

Walker, D. and Walker, P. M., 1961. Stratigraphic evidence of regeneration in some Irish bogs. *Journal of Ecology*, 49, 169–185.

Walsh, T., O'Hare, P. J. and Quinn, E., 1958. The use of peatland in Irish agriculture. *The Advancement of Science*, 14, 405–416.

Watson, A. and Miller, G. R., 1976. Grouse management. *The Game Conservancy and the Institute of Terrestrial Ecology*, U.K. Revised edition.

Webb, D. A., 1967. *An Irish flora*. Dundalgan Press, Dundalk.

White, J. M., 1930. Re-colonisation after peat-cutting. *Proceedings of the Royal Irish Academy*, 39B, 453–476.

White, J. M., 1932. The fens of North Armagh. *Proceedings of the Royal Irish Academy*, 40B, 233–283.

Wilcock, D. N., 1977. The effects of channel clearance and peat drainage on the water balance of the Glenullin basin, County Londonderry, Northern Ireland. *Proceedings of the Royal Irish Academy*, 77B, 15, 253–267.

Wilcock, D. N., 1979a. Post-war drainage, fertilizer use and environmental impact in Northern Ireland. *Journal of Environmental Management*, 8, 137–149.

Wilcock, D. N., 1979b. The hydrology of a peatland catchment in Northern Ireland following channel clearance. G. E. Hollis (*Edit.*), *Man's impact on the hydrological cycle in the United Kingdom*, 93–107.

Wishart, J. N., 1978. *Changing peatland in North Antrim*. Unpublished M.Sc. thesis, New University of Ulster.

CHAPTER X

Vegetation

ROY W. TOMLINSON,
Lecturer in Geography, The Queen's University of Belfast

Organizations of naturalists have been in existence in Northern Ireland since the last century and there have been many notable individual workers, for example Praeger, Stewart and Corry, but it remains true that published material on vegetation is limited. In consequence the first task of this chapter is to attempt a description of some of the communities which exist; a second aim is to assess these communities as resources for the people of Northern Ireland.

History of the vegetation

Symons (1963) demonstrated that in most counties of Northern Ireland more than 80% of the area was in 'improved' land. Although this figure was derived from surveys conducted in 1953, Hill (1963) felt able to conclude that the broad pattern of land use remained the same: since the main factor in the distribution of 'improved' and 'unimproved' lands was altitude, it may be expected that the distribution pattern continues to be generally true today despite the encroachment into the 'wild lands' as a result of government grants and subsidies and the expansion of forestry (Table 10.1). Areas of natural or semi-natural vegetation are therefore small and further, because of the prevailing climatic, geological and physiographic factors, the variety of such vegetation is also limited; peat-bog predominates in the wild-lands.

Although vegetation may reflect the current physical environment of Northern Ireland, its origin and development owes much to the activities of man over many centuries. A detailed account of the evolution of the vegetation has been admirably presented by Mitchell (1976), but a brief summary may help to place the current vegetation and its possible utility in perspective.

Although plants of an open habitat may have survived the Midlandian Cold Stage (70,000 to 10,000 years ago) and the short Nahanagan Stadial (10,500 to 10,000), vegetation only began to progress to its present form about 10,000 years ago at the start of the post-glacial period. As temperatures began to rise at the beginning of the Littletonian Warm Stage, animals and plants quickly moved back into Ireland via the land bridges connecting Ireland, Britain and Europe. These land bridges probably were short-lived; Mitchell postulates that links across the Irish Sea lasted no more than 1,500 years, from about 10,000 to 8,500 years ago. Although colonization was rapid,

TABLE 10.1

Land Use in Northern Ireland (February 1980)

Land Use	Total Grass		Total Crops		Forests		Woods+ Plantations		Other land on Agric+Holdings		Rough[1] Grazing	Total[2] Agric Area	Total Improved Land
	A	B	A	B	A	B	A	B	A	B	A	A	A
Antrim	52	80	6.0	9.5	3.3	5.1	0.7	1.0	2.7	4.0	19.0	80	65
Armagh	69	87	5.5	7.0	2.0	2.5	0.5	0.7	2.0	2.6	5.0	82	79
Down	60	80	10.6	14.0	1.6	2.1	1.0	1.3	2.0	2.7	5.6	79	75
Fermanagh	64	83	0.3	0.4	9.8	13.0	1.0	1.1	2.0	1.7	13.0	80	77
Londonderry	49	74.5	9.5	14.0	4.1	6.0	0.8	1.2	2.5	3.8	20.0	82	66
Tyrone	56	84	3.0	4.6	3.8	5.7	1.1	1.7	3.0	4.3	21.4	85	67
Northern Ireland	57		6.0		3.9		0.8		3.5		17.0	81	70

[1]Rough grazing on forest land not included in county totals (figures not available)
[2]Not including forestry
A Per cent of the total land area
B Per cent of total 'improved' land. 'Improved' land excludes rough grazing, includes forestry

208

the severance of land connections after such a relatively short time and so early in the migratory sequence has meant that the variety of plants native to Ireland is only two-thirds the number that are native to Britain. It must be remembered also that the plants were migrating from Europe and that the mainland of Britain was already at the outer edge of the ecological range of some plants; many plants reached south-east England, but did not progress further.

There has been relatively little research on the migration of plants into Ireland in general or into particular pathways of movement. Different localities with their differing physical and biological environments must surely have had contrasting communities and varying rates of vegetational development; succession depends on the species available and an enclosed valley away from the main lines of plant movement would not have the same vegetational history as a site within such pathways. In the absence of such detailed study it may be sufficient here to offer a generalised diagram of the development of vegetation up to the so-called climax woodland (Figure 10.1). In the period 7,000 to 5,500 B.P. therefore, the lowland sites with good soils and drainage were covered by a dense deciduous woodland dominated by alder, oak and elm whereas the uplands had a birch and pine community. Temperatures in this period may have been at the highest within the Littletonian Stage, but moisture was also high. Bogs had developed throughout the earlier part of

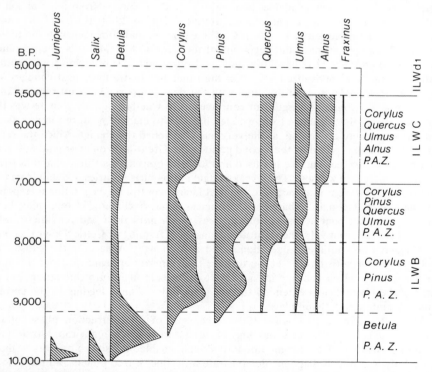

Figure 10.1 Generalised diagram of the development of vegetation in Ireland to the 'climax' woodland. (from Mitchell, 1976)

the Littletonian in the inter-drumlin hollows and lakes, left after retreat of the ice: the deposition of litter from floating aquatics and submerged plants gradually allowed reeds to enter the shallower waters, and as these in turn were deposited, fen peat and carr lands were formed. The onset of wetter conditions in the climax period saw the change to more acidic peat environments and the beginning of the *Sphagnum* dominated raised bogs (see Chapter 9). The scene at the climatic optimum is of lowland forest, interspersed by bogs and a few lakes, with a thinner, less luxuriantly wooded upland. Into this landscape, at around 5,500 B.P., came the Neolithic farmers clearing small patches of woodland, probably those of better soil on which the elm was dominant, and no longer was the vegetation a response solely to the physical conditions. However, despite the abundant evidence of woodland clearance which is shown in pollen diagrams, as late as Tudor times lowland Northern Ireland was mostly in forest (McCracken, 1971). One or two small areas of woodland which exist today may be direct descendants of this forest.

Whereas much of the lowlands remained under forest, albeit secondary, through to recent times, the uplands had a markedly different development; clearance of the woodlands by early man was permanent. Varying altitude and local topography, for example rock basins within the upland plateaux, have created differing vegetational histories: blanket peat was initiated first in such basins. However, from the numerous radio-carbon dates now available, two major periods of change from mineral soil to blanket peat seem to be apparent; one around 1,700 to 2,000 B.C. and the other within one or two centuries of 700 B.C. The earlier period coincides with the major expansion in agriculture at the beginning of the Bronze Age, and it is often claimed that this expansion led to soil acidification, podsolization and subsequent peat accumulation on the wet, podsolized soils. On the other hand, stratigraphical changes are apparent in lowland bogs at this time with the peat composed of plant remains of a wetter bog environment. Argument continues as to whether man or climate was the primary cause of the change from wooded hillsides to blanket peat, but in any event man was certainly active and, at the very least, hastened the change. Much the same kind of problem is posed by the second period. The Grenz horizon of around 600 B.C. is a major recurrence surface in raised and lowland bogs across Europe, and as such, indicates increased wetness. The level and date of this surface varies in detail from bog to bog, and it is clear that local hydrological factors control the vegetational response to the regional climatic change. Nevertheless, such a climatic change may have initiated blanket peat accumulation in areas which until then had remained under mineral soil: alternatively, the vigorous expansion of farming by Celtic 'Dowris' people may again have initiated vegetational and soil changes. Whatever the cause, the uplands of Northern Ireland began to have their present appearance from this time onward; marginal areas of the hillsides were at times brought into cultivation, but on others, the blanket peat extended further. The major change leading to the current peat vegetation had taken place.

Mitchell (1976) marks A.D. 300 as the start of his destruction phase of the Littletonian (I.L.W.d_2). The technology of agriculture began to make rapid strides; the coulter plough, and later the mouldboard plough, enabled the soil to be worked more efficiently and pollen diagrams demonstrate a decline in tree pollens, an increase in *Plantago lanceolata* and other weeds of cultivation, as well as cereal pollen. Farming in small clan groups and later in common fields became widespread, and as agriculture

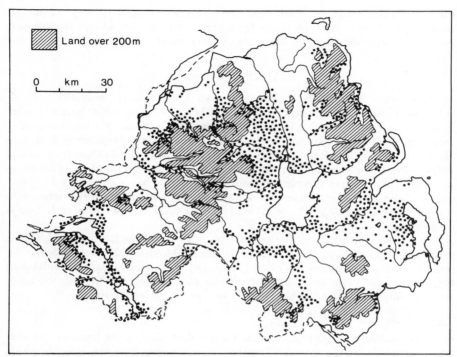

Figure 10.2 Probable distribution of woodland *c.* 1600 A.D. (after McCracken, 1971)

became more efficient or productive, so population grew leading to further expansion. In southern Ireland a major increase in agricultural activity came with monastic settlement and with Anglo-Norman settlement in general. The distribution of these settlements was largely confined to the areas of better soils and drier climate, thus in the north of Ireland such settlements largely were restricted to the south and east. Anglo-Norman effects on the vegetation were not therefore as great in Northern Ireland as in the rest of the island; a high proportion of the lowlands continued to be covered by woodland and remained so until the Tudor exploitation of the countryside (Figure 10.2). To the northwest of Lough Neagh, in the Glens of Antrim and in parts of Armagh the woodland was quite dense, but in County Down it was largely restricted to the sides of drumlins with small lakes and bogs between (McCracken, 1944; 1971).

The settlement of English and Scots in Ireland meant not only a further expansion of agricultural practice, but also, as McCracken (1971) observes, 'a sort of industrial revolution in the country'. Imports of iron were no longer necessary as pig and bar iron was produced locally, and this created a greater demand for timber to supply fuel. In addition, wood was needed for house and farm building, for barrels and boxes and in many other industries: by the eighteenth century local supplies of timber were insufficient to meet demand. This failure of supply may reflect widespread deforestation or simply lack of the required variety of wood, but it should be noted that timber offered for sale was in fairly inaccessible places. By the nineteenth century, apart from small woods on demesnes, the only remnants in Northern Ireland of the once extensive woodlands were in isolated valleys, in the Sperrins and Glens of Antrim; the lowlands were now "improved" land, or under lake or bog.

Meres and mires

The wetlands may be broadly divided into two types; those in which acid, nutrient-poor conditions prevail – the so called mires, and those wetlands which have soil water of neutral to alkaline reaction, and are of higher nutrient status – the meres. Whereas the latter are rare in Northern Ireland, the mires or peat bogs are widespread. Hammond (1979) estimated that there are 161,552 ha of peatland in Northern Ireland and 9,713 ha of mere or fen, representing 12% and 0.7% respectively of the total land area. However, much of this peatland and all the fenland has been modified by man; peat has been dug for fuel, drained for forestry or totally reclaimed for agriculture with the result that only 104,000 ha or 7.7% of the total land area of Northern Ireland is occupied by "unmodified" peat.

The peatlands lie for the most part in the counties of Antrim, Londonderry, Tyrone and Fermanagh; small patches of blanket bog in the Mourne Mountains comprise the only peatland of any extent in County Down, and in Armagh bogland is confined to the north where mires occur intermixed with fenland (meres). In both the latter counties, small, inter-drumlin bogs occupy the sites of former small lakes.

Blanket bogs

Extensive areas of blanket peat occur on the Antrim plateau, the Sperrins and other upland areas. Such areas are often described as monotonous in appearance, but a wide variety of plant communities does occur: this variety can be observed both on a country-wide basis and also within the major areas of blanket peat. Dickson (1966) utilized a modified version of Poore's (1955) method of vegetation description and recognised several communities in his three study areas – Ballypatrick Forest, Beaghs Forest (both in north Antrim) and Lough Navar Forest (Fermanagh). For example, he divided the vegetation initially into those areas of flushed peat and unflushed peat i.e. peat which has/has not some mobile water flowing either over or through it. In the unflushed areas, most of the vegetation had no one dominant species. The structure tended to be an open one although cushions of *Sphagnum* spp. were conspicuous. *Trichophorum caespitosum* (Deer Sedge), *Calluna vulgaris* (Ling), *Erica tetralix* (Cross-leaved Heath), *Narthecium ossifragum* (Bog Asphodel) all occurred together with *Drosera rotundifolia* (Sundew), and *Hypnum cupressiforme*. However, even in this nodum there were variations; at the more westerly Lough Navar site *Carex panicea* (Carnation grass) and *Sphagnum plumulosum* were constants.

Hummocks and hollows, so typical of raised-bogs, do occur also in areas of blanket peat, though such areas are sometimes raised bogs which have become incorporated as the blanket bog has developed. At Lough Navar, however, Dickson felt that the hummock-hollow area had a convex profile because of the underlying land form and not because it was an incorporated raised bog. The higher hummocks were dominated by *Calluna vulgaris* with *Eriophorum vaginatum* (Common Cotton-grass), *Hypnum* spp., *Cladonia* spp., and *Rhacomitrium lanuginosum* (Woolly hair moss) also present. In the hollows the dominant species was *Trichophorum caespitosum* with *Narthecium ossifragum, Eriophorum angustifolium* (Cotton-grass), *Erica tetralix, Sphagnum cuspidatum, S. papillosum* and *Carex panicea.*

Other unflushed communities, which owe their distinctive plant assemblages to slope and drainage factors can be recognised. On the Antrim plateau, for example, the peat is thinner around rock outcrops and drainage through the peat here is much better; on these sites *Nardus stricta* (Mat-grass), *Molinia caerulea* (Purple moorgrass), *Potentilla erecta* (Common Tormentil), *Calluna vulgaris* and *Erica cinerea* (Bell-heather) are all abundant whilst *Festuca rubra* (Creeping Fescue), *Sieglingia decumbens* (Heath Grass), *Carex panicea* and *Carex bigelowii* (Stiff Sedge) occur immediately around the well drained rock outcrop.

Dickson divided the flush communities into those areas which were only intermittently flushed and those strongly flushed. In the former, although the *Sphagnum* cover remains high the vegetation is dominated by tussocks of *Eriophorum vaginatum;* *Deschampsia flexuosa* (Wavy hair-grass) is constant and *Juncus squarrosus* (Heath Rush) may also occur. In the moss layer *Polytrichum commune* (Hair moss) and *Aulacomnium palustre* are common. At the Lough Navar site *Molinia caerulea* is dominant, whilst *Myrica gale* (Bog Myrtle), *Carex panicea* and *Succisa pratens* (Devil's-bit Scabious) are common. It is a matter of interest that *Myrica* is absent from the high level blanket peat of Antrim. In the strongly flushed areas *Juncus acutiflorus* (Sharp-flowered Rush) is dominant together with *Holcus lanatus* (Yorkshire Fog), *Nardus stricta* and *Poa* spp. (Meadow grasses). Such communities are only found around springs or at surface seepage zones. At the Lough Navar site *Schoenus nigricans* (Bog-rush) is the diagnostic species of this community. The Killeter Forest NR (G.R. H 086821, H 090808) also demonstrates the variation in vegetation with slope and drainage: this can be seen in Figure 10.3 taken from the work of Parker *et al.* and reproduced by kind permission of the Conservation Branch, DoE.

Kertland (1928) also demonstrated the variation in plant communities to be found in areas of blanket peat: thus, on Divis Mountain, north of Belfast, she found that the summit area had remnants of a once continuous deeper blanket peat on which *Calluna vulgaris* and *Eriophorum angustifolium* were abundant. On the surviving haggs *Vaccinium myrtillus* (Bilberry) was frequent whilst in hollows *Sphagnum* spp. and *E. angustifolium* dominate. In the eroding channels *Nardus stricta, Juncus squarrosus* and *Calluna vulgaris* occupy any small pockets of peat left between the boulders. Around this summit area *Calluna* dominates with *Erica cinerea,* a species which indicates the drier conditions and shallower nature of the peat (0.5 m). *Vaccinium myrtillus, Galium saxatile* (Heath Bedstraw) and *Potentilla erecta* are also frequent. This kind of community is also common in the Mourne Mountains (Armstrong, Ingold and Vear, 1934), and indeed on the hillsides, *Erica cinerea* may be the dominant species. This heather community passes downslope into grassland in both areas and *Molinia caerulea,* together with *Trichophorum caespitosum* on wetter sites, may be the most abundant species. In flush sites *Juncus* spp. dominate.

Lowland bogs

The vegetation of lowland bogs is not greatly dissimilar to that of blanket peat and differences are drawn between the two largely on their mode of origin and their structure and morphology. The lowland bogs of Northern Ireland are essentially of two types (i) those that have developed into a raised bog, that is they have a convex profile

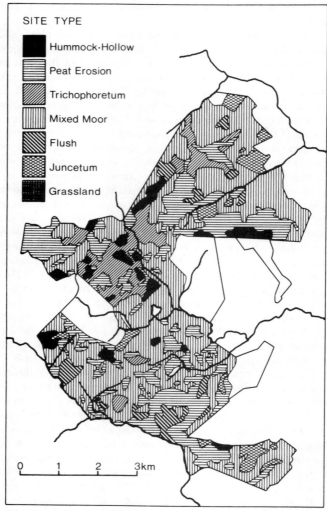

SITE TYPE

- Hummock-Hollow
- Peat Erosion
- Trichophoretum
- Mixed Moor
- Flush
- Juncetum
- Grassland

0   1   2   3km

Figure 10.3 Variation in plant communities within a peatland area: Killeter forest, County Tyrone. (after Parker *et al.* [MS], Conservation Branch, Dept of the Environment, N.I.)

and a perched water table, and (ii) those not raised in character. Whilst the former are always ombrotrophic, receiving water and dissolved nutrients only from rainfall, the latter may receive some groundwater and can be expected under such circumstances to be slightly richer in species composition. It is unfortunate that many of the raised bogs, and indeed many of the lowland bogs in general, have been extensively cut over so that good examples are not common. Some of the more notable sites have been preserved, however, either as Nature Reserves, Areas of Scientific Interest or as Forest Nature

Reserves; Meenadoan (G.R. H 244718) and the Fairy Water or Garvaghgullion (G.R. H 370765), both in County Tyrone, offer good examples of a raised bog.*

The Fairy Water above Omagh, flows in a broad valley which falls only slightly, less than 3 m in 12 km. On the floor of this valley, several raised bogs have developed over basins or depressions which mark the position of former lakes. Many of these raised bogs have been cut-over, but Fairy Water South Bog (Morrison, 1954), or Garvagh-gullion, has suffered little disturbance, and thus exhibits the classical features of a raised bog: in the northern part, a well-marked hummock-hollow complex (a term to be preferred to the older, suspect 'regeneration-complex') is surrounded by a *Trichophorum* dominated zone, and in turn this gives way on the steeper, bounding slopes to a *Myrica-Calluna* community.

The hummocks are composed largely of *Sphagnum imbricatum* – unusual in Britain – accompanied by *Calluna vulgaris* and *Cladonia impexa*. The taller hummocks are dominated by *Rhacomitrium lanuginosum*, while in the intervening pools *Sphagnum cuspidatum* and *S. subsecundum* are most abundant along with *Menyanthes trifoliata* (Bog Bean), *Utricularia minor* (Lesser Bladder-wort) and, in shallower parts, *Eriophorum angustifolium*. Towards the edges of the pools *Sphagnum papillosum*, *S. magellanicum* and *S. plumulosum* lead away from the water towards the *S. rubellum* of the hummocks: in short a classic example of the relationships between species occurrence and height above water table.

Trichophorum caespitosum dominated zones are not common on the raised bogs of Northern Ireland, at least in the lowland examples. This is because cutting has not only removed such peat, but also has increased drainage and thus allowed more *Calluna* domination. At Garvaghgullion, however, this zone is well developed and presents a sward-like appearance, but on closer inspection the *Trichophorum* can be seen growing in low well-formed tussocks. Both *Eriophorum angustifolium* and *E. vaginatum* occur within this zone together with *Narthecium ossifragum*; *Sphagnum tenellum* is most frequent in the ground layer with *Cladonia impexa* only in small patches.

Meenadoan Bog, in west Tyrone, provides another good example of a raised bog, but shows even more clearly than Garvaghgullion, the development sequence: unusually, this bog has a continuous record of growth from the late-glacial period (Godwin Zones I, II and III) (I.L.W.A. of Mitchell, 1976) to the present day.

Meres

Although some areas of fen vegetation occur in and around inter-drumlin lakes e.g. Ballyalloly Lake, near Comber in County Down, (G.R. J 453681) (McKeague, 1935), the most extensive fenland in Northern Ireland lies around the shores of Lough Neagh, especially to its south. Here, centuries of winter flooding have flushed the low-lying areas and under these neutral to alkaline conditions, fen peat has developed. Once this fen peat builds up above the level of such flooding, conditions quickly become acid and nutrient poor so that mire is formed; several distinct communities, aquatic, fen and moor, now can be found in north Armagh though they are not as extensive as formerly. Not all fenland areas are natural; many result from the digging of peat. When peat has

---

*Ordnance Survey Grid References are supplied in this chapter as frequently reference is made to specific sites.

been removed down to and below the water table, thus enabling the neutral/alkaline waters to enter, fenland may develop.

In the open drains it is possible to find communities of plants with submerged leaves e.g. *Elodea canadensis* (Water Thyme), *Hippuris vulgaris* (Mare's tail), *Myriophyllum* spp. (Water-milfoil), *Utricularia* spp., or of plants with floating leaves e.g. *Hydrocharis morsus-ranae* (Frog-bit), *Nuphar lutea* (Yellow Water Lily), *Lemna* spp. (Duckweed). These communities gradually give way to open reed swamp and closed reed swamp with *Typha* spp. (Bulrush, Reedmace), *Sparganium* spp. (Bur-reed) and *Phragmites communis* (Common Reed). The fen communities which succeed the reeds vary, depending on their height above the water level, thus some areas may be dominated by *Molinia* whereas others have one or other species of *Juncus* dominant. Over time, trees and shrubs have invaded those fenland communities to form carr-lands. Initially the *Myrica gale* and *Salix alba* (White Willow) have little effect on the ground flora, but as a closed canopy develops with *Alnus glutinosa* (Alder), *Salix alba, S. caprea* (Sallow, Pussywillow), *S. purpurea* (Purple Osier) and *S. viminalis* (Osier) the ground layer is reduced. Such a "woodland" can be found not only to the south of Lough Neagh but also to the east, for example at Rea's Wood in Antrim Bay (G.R. J 140850). This site has a sequence of vegetation development from the coastline; in particular it demonstrates the effect of past lowerings of the level of the Lough.

The effects of peat cutting leading to the formation of fens is nowhere better demonstrated than at Brackagh "Bog", beside the Upper Bann near Portadown, (G.R. J 020510), indeed it has been acclaimed by a national group of freshwater ecologists as being in the top five examples of fenland in the U.K. Here is a mosaic of small patches of different habitats, open water, floating aquatics, reed swamp, alder/willow carr, through to acidic cotton grass and *Molinia* moor (Figure 10.4); in addition several rare species of plants are recorded.

Given sufficient time and lack of environmental change, it is clear that fenlands may develop into woodland. At Rea's Wood, older, natural woodland can be found in the north and centre of the Reserve; these woods are wet-floored and indeed in parts are on overgrown swamps. Alder predominates throughout such areas, but birch *(Betula pubescens* and *B. pendula)* is scattered; the willows occurring are mainly *Salix atrocinerea* (Sally), *S. alba,* and *S. fragilis* (Withy). In drier parts ash *(Fraxinus excelsior)* can be found, whilst the rare alder-buckthorn *(Frangula alnus)* also occurs here. The ground cover includes *Cardamine amara* (Lady's Smock), *Scirpus sylvaticus* (Wood Club-rush), *Carex vesicaria* (Bladder Sedge) and *Solanum dulcamara* (Bittersweet).

Woodlands

The extensive woodlands of the climatic optimum, 7,000 to 5,500 B.P. (I.L.W.C. of Mitchell, 1976) were cleared piecemeal, first by Neolithic and Bronze Age man, but later in a more extensive and systematic manner by the Scottish and English settlers. Of the woodlands today, a few may be native, escaping clearance by man, whereas others exist because of planting and management over a considerable period, and give the appearance of being "natural". Rock, soil and slope changes, amongst other environmental variables, have led to the creation of distinct types of woodland – for example, ashwoods in some of the limestone areas, native oakwoods on basalt, granite and other rock types – whilst many areas of mixed woodland are also found.

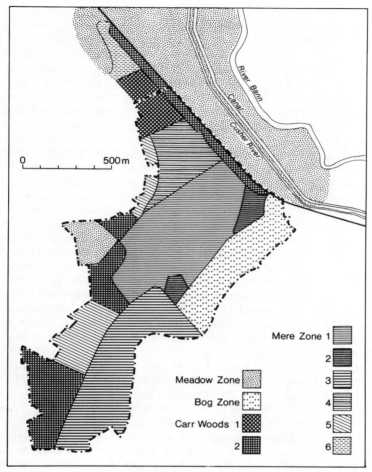

Figure 10.4 Brackagh Bog: vegetation 1930, with limits of present National Nature Reserve. (based on White, 1930)

Key Explanation:

Meadow Zone	Meadow Grasses, *Ulex europaeus*, *Carex* spp., *Pteridium aquilinum*, *Juncus* spp.
Bog Zone	*Calluna vulgaris*, *Eriophorum angustifolium*, *Sphagnum* spp.
Carr Woods 1	*Salix* spp., *Osmunda regalis*, *Molinia caerulea*
Carr Woods 2	*Salix* spp., *Alnus glutinosa*
Mere Zone 1	*Typha latifolia*, *Carex* spp., *Myriophyllum* spp., *Spiraea ulmaria*, *Juncus* spp., *Equisetum* spp.
Mere Zone 2	*Typha latifolia*
Mere Zone 3	*Spiraea ulmaria*, *Juncus* spp., *Carex* spp., *Menyanthes trifoliata*
Mere Zone 4	*Menyanthes trifoliata*, *Myriophyllum* spp., *Carex* spp., *Spiraea ulmaria*
Mere Zone 5	*Equisetum* spp., *Carex* spp.
Mere Zone 6	*Menyanthes trifoliata*, *Hippuris vulgaris*

Mixed deciduous woods

One example of such a mixed woodland is to be found at the Correl Glen NR in County Fermanagh (G.R. H 075544), a woodland composed of three parts to the west of Carrick Lough. The southwest and northwest parts are on slopes, sometimes rocky, above which is heathland. In the upper reaches of the wood, oak and birch trees are developed with an acidophilous ground layer, but in the valley bottoms ash is found. The eastern portion of the wood is on flatter ground and the trees are correspondingly larger; a shrub layer has developed beneath the oak and ash comprised of holly *(Ilex aquifolium)*, hazel *(Corylus avellana)*, rowan *(Sorbus aucuparia)*, willow *(Salix* spp.) and alder *(Alnus glutinosa)*. The species of the ground layer are calciphilous. At Castle Archdale NR, on the north-east shore of Lough Erne, (G.R. H 150604, 158588) and particularly Inishmakill Island, there are several kinds of wood intermixed, some of which represent development following the lowering of the Lough in the 1890s. Two zones are found immediately inland of the water's edge, consisting first of mixed scrub and then a zone of ash-alder scrub. Behind these two zones, both wet and dry oakwoods occur, with the dry *Quercus petraea* (Sessile Oak) wood to the west of the island. Some of the oak trees are well developed, but there is little sign of regeneration, rather birch and ash seedlings and saplings growing between the oaks. *Luzula sylvatica* covers much of ground, but *Pteridium aquilinum* (Bracken), *Blechnum spicant* (Hard-fern), *Dryopteris* spp. (Male Fern) and some *Vaccinium myrtillus* and *Calluna vulgaris* can also be seen. On poorly-drained areas, the oaks are less well developed and many are wind-thrown. The ground layer under such conditions is composed of *Iris pseudacorus* (Yellow Flag), *Mentha aquatica* (Water Mint), *J. effusus* (Common Rush), *Carex* spp. and *Ranunculus repens* (Creeping Buttercup). A small area dominated by ash also occurs and one of ash-sycamore, though mature trees of the latter have been ring-barked by the Nature Conservancy Branch in an attempt to reduce the infiltration of that species. Several of the islands in Lough Neagh also have mixed woodland, for example Tolan's Flat, Croaghan and Shallow Flat.

The lower parts of Banagher Glen NR in south-east County Londonderry (G.R. H 672045), areas of Peatlands Park NR, County Armagh (G.R. H 912606) and Glenariff Glen NR, County Antrim (G.R. D 210205), also provide further sites of mixed woodland. Although the Quoile Basin, County Down is noted largely for its aquatic and reedswamp communities and for the bird-life, Ballyhassen Wood, though not native, provides another location of mixed woodland. *Sambucus nigra* (Elder) and *Acer pseudoplatanus* (Sycamore) together with *Fraxinus excelsior* (Ash) comprise the tree layer but a more varied ground flora is evident. Gilbertson (1969) divides the woodland into various types largely on the basis of the predominant ground-flora but the sample size and analysis seem insufficient to justify these. *Pteridium aquilinum, Dryopteris dilitata* (Broad Buckler-fern), *Oxalis acetosella* (Wood Sorrel), *Endymion non-scriptus* (Bluebell) and *Luzula sylvatica* all flourish in one area or another or throughout the wood.

Oakwoods

Fortunately there are thought to be examples in Northern Ireland of native oakwoods, or at least of successors to such. Banagher Glen NR, especially in the upper slopes, has sessile oakwood *(Quercus petraea)* although birch and rowan also accompany. On these slopes ground conditions are base deficient, and the ground flora is correspondingly acidophilous. Boorin NR, County Tyrone (G.R. H 497846) although most notable for its heathland contains a small area of oakwood, with birch inter-mixed. Both species of oak and the hybrid grow here but the woodland has been used for coppice. Breen Wood, County Antrim (G.R. D 125338) is also mainly sessile oak but some pedunculate oak *(Q. robur)* also is found. Small units of planted conifers disturb the woodland, and alder and birch fringes the wetter parts; rowan is common throughout and hawthorn *(Crataegus monogyna),* holly and hazel are found as an understorey. On the wetter areas *Holcus mollis* (Creeping Soft-grass), *Oxalis acetosella, Blechnum spicant, Dryopteris aemula* (Hay-scented Buckler fern), *D. dilitata* and *Rhytidiadelphus loreus* compose the ground layer whereas in the more acidic parts *Vaccinium myrtillus, Calluna vulgaris, Deschampsia flexuosa, Potentilla erecta* and *Galium saxatile* are found. *Luzula sylvatica* is particularly common on flushed slopes, but also appears to be spreading vigorously since the withdrawal of grazing.

Other examples of oakwoods in County Antrim are to be found in the Glenshesk Valley (south of Ballycastle), where the mature oaks reach heights of 20 m or more and have developed a closed canopy with a hazel shrublayer, and at Shane's Castle which is quite similar. Craigagh Wood, north-east Antrim (G.R. D 227321) was planted sometime between 1830–1835 (Surgin, 1978), and contains many mature trees of 125-150 years in age. However, few of these older trees are oaks, these having been felled, and the oaks fall largely into the 25-75 year age classes. Nevertheless, oak accounts for 24% of the cover, with beech 32%, sycamore 10% and ash 9%. The oak is more frequent than the beech (88% to 54%), but because of the age difference, the beeches are better developed. Hazel, birch, rowan and holly make up an understorey together with saplings and young trees 3-6 m in height; the canopy being up to 16 m. The field layer is poor with bracken where the canopy thins but typically the beech casts a heavy shade and bare ground with litter and occasional clumps of moss is usual.

In County Down, the Rostrevor NR (G.R. J 186170) is predominantly oakwood. Plots investigated in 1972 revealed that 79% of mature trees were oak with only small frequency of ash, sycamore, cherry *(Prunus avium)* and rowan. A spatial variation exists in the woodland with ash more frequent along the southern and eastern boundaries and oak in an almost pure stand in the north. Tree-ring dates establish a major growth phase beginning in 1740 and continuing for about 25 years. This sequence has been interpreted as natural regrowth after possible felling of mature oaks in the 1730s (Pilcher, 1979). The Rostrevor oakwood, therefore, may be a successor of the extensive native mixed oakwoods of Ireland and have escaped complete clearance because of the steep, inaccessible nature of the slopes on which the Rostrevor wood occurs.

Ashwoods

While ash is quite common in some oakwoods, as at Rostrevor, there are woods in which the ash itself is the dominant species. One of the best examples is to be found in the Marble Arch NR of Fermanagh (G.R. H 123350), (Figure 10.5) where except for a few small areas of conifers, beech or oak woods, ash is the dominant species throughout. The beech and the conifers are clearly exotic, but the oaks too have been planted as is evidenced by their even size and spacing. These ash woodlands have been subdivided into three zones. In the north and north-west quarters, ash is dominant with little or no oak nor beech. Birch, willow *(Salix caprea)*, wych elm *(Ulmus glabra)*, alder, rowan and hawthorn are common, and in the north-west, hazel, which occurs as an undershrub throughout forms a coppice. In this ashwood zone, the ground flora is dominated by the Umbelliferae: the wood floor is carpeted with *Angelica sylvestris* (Wild Angelica) and *Conopodium majus* (Pignut); *Endymion nonscriptus* and *Filipendula ulmaria* (Meadow-sweet) also are abundant. Few grasses or rushes occur and little moss cover is visible.

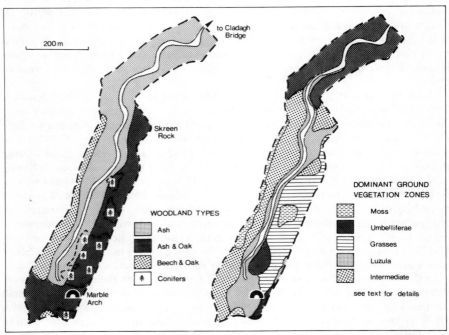

Figure 10.5   Marble Arch National Nature Reserve: Vegetation. (based on MS in Conservation Branch, Dept of the Environment, N.I.)

The beech-with-oak zone is confined to the west side of the gorge and a small area in the south: ash is present, together with other tree species, but the beech is always dominant in these areas. In consequence, as at Craigagh Wood, the ground flora is poor and dominated by mosses. *Primula vulgaris* (Common Primrose) and *Lonicera periclymenum* (Honeysuckle) are common whereas *Vaccinium myrtillus* and *Erica tetralix* are only locally present. The hazel coppice struggles to survive, again probably a response to the deep shade and the litter cast by the beech.

The third, ash-and-oak, zone is the most mixed of the subdivisions. In the extreme south of the reserve and along the eastern boundary the oak *(Quercus robur)* is dominant and, as described above, appears to have been planted. Elsewhere ash is the major species though the oak is always present. Above Skreen Rock, birch is intermixed with, and co-dominant with, oak and ash but the area is complicated by plantations of conifers. Where the oaks and the conifers give an open or incomplete canopy *Brachypodium sylvaticum* (Wood False-Brome), and *Deschampsia cespitosa* (Tufted hair-grass) are abundant with *Zerna erecta* (Upright Brome), *Dactylis glomerata* (Cocksfoot) and *Poa trivialis* (Rough Meadow-grass) common. In the eastern boundary area, and especially above Marble Arch, *Luzula* spp. form an almost complete cover.

Ash woods can be seen at Hanging Rock NR (G.R. H 110363), also in Fermanagh, but examples may be seen in County Antrim too; the Linford Water Valley (G.R. D 310087) has rich woodland most of which has been cut-over or coppiced but areas of older woodland are extant, especially below 140 m O.D. *Ulmus glabra* (Wych Elm), *Quercus petraea* and *Q. robur* are scattered throughout these remnants but ash is prevalent. The ground flora of these areas has *Festuca altissima* (Wood Fescue), *Milium effusum* (Wood Millet) and *Melica uniflora* (Wood Melick) whilst the base rich nature of the soil is indicated by the presence of *Allium ursinum* (Wild Garlic), *Ranunculus auricomus* (Goldilocks) and *Galium odoratum* (Woodruff). Where ground becomes wetter *Carex pendula* (Pendulous Sedge) and *C. laevigata* (Smooth-stalked Sedge) are located, but along the rocky stream margins *Luzula sylvatica* is common. The Linford Water Valley also demonstrates much secondary woodland and scrub.

Other types of woodland in Northern Ireland tend to be of scrubland. In addition to sites previously mentioned, birch woodland can be examined at Peatlands Park NR (G.R. H 912606) in north Armagh, where it is developed on both clay and peat. Hazel woodland is observable on the northern slopes of Cave Hill near Bellvue: this hazel scrub has managed to withstand the activities of children and adults over many generations. Hazel scrub is also developed at Garron Point, high on the slopes of Glenariff and at Straidkilly (G.R. D 298162) (all in County Antrim), and at Crossmurrin, County Fermanagh, (G.R. H 112348).

Within Northern Ireland examples of woodland types therefore may be seen but in general, over the centuries, man has removed most of the natural vegetation cover. Whereas in England those cleared areas which have not been improved have often reverted to heathland and only to bogland on the higher or shallower slopes, in Northern Ireland, because of the more oceanic climate, blanket peat covers most of the upland, and heathland is scarce.

Heathland

Heathland is not only scarce in Northern Ireland, but is scattered in its occurrence. Two forms of heathland are found: very small areas on drier slopes within largely blanket peat areas, and that of some mountain summits. Even adding the areas of these two types together, they occupy much less than 1 % of the land area of Northern Ireland.

At Boorin NR, County Tyrone, (G.R. H 497846) *Calluna vulgaris* is dominant and remains so because of a policy of burning to preserve the food resource for grouse. In the lower parts of the Reserve, *Molinia caerulea* is dominant, whereas in flush sites, *Juncus effusus* is the primary species with a moss layer composed of *Polytrichum commune* and *Sphagnum recurvum*. Bell heather is associated with *Calluna* on drier parts of the heath and with cross-leaved heath in more poorly drained sites. The grass species are similarly divided in their occurrence – *Anthoxanthum odoratum* (Sweet

Vernal-grass), *Agrostis* spp. and *Nardus stricta* on drier sites, but *Deschampsia flexuosa* and *Molinia caerulea* on the wetter. Nevertheless ling is dominant throughout, and because of repeated burning, there are visual differences in age and structure. Such variations were first described by Watt (1955) in East Anglia and have been shown by many others since (Gimingham, 1972). In the Boorin heath, Magurran (1976) identified four age divisions and these have been mapped along with other elements of the vegetation (Figure 10.6) – I Pioneer Stage – plants up to 2 years old; II Early building Stage (2-6 years); III Late Building/Early Mature (6-16 years), Late Mature (16 years+). Other species which are important in the composition include *Juncus effusus, J. squarrosus, Carex binervis* (Green-ribbed Sedge), *C. nigra* (Common Sedge), *C. echinata* (Star Sedge), *Potentilla erecta, Galium saxatile, Vaccinium myrtillus, Trichophorum caespitosum* in wetter places and *Eriophorum* spp.

A different heathland type is that of the mountain summits, as for example on Slieve Donard and other Mourne Mountains (Armstrong *et al.*, 1930). Here, over the greater part, *Rhacomitrium lanuginosum* is dominant with the sheep's fescue *(Festuca ovina)* being very abundant and ericaceous species also extremely common *(Empetrum nigrum, Vaccinium myrtillus, V. vitis-idaea, Calluna vulgaris)*. The summit nature of the community is exemplified by the presence of *Salix herbacea* (Least Willow). Whilst *Rhacomitrium*-dominated heath occupies the summit, on the south side *Festuca ovina* grassland is dominant and on the south-eastern slopes, which have a considerable amount of scree, a *Vaccinium myrtillus* community is present. Slieve Commedagh has a similar range of communities, and being less disturbed, probably provides an even better example of summit heathland.

Whereas in the uplands, blanket peat and occasional areas of woodland or heathland provide some 'wildscape', the lowlands of Northern Ireland for the most part have been 'improved'. Even so there are features of interest to the ecologist; fields have to be delineated and if this is not by dry stone wall, ditch, or fence then the hedgerow will form the boundary.

Hedgerows

In Britain, hedgerows can be of almost any age from early-medieval to nineteenth century, but in Northern Ireland the pattern of field enclosure is predominantly of the eighteenth and nineteenth century. The drumlin belt in Counties Down and Armagh was enclosed to a large degree by 1708 (Robinson, 1977), but even as late as the nineteenth century much of the north and west remained unenclosed: indeed Robinson demonstrates that the majority of hedges in Northern Ireland date from the period 1750–1850. Unfortunately, the species composition of these hedgerows is not given by Robinson although he indicates that a regional survey is in progress. At a general level, however, it seems that those hedges established before 1760 have 4-9 woody species, whereas those of post-1830, contain only 1-3 species.

The Forest Service, Department of Agriculture for Northern Ireland, has recently undertaken a census of private woodlands and hedgerows, and the preliminary survey for Antrim is now complete *(Forest Research 3/1979)*. This reveals an average density of hedgerow in the County of 110 m/ha, considerably higher than the average for Great Britain of 44 m/ha, but also shows that slightly over one-third of the County has no hedgerows: both these factors are in some degree a reflection of the physical

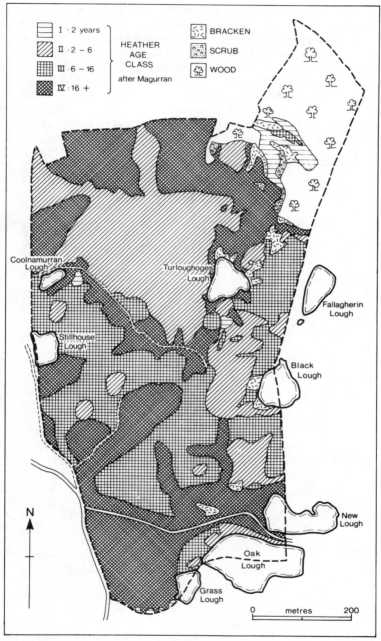

Figure 10.6 Boorin National Nature Reserve, County Tyrone: Heather Age Classes. (after Magurran, 1976)

environment. Of the hedgerows in the County, 56% of the total surveyed lengths contain hawthorn, 23% contain ash, 11% whin *(Ulex europaeus)*, 4% alder and 3% blackthorn *(Prunus spinosa)*. Of these species only hawthorn, whin and blackthorn compose hedgerows in which they have a stocking density of 70% or more, that is pure-stands or almost so, but 71% of the sampled hedgerows had only 1-3 species, while only 22% contain 4-7 species. These results compare favourably with the indicators mapped by Robinson (1977). One sample area of 1 sq. km. is reproduced in Figure 10.7 and the predominance of hawthorn can be seen together with planted trees of ash and sycamore; beech *(Fagus sylvatica)* often tends to have been reserved for approaches to large country houses.

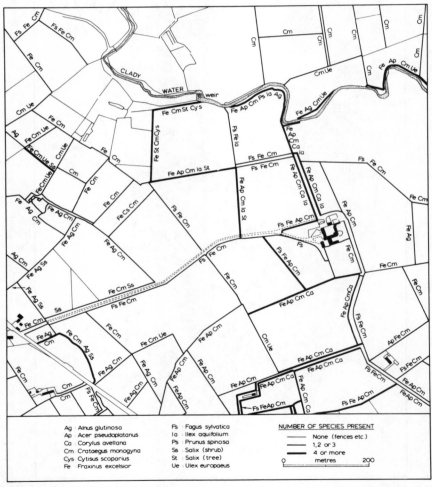

Figure 10.7 Example of the hedgerow survey of the Forest Service, Dept of Agriculture, N.I.: a 1 km² at Ballytweedy, County Antrim.

Grasslands

Much of the improved land in Northern Ireland is under pasture which, to the superficial view, appears lush and suited to pastoral agriculture. On closer examination, it is soon evident that the composition and value of this pasture varies considerably. Differences in management practices accounts for a great deal of this variation, for example reseeding and fertilizer applications, but the effects of the physical environment are also to be seen. On the basalts of County Antrim, on slopes where drainage is good, the rock may weather to almost a crumb-structure and give rise to a base-rich soil on which calcicolous species occur, species which are rare or absent from other parts of Northern Ireland. On the other hand where drainage is poorer and pH considerably reduced, the herbage is composed of moorland species such as *Nardus stricta, Deschampsia cespitosa, Agrostis tenuis* (Common Bent), with the fescues, a variety of sedges and rushes. Some *Cynosurus cristatus* (Crested Dog's-tail), *Holcus lanatus, Anthoxanthum odoratum* and *Trifolium repens* (White Clover) may also be found.

One small area of true calcareous grassland also occurs in this north-east part of County Antrim, in the Goodland Townland (G.R. D 197407). This small area has something of the appearance of chalk downland, but the northerly position, altitude and exposure of the site, limit the species composition. The 'downland' appearance is created in the main by *Festuca rubra* (Creeping or Red Fescue) growing in a close, very short sward created by centuries of sheep and rabbit grazing. Other species which occur here are also non-remarkable – *Thymus serpyllum* (Thyme), *Linum catharticum* (White Flax), *Lotus corniculatus* (Birdsfoot-trefoil) *Viola riviniana* (Common Violet), *Ranunculus bulbosus* (Bulbous Buttercup) amongst many others, suggesting simply a relatively dry meadow. Nevertheless although quite similar areas occur all round the chalk outcrop this "downland" patch is unique in Northern Ireland. Grasslands associated with hard, Carboniferous limestone occur in Fermanagh, but little botanical work has been carried-out. A small area has been set aside, however, as a Nature Reserve (Crossmurrin, G.R. H 112348).

In the west, the proportion of 'permanent' pasture increases. The catchments of the Upper and Lower Erne are characterized by "cold, sticky clays of poor physical condition, hard to drain and hard to cultivate" (Linehan *et al.*, 1948), and as a result pastures are both poor as regards feed and in species composition. *Agrostis tenuis, Holcus lanatus,* the fescues and *Poa* spp. (Meadow grasses) comprise these grasslands with occasionally some *Alopecurus* spp. (Foxtails) and *Phleum pratense* (Timothy). Such a composition might be found in any of the damper areas with permanent pasture. In the south of the country on the other hand, leys are far more common and species composition will depend even more markedly on management techniques – but these are better left to discussion on grasslands as a resource.

Vegetation as a resource

Vegetation may be assessed, first, for its value as the primary converter of the energy of sunlight, in terms of its provision of energy for herbivores, principally of course domesticated, or as material for man to use as timber – in construction and paper-making – or as fuel. Secondly, the ecological value of the vegetation can be assessed by consideration of its aesthetic appeal, recreational opportunities, shelter, and conservation value for education (see Buchanan in "Landscape" Chapter 12). Some people would argue also that specific plant communities have an intrinsic conservation value – that they should be maintained as last remnants of past plant assemblages and that this is part of their educational value. Such an argument has appeal, if recognising that conservation should be for man's benefit.

Forestry and peatland

Although occupying less than one tenth of the area of peatland, forest is the most evident use of the peat areas in the public mind. The development of forestry in recent years follows the aims set out in a White Paper in 1970 (Cmd 550) which called for considerable expansion of the industry so that by 2000 A.D. it was planned to have approximately 90,000 hectares planted by the Forest Service, DoA. This development was seen to be financially difficult – "at current high rates of interest there will be a substantial subsidy to forest" – but this subsidy was justified on three grounds. First, the expansion would provide employment, especially "in regions with otherwise falling populations". Such an increase in labour would not only occur as a direct result of forestry but as a consequence of the growth in "rural-based wood-using" industries. Second, there would be a financial return on the long term investment of funds and finally, the target area of 90,000 ha would produce sufficient timber to meet the demands of Northern Ireland and indeed "any surpluses which arose should find a market in Great Britain"; there would therefore be a saving in import costs.

By 1978 the planted area in Northern Ireland was 52,113 ha and the annual rate of planting 945 ha, the same as for several years previously [*Northern Ireland Trading and other Accounts*] (HC 161 1978-79). This rate is well below that necessary to achieve the target area in 2000 A.D. and reflects the difficulties of land acquisition, especially in the better, agriculturally marginal, uplands. Approximately 60% of the forest is on deep (>50 cm) or shallow (5-50 cm) peats on which, until recently, mainly Sitka spruce had been planted: Sitka *(Picea sitchensis)* constitutes some 60% of the plantations with Lodgepole pine *(Pinus contorta var latifolia)* and Norway spruce *(Picea abies)* accounting for a little under 10% each. Production from these forests by the turn of the century is by no means easy to calculate and much will depend on the management policies adopted; if the present policies of the District Forest Officers are maintained then the estimated annual production may total 362,000 m³ (270,000 m³ from felling, remainder from thinning). However, because of the confinement of forests to peatlands and other poor soils, forestry is extremely difficult and new management practices may have to be adopted, such as shortening the forest rotations and reducing the thinning. Sitka spruce on wetlands would thus be harvested some ten years before the time of the rotation of the maximum mean annual increment. Such stands would go unthinned whereas other soil areas would receive normal management. Given such a policy the mean annual production could be as high as 591,000 m³ in 2000 A.D. That early felling will give higher production may seem surprising but this only serves to emphasise the difficulties of the physical environment for if left to mature, many trees, and indeed whole areas of forest, could be lost due to windthrow. It seems appropriate therefore to evaluate the physical environment of the peatlands with regard to forest production.

Research has demonstrated that waterlogging, windthrow, exposure and nutrient supply impose limitations on forest production in the peatlands. Waterlogging inhibits root development, since in a waterlogged soil environment, there is a lack of oxygen: this limitation also means that the trees become more susceptible to windthrow and the uptake of nitrogen is reduced (Savill, 1977). Early tree growth is greater, therefore, the larger the upturned sod on which the tree is planted, and the greater the intensity of drains. The occurrence of ditches may themselves limit the spread of the root system, and thereby increase the risk of windthrow. It has been proposed that some initial growth be sacrificed in order to enable wide root-plates to be formed, and so reduce windthrow risk (Savill, 1977). MacKenzie (1976) also comments on management variables and windthrow, and agrees that ploughing should be kept to a minimum on high risk sites and that trees should be widely spaced, presumably to allow greater root spread. Equally, roads and rides should be kept to a minimum and orientated as far as is possible in the direction of the prevailing winds.

Exposure to wind will reduce yield classes of timber, as has been demonstrated by Savill (1974) using the correlation of growth rates and flag tatter (Lines and Howell, 1963). Reduction in yield affects the economic viability of tree production, and since exposure increases with altitude, there is an altitudinal limit to economic planting – a limit which occurs in the peatlands. From the effects of waterlogging, windthrow possibilities and reduced yields due to exposure, the peat areas do appear to offer a limited resource for timber production. Further, the peatlands are proving to be very limited in nutrient supply, particularly with regard to Sitka spruce. Again, Dickson and Savill (1974) have demonstrated that irrespective of treatment at the time of planting or of checked crops, Sitka spruce on oligotrophic peat will be limited by nitrogen deficiency 6 to 8 years later. Nitrogen fertilizer will have to be applied repeatedly to maintain satisfactory growth. "The economic implications of this are so daunting that it seems appropriate to question whether Sitka spruce should be planted at all on oligotrophic peats in future" (Savill, 1977). Hence the decision to expand the use of Lodgepole pine so that plantings of the two species were to reach "near parity within the next few years" (Forest Service, DoA, 1976-77), each at about 40% of the total. However, Lodgepole pine is not without its difficulties; 'basal sweep' occurs in the South Coastal provenances giving unstable, low-quality timber and as a result, from a peak of 42% of plantings in 1978, the proportion declined in 1979 to 34%. More northerly provenances are now being planted (Forest Service, DoA, 1979).

It may well be asked, in view of the above, whether the upland peat areas are suited to forestry at all – the costs of land acquisition, initial fertilizer application, repeated nitrogen fertilizers, drainage maintenance and weeding costs – all make this doubtful even bearing in mind that the yields will not be obtained until 30 or so years from planting. Indeed in the *Annual Report 1976-77* para. 3.3 (Forest Service, DoA) the position for Northern Ireland is summed – "maintenance work . . . has been one of the factors defying attempts to produce crops likely to show an economic return".

Economics of forestry

Published figures for the costs incurred in forestry in Northern Ireland, and for the returns obtained, are neither full nor precise; indeed the annual reports do not discuss financial matters at all. The various costings and returns have to be obtained therefore

Plate 10.1 Marginal hill land in north-east Antrim, where there is competition between forestry and sheep grazing.

from a variety of sources, and as a result, any estimate of the future returns from forestry are extremely tentative and must be regarded with some scepticism. The important point, bearing in mind these reservations, is that the probable future return from forestry does not meet the *current* return from sheep rearing in the hill lands.

The position of forestry in Northern Ireland is summarised well in the final comment in the '*Northern Ireland Trading and Other Accounts 1975-76*' (HC 156 1976-77)

> "It is important to realise that decisions to invest in forestry in Northern Ireland have often been based on strategic and social rather than purely commercial factors, and that in addition the long time scale involved in forestry operations militates against the presentation of a single year's accounts in a form which is realistic in the ordinary commercial sense".

Thus, by being restricted to hill, peatlands and areas marginal for agriculture, forestry cannot hope to be profitable at least in the short term and only a radical shift in world prices and in location of our forests seem likely to make the future harvests any more profitable. It is ironic that employment in forestry will not expand in the manner of the 1970 White Paper because of increased efficiency: any expansion in labour force has been in temporary, unemployment relief schemes but in 1979 there was a decline in the numbers employed through the Urban and Rural Improvement Campaign. One of the reasons for the location of the present forests has been a failure – not only costing forestry a considerable amount and resulting in poor growth but also not using labour.

Further, the anticipated area of planted forest has not been reached, nor with declining rates of planting (Forest Service, DoA, 1979) will the planned area for 2000 A.D. be achieved. The 1970 plan envisaged that the acreage would meet the demand of

Plate 10.2 Northern slopes of the Mournes, near Tollymore Park, where there is continual change in land use and vegetation.

Northern Ireland for timber, but it is clear that, as now, the vast majority of our timber products will be imported.

The difficulties of forestry in the hill, mainly peat, areas have been outlined and indeed it has been questioned whether forestry is a viable use of the peatland resource. Forest areas do have other uses than the strictly economic, for example recreational, conservational and educational. Tollymore Park, an area of some 48,580 ha on the north-east side of the Mournes, was opened in 1955 as Northern Ireland's first Forest Park and indeed remained the only one for ten years; by 1965 approximately 34,000 cars, representing perhaps 160,000 people, visited the park with most of them coming from Belfast, County Down and south County Antrim (>70%). Most of the visitors appreciated the quiet of such a place and suggestions for improvements were generally limited to small 'cosmetic' changes (Kilpatrick, 1965). Over recent years there has been an increase in the number of forest parks (Table 10.2 and Figure 10.8) and the number of visitors also continues to grow. The totals in the table are considerable underestimates of the number of people involved in recreational activities in forest areas since it does not include those sites which may be visited without paying – for example Belvoir Forest is a popular centre for residents of south Belfast – nor does it refer to forests where only picnic sites and walks are provided and yet these constitute a valuable and much used recreational resource, especially for the week-end car-ride.

Another aspect of the amenity value of forests and woodlands in Northern Ireland is their aesthetic appeal; this contributes both to recreational use of the countryside and also to the living conditions of the residents. In 1977-78 Wright attempted to evaluate woodland on the basis of its aesthetic appeal to local residents. Her study, conducted

TABLE 10.2

Paying Visitors to Forest Parks and other Forests

Source: *Annual Report 1979,* Forest Service, DoA

Forest	Numbers of Visitors in thousands				
	1975	1976	1977	1978	1979
Tollymore	126	149	135	128	129
Castlewellan	83	91	77	75	72
Gortin Glen	33	41	39	39	39
Drum Manor	26	27	25	20	25
Gosford	24	25	25	25	29
Glenariff	20	22	57(a)	44	49
Davagh	—	—	—	—	6(a)
Rostrevor	18	20	21	17	25
Slieve Gullion	5	4	4	3	4
Lough Navar	18	19	15	13	17
Ballycastle	33	5	7	4	7
Ballypatrick	—	24	14	16	15
Portglenone	11	11	14	7	7
Car Permit Holders	19	17	22	25	19
Hillsborough	19	33	23	16	(b)
TOTAL	435	488	478	432	443

(a) Opening of Forest Park
(b) Admission charge discontinued

amongst a cross-section of residents in the Dundonald area, was limited both in the techniques employed and in the results – for example Wright (1978) pointed out that the surrounding countryside in which the woodland was located affects perception as does the previous experience of the observer. The results did show a clear preference for areas of mixed woodland, that is woods with both deciduous hardwoods and deciduous and evergreen conifers. Such woods have a variety of tree form, texture and colour and allow a varied understorey to be developed. Noteworthy among the species common to the preferred woodlands was beech, but where this species achieved complete cover, that wood came relatively low in the list of preferred sites. Similarly sites of almost completely conifers, whether spruces or pines, were the least favoured locations.

Clearly commercial forestry could not be organised so as to produce mixed woodlands of the type preferred, it would not be economic or practical to do so, but there may well be an argument for a variety of tree species to be planted along routeways within forest parks.

With regard to the educational and conservational value of forests, little further need be said since much of the description of woodlands is based on nature reserves – many of which occur within forestry areas. Indeed in May 1980 there were 14 National Nature Reserves established on Forestry land, and 27 Forest Nature Reserves, which serves to emphasise the very good record of the Forestry Service in Northern Ireland in this field (Figure 10.8). Further, many of these have educational centres of value both to the public at large and to parties of school children. At Castlecaldwell, for example, the visitors' centre had over 1,200 people attending illustrated talks on forestry conservation and wildlife in 1977. Approximately 60% of these people were school children: they also made great use of the Seskinore Game Farm in 1977 with 6,500 educational visits. The Forest Service also maintain eight arboreta, including the National Arboretum at Castlewellan, and this has recently been expanded by the rehabilitation of Drumbuck Wood.

Hill peatland agriculture

The majority of the upland peat vegetation is used as sheep range. Sheep production on peatlands, which constitute such a large proportion of the hill land, is far from easy, and again, is a reflection of the poor nutrient status of this environment. The quantity and quality, that is both palatability and digestibility, of the herbage is poor. The digestibility of hill pasture is at a maximum of around 75% in May-June after which it declines gradually until there is a sharp drop in the autumn: a minimum level of 50% is reached in February. There is, therefore, a severe shortage of nutrition in winter, but perhaps of even more importance is the quality of pasture in spring and late summer. If suitable management practices were adopted to halt or delay the summer decline in digestibility, then the ewe flocks would have higher conception rates, there would be a decline in the loss of body weight in the early stages of pregnancy, and they would have also greater fat reserves on which to draw over winter. Under-nutrition in spring – that is late – pregnancy reduces milk yields and the quality of the milk, thereby reducing the growth rates of lambs. Lamb birth weight is in any case lower because of the poor nutrition at this period, and mortality shows an increase. Lack of palatable herbage also limits lamb growth rate once weaned from the milk. In addition to improvement of late summer herbage, there is therefore a need to improve the quantity and quality of spring and early summer herbage. This is clearly difficult in the peatlands and can only be achieved on drier slopes and on the margins. Such herbage improvements on hill farms will be restricted to in-bye land, where the sheep are grazed at tupping and lambing times. This in-bye land constitutes only 16% on average of the hill farm, and it is highly unlikely, therefore, that the peatlands offer much scope for expansion as a resource for sheep grazing. The only other alternative is the use of concentrates, hay etc. at these two periods of the year, that is late summer and spring, but this will cut into the gross margins. As can be seen in Table 10.4, the input in variable costs is much lower for hill farms, but gross margins will fall even further behind those of other sheep farms if these variable costs are increased by greater use of concentrates. In spite of improving prices for sheep meat, it would seem unlikely that there will be any great change in utilization of the hill land and its vegetation. Indeed the improving prices are mainly for the better quality upland and lowland sheep as can be seen from the average gross margins per ewe (calculated from Brown and Tease, 1979) at the bottom of Table 10.3. Although the margins for sheep include subsidies (though not in Table 10.3) and although the farmers will benefit from other hill farm subsidies, the figures more than stand comparison with forestry. The hill lands are probably therefore going to change little, with peatland vegetation offering only a poor resource in economic terms: as centres for recreation, both active and passive they may have a more important role in the future.

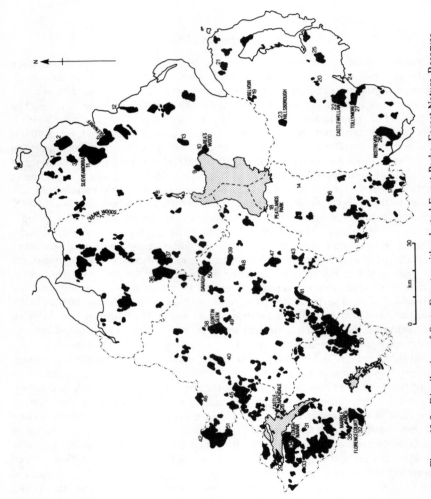

Figure 10.8 Distribution of State Forests, with selected Forest Parks, Forest Nature Reserves and National Nature Reserves.

Key to Forest Parks, Forest Nature Reserves and National Nature Reserves

Map No.	Name	Status	Map No.	Name	Status
	Antrim			*Fermanagh*	
1.	Ballycastle	FP	28.	Castle Archdale	NNR
2.	Ballypatrick	FP	29.	Castlecaldwell	FNR
3.	Breen	NNR	30.	Cornagogue Lough, Tully	FNR
4.	Garry Bog	FNR	31.	Correl Glen, Conagher	NNR
5.	Glenariff	NNR/FP	32.	Florencecourt	
6.	Kinramer, Rathlin Is.	FNR		Aghatirourke	FNR
7.	Loughram Is., Bann Woods	FNR		Dohatty Glebe	FNR
8.	Portglenone	FP	33.	Lough Naman Bog	NNR
9.	Randalstown	NNR	34.	Magho, Lough Navar	FNR
10.	Rea's Wood, Muckamore	FNR	35.	Marlbank	
11.	Slieveanorra	NNR		Corry Point Wood	FNR
12.	Straidkilly, Carnlough	NNR		Crossmurrin	NNR
13.	Tardree	FNR		Hanging Rock	NNR
	Armagh			Killesher	FNR
14.	Brackagh Bog	NNR		Marble Arch	NNR
15.	Carnagh	FNR		*Londonderry*	
16.	Gosford	FP	36.	Banagher Glen	NNR
17.	Hawthorn Hill, Slieve Gullion	FNR/FP	37.	Craig-Na-Shoke, Moydamlagh	FNR
18.	Peatlands Park	NNR		*Tyrone*	
	Down		38.	Boorin, Gortin	NNR
19.	Bigwood, Belvoir	FNR	39.	Drum Manor	FP
20.	Bohill	FNR	40.	Fairy Water (Garvaghullion)	NNR
21.	Cairn Wood, Ballysallagh	FNR	41.	Favour Royal	FNR
22.	Castlewellan	FP	42.	Killeter Bog, Glenderg	NNR
23.	Hillsborough	FP	43.	Knockaginny, Caledon	FNR
24.	Murlough Dunes	NNR	44.	Knockmany	FNR
25.	Quoile Pondage, Downpatrick	NNR	45.	Meenadoan, Lough Bradan	NNR
26.	Rostrevor	FNR/FP	46.	Moneygal Bog	FNR
27.	Tollymore	FP	47.	Parkanaur	FNR
			48.	Pomeroy	FNR
			49.	The Murrins, Killens	NNR
			50.	Slaghtfreedan, Daragh	FNR
			51.	Slievedoo	
				Goose Lawns	FNR
				Mullyfamore	NNR

TABLE 10.3

Financial results from surveyed farms 1976
Source: Department of Agriculture for Northern Ireland 1977

Enterprise Output	Lowland £ per ewe	Upland £ per ewe	Hill £ per ewe
Lamb	30.21	25.77	16.30
Wool	1.96	1.77	1.61
Subsidies	—	2.58	3.50
Flock Replacement Costs	−0.28	−0.38	+3.06
Total Enterprise Output	31.89	29.74	24.47
Variable Costs	5.58	4.60	2.77
Gross Margin	26.31	25.14	21.70
Gross Margin 1978-79 (Brown and Tease, 1979)	c. 36.00	c. 30.00	c. 21.00

Grasslands and hedges as resources

In the analysis of grassland as a resource much will depend upon the species composition of the grassland, for some species are more desirable than others because of their higher levels of palatability and digestibility. Since the time of the first Grassland Survey of England and Wales in 1939-40 (Davies, 1941), the proportion of perennial rye grass *(Lolium perenne)* in the sward has been taken as a mark of the standard of the grassland – the higher the proportion, the better the quality. This was the basis of the examination of grasslands of Northern Ireland conducted by Linehan *et al.* (1948): they classified grasslands on the proportion of Perennial Rye grass and white clover (high proportions being good pasture) and bent *(Agrostis)* (high proportions of this species indicative of poor to very poor pasture). The results of this survey are presented in Table 10.4 – from which it will be seen that in their natural state the grasslands of Northern Ireland are not a very valuable resource. The results suggested that management practices were the most important factors governing the quality of pasture. A more rigorous investigation of pasture quality is that of Sutton (1973) who worked in a small area of County Armagh. She found that three components accounted for most of the variation in pasture composition in this area. The first component separated those fields with a high occurrence of *Lolium perenne* and *Phleum pratense*, from those with *Anthoxanthum odoratum, Cynosurus cristatus, Agrostis* spp. and *Festuca rubra*. Sutton interpreted this component as one of age and management: those fields with high levels of *Lolium perenne* and *Phleum pratense* being recently sown, and on soils with higher available calcium and phosphate. Lower clay content was also important. The second component referred to the use and intensity of use of fields, though this was not a clear effect: the third component reflected the influence of drainage and in particular the clay content of the top soil, so that *Dactylis glomerata* (Cocksfoot) and *Ranunculus repens* were particularly associated with higher clay content.

TABLE 10.4

Classification of lowland grasslands of 4 Years of age or more

Source: Lineham *et al.* (1948)

Catchment	Good %	Fair %	Poor %	Very Poor %
Upper and Lower Bann and tributaries	11	32	51	6
Lagan and East County Down rivers	21	33	39	7
Upper and Lower Erne	1	15	70	14
Foyle and tributaries	5	27	56	12

In view of the high percentage of poor pasture in Northern Ireland revealed by Linehan *et al.* (1948), it is not surprising that livestock production at that time was also low. The average productivity of grassland in Northern Ireland for beef cattle in *c.* 1947-50 was between 10-15 cwt starch equivalent (S.E.) per acre, yet many case studies showed that this could be doubled; Kernohan (1947) in County Down found that it was possible to raise these values to 27.7 cwt starch equivalent per acre, Linehan and Lowe (1946) in County Antrim obtained values of 21-28 cwt S.E. per acre, and Turner (1948) 21 cwt S.E. per acre in County Armagh. Even in the more marginal areas improvements were made. The studies referred to above all involved reseeding with mixtures of Italian and Perennial Rye grass, clovers and Timothy grass, but the study made by McDowell (1954) also included plots which had only fertilizer treatment and controlled grazing. The experimental site in this case was not above 300 m O.D., but was in an exposed location and hence its marginal nature. The 'indigenous' sward was composed of *Sieglingia decumbens, Nardus stricta, Deschampsia cespitosa, Agrostis* spp., fescues, rushes and sedges. The plot which was only fertilized and grazed, i.e. not reseeded, was topped with ground limestone and superphosphate, and in the following spring triple superphosphate was applied. Two years later *Sieglingia, Nardus,* sedges and rushes had almost disappeared to be replaced by rough stalked meadow grass *(Poa trivialis)* with *Agrostis* and *Holcus lanatus* also increasing in occurrence. This fertilizer application led to an increase of 150% in output, to a mean of 15 cwt S.E. per acre, while treatments with fertilizer and reseeding had a 266% increase, to a mean of 23 cwt S.E. per acre.

Such results are achieved by considerable expenditure on reseeding and fertilizer, but they are not always long-lived. Porteous (1964) working in Fermanagh, found that on one of his experimental sites the liveweight gain was achieved at considerable cost in added fertilizer, which left little margin for profit, and without subsidies there would have been none. On his second site, he concluded that the liveweight gain was not good, considering the extent of treatment, and he pointed out that pasture improvements were short lived, with indigenous species quickly recolonizing. Recently, however, the amounts of mineral fertilizer added to grasslands have come under closer scrutiny, and indeed there has been wider use of natural fertilizer, particularly of slurry. McAllister (1971) and McAllister and Adams (1975) have proposed that the nutrient budget of the farm as a whole should be estimated, and have suggested that by such investigations the application of mineral fertilizers may be reduced. This approach consists of balancing the amounts of nutrients produced by the farm livestock, particularly phosphorus and potassium, against the amounts needed by the crops at optimum growth: applications are such as to reduce the imbalance. Adams (1976) has reported that in farm trials of this policy "on average they have saved £200 a year – some as much as £500 by limiting applications to the needs shown on their farm's nutrient 'balance sheet' ".

The lush green grasslands of Northern Ireland are not, therefore, as valuable a resource as a superficial view would lead one to believe: considerable improvements are needed, and, in spite of new policies on the farms, at some cost. Such improved grasslands will only warrant expenditure if market prices for livestock produce are sufficient to offset the considerable cost and give a reasonable profit – or unless subsidies are sufficient to enhance livestock income.

With regard to the boundaries around fields, there has been a limited amount of work on hedgerows in Northern Ireland: only Moles (1974) has examined in any detail the ecological importance of hedgerows. His extensive field study is somewhat limited by a qualitative classification of hedges, which depends on their height, width and density. As might have been expected the taller, wider and denser the hedge, the more ecologically diverse it was – diverse in terms of birds, herbaceous and woody plants, butterflies and fieldmice. The dominant hedge species was important, however, so that blackthorn, for example, was of little value to the maintenance of wildlife diversity. If tall, wide and dense hedges could be maintained Moles showed that short and narrow hedges could be lost without too much damage to the wildlife diversity. Hedge clearance and field enlargement is an increasing trend in Northern Ireland, especially in arable areas of County Down, but nowhere is the ecology threatened on the same scale as, for example, in Eastern England. The undulating character of the land, especially in drumlin country, prevents the creation of really large fields and therefore ensures survival of the hedgerow. What may be more serious is the loss of the tall, dense and wide hedge, as this is replaced by shorter more open hedges which result from mechanical trimming and the absence of correct laying of the hedge.

Conclusion

In this increasingly technological age it is refreshing that renewed interest is taking place in what used to be described as 'natural history'; witness the growth in guide-books, floras, bird-watching keys and in the number of wildlife programmes on both national and local television networks. Northern Ireland is well placed to supply this interest. Despite the high proportion of the landscape lying in 'improved' land, the number of Nature Reserves and other conservation sites is large and increasing and the variety of such sites is wide. There is no part of Northern Ireland which is far from such a site and indeed most areas would have examples of several different types of community within easy travelling distance. For both scientist and interested layman, there are therefore ample opportunities to conduct rewarding and valuable study. Some areas of vegetation may be regarded as a resource of a different kind, an economic resource, but the monetary value of vegetation is difficult to assess. Such assessments as can be made suggest that the hill lands will remain much as they are at present. This conclusion need not be regarded as a loss or a waste since vegetation has another value – its aesthetic value (see Buchanan in Chapter 12). Leaving aside its importance in the circulation of oxygen and water, this may indeed be its ultimate value. Any examination of the natural resources of Northern Ireland must consider vegetation – from the point of view of its appearance and composition, its conservation value, economic value, its provision of leisure and recreational opportunity and its aesthetic appeal.

REFERENCES

General
Dickie, G., 1864. *A flora of Ulster and botanists guide to the North of Ireland.* Aichison. Belfast.
Hill, D., 1963. Land Use: Introduction, Symons, L. *(Edit.)* *Land Use in Northern Ireland.* University of London Press.
Mitchell, G. F., 1976. *The Irish Landscape.* Collins. London.
Praeger, R.Ll., 1934. *The Botanist in Ireland.* E.P. Publishing Wakefield (1974 reprint).
Small, J., 1952. Botany. Jones, E. *(Edit.)* *Belfast in its regional setting.* British Association for Advancement of Science.
Stewart, S. A. and Corry, T., 1938. *A flora of the North-East of Ireland.* Quota Press. Belfast.
Webb, D. A., 1967. *An Irish Flora.* Dundalgan Press. Dundalk. 5th edition.

Meres and Mires
Armstrong, J. I., Calvert, J. and Ingold, C. T., 1930. The ecology of the Mourne Mountains with special reference to Slieve Donard. *Proceedings of the Royal Irish Academy,* 39B, 440–452.
Armstrong, J. I., Ingold, C. T. and Vear, K. L., 1934. Vegetation map of the Mourne Mountains. *Journal of Ecology,* 22, 439–444.
Browne, D. and Tease, D., 1979. Farm Management Standards. *Agriculture in Northern Ireland,* 53, 240-50.
Council of Scientific Research and Development. 1956. *The Northern Ireland Peat-bog Survey,* H.M.S.O., Belfast.
Department of Agriculture, Northern Ireland. 1977. *An economic analysis of ewe flock performance in Northern Ireland, 1975 & 1976.*
Dickson, D. A., 1966. *The relation between vegetation and mineral nutrient content of some areas of deep peat in Northern Ireland, with particular reference to afforestation.* Ph.D. Thesis Unpubl. Q.U.B.
Duff, M., 1930. The ecology of the Moss Lane Region, Lough Neagh. *Proceedings of the Royal Irish Academy,* 39B, 477-96.
Hammond, R., 1979. *The peatlands of Ireland.* An Foras Taluntais. Dublin.
Irwin, J. H. D., 1971. Profit from the hills. *Agriculture in Northern Ireland,* 46, 78-82.
Irwin, J. H. D., 1971. Hill sheep production. *Agriculture in Northern Ireland,* 49, 86–90, 152–158, 217–223, 255–260.
Jameson, R. A., 1971. *Peat erosion in the Mourne Mountains.* B.Sc. Thesis Unpubl. Q.U.B.
Kertland, M. P. H., 1928. The ecology of Divis. *Journal of Ecology,* 16, 301–322.
McKeague, M., 1935. *The ecology of Ballyalloly Lake.* M.Sc. Thesis Unpubl. Q.U.B.
Morrison, M. E. S., 1954. *The ecology and post glacial history of a County Tyrone bog.* M.Sc. Thesis Unpubl. Q.U.B.
Morrison, M. E. S., 1958. *Palynological and ecological studies in Northern Irish bog sites.* Ph.D. Thesis Unpubl. Q.U.B.
Poore, M. E. D., 1955. The use of phytosociological methods in ecological investigations. *Journal of Ecology,* 19, 226–269.
Small, J., 1931. The Fenlands of Lough Neagh. *Journal of Ecology,* 19, 383–388.
White, J. M., 1930. Recolonisation after peat cutting. *Proceedings of the Royal Irish Academy,* 39B, 453–476.
White, J. M., 1932. The Fens of North Armagh. *Proceedings of the Royal Irish Academy,* 40B, 233–283.

Woodlands
Adams, S. N., Jack, W. H. and Dickson, D. A., 1970. The growth of Sitka spruce on poorly drained soils in Northern Ireland. *Forestry,* 43, 125–133.
Cmd Paper 550. 1970. *Forestry in Northern Ireland.* H.M.S.O., Belfast.
Dickson, D. and Savill, P., 1974. Early growth of *Picea sitchensis* (Bong.) Carr. on deep oligotrophic peat in Northern Ireland. *Forestry,* 47, 57–88.
Gilbertson, M., 1969. *The ecology of the Quoile river.* Unpubl. M.Sc. Thesis Q.U.B.
Jack, W. H., 1965. Experiments on tree growing on peat in Northern Ireland. *Forestry,* 38, 20–40.

Jack, W. H., 1968. The growth of trees on peat in Northern Ireland. *Proceedings of a Symposium on peatland forestry.* NERC, Edinburgh.

Kilpatrick, C. S., 1965. Public response to forest recreation in Northern Ireland. *Irish Forestry,* 22, 3–15.

Lines, R. and Howell, R., 1963. The use of flags to estimate the relative exposure of trial plantations. *Forest Record,* No. 51 H.M.S.O., London.

McCracken, E., 1944. *The composition and distribution of woods in Northern Ireland from the sixteenth century down to the establishment of the Ordnance Survey.* M.Sc. Thesis Unpubl. Q.U.B.

McCracken, E., 1971. *The Irish woods since Tudor times.* David and Charles, Newton Abbot.

MacKenzie, R. F., 1974. Some factors influencing the stability of Sitka spruce in Northern Ireland. *Irish Forestry,* 31, 110–129.

MacKenzie, R. F., 1975. *Growth and stability of Sitka spruce in relation to certain environmental factors.* Ph.D. Thesis Unpubl. Q.U.B.

MacKenzie, R. F., 1976. Silviculture and management in relation to risk of windthrow in Northern Ireland. *Irish Forestry,* 33, 29–38.

Ministry of Agriculture, Northern Ireland. *Forest Service Annual Reports,* 1976-77, 1977-78, 1979.

Northern Ireland Trading and other Accounts. 1975–1976 (HC 156 1976-77).

Northern Ireland Trading and other Accounts. 1977–1978 (HC 161 1978-79).

Parker, R. E., 1957. Some problems arising in the afforestation of peatland in Northern Ireland. *Irish Forestry,* 14, 118–121.

Parkin, K. F., 1957. Afforesation of peatlands in Northern Ireland. *Irish Forestry,* 14, 111–117.

Savill, P. S., 1974., Assessment of the economic limit of palatability. *Irish Forestry,* 31, 22–35.

Savill, P. S., 1977. *Environmental and soil factors affecting the growth of conifers in Northern Ireland.* Ph.D. Thesis Unpubl. Q.U.B.

Surgin, W. A., 1978. *Craigagh Wood: an historical and vegetational study.* B.A. Thesis Unpubl. Q.U.B.

Wright, P. M., 1978. *Landscape evaluation of selected areas of woodland in Northeast County Down.* B.Sc. Thesis Unpubl.Q.U.B.

Heathlands

Gimingham, C. H., 1972. *Ecology of heathlands.* Chapman & Hall, London.

Magurran, A., 1976. *An ecological investigation of Boorin Wood Nature Reserve, Gortin, County Tyrone.* MS, Conservation Branch, Department of Environment Northern Ireland.

Watt, A., 1955. The life-cycle of *Calluna. Journal of Ecology,* 43, 490–000.

Hedgerows

Forest Service, Department of Agriculture, Northern Ireland, 1979. *Forest Research 2/79.*

Forest Service, Department of Agriculture, Northern Ireland, 1979. *Forest Research 3/79.*

Moles, R. T., 1974. *Wildlife diversity in relation to agricultural management in lowland County Down, Northern Ireland.* Ph.D. Thesis Unpubl. Q.U.B.

Robinson, P., 1977. The spread of the hedged enclosure in Ulster. *Ulster Folklife,* 23, 57–69.

Grasslands

Adams, S. N., 1976. Nutrient balance sheet shows a profit. *Farmer's Weekly,* September 24th, pp. v-vii.

Davies, W., 1941. The grassland map of England and Wales: Explanatory notes. *Agriculture London,* 48, 112–121.

Field, E., 1973. *Vegetation and soil studies in relation to landuse history on hill grazing land in the Sperrin Mountains.* M.Sc. Thesis Unpubl. Q.U.B.

Kernohan, J. T., 1947. Grassland output on a County Down farm. *Journal of the British Grassland Society,* 1, 78–81.

Linehan, P. and Lowe, J., 1946. The output of pasture and its measurement I. *Journal of the British Grassland Society, I,* 7–35.

Linehan, P., Lowe, J., and Stewart, M., 1947. The output of pasture and its measurement II. *Journal of the British Grassland Society,* 2, 145–168.

Lowe, J., 1951. *Output . . . in botanical composition of grassland swards under certain systems of seeding, manuring, and management.* M.Agric. Thesis Unpubl. Q.U.B.

McAllister, J. S. V., 1971. Nutrient balance on livestock farms. *The Potassium Institute Limited.* 1st Colloquium, 113–121.

McAllister, J. S. V. and Adams, S. N., 1975. Nutrient cycles involving phosphorus and potassium on livestock farms in Northern Ireland. *Journal of Agricultural Science, Cambridge,* 85, 345–349.

McDowell, K. A., 1954. Grassland output on a County Londonderry hill farm. *Journal of the British Grassland Society,* 9, 173–181.

Porteous, C. B., 1964. *Studies on sward constitution and animal output on County Fermanagh grasslands.* M.Agric. Thesis Unpubl. Q.U.B.

Restrick, G., 1970. *Soil and vegetation change in abandoned farmland in selected areas of County Tyrone.* B.Sc. Thesis Unpubl. Q.U.B.

Sutton, J. M., 1973. *A study of the interaction of botanical composition, soil and farm management variables . . . to agricultural classification in Northern Ireland.* Ph.D. Thesis Unpubl. Q.U.B.

Turner, R. R., 1948. Grassland output on a dairy farm in County Armagh. *Journal of the British Grassland Society,* 3, 95–102.

CHAPTER XI

Energy Resources

PALMER J. NEWBOULD,
Professor of Environmental Science, New University of Ulster.

Introduction

A superficial view might suggest that Northern Ireland has no energy resources and that therefore this chapter is unnecessary. On the other hand an optimist would point to the old coal mines at Ballycastle and Coalisland, to the lignite deposits under Lough Neagh, to the extensive areas of peat, the prospecting for oil, both inland and submarine, and for uranium in County Tyrone, and to the sun, wind, rain, tide and wave energy waiting to be tapped. A balanced evaluation of the situation lies between these two extremes; the indigenous energy resource actually being used is minimal, but the potential is significant. So is the potential for the environmental energy sources.

Current energy use*, and future trends

Resources are best discussed in relation to the demands made upon them rather than in the absolute. Current and recent energy use in Northern Ireland is shown in Figure 11.1. The quantities listed are primary energy (as opposed to delivered or end use energy) and represent energy imports to Northern Ireland, including the fuel imported by the Northern Ireland Electricity Service (NIES) for making electricity. All quantities are expressed in Petajoules (PJ, 10^{15} joules) which is a convenient unit since the total primary energy use in Northern Ireland is running a little under 200 PJ year^{-1}. The cross-border electricity link has been inoperative for a few years, so there has been no net import or export of electricity that way. There are a number of minor inaccuracies. Peat imports from the Republic of Ireland are not shown. In 1978 they totalled 24,313 tonnes of machine turf and 13,128 tonnes† of briquettes. These figures are equivalent to approximately 0.32 PJ and 0.24 PJ respectively, totalling 0.56 PJ (Duddy, personal communication). No figures are included for locally cut peat or for firewood, but both are taken to be very small (see later sections). Nor is any account taken of a very small amount of hydro-electricity or wind electricity generated

* the term "energy use" which might appear to contravene the first law of thermodynamics is convenient shorthand for conversion of fuel energy into heat or mechanical energy directly useful to man, or a similar conversion of environmental energy.

† tonne=metric ton=1,000 kg   tonne=0.984×ton

privately. And no figure is included for imported bottled gas, but again it would be negligible on the scale of Figure 11.1. In the opposite direction some small components of the oil imports are used, e.g., for lubrication and do not represent usable energy.

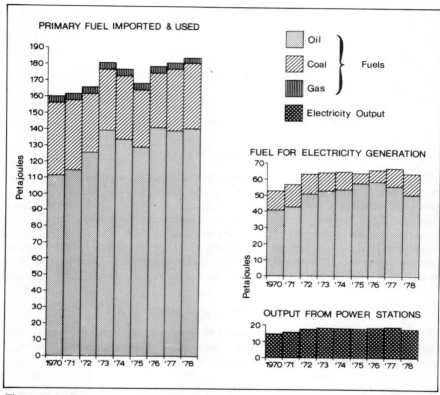

Figure 11.1 Energy imports into Northern Ireland, and fuel used in electricity generation. As shown, the supply and consumption of energy has been almost static since 1973, and, not shown, has fallen in the subsequent period 1979-1981.

The figures illustrate the steady increase in energy use occurring between 1970-73, which is a continuation of the expansion of the 1960s. In autumn 1973 there was a steep increase in the cost of oil, largely due to the OPEC countries putting the price up and this, combined with economic depression and perhaps some local factors, has caused a much more static situation from 1973-78.

It seems possible that energy use will remain around its present level for some time into the future. The 1980 recession was actually accompanied by a reduction in energy use. The 1980-81 electricity sales were 7.9% lower than in the previous year. In Britain population growth is now virtually nil. In Northern Ireland birth rate (*c.* 16/1,000) is still substantially greater than death rate (*c.* 11/1,000) so that official predictions indicate that the population (1,529,000 in 1979) will increase to 1,596,000 in the year 2000, an increase of just over 4% in 21 years. So population growth alone is unlikely to be responsible for much increase in energy use. Another argument sometimes used is that Northern Ireland is lagging somewhat behind the rest of the U.K. in economic development, and that there may therefore be some catching up in energy use per caput.

It seems that the main energy supply problem facing Northern Ireland will be not so much meeting increased demand but how, within a static energy demand, to decrease oil dependence, as oil becomes scarcer and more expensive. The energy system is small, not at present coupled to any other, heavily dependent upon oil (over 75%), and upon import by boat. These matters will be discussed further in a later section where the need for an energy policy and its possible nature will be reviewed.

Fossil fuel resources

Historically two small coalfields have been exploited in Northern Ireland, one at Ballycastle and the other near Coalisland and Dungannon in County Tyrone (Wilson, 1972; Roberts, Chapter 7). Both are Carboniferous; the Tyrone coalfield is a much faulted area of Namurian and Westphalian strata while the Ballycastle coalfield consists of Visean coals beneath Fair Head. Some beds of low grade oil shales occur in the Visean and Namurian strata. The Tyrone coalfield has been extensively worked, but some faulted, thin seams probably remain. The eight distinct coal seams of workable thickness at Coalisland have been virtually worked out, production finally closing 1967. There are fairly large reserves of low quality Visean succession in the Ballycastle coalfield. Yields of up to 77 litres tonne^{-1} were reported in 1917 (Wilson, 1972), but the shales are of no economic importance now.

Recent geophysical evidence indicates that sedimentary basins exist under the Antrim basalts, both at Larne and between Ballymoney-Ballymena, and these basins may contain coal measures at some depth, but this is unproven. There is also the possibility that oil and natural gas may occur in sedimentary basins in Antrim coastal areas. In the 1960s, a borehole near Larne went to 1,280 m and one near Ballycastle to 1,840 m, both without reaching any coal deposits. A third hole at Magilligan Point found two thin coal seams at depths of well over 1,070 m. A good deal more exploration has been going on in recent years, and in 1979, the British Government announced it was to spend about £¼ million a year for several years on coal prospecting in Antrim, Londonderry and Tyrone. In 1981, the Department of Commerce for Northern Ireland issued a licence to prospect for petroleum over an area of 465 square miles (1,200 km^2) of land and 85 square miles (220 km^2) of sea in the north of Counties Antrim and Londonderry to a consortium consisting of Ulster Natural Resources Ltd, North Sea Petroleums Ltd and Exicon Exploration Ltd. The sea area covers a three mile wide strip from Castlerock to Ballintoy and is adjacent to that licenced in 1980 to Energy Sources (N.I.) Ltd in respect of the Rathlin basin. The general configuration looks suitable but it will probably require two years exploration to see whether there is an economic find of oil or gas.

Small gas shows were recorded in the 1960s from bores in the Carboniferous rocks of County Fermanagh, and in 1981 a more extensive find was reported straddling the Border between Cavan and Fermanagh and said to be nearly as large as the Kinsale natural gas field (Irish Times 10.4.81). Enthusiasm for this new gas field seemed to wane later in 1981. No doubt there is a lot of gas there, but the economics (and, indeed the politics, since the field runs across the Border) of its extraction and transport may be less favourable.

There are substantial beds of lignite, of early or mid-Oligocene age in the Lough Neagh clays and these have been worked as fuel on a small scale in the past. McMullan, Morgan and Murray (1976c) consider the Lough Neagh lignite deposits are not really economic to work since there is only enough to keep a 100 MW power station running for 10 years. Assuming a 55% load factor and 35% efficiency, this means that the lignite resource is equivalent to about 50 Petajoules.

Peat resources

Peat is intermediate between the non-renewable fossil fuels and renewable resources like biomass. While active peat formation is still occurring in some areas, exploitation is much faster than formation, so that peat is effectively a non-renewable fossil fuel resource.

Hamilton (Chapter 9) reviews the availability of peat fuel in Northern Ireland. The 1952-53 survey by the Council of Scientific Research and Development estimated total peat resources at 300 million tons* (about 3,780 PJ), but only 7 million tons (88 PJ) were believed exploitable by machine cutting. This would keep the NIES system running for just over one year, or a 20 MW power station running for 85 years. However, there are reasons why this is not a feasible proposition. Some of the peat would have to be transported too far and the individual bogs are not really large enough to warrant Bord na Mona type large scale exploitation. Only 6 areas are larger than 500 acres and suitable for large scale peat harvesting (Howard, 1968). A new machine called the Herbst Difco was introduced to Ireland in 1981. It produces compact cylindrical "Turfbricks" and will reduce the size of bog economically exploitable by machine.

The Electricity Supply Board (ESB) in the Republic run a number of small peat-fired power stations, such as the 5 MW one located at Gweedore in the Gaeltacht part of Donegal. This uses 25,000 tonnes of sod peat (0.35 PJ) per year which is provided by local farmers. Some 300 peat cutters supply anything between 20 and 800 tonnes per year, the smaller quantities representing hand cutting and the larger quantities the smaller type of one-man peat cutting machine costing about £10,000. While small power stations such as this may not give a good return on investment, they do provide employment in rural areas. This point was made forcefully for Northern Ireland by the Rural Industries Development Committee in 1964, but has not been acted upon.

Even if commercial peat cutting is not economically viable in Northern Ireland, individual peat cutting for domestic fuel is still very widespread. It is difficult to estimate the scale of this. Wishart (1978) studied peat cutting on three bogs in north Antrim (Garry, Moycraig and Cloonty), and estimated that 219 peat cutters (and their families) were cutting about 1,500 tonnes of peat (c. 7 tonnes each per year). Over half

*1 ton = 1.016 tonnes

the peat cutters lived within 4 km of the bog they were from and three-quarters lived within 5.6 km, i.e. within a circle of 100 km² area.

Suppose this density of peat cutters and peat cutting existed all over Northern Ireland, the annual yield of peat would be 3.9 tonnes km⁻² or 53,000 tonnes. At 1,092 kJ kg⁻¹ (Wishart's value) this would represent an energy yield of about 0.5 PJ. This is presumably an overestimate, but it may be that the true value is 0.1–0.2 PJ. Henry (1976) gives an estimate for 1973 of what he terms "Farmers' peat" of 320.7×10^3 TOE (Tonnes Oil Equivalent) per year for the Republic of Ireland. This works out at 13.5 PJ which is 12 tonnes km⁻² or three times as much per unit area of land as the estimate given above for Northern Ireland. Given the much greater peat resource and peat cutting tradition of the Republic of Ireland, this is not unreasonable.

Uranium resources and nuclear power

A Canadian company, Sabina Industries Ltd, are prospecting for uranium over 302 square miles (780 km²) of south Tyrone and Fermanagh (DoC, 1978). The commercial value of any find will depend upon the value of uranium in the world market, which in turn determines how lean and inaccessible an ore is worth exploiting. It will also be affected by political factors, such as whether Australia declines to export uranium, and the rate of development of the world nuclear power programme including the transition from thermal to fast breeder reactors. In 1980-81 uranium prospecting was very active across the border in Donegal, especially in the granites around Fintown and Doochary, where it has aroused considerable local opposition. The amount of prospecting effort suggests there must be some chance of an exploitable find.

Currently the nuclear power option does not seem especially attractive in Northern Ireland. Nuclear reactors are mainly used to supply base load electricity, that is they are kept running at a high load factor all the time. Minimum demand in the Northern Ireland system at present is about 250 MW (Gaston, personal communication). The minimum size of nuclear reactor currently available would be about 600 MW, which would represent too many eggs in one basket. While the proponents of nuclear power claim that the reliability of nuclear reactors is high, the fact remains that if they go wrong, the repair may take quite a long time because of the hazard of radioactivity. So the electricity system might need to remain functional for considerable periods without the nuclear reactor. The combined systems of the NIES and the ESB might well be large enough to include one nuclear power station providing the N-S interconnector can be repaired and maintained functional (McMullan, Morgan & Murray, 1976a).

However, winning public acceptance of the first nuclear power station in a non-nuclear country might take a long time. Probably the escalation in the price of electricity will depress demand and the new power station at Kilroot will ensure ample generating capacity for Northern Ireland, even if some of the older generating sets are decommissioned. Hence, even if it can be unequivocally demonstrated that nuclear electricity is both acceptable and cheaper, it may be still cheaper to continue using efficient new oil fired generating capacity than to decommission or underuse it in favour of building a nuclear power station. Furthermore, the U.K. Government has recently allocated £370 million to sorting out the problems of the NIES and may not wish to make a further substantial capital grant in the near future.

Environmental energy sources

The so-called environmental energy resources mainly derive from the sun. The sun's heating causes atmospheric circulation which is the source of wind-power and wave-power. Water evaporated by the sun falls as rain and is the basis for hydro-power. Direct solar energy can be used for heating or via photovoltaic cells to make electricity. Photosynthesis is the process whereby plants convert solar energy into bound chemical energy, and there has been much recent research on growing crops specifically for energy conversion, called energy crops or biomass crops.

The two main non-solar sources are tidal energy, the tides being caused by the moon's gravitational pull, and geothermal energy, the heat from the centre of the earth which derives from radioactive decay. The potential of these various energy sources in Northern Ireland will be reviewed. It is interesting to note that Johansson and Steen (1978) in their plans for Solar Sweden 2015 envisage 26% of the energy from hydropower, solar cells and windpower, 62% from biomass and 12% from solar heating.

Annual solar radiation incident on a horizontal surface in Ireland is about 1,000 kWh m^{-2} (Lalor 1975, Solar Energy Society of Ireland 1978). In terms of the units used earlier this is 3.6 PJ km^{-2}. In theory this value can be increased by about 15% if the surface is optimally inclined. This is about half the radiation available in the most favourable parts of the world. However, one major difficulty arises from its distribution around the year since more than 50% arrives in the 3 months May–July and less than 10% in the three months November–January. The economics of photovoltaic cells are still not very good so they seem unlikely to find much application in Ireland. So the main direct applications of solar energy are likely to be space heating and water heating. Hand et al. (1977) feel that the prospects for solar water heating in Ireland are quite good. Since at least 60% of the insolation is diffuse, in practice the orientation of the solar panel is relatively unimportant. They feel it is preferable to have a single stage system where the water heated by the sun is used, rather than have a heat exchanger. However the single stage system requires precautions against freezing up in the winter. The Solar Energy Society of Ireland (1978) develop a scenario which involves the fitting of solar water heating into 60% of new houses and solar space heating into 5% of new houses (O'Rourke et al., 1976). Both systems would require supplementary electrical heating in the winter, but around the year would supply 25-50% of the heat energy required, saving 1.2–3.2 PJ year^{-1}. This figure refers to the Republic, in which case the relevant figure in Northern Ireland would be about half (0.6–1.6 PJ year^{-1}).

While Ireland may seem a bit short of sunshine hours, because of its low population density the available solar radiation per head is about six times that in the U.K. The total solar input is about 800 times the primary energy demand, as opposed to 80 times in the U.K. (Department of Energy, 1976).

The heat pump is another way of using environmental heat. A heat pump is like a refrigerator in reverse and combines the electricity needed to drive the compressor with environmental heat from air or water. McMullan, Morgan & Murray (1976b) suggest that a heat pump should attain a Coefficient of Performance (COP) of 2.5 which means that 1 Joule of electrical energy would provide 2.5 Joules of heat energy. Research at University College Galway (Alstrom, 1979) suggests that a seasonally averaged COP of 2.6 is easily attainable. However, their heat pump is designed to take care of all heating when the outside temperature is above 2°C. When the air temperature falls below 2°C direct electric heating is required and the effective COP is reduced. The main problem is that the cost of installing a heat pump heating system is quite high and the payback time correspondingly long.

Biomass can be subdivided into its traditional form, firewood, and its new form, energy crops. The amount of firewood used is anyone's guess. Earl (1975) gives a figure for the U.K. as a whole of 4 kg coal equivalent per head per year. Transferred directly to Northern Ireland this would give 0.17 PJ year^{-1}. Earl also suggests that the U.K. derives about 0.1% of its total primary energy from firewood and this would give a very similar figure, 0.18 PJ. J. M. Sanderson of the Forest Service, DoA, (personal communication), suggests that peat burning is about twenty times greater than firewood burning. If we include imported peat this would give a maximum value of 0.1 PJ for firewood. Another suggestion is that about 1% of households burn wood (say 5,000 households) and their annual consumption averages out at about 3 tonnes of firewood per household. Assuming an energy content of about 10 GJ tonne^{-1}, this would give a value for firewood burnt of 0.15 PJ, so it seems reasonable to suggest that the true value does not exceed 0.20 PJ year^{-1}. However, it is also clear that householders are installing modern woodburning stoves at a considerable rate, and the consumption of firewood may increase greatly in the next two decades. This is a good reason for managing hedgerow and copse timber on a proper sustained yield basis instead of the present chainsaw and no replacement approach.

In fact the organised growth and use of plant biomass as a renewable and storable energy resource has attracted increasing attention in recent years. A substantial research and development programme is under way within the EEC and much of it is based in the Irish Republic (Owen Lewis, 1978). The situation there is especially favourable for biomass production because:–

(i) in Ireland the ratio of land area to energy requirement is the highest of all the EEC countries.

(ii) as a corollary of this there are substantial areas of under-used land, e.g. the western blanket bog areas or the poorly drained gley soils of the Leitrim drumlins;

(iii) the maritime climate is favourable for biomass, i.e. lignin/cellulose production;

(iv) the Irish experience in large scale peat harvesting (include adaptation of machinery) and in the production of electricity from peat would be relevant to biomass production and conversion.

The problem is to determine to what extent biomass might have a role in Northern Ireland. There are several factors affecting this. Perhaps the most important is the availability of suitable land which in turn depends upon the EEC Common Agricultural Policy (e.g. the price of lamb, mutton, wool or other commodities).

The favoured biomass crops for poor soils in humid temperature regions are short rotation forestry, either coniferous or broadleaved. The conifer crop would have to be replaced after each harvest and unless extremely high planting densities are used, the first few years are relatively unproductive. Minimum rotation time might therefore be 15-20 years. The alternative is coppiced willow, alder or poplar, harvested on a 1-4 year coppicing cycle and allowed to regrow from the rootstock, known as the stool. Some rather small scale experiments at Loughgall Horticultural Centre have given yields up to 41.65 tonnes ha^{-1} year^{-1} from *Salix* x *"aquatica gigantea"* grown at a close spacing (40,000 ha^{-1}) and with added nitrogen. In fact the effect of nitrogen was not great but this may be because the soil was already relatively fertile. These yields would be equivalent to about 20 tonnes ha^{-1} year^{-1} dry weight. More extensive experiments at Newtownbutler and Castle Archdale in County Fermanagh, on heavy gley soils and in exposed sites indicate that the same species, harvested on a three year rotation, will give a sustained yield of at least 14.6 tonnes ha^{-1} year^{-1} dry matter.

Many decisions remain to be taken but a possible scenario might involve an area of land of mixed quality where poplar could be planted on the better and drier sites, willow in most of the wet sites and alder where nitrogen deficiency seemed severe. The crop would be machine harvested on a 1-4 year rotation and either bundled or chipped as part of the harvesting process. If bundled it may be chipped at the conversion plant.

This biomass material may be used to make electricity and Neenan and Lyons (1977) propose a model with the parameters set out below:–

Area of plantation	117 km²
Productivity	12.5 tonnes ha^{-1} year^{-1} dry matter
Calorific value	16.9×10⁹ J tonne^{-1}
Yield	*c.* 2.5 PJ year^{-1}

This would fuel a 50 MWe* power station, working with a conversion efficiency of 35%, a load factor of 55% and produce 0.8–0.9 PJe* year^{-1}. These figures must be related to Northern Ireland land/use statistics, which are set out below:–

	km²
State Forestry	671
Woodland	131
Total agricultural, including rough grazing	10,409
Total land area	13,580

So 117 km² is 0.9% of the total land area or 17% of the present state forest area. Thus the requirement in terms of land area is quite considerable, and the energy saving, 2.5 PJ primary energy, is only about 1.4% of present energy demand. Stott *et al.,* (1980) suggest there are at least 200 km² of disadvantaged land in Fermanagh and west Tyrone immediately available for biomass production with another 200 km² becoming available once the crop proves successful.

But there are additional reasons for adding a substantial element of biomass to the energy mix. It is a versatile fuel. In its chipped form it can be made into briquettes which would be a very convenient product for domestic woodburning stoves. Biomass can also be converted to methane, methanol or ethanol for use as a gaseous or liquid fuel. These conversion plants could be designed to accept organic wastes, such as domestic or industrial wastes, animal manure, plant residues, etc. thus helping with the problems of solid waste disposal and the pollution it often causes. If anti-pollution legislation requires a high standard of treatment for organic wastes, the economics of extracting their energy content will become more favourable, and will support the biomass programme.

A major problem of EEC agriculture is that production varies from year to year, due to climatic and other factors to the extent of ±20% while demand remains constant.

* e signifies electrical

One suggestion for reducing the effect of this is that agriculture should diversify into non-food crops and biomass fits the bill quite well. Farmers could grow a few hectares of willow coppice under contract, either harvesting it themselves, or having it harvested by the central biomass conversion plant.

Wind power warrants discussion on two scales. Small aerogenerators in the range 5–30 kW may be used to provide electricity for individual houses or farms, and large generators in the range 0.5–2.0 MW could provide electricity for the grid, either directly or by pumping water into a pumped storage scheme. Much of the west coast of Ireland averages a power density of more than 4 MWh m^{-2} whereas most of Northern Ireland is nearer to 2 MWh m^{-2} (Allen and Bird, 1977). McMullan, Morgan and Murray (1976*c*) show that the use of normal meteorological data, and averaging them, seriously underestimates the power available from the wind. Haslett and Kelledy (1979) stress the significant annual variability of wind power which emphasises the need for pumped storage.

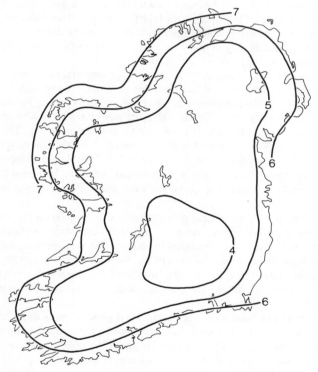

Figure 11.2 Mean annual wind speed, measured in metres per second, for Ireland 1951-1970 (from Rohan, 1975).

On the domestic scale, Bogle, 1978, Bogle *et al.,* 1979, examined the energy potential of the wind at Aldergrove based on hourly weather data for wind speed and air temperature collected over the period 1949-75. They constructed a theoretical simulation model consisting of a wind generator, a house and a heat store, and by varying the size and performance of these three components, they examined the potential of wind power for domestic heating. Aldergrove is not in a particularly windy area, but comparable with much of central Scotland and England. Various storage systems are available, but Bogle concludes that batteries are too inefficient and expensive, hydrogen though perhaps the best is unsuitable on a domestic scale and thermal storage, probably in water, is to be preferred. A favourable system might be based on a 6 kW aerogenerator (blade diameter 15 m) operating at windspeeds between 5 and 30 knots (2.6–15.4 m sec^{-1}) and a heat store operating between 60 and 80° C. Supplementary electric heating, perhaps up to 3,000 units in the year will be needed. The better the house and the tank are insulated, the less supplementary heating will be needed. The economics of the system depend upon how the price of electricity increases. If it increases simply in line with inflation, a relatively small heat store is needed (i.e. it pays to supplement considerably). Where electricity prices rise much faster than inflation, a large heat store, say 25 m^3 of water, is best. This then begins to look like the 'swimming pool in the basement' idea, and poses its own architectural and engineering problems. In general, homes heated by wind power look as if they will soon become an economic proposition for new housing developments. If they become common, the supplementary heating required during calm spells in the winter could create an awkward peak demand for the electricity system.

On the domestic scale there seems scope for experimentation with different types of aerogenerator, including vertical shaft machines. On the large scale the engineering problems are more difficult and most large aerogenerators end up by sustaining severe wind damage or blowing down. The fact that the power available is proportional to the cube of the wind speed means that gales contain enormous power. The most suitable design for large machines is probably the horizontal shaft high speed type. There may be a limit to the economies of scale (Nolan, 1978). It is simply difficult to make the large machines strong enough. A 1 MW generator needs to be about 80 m high. The 660 kW generators at Aalborg in Denmark have 54 m diameter polyester resin blades on 45 m towers (Power, 1979).

Sorenson (1978a, b) claims that up to 25% of the average Irish electrical load could be supplied by wind generators acting in a fuel saving mode, without storage. This means that they do not reduce the need for conventional generating capacity. If some storage capacity is included the fraction of the total load carried can be increased and wind generating capacity begins to substitute for other forms of generating capacity. This strengthens the case for pumped storage, with the wind generators pumping water direct to storage.

The environmental impact of large scale wind generation is quite significant. The machines are certainly dangerous. Wind farms on hill tops would be unsightly to many people. They are also inclined to be noisy. However the resource is free, and abundant, and some significant contribution from wind energy must be sought.

Northern Ireland used to have very many small watermills (Gribbon, 1969). A hydro-electric installation at Bushmills was in use from 1883 onwards to power the Giant's Causeway tram. Also, at Limavady the generation of hydro-electricity started in 1894 and continued to the 1960s when the turbines at Largy Green and Roe Mill were producing about 1 million units of electricity (0.0036 PJ), saving fuel equivalent to 0.01 PJ each year.

Despite these examples from the past, there are no significant sources of hydro-electricity in Northern Ireland now. The topography is such that there are few extensive areas of high ground. McMullan, Morgan and Murray (1976c) suggest that in an area with a rainfall of 1 m, and assuming all the rain runs off, a collection area of 30 km² is necessary to produce 10 kW averaged through the year. In practice no more than two thirds of the rain would run off, and if rainfall were unevenly distributed around the year, storage might be a problem, so that 50 km² might be a more realistic estimate. Also extensive arterial and land drainage has made the hydrological regime of the rivers more flashy and thus less suitable for hydro-electric schemes.

An alternative approach is via the empirical equation (McMullan, Morgan & Murray 1976c).

$$P = 9.8 \, FH$$

where P is the average power yield in kW, F is the flow rate in m³ sec⁻¹ and H is the head of water in metres. The efficiency of generation of hydro-electricity is extremely high, typically 80-90%.

The Republic of Ireland has two major hydro-electric schemes, one on the Erne and one on the Shannon. Their vital statistics (Tinney 1980, personal communication) are set out in Table 11.1. Lough Neagh is often suggested as a possible source of hydro-electric power, and certainly it is a large reservoir with a large catchment but the difficulty is that it is too low (operating level about 12.5 m above mean sea level Belfast) and also too far from the sea. It contrasts with Lough Erne, where the operating level is about 46 m above sea level and there is a relatively short and abrupt fall to Ballyshannon. The actual contribution of the Shannon and the Erne to the Republic of Ireland energy economy is about 2 PJ year⁻¹ end use which represents a primary fuel saving of about 6 PJ.

It seems unlikely that any Lough Neagh scheme could produce more than about 10 MW. There is also a potential conflict between the use of large existing lakes for hydro-electricity and some of their other uses such as pleasure boating which require a fairly stable water level. The stable water level limits the timing of power generation; one cannot run the reservoir low to meet a heavy demand. It does not however affect the amount of electricity generated. The recent consultants' report on the Erne

TABLE 11.1

Vital statistics of Shannon and Erne hydroelectric schemes with some comparative data on Lough Neagh

	Catchment km²	Average annual rainfall mm	Average annual flow m³ s⁻¹ F	Average head H	Potential power yield 9.8FH MW	Actual Electrical yield* MW
Shannon	10,400	967	194	28.3	53.8	35.4
Cliff				10.0 ⎫	10.0 ⎫	
Erne	3,950	1,050	102	⎬	⎬ 38.5	31.4
Cathaleen's Fall				28.5 ⎭	28.5 ⎭	
Lough Neagh (tentative)	5,807	1,030	113	8.0	9	—

*ESB figure for average generation of units divided by number of hours in a year.

catchment (Brady-Shipman-Martin & P.A. International, 1980) maintains that potential conflicts of this type can easily be overcome.

There remains the possibility of a number of small schemes in the Mournes, Sperrins or Antrim plateau. If sources such as wind, tide or nuclear power were to be developed, a pumped storage scheme would be desirable if not essential. Indeed, one was planned for Camlough in the Mournes. The two 115 MW pumping/generating turbines have actually been made and are being stored, but there was considerable local opposition to the scheme which has been deferred. The ESB have a similar pumped storage scheme at Turlough Hill which is rated at 292 MW and is used to produce 250-300 million units (*c.* 1 PJ) per year.

Serious and intensive research and development related to wave power has only been proceeding during the past decade (Ross, 1979). It is too early to decide which of the main systems will be the best, but it may be worth reviewing the characteristics of wave power.

(i) Available energy: Lewis (1977) suggests that Atlantic waves, which contain as much as $50 \, kW \, m^{-1}$ energy in the winter, average $38 \, kW \, m^{-1}$ over the whole year. Ross (1979) quotes Ian Glendinning as giving the maximum continuous rating as $50 \, kW \, m^{-1}$ which with a load factor of 60-70%, 80% conversion efficiency and 90% transmission efficiency leaves landed and available power of about $24-30 \, kW \, m^{-1}$. Taking a figure of $25 \, kW \, m^{-1}$, this becomes $25 \, MW \, km^{-1}$ and means that the total electrical capacity of Ireland North and South could be met by about 200 km of wave generators, i.e. the available energy is vast. Wells (1977) describes the wave power impinging on the coastline of Ireland from Tory Island to Carnsore Point as equivalent to 12,000 MW. The period of high wave energy extends from October to February and corresponds quite well with the main need for space heating. Wave energy is more consistent in its rate of incidence than wind energy because it has larger momentum. Probably wave generators would be best located in about 50 m depth of water, perhaps 5 km out from the coast.

(ii) The engineering problems are considerable. The structure must stand up to very high seas without damage. North Sea oil platforms and drilling rigs are quoted as comparable examples, but there has been considerable damage and loss of life in this operation and the North Sea is not as rough as the Atlantic. As with wind generators it may be best to design the wave generator so that it avoids the very strongest waves. There is an additional problem in bringing the power ashore as electricity. No cables will stand repeated flexure. No full size wave generators are yet working in the open ocean. One advantage is that the wave generators are likely to be modular, that is the power generated will come from relatively small units, like wind power but unlike hydro-electric or tidal power.

(iii) Available technologies: The best known of the technologies are Salter's Nodding Ducks and the Cockerell wave raft. In the 'Duck' a cam-shaped float pivots about a cylindrical spine and is rotationally displaced by the passage of a wave. High efficiency is claimed, and in scale model tests the contrast between the waves on one side and the calm sea on the other is very striking, showing that the device really has extracted most of the energy. In very rough seas, the largest waves break right over the device.

The wave raft is essentially a series of pontoons hinged to one another with pumps located at the hinge points which are activated by the passage of waves.

Another promising technology is the Matsuda resonant tube buoy, which is anchored to the sea bed. As the water rises and falls in the tube it alternately drives air out of the tube or sucks it back in again, and this air rotates a turbine . The turbine is so designed that it rotates in the same direction whether the air is being sucked in or blown out. This allows high speeds to be attained. This design has been further developed and tested by Professor A. A. Wells, formerly of The Queen's University, Belfast.

Various other ingenious devices are being developed. It is difficult to select one winner at present; on the other hand fairly substantial investment is required to test these designs at full scale in the Atlantic Ocean. There may be penalties as well as rewards for being the first fully operational technology in such a field.

(iv) A particular benefit for Northern Ireland is that the manufacture of wave generator units is regarded as possible work for shipyards as shipbuilding declines.

(v) The Republic of Ireland is as well located as anywhere in Europe to take advantage of wave energy. Northern Ireland has less open ocean coastline but the North Coast from Magilligan Point to Fair Head would still be a very good area for collecting wave energy.

(vi) Environmental aspects: Wave generators are a potential hazard to shipping and will have to be well beaconed and located away from main shipping routes. They will of course reduce the amount of wave energy reaching the coast, but in some cases this may be beneficial. Possible effects on inshore fisheries are uncertain. No energy technology can be either safe or environmentally harmless but wave energy looks to be one of the better ones.

In a few countries, such as Iceland and New Zealand, geothermal energy (earth heat!) comes bubbling out of the surface of the ground as hot springs. Elsewhere man has to work for it, usually by drilling deep holes and pumping cold water down and hot water up again. The rock temperature at different depths, dependent upon radioactive decay in the earth's core or in deeper parts of the crust, is very variable from place to place. Antrim is cited (O'Sullivan, 1980) as a proven geothermal source with water at 35° C only 500 m down. This requires further exploration, but in general geothermal energy is not particularly promising. Mostly it only produces warm water, a form of energy currently in surplus, and being discharged into the environment as thermal pollution rather than being conserved as useful heat. Nonetheless a plan to drill a 3,600 m borehole near Larne for geothermal energy, at a cost of over £2 million was announced by David Howell, Minister for Energy, on September 12, 1980. Drilling began in the spring of 1981.

Tidal power is generally less favoured than wave power. It requires an appropriate estuary or sea lough configuration where tidal ebb and flow is constricted. It is obviously best in areas with high tidal range. The best known, operative system is that at La Rance, near St Nazaire in Brittany.

The scheme most often suggested for Northern Ireland is Strangford Lough. In comparison with La Rance, Strangford has a much larger reservoir but a smaller tidal range. Wilson (1965) made a feasibility study of Strangford and Carlingford Loughs coupled with pumped storage at Rostrevor. McMullan, Morgan and Murray (1976c) make a comparison between the potential of Strangford and La Rance (see over page). The actual electricity generated would be about 20% of this and they suggest 100 MW in perpetuity amounting to about 500 million kWh per year. La Rance actually produces about 550 million units per year.

	Mean tidal range, m	Basin area km^2	Mean Power MW	Potential Annual Production 10^6 kWh
Strangford	3.6	125	350	3070
La Rance	8.4	22	340	3060

There is a problem in determining tidal range because it varies between neaps and springs. Equally the size of the basin varies with the height of the tide. Wilson's figures for Strangford and Carlingford are as below.

	Mean, tidal range, m		Basin area km^2 High Low Tide Tide Mean			Generating capacity to be installed MW	Proposed electricity production 10^6 kWh
Strangford	2.0–4.1	3.1	136	90	113	$35 \times 5.8 = 203$	330
Carlingford	1.7–5.6	3.7	38	26	32	$16 \times 7.6 = 122$	170

The Strangford scheme was re-examined in 1980-81 by Wilson and Cochrane culminating in a preliminary feasibility study published by the Northern Ireland Economic Council in August 1981.

The favoured engineering solution involves a barrage about one third of the way up the narrows, from Kilclief Point to Carrstown Point. Electricity would be generated on the ebb flow only rather than ebb and flood generation as at La Rance. There would be 30 turbines of 7.6 m diameter, each rated at 7 MW and 18 sluices of 12 m square to let the tide back into the Lough. There would also be a lock to allow boats in and out. The favoured option is calculated to produce 528 GWh of electricity per annum, about 10% of present production. This could be accepted directly into the grid as and when available without the need for pumped storage. It represents 1.9 PJe* or a fuel saving of 5.7 PJ per annum.

The barrage would be formed of concrete or steel caissons which would be floated into position and sunk; North Sea oil exploitation is based on similar technology which is now reasonably well known. If steel were the chosen material, this might create employment for the Belfast shipyards. The U.K. government might like to use the Strangford barrage as a test-run for the much larger and more expensive Severn barrage.

Initial construction costs of the preferred option are a little over £300 m at 1979 prices. The preliminary cost-benefit analysis of the scheme looks promising but is sensitive to some of the assumptions on which it is based. These mainly concern the future demand, cost and fuel source of electricity plus the chosen discount rate. The base case, i.e. the assumptions thought most likely to be correct, including a 5% discount rate, shows a 1980 Net Present Value of £154 m. At a 7.5% discount rate this becomes a small Net Cost of £12 m. The benefits are largely assessed in terms of fuel saving since the discontinuous nature of the tidal electricity means it cannot save generating capacity.

The cost-benefit analysis is based only on energy costs and benefits. The wider context would include environmental costs and benefits, local employment and the value of the road across the top. If the base assumptions can be upheld, the question will be whether the likely net environmental harm is worth more or less than £154 m.

*e signifies electrical

The major environmental impact will result from the changed tidal regime within the Lough. The tide will never go more than half way out. This will severely truncate the intertidal zone and also reduce the overall water circulation including the import of plankton and particulate organic matter from the Irish Sea. This would greatly reduce the food supply of all the filter-feeding marine organisms in the Lough. The pattern of sediment erosion and deposition will also change, probably involving more deposition of fine sediment. The freshwater inflow will receive less saline dilution as will any sewage inflow or other pollutant, though due to the great preponderance of tidal inflow over inflow from the catchment, this is not likely to be important.

The new tidal regime would affect land drainage around the Lough. The present Quoile barrage would be unable to discharge which would either mean installing pumps or a reversion to marine conditions in the Quoile Pondage and renewed flooding around Downpatrick. However the use of the barrage to exclude the highest high tides could reduce flooding problems in this and some other areas such as Newtownards. The barrage itself might deter the movement of seals and of the very large skate and tope which come into the Lough to spawn. The problem is to make any precise evaluation of the present conservation value of Strangford and of the likely diminution in this value if the barrage were installed according to present plans. There is no doubt that Strangford is a site of international conservation value. Its marine biology is very rich in terms of species and community diversity, related to its configuration of deep channels and shallow mudflats, with the massive inflow/outflow of sea water. There seems to be no other site at all similar in Britain or Europe. In fact the features which make it so attractive as a source of tidal power also contribute greatly to its conservation value.

The overwintering bird populations are outstanding. The International Waterfowl Research Bureau defines estuaries as being internationally important if they support a wintering population of 20,000 waders. Strangford usually has double this number. The Ramsar Convention recognized a standard of 10,000 wildfowl for wetlands to be of international importance: again Strangford has double. The peak winter population of pale-bellied Brent geese, usually 10-12,000 represents about 40% of the world population of that race. These birds are largely dependent upon feeding on the intertidal mudflats, either when they are exposed or in the case of Brent geese, feeding on eel-grass (*Zostera*) when it is in very shallow water. The area of available feeding ground is likely to be halved or worse.

Other environmental effects might include safer small dinghy sailing and a general increase in recreational use. This in itself will require careful management to prevent recreation pressure exceeding carrying capacity and seriously damaging conservation values. The present large oyster-farming operation is based on trays supported on short stilts over the mudflats and would be very severely affected.

The economic evaluation is favourable and the environmental evaluation unfavourable. More information is required on engineering feasibility, economics and environmental impact and if there is still a presumption in favour of proceeding with the scheme, a public enquiry will presumably be held. Some compromise is possible, for example, a change to an ebb and flood generating scheme would have less environmental impact. The big problem is the uncertainty of prediction, which can only be tested by completing the scheme.

Conclusions: the need for an energy policy

It is commonplace to say that we need an energy policy, but much easier said than done. It is also commonly assumed that demand is the independent variable and cannot be manipulated and supply must always be adjusted to meet demand (see, for example, Republic of Ireland's Department of Industry, Commerce and Energy, 1978).

This is not necessarily so. One way of reducing demand is energy conservation, that is getting the same amount of heat, or work or light or whatever for a smaller amount of energy. The simple methods such as roof insulation, or cavity wall insulation, or factories using their own waste steam can be very cost effective, but more sophisticated methods, such as the heat pump, have a longer pay-back time. There can also be unexpected side effects or consequences. Minogue (1980) showed that house insulation may simply lead to warmer houses rather than fuel saving. Fremlin (1980) suggests that insulation involving fewer air changes will increase the level of radon in living rooms, increasing, however infinitesimally, the cancer risk to the householders.

Energy rationing is usually dismissed as politically unacceptable, i.e too authoritarian. It would be difficult to implement fairly. Fiscal control by heavier taxes on fuel tends to hit the less well-off though an increase in the cost of energy relative to that of labour might help reduce unemployment. Again there are social problems, old people die of hypothermia, people cannot regulate their electricity bills, and the cost of energy shows up as a significant element in the cost of living index.

There is no evidence to suggest that the general level of human welfare is higher in a high energy society than in a medium energy society (Illich, 1974). The social benefits deriving from air travel, for example, seem minimal. However, the political reality is that in the main energy policy means tailoring supply to meet an increasing demand over which government has little or no control. And the other reality is that between now and the end of the century, or perhaps 2010, the reduction in oil supply can only be compensated by an increase in the use of coal and/or nuclear power, probably both. Beyond that time period, especially if we act quickly and resolutely in the right direction now, renewable sources of energy could have an increasing role, eventually meeting 100% of the energy demand.

So what are the options open for Northern Ireland? First it is necessary to establish likely demand, both for electricity and for fuel, and the security, that is the consistency and reliability of supply required. Electricity utilities normally work with generating capacity which is at least 20% greater than the maximum demand. The NIES has been operating with 30-40% spare capacity even before Kilroot has been completed. Society has become very dependent upon a secure supply of electricity, e.g. hospitals, supermarkets, traffic lights, petrol pumps, cash registers, continuous process industry, intensive livestock farming, etc. are all badly hit by a switch-off. The electricity failure in New York in 1977 led to serious vandalism and looting. In a less dramatic way the problems associated with severe electricity cuts were seen in Northern Ireland during the Ulster Workers Council strike in 1974. So the idea of reducing the margin between demand and capacity, economically attractive, seems politically and socially rather risky. So probably both in the electricity and non-electricity sectors, demand will remain at its present level, or increase slightly, say 2% per year. Kilroot (600 MW), Ballylumford B (960 MW) (see Plates 11.1 and 11.2) and Coolkeeragh (360 MW) would supply all the capacity needed until the end of the century though as currently

Plate 11.1 The new power station at Kilroot, shown under construction. Photograph from Northern Ireland Electricity Service.

Plate 11.2 Ballylumford B power station on Larne Lough, which is the station with the largest generating capacity in Northern Ireland.

planned this would mean 100% oil-fuelled electricity. This 1920 MW of oil-fired capacity is backed up by 240 MW of gas turbines to cope with peaks of demand. The ageing Belfast West power station (240 MW) is the only remaining coal fired capacity in the system and in 1980-81, in order to maximise the contribution of coal-fired electricity which was cheaper than oil fired, this station achieved a higher load factor than any of the others. The possibility of converting some existing generating capacity from oil to coal is under active consideration.

It seems desirable physically to link the Northern Ireland energy system both with that of the Republic of Ireland and that of Britain. This should give greater security of supply, should help to even out the peaks and troughs of demand and would allow us to draw energy supplies from a greater variety of energy resources. Possible links are electricity transmission wires or gas pipelines.

The Irish Government are building a gas pipeline from Cork to Dublin, so that the natural gas from the Kinsale field can be brought to the Dublin consumers. There is now considerable discussion about extending the pipeline from Dublin to Belfast. Feasibility and availability of supply seem not to be in doubt and discussion is concentrated on the price of the gas. Another option more regularly canvassed is a pipeline from Scotland to Belfast, bringing North Sea gas to Northern Ireland. The problem with gas is that the present consumption is so low. The heavy investment in a gas pipeline would need a substantial increase in the number of consumers and the amount of gas consumed to justify it.

In 1976, the Department of Commerce commissioned the International Consultancy Service of the British Gas Corporation to carry out a study on the future of gas in Northern Ireland. The consultants considered seven options including piped natural gas from Scotland or from the Republic of Ireland, and various forms of importation of liquefied natural gas. Given tariffs about halfway between those in Britain and those in Northern Ireland at present, and considerably increased sales, all options are quite costly ranging from capital costs of £45-£76 million at 1976-77 prices and losses over the first 12 years ranging from £62-£135 million. Of course the costs of closing down the gas industry in Northern Ireland, in terms of compensation to existing consumers, and redundancy payments to employees would also be considerable, but not on-going. The figures have been hotly argued, and according to one's vested interest and initial assumptions, it is possible to prove viability or non-viability of almost any scheme. The argument continued vigorously in 1981. It is believed the pipeline would attract an EEC grant, which is regarded as a free good, not costing anyone anything and thereby bringing down the cost of the scheme. The two crucial factors are:

(i) the necessary increased consumption of gas would be mainly at the expense of electricity consumption;

(ii) uncertainty about the duration of supply of natural gas.

The NIES, even before the completion of the first two units of Kilroot, had surplus generating capacity. Any reduction of electricity consumed is likely to increase their unit costs. Since they are already receiving government subsidy of more than £370 million over 6 years, the Government are reluctant to subsidize direct competition which is likely to increase their unit costs.

By 1980 production of natural gas in the North Sea had levelled off and was showing the first indications of decline (European Communities Commission 1980). It is argued that when the natural gas runs out, the pipeline can still be used to supply synthetic natural gas (SNG) probably made from coal. But the scale and economics of this seem uncertain.

The electricity links look more promising. The 300 MW cross-border link functioned for some years, but has several times been destroyed by terrorist activity, to which it is certainly vulnerable. It would (and did) achieve considerable savings for both the ESB and the NIES, especially in terms of what is called spinning reserve, the amount of plant kept running to meet any sudden increase in demand. These savings are achieved without any overall net transfer of electricity north or south. Had the interconnector been functional throughout 1979-80 the potential savings are estimated at £5-6 million in the year.

If the link were functional and reliable at present, it might allow the ESB to defer some of their new power stations and rely instead on the surplus plant of the NIES. This argument only really holds if the ESB are planning further oil-fired plant. Most of their plans are focussed on coal, peat and possibly nuclear power. However the purchase by the ESB of electricity from the NIES was supported in 1980 by the then Minister for Energy, Mr George Colley (Irish Times 1.9.80).

If the ESB do proceed with a nuclear power station (and the lead time including public enquiries would be at least 10 years) this might provide relatively cheap off-peak electricity to the NIES. As fuel assumes an increasing proportion of the cost of electricity, as seems likely with oil-fired electricity, the less off-peak discount is possible. Another future dimension here is that as petrol escalates in price, the electric car becomes a more attractive proposition, especially if cheap off-peak electricity is available for nocturnal recharging. However an electric car recharged with oil-fired electricity is not such a good proposition.

An underwater cable to Scotland is obviously technically more difficult and much more expensive than restoring the cross-border link, but it is technically feasible. In the 1990s, the link with Scotland could well prove the favoured option as against building more plant here, and would allow Northern Ireland to buy surplus nuclear, coal- or hydro-electricity from Britain, as well as having the logic of unifying the United Kingdom electricity system.

There seems little doubt that the real cost of supplying energy sources such as oil, gas, coal or electricity is greater in Northern Ireland than in the rest of the U.K. This is because none of the resources are indigenous, so that significant transport charges are involved, the scale of the operation is small and the local energy system is not linked to any other. The question then arises as to whether and to what extent the U.K. Government should subsidize the cost of energy here, perhaps at the expense of the British energy users. Energy subsidies are bad because they tend to increase the rate of use of this scarce and dwindling resource but they may be politically expedient. It is also hazardous for governments to manipulate costs between different forms of energy though it is frequently done. The Irish Government promoted peat fired electricity in order to provide employment and to save energy imports. This investment is now paying off handsomely (Noone 1980, O'Donnell 1974). The U.K. Government have invested heavily in the provision of electricity in Northern Ireland without corresponding subsidies to oil or coal or gas. One of their main objectives has been to attract or retain heavy electricity-using industries, but since most of the electricity here is oil-generated, this policy now appears short sighted. Pressure for a similar subsidy to the gas industry is mounting.

Giles Shaw, the Parliamentary Under Secretary of State with responsibility for energy made a statement on the 23rd July 1979 about Energy Policy in Northern Ireland. He established that the main aim of the energy strategy was to maintain high security of supply. The second aim is to ensure that energy prices should not produce unbearable problems for the poorest sections of the community or lead to a weighting of industrial costs which could be seriously damaging to production and employment. On the other hand there is no reason why energy prices should be the same as in the rest of the U.K. Indeed since there is considerable regional variation anyway, it is not meaningful.

The strategy set out at that time says no to a gas pipeline, seeks the restoration of the cross-border electricity link, suggests an examination of whether generators 3 and 4 at Kilroot could be converted to coal and issues the customary exhortation to conserve energy. In the summer of 1980 work was halted on generators 3 and 4 at Kilroot pending a firm decision on their future. It is interesting to note that their cancellation or postponement was recommended in 1976 by the Shepherd Committee on the structure of the electricity service in Northern Ireland. This recommendation, after a crucial delay of nine months was turned down by the Government, mainly on the grounds that the savings involved would be too small to justify the upheaval and loss of jobs in Larne and Belfast. It seems likely that the Government were still using estimates of growth in demand for electricity which were much too high.

In 1981 the U.K. Government decided not to proceed with the construction of generators 3 and 4 at Kilroot and also, from 1982, to set electricity tariffs in Northern Ireland at a level corresponding with the highest tariffs in England and Wales and to maintain this relationship permanently. Dependence on oil and the existence of excess generating capacity are therefore no longer a cause for concern to consumers here. The danger is that this will also deter the NIES from looking for new and cheaper sources of electricity. Also the Government in relating electricity prices, but not those of coal, oil and gas, to the prices prevailing in England and Wales may be held to be discriminating in favour of electricity.

Long-term strategy

The trouble with these difficult short to medium term problems is that they divert attention (and investment) from the real long-term solutions which must be based on environmental sources of energy. Investment in wind energy and biomass energy is needed now, plus more detailed examination of the Strangford Lough tidal barrage (including of course its environmental consequences) and of the possibility of geothermal energy. Wave energy should await the results of current research and development work in Britain but looks promising. Environmental sources of electrical energy may require the revival of the Camlough pumped storage schemes – the turbines have already been made and are in storage.

However electricity being only about 10% of energy end use (about 37% of primary energy use) energy policy must concentrate in other areas. Partial solar space heating and water heating must be incorporated in all new housing schemes. Improved and versatile solid fuel heaters, capable of using peat, biomass or conventional firewood should be incorporated as well as greatly improved insulation.

In terms of technical feasibility, and environmental and social acceptability, Northern Ireland should be aiming at an energy system for the year 2010 which would include the following characteristics:–

   (i) Electricity system to be interconnected both with Scotland and the Republic, and also to include a pumped storage scheme;

  (ii) Wave energy to be a major source of electrical energy; possibly also tidal power;

 (iii) Fluidized bed coal combustion as the other main fuel for electricity;

 (iv) Wind generators in the 1 MW range to contribute to the electricity grid;

  (v) More houses and farms in rural areas to have their own wind generators in the 10-20 KW range;

 (vi) Small-medium sized hydro-electric schemes to be sought in the Mournes, Sperrins and Antrim hills but with careful regard for amenity;

 (vii) Oil to be used for electricity only in so far as it is difficult to find other uses for the heavier fractions;

(viii) Petrol or diesel fuelled transport to be replaced by ethanol-fuelled or electric transport;

 (ix) More positive incentives for energy conservation, in the first instance insulation in the home and the factory and by combined heat and power schemes where possible. Improved public transport and freight systems should decrease transportation energy. More energy could be extracted from waste materials. Agriculture could reduce its energy dependence;

  (x) An increasing role for energy from biomass, involving not only short rotation willow, alder and poplar coppice but also conversion of domestic and agricultural wastes, perhaps to methane, and more use of firewood from the hedgerows and copses;

(xi) Continuing exploitation of peat;

(xii) New housing, and also industrial and commercial premises to contain an element of solar space and water heating.

This scenario reflects the author's personal conviction that small is beautiful, that there is a diminishing future for heavy industry especially when it is located away from its resource base, that employment is an important human need and that energy consumption per caput is more likely to fall than to rise.

Different scenarios are possible . . . . . .

Acknowledgements

I am most grateful to Mr J. Duddy of Bord na Mona, Mr John Gaston of the Northern Ireland Electricity Service, Mr J. M. Sanderson of the Forest Service, DoA (Northern Ireland), Mr R. A. Sterling of the Department of Commerce (Northern Ireland), and Mr Sean Tinney of the Electricity Supply Board, for their helpful responses to my requests for information. They are in no way responsible for any opinions expressed in this chapter.

REFERENCES

Allen, J. and Bird, R. A., 1977. The prospects for the generation of electricity from wind energy in the U.K. *Department of Energy, Energy Paper 21*. Energy Technology Support Unit. H.M.S.O.

Alstrom, D., 1979. Pumping heat in Galway. *Technology Ireland*, 11 (8), 29–31.

Bogle, A. W., 1978. *An analysis of wind power potential for domestic heating at Aldergrove*. Unpublished B.Sc. dissertation, New University of Ulster.

Bogle, A. W., McMullan, J. T., Morgan, R. and Murray, R. B., 1979. Modelling of a domestic wind power system including storage. *International Journal of Energy Research*, 3, 113–127.

Brady-Shipman-Martin and P. A. International, 1980. *Erne Catchment Study Vol. 1, Summary Report*. Prepared for the Governments of the United Kingdom and Ireland and the Commission of the European Communities.

Commerce, Department of, 1978. *Mineral Development Act (Northern Ireland) 1969. Statement for the year ended 28th February 1979*. H.M.S.O.

C.S.R.D. (Council of Scientific Research and Development), 1956. *The Northern Ireland Peat Bog Survey*. Final report of the preliminary survey. H.M.S.O., Belfast.

Duddy, J., 1979. Personal communication. 25.9.79.

Earl, D. E., 1975. *Forest energy and economic development*. Clarendon Press, Oxford.

Energy, Department of, 1976. Solar energy: its potential contribution within the U.K. *Energy Paper* 16, Energy Technology Support Unit, H.M.S.O.

European Communities Commission, 1980. *Gas: maintaining supplies*. Background Report ISEC/B39/80.

Fremlin, J. H., 1980. The pros and cons of heat saving in houses. *Conservation News*, 77, 7.

Gaston, J., 1980. Personal communication. 8.9.80.

Gribbon, H. D., 1969. *The history of water power in Ulster*. David and Charles.

Hand, F., Asare, B. and Haslett, J., 1977. Domestic hot water and solar energy in Ireland. *International Journal of Energy Research*, 1, 249–257.

Haslett, J. and Kelledy, E. 1979. The assessment of actual wind power availability in Ireland. *International Journal of Energy Research*, 3, 333–348.

Henry, E. W., 1976. *Energy Conservation in Ireland 1975-85*. Stationery Office, Dublin.

Howard, A. J., 1968. *Transactions of the Second Internation Peat Congress, Leningrad 1963*, H.M.S.O., Edinburgh.

Industry, Commerce and Energy, Department of, 1978. *Energy Ireland*. Discussion document on some current energy problems and options. Stationery Office, Dublin.

Illich, I., 1974. *Energy and equity*. Calder & Boyars, London.

Johannson, T. B., and Steen, P., 1978. Solar Sweden. *Ambio*, 7, 70–74.

Lalor, E., 1975. *Solar energy for Ireland*. National Science Council, Dublin.

Lewis, A. W., 1977. Waves: an alternative source of energy for Ireland. *Technology Ireland*, 9, (1), 16–18.

Minogue, P., 1980. Energy conservation in buildings – Potential savings from insulation in *Aspects of Energy Conservation*, Proceedings of a seminar. An Foras Forbartha, Dublin.

McMullan, J. T., Morgan, R. and Murray, R. B., 1976a. Energy in Northern Ireland. *Technology Ireland*, 8, (4 & 5), 41–44.

McMullan, J. T., Morgan, R. and Murray, R. B., 1976b. Improvements in heat pump design. *Technology Ireland*, 8 (6), 8–10.

McMullan, J. T., Morgan, R. and Murray, R. B., 1976c. *Energy resources and supply*. John Wiley.

Neenan, M. & Lyons, G., 1977. *Energy from biomass*. An Foras Taluntais. Dublin.

Nolan, D., 1978. Windpower research in Ireland. *Technology Ireland*, 10, (1), 27–30.

Noone, B., 1980. Turf is still cheapest. *Technology Ireland*, 11, (10), 46.

Northern Ireland Economic Council, 1981. *Report No. 24. Strangford Lough Tidal Energy*. N.I.E.C. Belfast.

O'Donnell, S., 1974. Ireland turns to peat. *New Scientist*, 63, 18–19.

O'Rourke, K., Lewis, J. O. and O'Connell, D., 1976. Solar energy for domestic space heating. *Technology Ireland*, 8, (6), 23–25.

O'Sullivan, A., 1980. Hunt for natural hot water in Ireland is only beginning. *Irish Times* 16.7.80.

Owen Lewis, J., 1978. Current Irish work on solar energy. *Technology Ireland*, 10 (3), 46–51.

Power, H., 1979. Tilting at windmills. *Technology Ireland*, 10 (10), 20–24.

Rohan, P. K., 1975. *The climate of Ireland*. Stationery Office, Dublin.

Ross, D., 1979. *Energy from the waves*. Pergamon.

Rural Industries Development Committee of the Northern Ireland Council of Social Service. 1964. *Increasing employment in rural areas in Northern Ireland. A report on the past, present and future use of peat lands*.

Sanderson, J. M., 1979. Personal communication. 24.8.79.

Shaw, Giles, 1979. *Energy policy in Northern Ireland*. Statement made on 23.7.79. Dept. of Commerce, Belfast.

Shepherd, G. T., Chairman, 1976. *Report on the present and projected financial position of the Northern Ireland Electricity Service*. H.M.S.O., Belfast.

Solar Energy Society of Ireland 1978. *Towards energy independence*. S.E.S.I.

Sorenson, B., 1978a. Wind: large scale utilization. *Proceedings SESI/IIRS/IDA Conference* 'Wind, Wave, Water'. April 1978.

Sorenson, B., 1978b. On the fluctuating power generation of large wind energy converters with and without storage facilities. *Solar Energy*, 20.

Stott, K. G., McElroy, G., Abernethy, W. and Hayes, D. P., 1980. Coppice willow for biomass in the U.K. *Proceedings of the Energy from Biomass Conference*, Brighton, November 1980.

Tinney, S., 1980. Personal communication, 22.1.80.

Wells, A. A., 1977. Wave power: Ireland's future power resources. *Technology Ireland*, 9, (7), 26–31.

Wilson, E. M., 1965. Feasibility study of tidal power from Loughs Strangford and Carlingford with pumped storage at Rostrevor. *Proceedings of Institute of Civil Engineers*, 32, 1–29.

Wilson, H. E., 1972. *Regional geology of Northern Ireland*. H.M.S.O.

Wishart, J., 1978. *Changing peatlands in North Antrim*. Unpublished M.Sc. Dissertation, New University of Ulster.

CHAPTER XII

Landscape

The recreational use of the countryside

RONALD H. BUCHANAN
Director of the Institute of Irish Studies and Reader in Geography,
The Queen's University of Belfast

The idea that townspeople would spend much of their leisure time in the countryside would never have occurred to an older generation for whom leisure meant little more than a rest on Sunday or a day off work for one of the major church festivals. Mass leisure has developed only in the present century, as more people have acquired the time, the money and the means of transport to visit the countryside and the coast: in our time, these have become the recreation areas for an increasingly wide cross-section of the urban population. Many who visit the countryside do so for a specific purpose; they enjoy cycling or hill-walking, horse-riding, mountaineering or bird-watching, or perhaps they head for the rivers and coasts to fish, canoe, water-ski or sail. They may go as individuals, as members of clubs, or if they are younger, in groups sponsored by education authorities, to participate for example in programmes such as the Duke of Edinburgh Awards scheme. Those who engage in active recreation are attracted to the countryside for the special resources it has to offer: the challenge of a difficult rock face to the mountaineer, a good trout stream for the game fisherman, or the foaming rapids of a river gorge which test the skills of the canoeist. Often these activities take place in countrysides where the fine scenery enhances the enjoyment of a particular sport. In this way the appreciation of landscape for its scenic beauty merges with the more active use of the countryside for specific types of recreation.

In fact it is the visual pleasure derived simply from viewing landscape that draws most people to the countryside: "perception of the appearance of the landscape remains the most common denominator in the public enjoyment of the countryside", state Coppock and Duffield on the basis of survey experience (Coppock and Duffield, 1975, 112).* Kenneth Clark's comment is a little more perceptive ". . . with the exception of love, there is perhaps nothing else by which people of all kinds are more united than by their pleasure in a good view" (Clark, 1979, 147). In Britain generally there is "a widespread preference for natural over man-made countryside, for wilderness devoid of human impact over landscape altered by human occupance" (Low-

---

*Page numbers are provided with references in this chapter as specific pages, or parts of pages, are being referenced in most cases.

enthal, 1978, 385). Variety in landform and vegetation, in shape, colour and texture, adds to visual enjoyment, as does water, whose surface reflections add an extra dimension. Hence the coast is one of the most favoured locations, since it provides a wide range of resources for active recreation as well as for passive contemplation. Most people in Britain prefer landscapes dominated by nature, and in England at least, many prefer a countryside which is "tamed and inhabited, comfortable, humanised" (Lowenthal and Prince, 1965, 190). Man should be in control, faintly visible in a landscape which he has ordered according to his tastes and needs.

Those who seek recreation in the countryside come from many different back-grounds and interests, but they share one thing in common: they want the countryside to stay as it is, unchanging; or if change is to occur, it should be in scale and in keeping with the remembered landscapes of the past. This, of course, cannot be, for the old landscapes of both lowlands and uplands were fashioned when power was provided by the muscles of men and animals, and its scale, in fields and buildings, was adapted to needs very different from those that prevail today. If farming is to remain efficient as an industry it must use whatever equipment and techniques are necessary to remain profitable, and since farm land must be adjusted to these activities, it is inevitable that the rural landscape itself will change. The new landscape need not be ugly, but it will be different, just as the present landscape of hedged fields differs from the open landscape which it replaced more than two centuries ago, with the agricultural innovations of the eighteenth century.

Farming activities are the dominant influence in shaping the rural landscape, but they are not alone in causing change. Recreation pressure has itself brought change, with its demand for car-parks and caravan sites. In the uplands, afforestation has been a major development extending steadily over the past half century; mineral extraction and quarrying affect uplands and lowlands alike in many areas; new reservoirs, electricity generating stations and power lines, the buildings of manufacturing industry itself, road construction and drainage operations all affect the appearance of the countryside in many parts of these islands. These developments are important to the national economy, and locally they often provide much-needed employment in rural areas. But because they cause change in landscape, they elicit a negative response in the townsman, anxious to retain the traditional landscapes in which he finds the solace and enjoyment of true recreation.

So apparently irreconcilable are the differences between those who make a living in the countryside and those who seek recreation from it, that the question of what the planners term "rural amenity" has at times become a major political battlefield. Often the issues are represented by the extremes of exploitation versus preservation – but between them there is a middle ground, represented by conservation, which may be defined as: "the sensible use of natural resources to ensure the perpetuation or enhancement of all their benefits for man and other living things, dwelling in harmony with one another and with their surroundings" (Forsyth & Boyd, 1970, 84).

Landscape conservation

Policies on conservation and the use of the countryside for outdoor recreation were developed in Britain after World War II, and the strategies devised there have been followed in Northern Ireland. Two methods have been used: in one, land is protected

266

through public ownership, which is the most effective way of ensuring management for conservation; in the other, land considered worthy of protection is designated and its conservation attained through statutory planning. The former approach was pioneered in the U.S.A., where some areas owned by the Federal Government were set aside at the end of the last century to be conserved as the world's first National Parks. In Britain the second approach was used, for little land is actually owned by the state. In fact it was a voluntary body, the National Trust, which pioneered the purchase of land and buildings to be preserved for the nation in perpetuity. Other bodies which protect landscape through ownership are those directly concerned with nature conservation, such as the voluntary County Naturalists' Trusts and the Royal Society for the Protection of Birds or the statutory Nature Conservancy Council. Local authorities exercise a similar role in the provision of County Parks many of which are former privately-owned estates.

The area of land in Britain protected through ownership, however, is comparatively small, and the more usual approach has been to conserve land by controlling development, using powers conferred by special planning legislation. Advocacy of this approach extends back before the First World War, and in the 1930s it became the policy of the newly founded Council for the Preservation of Rural England, and of the Ramblers Association (1931) (Hall, 1976, 169). Official backing for legislation came from the government-sponsored Addison Committee in 1931, whose major recommendations were later incorporated in the 1947 Report of the Hobhouse Committee, which laid the basis for the National Parks and Access to the Countryside Act of 1949. This Bill marks the real beginning of landscape conservation in Britain as part of accepted planning policy. Under the Act, a newly established National Parks Commission was given the task of designating National Parks and Areas of Outstanding Natural Beauty in England and Wales. Scotland was excluded, as the Scottish Home Office argued that pressures on the countryside were less severe than in England and Wales, and access was less impeded by legal constraints (Coppock, 1968, 204; Foster, 1974, 484). National Parks were conceived as extensive areas of wild scenery, whose natural beauty and wildlife should be protected and enhanced, and promoted for enjoyment by the public. Planning within each park was to be administered by a special committee, one-third of the members being nominated by central government and the remainder by the local authority in whose area the Park lay. Areas of Outstanding Natural Beauty (AONB) were to be smaller in extent than the National Parks, and the purpose of their designation was strict control of development: there was no remit to promote outdoor recreation, and planning was administered in the normal way by the local planning authority (Bell, 1975, 9).

In most respects the 1949 Act was extremely successful, but the rapid increase in outdoor recreation, and major changes resulting from structural change and technical innovation in farming, led to new legislation in 1968. The most important part of the new Countryside Act was the replacement of the National Parks Commission by the Countryside Commission, with functions similar to its predecessor but with a brief which now concerned the countryside as a whole, and included a remit to advise and grant-aid local authorities on the provision of amenities for outdoor recreation. Finally, in the 1972 reorganisation of local government, changes were made to the administration of National Parks, each of which in future was to be administered by a Park Officer under a single executive committee. One of its main tasks was to be the preparation of a National Park Plan which would include a statement on how the plan should be implemented. The conservation of scenic landscapes through designation was virtually completed in England and Wales by the early 1960s, and today there are ten National Parks, mostly situated in the uplands of the north and west, and 33 Areas of Outstanding Natural Beauty. A further National Park, the Cambrian Mountains in mid-Wales, was proposed in 1972 but rejected by the Government; since then the only new proposal involving designation has been the concept of the Heritage Coast, which provides for strict control of development along some 1,000 km of coastline. Meantime provision of facilities for outdoor recreation in the countryside has steadily increased, for example in the expanding network of long-distance footpaths and in state forests and water-catchment areas, many of which are now open for recreational use. Country Parks have proved to be a particularly popular innovation, especially among day-trippers out for a drive in the country. Intended to provide "a blotting paper function of relieving visitor pressure on the more beautiful areas" (Shoard, 1976, 70), some 130 Country Parks were established by local authorities between 1968 and 1976 (Waugh, 1981).

In 1967, a separate Countryside Commission was established in Scotland, with functions similar to those of its sister body in England and Wales. There are no National Parks in Scotland; development proposals in areas defined as National Park Forward Direction Areas are monitored by the Secretary of State. Similar planning safeguards, together with agreements on land management, are proposed in 40 National Scenic Areas identified by the Countryside Commission for Scotland in a Report, *Scotland's Scenic Heritage,* published in 1978. The Commission has also advocated (1974) a hierarchy of parks in Scotland, ranging in size from the city park to the country and regional park, and "special parks", situated in "countryside of considerable natural beauty and amenity" where facilities are necessary to meet "a national demand for recreational opportunity" (Countryside Commission for Scotland, 1978, section 5.10). So far, four country parks and five regional parks have been designated in Scotland.

In general, the system evolved in Britain for conserving scenic landscapes by statutory designation has worked well. This is especially true of the National Parks whose main problems have been due to lack of funds and the structure of their internal administration (Dennier, 1981, 50). The AONBs have also conserved landscape by strict control of development: but unlike the National Parks they have no special remit to prepare plans or provide for recreation, although most are under considerable pressure by virtue of their lowland location and accessibility to major urban centres. Marion Shoard has referred to the AONBs as "the second-class citizens of the world of protected landscapes" (Shoard, 1980, 144), and her judgement is confirmed in a recent policy review undertaken by the Countryside Commission (1977).

Landscape conservation through designation has not been able to resolve one problem which has assumed increasing importance in recent decades, that is, changes in land use resulting from the application of new techniques of farming. These have affected the lowland areas of arable farming in particular, but issues such as the reclamation of moorland on Exmoor have also raised questions of great importance to future conservation policy. To a large extent the problems have arisen because activities relating to farming and afforestation are both excluded from the provisions of the 1947 Planning Act, for the government of the day, well aware of the political issues involved, adopted the principle that farming would ensure the conservation of land-scape as well as of land (Sheail, 1975, 50). Today this is no longer necessarily true: indeed it can be argued that the diverse ecology which sustains Britain's most scenic landscapes can be kept only by a strategy of planned land use which would require farmers to cede at least some control over the management of their land (Newby, 1980, 219 and 245). So far no government has been willing to face the all-powerful agricultural political lobby on this issue, nor to initiate the type of comprehensive strategy for the countryside as a whole which many commentators believe to be the only way in which conflicts between farmers and amenity groups, and between major government departments such as the DoE and MAFF can be resolved (Coppock, 1974, 632; Davidson and Wibberley, 1977, 56). Advocates of this strategy will derive little comfort from the recent progress of the modest Countryside and Wildlife Bill, promoted by the Thatcher Government: at Committee stage in the House of Lords it had already evoked a record 560 amendments (The Guardian, 10th February 1981).

Landscape resources of Northern Ireland

In Northern Ireland, the increased use of the countryside for recreation and the resulting lobby for protective legislation has followed a similar pattern to Britain, but there are major differences in the degree of pressure imposed on the landscape, the type of legislation enacted and the way in which it has been implemented. These points will be examined in turn, but first the areas used for recreation will be identified, beginning with the nineteenth century tourists from Britain who were the first to draw attention to the scenic landscapes. For them, by far the most important area was the Antrim coast and expecially the Giant's Causeway. Thackeray made a special trip to see it and wrote as follows:

"The hill-tops are shattered into a thousand cragged fantastical shapes . . . The savage rock sides are painted of a hundred colours. Does the sun ever shine here? When the world was moulded and fashioned out of chaos, this must have been the bit left over – a remnant of chaos!" (Thackeray, 1887, 312).

Some years earlier, Mr and Mrs C. S. Hall, were also attracted to the North by the prospect of visiting the Causeway, but in the course of their journey they included visits to Carlingford Lough and the Mourne Mountains – "The most sublime scenery, with the wide expanse of ocean open before it" (Hall, 1843, 6). They saw Lough Neagh – "the most magnificent sheet of water in Great Britain" (Hall, 1843, 113), but their most enthusiastic prose is reserved for the Antrim coast, from the Gobbins in Islandmagee to Portrush.

Soon after the Halls' visit, the Antrim coast became more accessible, first with the opening of the coast road from Larne to Ballycastle, and then with a railway link between Belfast and Portrush which opened in 1885. Thirty years later the world's first electric tramway connected Portrush with the Causeway in a spectacular line which followed the cliff-edge for much of its length, while in 1880, a narrow-gauge railway was opened between Ballycastle and Ballymoney. The east coast of Antrim and the Glens remained inaccessible by rail, but the LMS-NCC Railway Company promoted tourism by providing a cafe and building paths at Glenariff and along the Gobbins cliffs in Islandmagee. Meantime the Belfast and Co. Down Railway was also promoting tourism within its territory, especially the Mournes which were made accessible to

Belfast when the line to Newcastle opened in 1869. The Company's *County Down Tourist Guide,* written by the naturalist Robert L. Praeger, and published in 1898, is a model of its type, detailing the antiquities and beauty spots to be found by following selected itineraries and using the Company's rail system. Sections of the Guide were devoted to fishing, boating, golfing, cycling, walking and sketching, and there was a full chapter of walks and mountain climbing in the Mournes.

Through special excursions to their resorts at Portrush and Newcastle and to Rostrevor on Carlingford Lough where the sponsor was the Great Northern Railway, the railway companies helped to establish the Mournes and the north Antrim coast as the most popular centres for the day tripper and holiday maker during the early years of the present century. They also encouraged commuting during the holiday season through concessionary weekly and monthly fares, encouraging development to spread along the shores of Belfast Lough, to Whitehead and Bangor respectively, and to the north Ards in County Down. This trend became accentuated with the advent of the car in the 1930s, the ribboning of coastal development, initiated by the railways, often being cited when the case for planning legislation was advocated after World War II.

Pre-war, most visitors to the countryside came from Belfast, but post-war tourism was promoted outside Northern Ireland, with the emphasis placed on scenic beauty as its principal attraction. Besides the traditional areas of the Mournes and the Antrim coast and glens, the modern tourist is invited to visit places which were largely unknown to the Victorian traveller.

"The Sperrins, in Londonderry and Tyrone, roll across half Ulster, and in places you might be on the moon for all the company between you and the far horizon" (Northern Ireland Tourist Board, 1980, 8).

Cuilcagh in Fermanagh and Slieve Gullion in Armagh are upland areas which the tourist is now invited to visit, and Lough Erne's attractions are described in glowing terms:

". . . 300 square miles of water simply undiscovered by you holiday-makers. The depths are full of fish and the surface alive with ducks. There are 154 islands with the myriad colours of oak, ash, birch, gorse, wild flowers and reeds" (Northern Ireland Tourist Board, 1980, 13).

Finally the man-made landscape is also given special mention:

"We've Stone Age dolmens, Celtic cashels and raths, Norman castles and Georgian mansions all over the country . . ." (Northern Ireland Tourist Board, 1980, 2).

Remoteness, a varied landscape and coast of great natural beauty, a heritage of ancient monuments and buildings, all these are envisaged as having great appeal to the modern tourist, especially when backed by resources for more active recreation, in cruising, golfing, fishing and pony-trekking. For those engaged in tourist promotion, the landscape is a capital asset of great economic value, providing the basis for a tourist trade with a turn-over worth £28.2 million in 1969 (Ulster Year Book, 1975, 113), before civil unrest and terrorist violence ended any immediate prospect of further expansion.

Visitors with interests more specific than the tourist also began to explore the countryside towards the end of the nineteenth century. These were members of field naturalists' clubs, the oldest of which, in Belfast, was founded in 1863. Under the leadership of men such as R. J. Welsh, the pioneer photographer, and the distinguished naturalist, R. L. Praeger, members of the field clubs wandered even further afield as they recorded Northern Ireland's flora, fauna and field antiquities (Evans and Turner, 1977, 14). Initially those involved were mainly business and professional people, but all the field clubs encouraged young people to join in their activities, and as field studies became an accepted part of the school curriculum after World War II, teachers and older children became increasingly involved. Estyn Evans, first Professor of Geography at Queen's University, was the key academic figure in stimulating this interest in field study, through his teaching of undergraduates and of adult students in extra-mural classes. His many books and articles on the countryside, dealing with the evolution of the landscape and the history and prehistory of rural communities, provided the basis for work now undertaken in many field study centres scattered throughout Northern Ireland. The children who attend these centres in increasing numbers now form a sizeable group of countryside users, and some of them at least will continue to seek recreation in the countryside in their adult years.

During the 1920s and 1930s walkers and cyclists were also beginning to explore the countryside in increasing numbers. Initially Down and Antrim were the favoured areas, and the first Youth Hostels, opened in 1931, were built in the Mournes and along the Antrim coast. By 1933 YHANI had established nine hostels, its aim being "a chain of fourteen, so that you could have a fortnight's walking tour staying one night in each hostel and then moving on to the next" (Youth Hostel Association of Northern Ireland, 1981, 25). More than any other organisation, YHANI encouraged young people, mainly from Belfast, to seek recreation outdoors in the countryside, and significantly, several of its founder members were also responsible for the establishment of the Ulster Society for the Preservation of the Countryside, a group with aims similar to its sister organisation, the Council for the Preservation of Rural England. Ten years earlier the National Trust had also decided to extend its activities to Northern Ireland, establishing its own semi-independent regional committee in 1936.

Pressure for legislation

By the late 1930s Northern Ireland had the nucleus of an amenity lobby, but unlike Britain there was no major campaign for planning legislation. Pressures on the countryside in the form of ribbon development, holiday houses and the first caravans, were becoming evident on limited sections of the coasts of north Antrim and north Down, but nowhere were they as severe as in Britain. Northern Ireland's total population in 1937 was only 1,280,000; only 53% lived in towns and cities, and even Belfast, the major urban centre had only 438,086. Belfast had expanded slightly during the 1930s, but like its British counterparts – Glasgow, Liverpool and Newcastle – the industries which sustained its working population had declined severely during the economic recession; unemployment was high and only a minority could afford day trips or weekends in the countryside. Not only was pressure from recreation insignificant, but ribbon development on the urban fringe and landscape dereliction through industrial activity were also of negligible importance in Northern Ireland. All these had a significant political impact in Britain during the 1930s, when the Labour Party was especially sympathetic to amenity interests. This was not the case in Northern Ireland, where the local administration, Unionist by title, but Conservative in attitude and political conviction, were unconvinced that land-use planning was a proper function of government. All this was to change in the post-war period. With the example of British planning and countryside legislation as its reference point, and the Unionist Government's avowed policy of moving step-by-step in legislation with Britain, the amenity groups began to press for landscape protection in Northern Ireland on the model now adopted in England and Wales.

The first public statement to acknowledge that the countryside was under pressure and that legislative action was necessary, came in a Report, *The Ulster Countryside,* issued in 1947 by the Amenity Committee of the Planning Advisory Board, a body which had been appointed a few years earlier by the Northern Ireland Minister of Home Affairs. The Committee included representatives of local government, civil service departments and business and professional organisations, as well as several prominent members of the USPC, YHANI, the National Trust, and an independent member, Estyn Evans. In a foreword to the Report, David Lindsay Keir, the Board's Chairman and also Vice-Chancellor of Queen's University, made the following statement:

"Ulster is probably as richly endowed by nature as any area of comparable size in the world. Contained within a relatively small compass, its mountains and moorlands, lakes and rivers, cliffs and strands provide unique attractions and opportunities for enjoyment not only for those whose homes are in the Province, but for many thousands who yearly visit our shores, many of them in order to find here a restfulness and unspoiled charm which are becoming increasingly difficult to discover elsewhere. The amenities which form the subject of this Report are indeed one of the Province's most valuable assets. Once destroyed, however, they are impossible to replace, and instances – happily not as yet numerous, though disturbing as portents – can already be cited of the infliction of irreparable damage by thoughtless and careless development. Scenes once typical of the beauty of Ulster have ceased to be so, not so much from any deliberate intention to despoil as from lack of taste and a sense of responsibility. Just because our area is so small we cannot afford to repeat the mistakes of the past, and it should be a matter of major concern to the whole community that the beauty of Ulster as it has come down to us should remain unmarred. This does not, of course, mean sterilising the development of our countryside and coast. What it does mean is that the process of development should be shaped with sympathy and intelligence" (The Ulster Countryside, 1947, 7).

In its recommendations, the Report advocated the establishment of five National Parks centred on the Antrim Glens and Coast, the Mourne Mountains, the Sperrins, Upper and Lower Lough Erne and Slieve Gullion (Figure 12.1). The purpose of the Parks was:

"to safeguard scenery of great beauty which is a national asset and not merely of local interest and concern; to protect the natural flora and fauna of the areas; and to ensure that the public generally – particularly the rapidly increasing numbers of young people who spend their holidays camping, walking and cycling – should have free access to them" (The Ulster Countryside, 1947, p. 17).

The Committee also proposed that the entire coastline, recognised as being under increasing pressure from development, should be designated an Area of Special Control, where particular attention should be given to the siting, design and materials used in new buildings. Nature Reserves should also be established for educational and scientific purposes, varying in size from areas of national importance to smaller sites which could be managed by local authorities. Field Museums were suggested as a means of introducing the public to the natural history and geology of Northern Ireland.

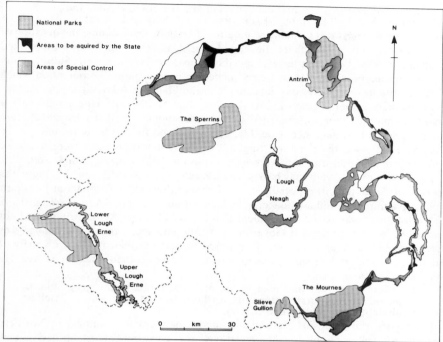

Figure 12.1 Recommendations in *The Ulster Countryside* Report 1947 for five National Parks and Areas of Special Control along the entire coastline, with certain important parts to be acquired by the State.

Management of National Parks, Nature Reserves and Ancient Monuments could be handled "most economically and efficiently" through a National Parks Commission, appointed and funded by government, and including representatives from the Ministries of Home Affairs and Agriculture, Queen's University, the Ulster Medical Society, the National Trust, the Ulster Tourist Development Association and the Youth Hostel Association. Finally the Committee also made a series of recommendations on other countryside matters, ranging from the encouragement of good design in building and the planting of trees, to the control of ribbon development, advertising and caravan sites.

The Planning Advisory Board's Report provided a comprehensive strategy for conserving Northern Ireland's scenic landscapes which, had it been implemented, would have provided for better standards of rural planning at an early date. In fact its proposals were greeted with almost total silence by the Government of the day, which not only ignored the Report, but also allowed the Board to fall into abeyance.

More than ten years were to pass before the question of amenity was raised again, this time in more specific terms, when Brian Faulkner, then Minister of Home Affairs, appointed a Committee in 1960 with the following terms of reference:

"To consider the protection of the natural fauna and flora and the physical features of scientific interest in Northern Ireland and to make recommendations on measures for their conservation and control, including the protection of wild life" (Nature Conservation in Northern Ireland, 1961, 1).

At its initial meeting, this Committee inquired if it could also examine the question of landscape conservation which it believed to be highly relevant, but following a pointed exchange of letters, this matter was specifically excluded from review. Subsequently the Committee proceeded to make recommendations on nature conservation which differed little in substance from those made in the Planning Advisory Board Report, fourteen years earlier. These were to the effect that Northern Ireland should have a system of nature reserves, managed by an independent Northern Ireland Nature Conservancy, whose members would be appointed and funded by government. The Committee stressed the need for "urgent" action, but several years were to elapse before some of these proposals were included in the 1965 Amenity Lands Act.

The decade of the 1950s may have seen little action on rural planning, but there was no lack of development, especially in the Belfast urban area. Throughout Northern Ireland planning was still administered by local authorities under Acts passed in 1931 and 1944; there was no local equivalent to the 1947 Planning Act in Britain, and not until 1960 was the Stormont Government finally convinced that some change was necessary. In that year it appointed Professor Robert Matthew of the University of Edinburgh to undertake a survey and prepare an advisory plan for the Belfast area. He was also requested:

"to relate the survey and plan in the broadest terms to the geographical, economic and cultural pattern of Northern Ireland as a whole" (Belfast Regional Survey and Plan, 1963, 7).

His report, published in 1962, inaugurated a new era for planning in Northern Ireland, for following his recommendations, the Government established a new department, the Ministry of Development, to co-ordinate planning; and although local planning functions were retained by the existing counties and county boroughs, government was now convinced of the need for new legislation.

In relation to the countryside, Matthew made several crucial comments. He noted that Northern Ireland had:

"an accessible and attractive countryside offering a great variety of interests for tourists and for leisure activities; roads still uncrowded for motoring . . . a type of environment of great potential value in the world of tomorrow, a type of environment becoming increasingly rare, and therefore more valuable, in Europe where past industrialisation has been allowed or has allowed itself more and more to destroy natural amenity. Once destroyed, it is difficult or impossible to replace" (Belfast Regional Survey and Plan, 1963, 7).

He went on to stress:

"The character of the Ulster countryside is one of the most precious assets, both for the well-being, enjoyment and stimulation of her people, and for those who visit the Province. Nevertheless there are all too many signs throughout the Region of neglect and indifference. There is little sign of appreciation of the value of the natural environment and in particular the special endowment with which many parts of the Region are blessed" (Belfast Regional Survey and Plan, 1963, 33).

Finally he commended the recommendations of the Planning Advisory Board, noting in a somewhat caustic aside, that the points made sixteen years earlier had not been implemented then and were even more valid today. He concluded:

". . . the maintenance and enhancement of amenities, as emphasised throughout this study, is not a matter of sentiment; it is a matter of making the best possible use of available resources. Northern Ireland, in this highly competitive modern world, cannot afford to neglect, or even unwittingly destroy, this resource" (Belfast Regional Survey and Plan, 1963, 34).

For Matthew, planning for amenity and landscape conservation made economic sense. By stressing this he made a shrewd assessment of the political climate in Northern Ireland at that time, for this was the one point calculated to justify amenity planning to the business and farming interests then dominant in the ruling Unionist Party. In 1965, three years after the Matthew Report was published, the Amenity Lands Act was passed by the Northern Ireland Parliament.

The Amenity Lands Act

The Amenity Lands Act formed the basis for developing a policy of landscape protection and nature conservation in Northern Ireland in much the same way as the 1949 Act had done in Britain and there were close resemblances in the provisions made within the legislation. The Northern Ireland Government now had power to designate National Parks and Areas of Outstanding Natural Beauty, but it could also acquire land, by vesting order if necessary, where this was essential "to preserve any area of natural beauty or amenity" or to establish "any area of scientific interest as a nature reserve" (Amenity Lands Act, 1965, section 1).

National Parks were defined as extensive areas of countryside which warranted special measures to "preserve or enhance the natural beauty or amenities of that area; protect wild life, historic objects or natural phenomena therein; promote the enjoyment by the public of the said area; and provide or maintain public access therein" (Amenity Lands Act, 1965, section 6). An AONB was stated to be an area of countryside other than a National Park which was thought to need "special protection by reason of its outstanding natural beauty" (Amenity Lands Act, 1965 section 10). Planning in National Parks was to be administered by a National Park Committee, eight of whose twelve members were to be appointed by government, but within AONBs responsibility would continue to be exercised by the relevant local authority in consultation with the Ulster Countryside Committee which would advise on all planning applications relating to the designated areas. The latter was to be established by the Act, its members appointed by Government with powers to advise the then Ministry of Development on the designation of National Parks and AONBs, and on "any other matter affecting the natural beauty or amenity of any place in Northern Ireland" (Amenity Lands Act, 1965 section 46). Nature conservation matters were to be handled by a second advisory committee, the Nature Reserves Committee, similarly appointed by government to advise the Minister on the establishment and management of Nature Reserves (NRs) and Areas of Scientific Interest (ASIs).

Amenity planning after 1965 was influenced by one further piece of legislation, the reorganisation of local government which took place in 1973. Under this Act, planning became a function of the provincial government at Stormont, and the new local authorities, known as district councils, had simply a consultative role. Following this, the UCC had no longer a statutory role in development control within designated areas, but could be invited by the Planning Service of the new Department of Housing, Local Government and Planning, to comment on those applications which the Department deemed to be appropriate.

Initially the UCC decided to concentrate on the designation of AONBs, "influenced by the fact that formal steps leading to National Park designation would take some time to complete and that some interim protection should accordingly be given to areas which might ultimately become National Parks" (Ulster Countryside Committee, 1966, 8). By 1972 eight AONBs had been designated, four within the first year of the Committee's existence (Figure 12.2). None have been added since, although Fermanagh Lakeland was first proposed in 1965 and Slieve Croob in County Down in 1974. Over a period of twelve years the Committee's *Annual Reports* note "with regret" that no progress had been made in Fermanagh. From the beginning the UCC was anxious to establish National Parks in each of the areas recommended in the 1947

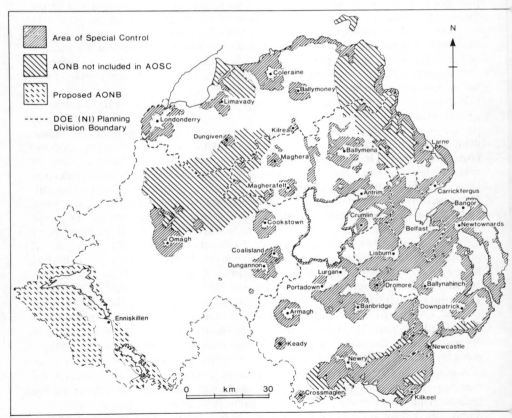

Figure 12.2 Areas of Special Control (ASCs) are the areas where development has been most rigidly controlled since 1978, but criteria used for establishment of ASCs varies with DoE Planning Divisions. West of the Bann, ASCs exist only as green belts around towns and to protect a few scenic areas. Much of the north coast, Rathlin, the middle section of Glenariff, the Sperrins and Fermanagh's Lakeland lie outside Areas of Special Control.

Report. Fermanagh was the first to be proposed, partly because a planning survey had been completed for the County Council two years previously as the basis for tourist development schemes. This proposal was accepted by the Ministry, but after strong local opposition, mainly from farmers, the UCC advised the government not to proceed with designation (Ulster Countryside Committee, 1968, 8). Subsequently National Parks were considered for south Armagh in 1968 on the initiative of the rural district council, and for the Sperrins in 1969, where two councils were involved. No action was taken on the south Armagh proposal, and in the Sperrins, Tyrone County Council agreed to the designation in principle as did Londonderry, but the latter made the provision that action to implement the Park should be deferred for a year. By 1970 no further progress had been made, and in its *Annual Report for 1970* the UCC stated its intention temporarily to abandon the attempt since "the impending reorganisation of local government has made it difficult if not impossible to designate and make arrangements for a National Park under the terms of the Amenity Lands Act". The Committee added the following comment:

"We consider that the National Park concept is a good one and we recommend that in the areas we have proposed as National Parks two main lines of action should be pursued. First the landscape should be preserved so that these outstandingly beautiful areas may be enjoyed by future generations, and secondly the recreational provision should be increasingly provided in a planned and orderly manner so that the growing number of visitors (who will come in any event) will enjoy the countryside without doing it harm" (Ulster Countryside Committee, 1970, 8).

No further comment was made concerning National Parks until 1978, when in a review of its functions the Committee adhered to its earlier comments, namely that the concept of National Parks was still relevant in Northern Ireland.

The purchase of properties which at first were known as "Amenity Areas" and later as "Country Parks" was also given a high priority by the UCC. The first two, at O'Cahan's Rock and the Ness Glen, were both in County Londonderry; later were added larger properties at Crawfordsburn (1972) in Down, and Castle Archdale (1974) in Fermanagh, the last a particularly ambitious project on Lough Erne where there was an extensive caravan site. A riverside walk in Londonderry, properties at Redburn and Scrabo in north Down – where a coastal walk of 17 km was negotiated to link Holywood and Bangor, two offshore islands in Lower Lough Erne and a former turf bog at the Birches in north Armagh, completed the list by the end of the 1970s. There was also the Lagan Valley Regional Park, comprising several properties linked by the River and its towpath. Originally sponsored by the UCC, the Park was provided in 1972 with a separate management committee which included representatives of the relevant local authorities and Government Departments.

Finally the UCC was also concerned with a wide range of topics relating to countryside planning and recreation, from sponsoring schemes to encourage tree planting, publishing its own design guide to building in rural areas (Ulster Countryside Committee: *Building in the Countryside,* 1976), and even undertaking its own pilot survey of the coast in order to convince government that the protection of coastal scenery was an important objective (The Ulster Countryside Committee, 1976, 28–50). It urged unsuccessfully for a survey of resources for outdoor recreation, and for a landscape evaluation survey which might provide a more objective basis for any further designations of scenic areas. Pressure to consider legislation on countryside access and rights of way did eventually elicit some response from government, and legislation for this is now being prepared. Mindful that the idea of conservation and the need for amenity planning had to be carefully presented to a public largely unaware of the issues involved, the Committee in its early years made genuine efforts to explain its policies through visits to local authorities, but during the 1970s this effort at public relations was gradually abandoned. As a result the amenity side of countryside planning lacked an authoritative voice in the increasingly complex local politics of that decade.

Meantime the Nature Reserves Committee was working to ensure that the "most important geological sites and the last remaining fragments of our natural habitats together with their wild life are not swept away because of ignorance or neglect" (Nature Reserves Committee, 1967, 10). In establishing priorities for designation, the Committee decided to concentrate on preserving a representative range of natural habitats, although it was also concerned with protecting individual species of plants and animals, especially where these were in any way endangered. Over the years the NRC has concentrated on its specific tasks, and working within these parameters it had established 34 NNRs and 44 ASIs by 1980.

Two decades of landscape conservation

Significant progress has been made in the conservation of landscape and provision for outdoor recreation in Northern Ireland since the passing of the 1965 Act. Many areas are now protected for amenity and wildlife purposes through direct ownership by government agencies and by voluntary bodies such as the National Trust, the Royal Society for the Protection of Birds (established in Northern Ireland in 1966) and the Ulster Trust for Nature Conservation (1978) (Figure 12.3). The National Trust has been particularly active, and now has more than forty properties, including mansions such as Castleward House in County Down and Springhill House in County Londonderry (see Plates 12.1 and 12.2), as well as some of the finest stretches of the north Antrim coast, at the Giant's Causeway and Murlough Bay. Its wildlife conservation scheme on Strangford Lough also helps to protect one of Northern Ireland's most important wildlife habitats.

Land managed specifically for recreation includes both Forest and Country Parks, the former managed by the Forest Service, attracting 4-5,000 visitors a year to its seven Forest Parks and other forest amenity areas. Country Parks, managed by the Conservation Branch of the DoE, have also proved popular, and some, like Crawfordsburn, near Belfast, attract large numbers of visitors. But most country parks are used by people living in their immediate locality, and their location does little to relieve pressure on Northern Ireland's more vulnerable scenic areas, a defect which is also apparent in the provision of country parks in Britain. This should be rectified in future developments, with new sites carefully chosen on the basis of recreational need rather than on the availability of land. Central government should have a continuing role in such provision, but local authorities should also be involved since recreation is now one of their major functions. Unfortunately with a few notable exceptions, at Craigavon and Newtownabbey for example, few schemes at this scale have been proposed by district councils during the past decade.

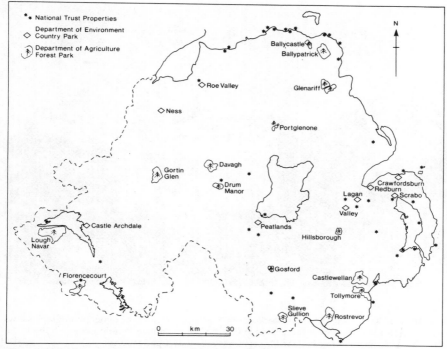

Figure 12.3 Map of Northern Ireland showing National Trust properties, DoE Country Parks and DoA Forest Parks. These are the main centres where special provision has been made for visitors to enjoy the landscape, an estate or a mansion house.

Local authorities have however, participated in one major project which involves a high degree of co-operation with other statutory bodies and private landowners. This is the plan for a long distance footpath, the Ulster Way, which when complete will encircle Northern Ireland with a total length of nearly 720 km (Sports Council for Northern Ireland, 1975). First mooted in 1931, the idea made little progress until it was backed by the newly established Sports Council for Northern Ireland in 1974, and under an energetic committee the negotiations for access are now well under way. The success of the scheme so far represents a notable achievement by one man, Wilfred Capper, who has been a prominent member of all local major amenity bodies since the 1930s.

Landscape protection through designation and development control made swift progress in the years immediately after the passing of the Amenity Lands Act, but the failure to establish National Parks meant that Northern Ireland's major scenic areas were denied the type of comprehensive management and the provision of facilities which have helped to make the National Parks a notable success in Britain. Opposition from farmers was a major reason for the failure to implement the proposal for a National Park in Fermanagh, but local politicians also expressed the fear that designa-

Plates 12.1 and 12.2   National Trust mansions in Northern Ireland. The upper photograph shows Castleward House (1764), near Strangford in County Down, and the lower photograph shows the 18th century Springhill House, near Moneymore in County Londonderry.

tion would hinder development in areas already suffering from unemployment. Senator Donaghy expressed this view in a Senate speech in 1967: "We cannot sanction any undertone in this call for the preservation of natural beauty spots that would appear to doom large areas of several counties to be nothing more than show pieces for the visitor and cheap recreation centres for the holiday maker" (*Hansard, 50,* No. 3, 507). Less explicit was the belief that through its nominations on the proposed National Parks Committees, the Unionist Government at Stormont could usurp the powers then exercised by local councillors in the management of areas which were largely Nationalist in political affiliation. Local government reorganisation in 1973 removed this particular objection since district councils were left with few executive powers. Planning – one of the more contentious local issues – was thereafter a function of the central administration, and Stormont officials saw no need to promote National Parks as one means of securing more consistent planning. Local politicians were no longer interested in amenity questions, confronted as they were with the more immediate issues arising from prolonged civil unrest; and after the imposition of direct rule from Westminster, the ever-changing succession of Government Ministers at the Northern Ireland Office saw no reason to become involved in peripheral issues which could only add to the complexities of a political situation that they already had difficulty in comprehending.

It has been argued that the combination of AONBs and Country Parks may be better suited to the needs of landscape protection in Northern Ireland than the promotion of National Parks (Rogers, 1974, 402). But this ignores the important point, clearly evident in England and Wales, that AONB designation highlights the negative side of amenity planning. This point was recognised in 1977 by the UCC ". . . the time is now ripe to adopt a more positive policy towards these areas. It is considered that the policies regarding Areas of Outstanding Natural Beauty should be reviewed and consideration given to such questions, among others, of making available sites for housing and workshop development as well as grant-aid to landowners for the visual improvement of their properties and the provision of facilities for visitors" (Ulster Countryside Committee, 1977, 14). In fact the UCC's recommendation was overtaken by events, for the DoE had already decided to appoint an independent Committee to review its planning policy in rural areas.

The problem confronting the DoE was public opposition to its development strategy which sought to concentrate rural development in existing settlements, mainly for economic reasons. This conflicts with a widely held desire in Northern Ireland to live in the open countryside, an attitude which farmers as landowners, were not inclined to discourage; unused to planning controls in their own business-related development, they resent what they regard as bureaucratic interference in their rights as property owners. Without local participation in the planning system, and in the absence of a democratically-elected provincial legislature at Stormont, planning decisions now seem remote from the needs and aspirations of individual citizens, despite the existence of a Planning Appeals Commission. Local councillors, who have no responsibility for planning other than a right to be consulted, were quick to express discontent with a system disliked for many reasons other than planning, and in appointing the Cockcroft Committee, the DoE no doubt hoped for a more objective review of its policy than was possible in the council chamber, or in the more rarefied atmosphere of Westminster. In the event the Cockcroft Committee conveyed to the Department views expressed by the councillors it had interviewed, untempered by any pretence at critical evaluation (DoENI, 1978*a*).

The Department responded by agreeing to relax its policy on development control, although it affirmed that "there are certain areas of Northern Ireland where the Department believes that rigid control should be exercised" (DoENI, 1978*b*, 4 section 3). These areas apparently are not the AONBs which already have statutory backing, but rather, new "Areas of Special Control", defined by methods not revealed, but with boundaries *agreed* between the Department and the District Councils in whose area the ASC is contained (Figure 12.2). The Department added that the UCC would also be *consulted*. This new policy could well undermine the system of conserving landscape by controlling development in designated areas carefully built up over the past 16 years. For in the absence of any firm statement to the contrary, it would seem that AONBs have no longer any major role in development control, and that the control formerly exercised within these will now be effected only within the ASCs. This might be an acceptable alternative if the ASCs were defined on agreed criteria in which landscape quality would be the guiding principle, but on the evidence available so far this is not the case. ASCs apparently are intended to act both as green belts around urban centres and to protect scenic areas, but in the latter case their designation has been inconsistent, apparently because adjoining planning divisions have failed to agree on the criteria to be used in definition, while certain major scenic areas are not even proposed for ASC status. It is impossible to have confidence in a system which, for example, protects the upper portion of Glenariff in County Antrim as an ASC, while the lower half – in a different planning division – is omitted; or which fails to include as an ASC one of the finest stretches of coastline in Britain, from Fair Head to Cushendun in County Antrim or the beach at Magilligan.

The prospect for landscape conservation

At present it seems unlikely that "the preservation and enhancement of natural beauty", one of the primary objectives of the 1965 Amenity Lands Act, can be attained under the present system. No National Parks have been established, yet their designation was intended as the keystone of the 1965 strategy, a point underlined by the success of the National Parks in England and Wales, which were given similar prominence in the 1949 Act in Britain. Instead of the positive management of scenic landscapes through National Park designation, Northern Ireland has been forced to rely on negative sanctions operated within the AONBs. Inevitably this has led the public to conclude that scenic beauty is to be equated with economic sterility, and in the absence of any significant leadership from local politicians, amenity planning has become expendable in the light of sustained public criticism of planning in general.

Relaxation of the 1965 policy might be justified if the pressures on scenic areas had themselves diminished in recent years, but this has not been the case. In the industrial sector, quarrying, and sand and gravel extraction continue to affect sections of the east Antrim coast, the northern Sperrins and the Mourne coastal plain, but the greatest potential threat is in oil exploration in north Antrim, scheduled to begin in 1981 in an area not yet defined as an ASC. The search for alternative sources of energy could also have a detrimental effect, especially in Strangford Lough, where the possibility of a tidal barage across the Narrows is currently being explored. The programme to

Plates 12.3 and 12.4 Torr Head (upper photograph) and the middle section of Glenariff (lower photograph) are two examples of scenic landscapes in County Antrim that are outside Areas of Special Control, and hence are not well protected from possible development.

upgrade roads, in some instances to motorway standards has had a major impact in several rural areas, but the current economic recession means that new projects have been temporarily delayed. Water abstraction is perhaps a more important issue, for proposals to build a new reservoir at Kinnahalla, which could have had a detrimental effect on the ecology and recreational use of Northern Ireland's one major mountain area, were abandoned only following a major planning appeal (Kinnahalla, 1980). Demand for water still exceeds supply and since the use of Lough Neagh as a natural reservoir is not favoured in current policy, the potential threat to the Mournes remains.

The drastic reduction in the number of tourists visiting Northern Ireland during the past decade of continuing terrorist violence means that recreation pressures have increased less dramatically than forecast. The potential for tourism remains high, and is still a major economic justification for landscape conservation if one is needed. Meantime, local participation in outdoor recreation has continued to rise, although reliable figures are not readily available. Water-sports, particularly angling, sailing and cruising have brought increased pressure especially to Strangford Lough, where a management scheme has yet to be implemented although described as "an urgent necessity" in a 1978 Report (Strangford Lough Working Group, 1978). Similarly there is growing demand for lakeside accommodation around Lough Erne, an area not yet covered by a formal designation for landscape conservation. The Mournes in particular have experienced a major increase in use, not least because of the heavy concentration of outdoor education centres, sponsored by individual schools, youth organisations and education authorities. Each year a new generation of school-children is introduced to the countryside through such activities, and this alone is responsible for creating additional pressures. When the tourist trade eventually revives, the increase in recreation use of scenic areas could be dramatic, for as a 1970 Conference Report stated, "the cultural and sporting facilities, and the relative solitude offered by Northern Ireland, form a resource increasingly attractive to a widening circle in an affluent and crowded Europe . . . the countryside of Ulster is a golden egg indeed" (Forsyth and Boyd, 1970, 11 and 90).

Landscape changes resulting from innovations in farming are much less dramatic than in England and Wales, for livestock rearing continues to be the dominant enterprise, and grass the main crop. Hedgerow removal and field enlargement are less significant in Northern Ireland, but the new industrialised farm buildings and silos are obtrusive in many areas. Because the farmed landscape has escaped major despoilation so far it is all the more valuable as a scenic resource, but it remains vulnerable to modern technology. Drainage schemes for example can have a detrimental effect on the landscape as well as triggering major ecological change, and insensitive implementation of early schemes has left ugly scars in several areas, including sections of the River Blackwater in County Armagh. Upland landscapes have been most affected by state afforestation in the recent past, but a drastic reduction in the rate of land acquisition means that a 1970 target of 90,000 ha. of forest in Northern Ireland by 2000 A.D. is now unlikely to be met.

Scattered housing, spreading along rural roads, remains the type of development which most affects the rural landscape, despite the constraints applied by the previous planning policy. The reasons for this lie in the preference for living in dispersed dwellings, and in the prevalence of small-scale ownership of rural land. Many townspeople have ties of kinship with farm families and the sense of obligation to provide a building site for a "friend", reinforces the natural inclination to maximise profit from land. But the scale of Northern Ireland's landscape is vulnerable to the sprawl of scattered development. In the traditional countryside new housing was absorbed within the existing framework of small hedged fields, not least because the dwellings themselves were small in size, simple in proportion and unobtrusive in the materials used. Today new buildings dominate a landscape increasingly divested of hedgerow trees and shelter belts, their urban designs the more obtrusive because the houses follow the roads along which services such as water, electricity and phone are aligned. In scenic areas, insensitive siting and design both of dwellings and farm buildings can degrade a landscape as easily as a power station or quarry tip: only the scale is different. Yet high standards of visual amenity cannot be achieved solely by strict control of development through statutory planning: there has to be positive inducement to encourage better design, and the obvious need for this alone warrants new policy initiatives.

It could be argued that the best strategy is simply to implement fully the provisions of the 1965 Act, but this is unrealistic on two counts. Firstly, in relation to National Parks, it would be difficult now to grant National Park Committees executive responsibility for planning in their areas since this function has been administered centrally by the DoE since local government reorganisation in 1972. Furthermore the political objections to nominated Park Committee Members would still hold today. For administrative and political reasons National Parks as originally conceived in 1965 do not seem an attainable objective. Secondly, the 1965 Act placed special emphasis on the role of the UCC as an advisory body, which would mediate between local government as the planning authority and central government as the policy maker in matters relating to rural amenity. This role was reasonably satisfactory until 1973, when following the assumption of planning responsibilities by the DoE the UCC was left in the position of advising the DoE only when and if the Department decided it needed advice; and even if advice was sought, the Department might listen but it need not react. The UCC is also inhibited by its advisory role from making public pronouncements on policy matters, and in the absence of a local Parliament its work lacks the stimulus of political scrutiny and debate. Externally its task is made more difficult through its close identification with the DoE, for its objectives are seen by the public simply as another restrictive element in an already unpopular planning process.

The doubtful viability of National Parks within the present administrative structure and political climate of Northern Ireland, and the emasculation of the UCC as an effective body in the promotion of rural amenity indicates the need for a complete reappraisal of the present system for preserving and enhancing the natural beauty and amenity of scenic landscape in Northern Ireland. A phrase used by Reg Hookway, then Director of the Countryside Commission, at the Northern Ireland 1970 Conference, suggests a starting point, for he urged his audience to "aim for quality, quality in the standards of your management and quality of environment" (Forsyth and Boyd, 1970, 100).

The identification of scenic quality is thus the starting point, and this indicates the need for a new survey of the countryside in Northern Ireland, using the wide range of techniques now available and known by the term "landscape evaluation". Professional doubts are expressed about the utility of this method of landscape appraisal (Appleton, 1975, 119–163; Fleming, 1976), but a recent study undertaken by the Countryside Commission for Scotland merits testing for possible application in Northern Ireland (Countryside Commission Scotland, 1978). Once the major scenic areas have been recognised, the next step is to establish what Hookway called "the pressure points", that is the places where pressure on resources exists or can be anticipated. Such a resource survey should involve an assessment of capacity, to establish the ability of scenic areas to undergo exploitation by different activities before they experience ecological damage or loss of visual amenity. From these two surveys would emerge a statement on those landscapes which are scenic and those which are under pressure: from this a strategy for landscape conservation could be devised and applied.

Such a strategy should recognise that not all landscapes are of equal quality, and that landscape conservation should be based on a graded hierarchy which recognises these differences. At the top of the hierarchy there could be *National Heritage Areas,* places of exceptional landscape quality in which all forms of land use and development would be strictly controlled to conserve the existing character. The second category would be areas less vulnerable to pressure than the NHAs, with capacity to absorb a wider range of uses and activities and consequently with less strict control on development. These could be new or existing *AONBs,* with boundaries modified following professional landscape evaluation, but extended to include scenic coastal areas. *Country Parks* could constitute a third category, their number extended and location determined to balance recreational demand with conservation needs. Ultimately the apearance of landscape is determined by land use, and within the designated areas land use should be managed rather than controlled. For management implies agreement between owners, users and policy-makers on how the land is to be conserved, on the basis of plans prepared for each area, in the manner of the National Park Plans in England and Wales (Dennier, 1981). Such plans would include positive proposals for landscape enhancement – in Nan Fairbrother's words "to rescue our vanishing natural vegetation" (Fairbrother, 1972, 341) – and again a precedent is suggested in the proposals made by the Countryside Commission in its *New Agricultural Landscapes.*

Finally, as Richard Mabey has wisely said: "the most difficult problem in establishing a conservation policy is not so much why we should do it, or which particular pieces of land or styles of management are involved, but *how* these decisions are reached and implemented, whose interests are legitimately involved, and what kind of political and economic machinery is needed for them to find expression" (Mabey, 1980, 227). If landscape conservation is to withstand the political pressures inherent in Northern Ireland and to achieve some co-ordination of policy between the often conflicting interests of such large government departments as the DoE and DoA, there is need for an independent agency, managed by a committee nominated by government, but with its own professional staff, financial resources and capacity to devise and implement policy. Its functions should be similar to the Countryside Commissions in Britain, that is, to advise government departments and local authorities on matters relating to rural amenity and outdoor recreation; but it should also have executive responsibility for management within designated areas. Here its work could be aided by local advisory committees, drawn from a cross-section of interests among those resident say within the redefined AONBs. Ideally the Committee's functions should be wider than those indicated, to include all aspects of environmental conservation, historic buildings and ancient monuments as well as wildlife habitats and scenic landscapes. Such a body in

Plates 12.5 and 12.6 Landscapes around the Mournes in County Down, such as Tollymore Forest Park (upper photograph) or Annalong Harbour (lower photograph) attract large numbers of visitors from urban centres like Belfast and Newry.

fact was proposed by the Planning Advisory Board thirty years ago, and experience of a different system now shows the wisdom of its recommendation.

The scheme for conserving Northern Ireland's scenic landscapes as outlined here is only one of several possible options. It is advanced in order to stress the need for a fundamental rethinking of existing policy, for in the present times fine rural landscape cannot be taken for granted. Without a clear statement on priorities by government, and the political will to implement accepted policy, the landscape of Northern Ireland will deteriorate to the irreparable loss of future generations.

REFERENCES

Appleton, J. *et al.*, 1975. Landscape Evaluation. *Transactions Institute of British Geographers*, 66, 119–164.
Belfast Regional Survey and Plan: Recommendations and Conclusions. 1963. Cmd. 451.
Bell, M. (*Edit.*), 1975. *Britain's National Parks*, (Newton Abbot).
Clark, K., 1979. *Landscape into Art*, (London).
Coppock, J. T., 1968. The Countryside (Scotland) Act and the Geographer. *Scottish Geographical Magazine*, 84, 201–212.
Coppock, J. T., 1974. Ideals for National Parks. *Geographical Magazine*, 46, No. 11, 627–633.
Coppock, J. T. and Duffield, B. S., 1975. *Recreation in the Countryside*, (London).
Countryside Commission, 1977. *New Agricultural Landscapes*, (Cheltenham).
Countryside Commission, 1978. *Areas of Outstanding Natural Beauty: a discussion paper*, (Cheltenham).
Countryside Commission, 1980. *Areas of Outstanding Natural Beauty: a Policy Statement*, (Cheltenham).
Countryside Commission for Scotland, 1974. *A Park System for Scotland*, (Battleby).
Countryside Commission for Scotland, 1978. *Scotland's Scenic Heritage*, (Battleby).
Davidson, J. and Wibberley, G., 1977. *Planning and the Rural Environment*, (Oxford).
Dennier, A., 1981. National Parks: Planning for Management, Gilg, A. W., *Countryside Planning Year Book*, (Norwich), 49–66.
Department of the Environment for N. Ireland, 1978*a*. *Review of Rural Planning Policy:* Report of the Committee under Chairmanship of Dr W. H. Cockcroft, (Belfast).
Department of the Environment for N. Ireland, 1978*b*. *Review of Rural Planning Policy: Statement by the DoE*, (Belfast).
Evans, E. E. and Turner, B. S., 1977. *Ireland's Eye*, (Belfast).
Fairbrother, N., 1972. *New Lives, New Landscapes*, (Harmondsworth).
Fleming, S. C., 1976. *Landscape Evaluation and the Northern Ireland Coast*, (unpublished BA dissertation, Geography Department, Queen's University, Belfast).
Forsyth, J. and Boyd, D. E. K., 1970. *Conservation in the Development of Northern Ireland*, (Belfast).
Foster, J., 1974. Parkland for Scotland, *Geographical Magazine*, 46, No. 9, 480–86.
Hall, C., 1976. The Amenity Movement, Gill, C., *The Countryman's Britain*, (Newton Abbot), 162–75.
Hall, S. C. and S. C., 1843. *Ireland, its Scenery and Character etc.*, (London).
Kinnahalla Scheme 1980. Appeal to the Water Appeals Commission, (Belfast).
Lowenthal, D. and Prince, H. C., 1965. English landscape tastes, *Geographical Review*, 55, 186–222.
Lowenthal, D., 1978. Finding Valued Landscapes, *Progress in Human Geography*, 2, No. 3, 373–418.
Mabey, R., 1980. *The Common Ground*, (London).
Nature Conservation in Northern Ireland, The Report of the Committee, 1961. Belfast.
Newby, H., 1980. *Green and Pleasant Land?* (Harmondsworth).
Northern Ireland Tourist Board, 1980 *Northern Ireland*, (Belfast).
Praeger, R. J., 1898. *Official Guide to County Down*, (Belfast).

Rogers, R. S., 1974. Where Beauty Contrasts the Troubles. *Geographical Magazine* 46, No. 8, 397–402.

Sheail, J., 1975. The Concept of National Parks in Great Britain, 1900–1980. *Transactions of the Institute of British Geographers.* 66, 41–56.

Shoard, M., 1976. Recreation: The Key to the Survival of England's Countryside. MacEwan, M., *Future Landscapes,* (London), 58–73.

Sports Council for Northern Ireland, 1975. *The Ulster Way,* (Belfast).

Strangford Lough Working Group, 1978. *Report,* (Belfast).

Thackeray, W. M., 1887. *(Edit.) The Irish Sketch Book,* (London).

The Ulster Countryside, 1947. (Belfast).

Ulster Countryside Committee, 1976. *Building in the Countryside,* (Belfast).

Waugh, M., 1981. *The Shell Book of Country Parks,* (Newton Abbot).

Youth Hostel Association of Northern Ireland, 1981. *Handbook,* (Belfast).

Abbreviations used throughout the text.

DoA	Department of Agriculture for Northern Ireland
DoE	Department of the Environment for Northern Ireland
DoF	Department of Finance for Northern Ireland
ASC	Area of Special Control (a local planning unit introduced in 1979)
ASI	Area of Scientific Interest (an area with some degree of protection under the Amenity Lands Act (N.I.) 1965)
AONB	Area of Outstanding Natural Beauty (an area with some degree of protection under the Amenity Lands Act (N.I.) 1965)
BOD	Biochemical Oxygen Demand (the amount of oxygen required to break down organic waste material)
FCB	Fisheries Conservancy Board for Northern Ireland
FFC	Foyle Fisheries Commission
NRC	Nature Reserves Committee for Northern Ireland
UCC	Ulster Countryside Committee
NNR	National Nature Reserve
FNR	Forest Nature Reserve
UDN	Ulcerative dermal necrosis disease in fish
m O.D.	Altitude measured in metres above Ordnance Datum, here understood as mean sea level.

SELECTIVE INDEX OF MAIN TOPICS

INDEX OF NORTHERN IRELAND PLACE-NAMES, EXCEPT COUNTY NAMES

NOTES

NOTES

NOTES

NOTES

NOTES

NOTES

NOTES

NOTES